IMAGINEERING
ATLANTA

THE HAYMARKET SERIES

Editors: Mike Davis and Michael Sprinker

The Haymarket Series offers original studies in politics, history and culture, with a focus on North America. Representing views across the American left on a wide range of subjects, the series will be of interest to socialists both in the USA and throughout the world. A century after the first May Day, the American left remains in the shadow of those martyrs whom the Haymarket Series honors and commemorates. These studies testify to the living legacy of political activism and commitment for which they gave their lives.

IMAGINEERING ATLANTA

The Politics of Place in the City of Dreams

CHARLES RUTHEISER

VERSO
London • New York

First published by Verso 1996
© Charles Rutheiser 1996
All rights reserved

The right of Charles Rutheiser to be identified as the author
of this work has been asserted by him in accordance
with the Copyright, Designs and Patents Act 1988

Verso
UK: 6 Meard Street, London W1V 3HR
USA: 180 Varick Street, New York NY 10014–4606

Verso is the imprint of New Left Books

ISBN 1–85984–800–1
ISBN 1–85984–145–7

British Library Cataloguing in Publication Data
A catalogue record for this book is available from the British Library

Library of Congress Cataloging-in-Publication Data
A catalog record for this book is available from the Library of Congress

Typeset by M Rules, London
Printed and bound in the United States of America

CONTENTS

LIST OF MAPS

ACKNOWLEDGEMENTS

A friend of mine once told me that writing a book was "an unnatural act." While I am not quite comfortable with that characterization, it surely is a bizarre, complex, and only partially solitary endeavor. In the course of researching and writing this book, I have enjoyed the inspiration and assistance of many people, only some of whom will I be able to mention here.

The Department of Anthropology and the College of Arts and Sciences of Georgia State University have been generous in their patronage of this project, providing a Research Initiation Grant in the summer of 1993 and course release and summer research funds during 1994 and 1995. My colleagues, especially Claire Sterk-Elifson, Kirk Elifson, and "Art Murphy," were a constant source of support. Rebecca Dameron and Deborah Duchon of the Center for Applied Research in Anthropology helped me make sense of the often baffling numbers on Atlanta's sociocultural diversity. Jeff McMichael, Director of GSU's Cartography Research Lab, did a masterful job in putting together the maps. Mark Witsaman and Joe Kendall provided invaluable research assistance, as did the students of Anthropology 420/620 and Anthropology 823 over the last three years. Particular thanks go to Sarah Heathcote, Frank Millard, Maureen Capozzoli, Ann-Marie Kuschinski, Kitty Kelly, and Susan Hart, as well as to the crew at Empty the Shelters.

I have lost track of just how many people I talked with in connection with this project, but the following have been of special importance: Lanfranco Blanchetti, Doris Betz, Patti Cooper, Loren Council, Charles Dove, Stephen Englemann, David Ethridge, Solomon Green, Suzanne Gwynn, Evelyn Hammond, Frank Johnson, Kristi Lawson, Rob Kadoori, Neill Matheson, Joy Martin, Sophia Mihic, Viranjini Munasinghe, Steve Newman, Andrew Steiner, Teresa Ward, and Elizabeth Young. Mike Davis saw merit in this project at an early stage, and Gary McDonogh, Don Moore, Bob Rotenberg, Neil Smith, and Sharon Zukin offered numerous helpful suggestions along the way. Michael Sprinker has been an *Übermensch* of an editor, reading and commenting extensively on the manuscript in its draft form, as did Melissa Gilbert, Meredith McGill, and Ruth Petrie. Jane Hindle, Isobel Rorison, and the staff at Verso deserve kudos for their patience and for giving new meaning to the concept of "just-in-time production." To Tassi Crabb, I owe more than can easily be acknowledged.

My family has always been supportive, especially my grandfathers – Frank Osheowitz and Jack Rutheiser – who, from an early age, taught me the value of a good argument, as well as the need to "stimulate conversation." It is to them that I dedicate this book.

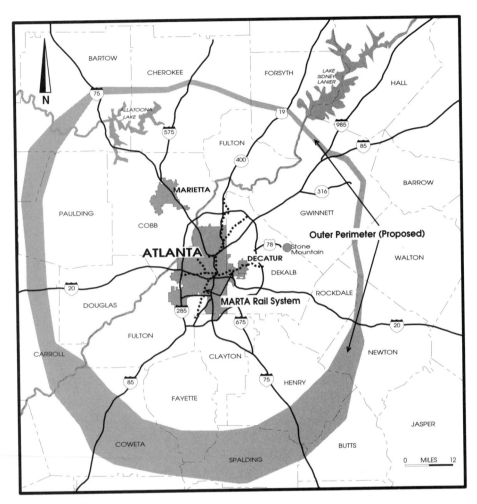

Map 1:   Atlanta Metropolitan Area

INTRODUCTION

No true secrets are lurking in the landscape, but only undisclosed evidence, waiting for us. No true chaos is in the urban scene, but only patterns and clues waiting
to be organized.

Grady Clay[1]

This book has its origins in the summer of 1992, when I took up a new job at
Georgia State University – a self-described "urban" university in the heart of the old
central business district. Soon after I arrived, Atlanta's civic and business leadership
returned from Barcelona, where they had been honored guests at the Olympic
Games. Although headlines around the world proclaimed "It's on to Atlanta!" neither the power elite nor most Atlantans were very happy. The local media intoned
a sense of serious concern about the city's lack of both preparedness and sense of
identity. Two years had gone by since Atlanta's selection as a host city, but no firm
plans had yet been revealed, much less construction begun.

The closing ceremonies in Barcelona had done much to turn expectancy into
high anxiety. Atlanta's Olympic mascot had made its long-awaited debut, but the
amorphous, blue, non-representational entity with bulging eyes and cheerily
demented grin – the rather appropriately named Whatizit – had been quickly and
resoundingly ridiculed at home and abroad. The ambiguity of the creature
prompted a wave of punditry speculating as to what "it" really was. The cultural
critic Robert Hughes, writing in the *New Yorker*, saw in the blue blob the repressed
image of a fetus, "a case of overspill, or precipitation, from a popular culture laden
with fetal obsession."[2] The cartoonist Matt Groening, creator of *The Simpsons*,
thought it "a bad marriage of the Pillsbury Doughboy and the ugliest California
Raisin."[3] Yet according to the design team that created it, Whatizit's lack of a
clearly defined identity was its chief virtue, for thanks to the wonders of computer-
generated animation, it could "morph" into any- and everything within the placeless
world of the video screen.[4]

To most Atlantans, however, Whatizit's purposeful ambiguity was exactly the problem. Old-time residents decried the lack of reference to traditional city symbols, like the resurgent phoenix (reportedly the runner-up to Whatizit and subsequently reincarnated as Blaze, the mascot of the Paralympic Games), or the ubiquitous peach.[5] One local newspaper columnist derisively dubbed it the "Olympic maggot,"[6] while many other Atlantans showed their displeasure by calling it "the slug." "Salt the slug" T-shirts quickly appeared among the wares of the city's street vendors, but just as rapidly, and mysteriously, disappeared from view.

Slightly embarrassed, but nonplussed, the brains trust of the Atlanta Committee for the Olympic Games, or ACOG, mobilized a team of Hollywood spin doctors to do a make-over. The decision to revise rather than abandon the problematic image was due in no small part to the fact that the widget had been the personal choice of ACOG czar Billy Payne, a real estate lawyer and former University of Georgia football star, who had emerged from relative obscurity to cheerlead Atlanta's bid for the Olympics. After a year of cosmetic retooling aided by a bevy of youthful focus groups, "it" looked much the same, but had been personified into Izzy, "an adventurous teenager who lives in a world of Whatizits inside the Olympic torch."[7] According to the back story provided by the image therapists, Izzy was on a quest to become the first Whatizit to compete in the Olympic Games.

The make-over proved somewhat successful, if only among the nation's population under twelve years of age, who, thanks to aggressive promotional efforts, actually seem to like the creature. In the summer of 1994, ACOG officials smugly displayed 85,000 fan letters on the floor of the Georgia Dome as testimony to Izzy's popularity among the Barney the Dinosaur set.[8] This has been most encouraging to ACOG, who wistfully envision Izzy as a licensed character worth potentially some $50 million in retail sales.[9] Marketing plans include not only towels, lunch boxes, dolls, pins, and other conventional ephemera, but holiday television specials, comic books, CD-ROM software, gigs at county fairs and parades, as well as placements – as a "product" – in films and TV shows.

By the summer of 1995, however, few of the more ambitious plans had been realized and a poll commissioned by ACOG showed that the vast majority of American adults were not familiar with Izzy (nor, for that matter, were they aware that Atlanta was the site for the 1996 Olympics). In response to their mascot's poor showing among American adults, Izzy's handlers planned a major public relations offensive for the year leading up to the Games, including live appearances at all of the theme parks owned by one of the official Olympic corporate sponsors, Anheuser-Busch. No doubt by the summer of 1996 most readers of this volume, especially those with young children, will be more acquainted with the creature.

Whether Atlantans realized it or not, Whatizit/Izzy was actually a most appropriate symbol for their city. Critics had often claimed that boosters talked about Atlanta as if it was a person. Much like the smiling slug, Atlanta was a striving, self-absorbed adolescent trying to find a place among more mature and established peers, the youngest city ever to host the Games. Both were possessed by a sense of mission and shameless hucksterism, as well as a propensity to turn seeming disasters, whether they be devastation in war or embarrassment before the world, into fame and profit. More to the point, thanks to a century's worth of labors by a dedicated cadre of entrepreneurs, journalists, and assorted other urban boosters, Atlanta's identity as a place was no less ambiguous than that of the aqua-toned creature. A nationwide poll found that the city had a very tenuous kind of name recognition amongst the American public at large, being far better known for the Cinderella exploits of its professional baseball team, the Braves (who had gone from last to first place in their division between the 1991 and 1992 seasons), than anything else, even *Gone With the Wind*.[10] This studied lack of definition – 20 percent of those surveyed could not come up with anything characteristic of the city at all – contrasted markedly with Atlanta's image in the global business press, which had regularly ranked the city as one of the most accommodating locales for investors. Much like Izzy, Atlanta's most appreciated and defining characteristic seemed its ability to morph, to reconfigure itself in response to the demands of capital.

To be sure, Atlanta's boosters had long worked to craft a distinctive, appealing image for the city. The "official" mythology promulgated in numerous publications, ads, and videos, sponsored by both Atlanta's predominantly white corporate elite and mostly black political establishment, posited the city as the embodiment of the *New New South* – not only a good place to do business, but hospitable, progressive, racially harmonious, and, owing almost exclusively to the efforts of native son Martin Luther King, Jr, the cradle of the modern human rights movement. Above all, however, this Atlanta is a bright and shiny city of the future, nothing less than the natural capital of the twenty-first century: "a city that has managed to shape a tech-nologically-advanced environment without compromising its moral vision or charming quality of life."[11] This bland, techno-oriented imagery reduced Atlanta's provincial and all-too-frequently racist past to "Southern hospitality," while obscuring an unresolved conflict between two historical legacies, one associated with the former Imperial Capital of the resurgent Ku Klux Klan, the other, the Black Mecca of W.E.B. DuBois and a large and prosperous African-American middle class. One did not have to look far beneath the shiny surface of the boosters' celestial Atlanta, however, to discover what was actually one of the poorest and most racially segregated central cities in the United States.

This book is intended as a critical introduction to the multiple manifestations of Atlanta, an exploration of its peoples, places, and politics, its myths and realities, as well as the processes that define, align, and produce them. "Critical" in this sense extends far beyond revealing that Atlanta is something less than what its boosters claim it to be by drawing attention to some of the taken-for-granted ways in which we talk about, explain, and experience cities and urbanity in contemporary society. It is an "introduction" in that no single account can be comprehensive enough to definitively convey the vast extent and contradictory complexity of any contemporary metropolis. Rather, it incorporates three years of observations, conversations, interviews, and archival research with a wide variety of previously published accounts in an effort to provide the reader with an elementary understanding of the political, economic, and sociocultural forces that shape Atlanta's impressive but profoundly uneven development.

Over the last two decades or so, a variety of writers have been sketching the contours of a new kind of urban form, a phantasmagorical landscape characterized by fragmentation, near-instantaneous communication, privatized public spaces, highly stylized simulations, and the subordination of locality to the demands of a globalizing market culture.[12] Atlanta is in many ways paradigmatic of this ageographic and generic urbanism. Its twenty-county metropolitan area encompasses a polynucleated sprawl of sylvan suburbs, slums, and shopping malls surrounding a central archipelago of fortified fantasy islands rising out of a sea of parking lots – the whole tenuously linked by expressways, television, and a fragile sense of imagined communitas. As such, it provides a fertile ground for investigating the play of culture, power, identity, and place within a "nonplace urban realm."[13]

Much like Los Angeles and other cities lacking any "natural" advantages, such as a harbor or a navigable river, Atlanta has from its inception been the object of a particularly intense form of boosterism, a creation of its own imagination. Under the influence of "the Atlanta Spirit," generations of entrepreneurs, politicians, journalists, and assorted visionaries have regularly reconfigured the reputation and built form of the city, turning a provincial railroad hub into an service-oriented, "informational"[14] metropolis of global reach. Appropriating a term from Walt Disney, I refer to these successive waves of organized promotion and redevelopment as linked, but not always well coordinated, acts of urban "imagineering." I am using this term in a more expansive way than the strict Disneyite sense of designing "futuristic solutions to theatrical and infrastructural problems,"[15] to encompass the manifold labors of public relations operatives and other "creative specialists" working in the seemingly boundless and placeless spaces of the mass media. The Olympic-inspired effort to recreate a sense of "traditional urbanity" in downtown Atlanta through the renovation of the public character of the city presents a particularly vivid example of the state of the art of what I refer to as "making place" through both urban design and an aggressive, relentless use of advertising. By using the notion of "imagineering" to refer to late-nineteenth-century as well as present-day practices of city building, I also wish to emphasize the historical continuities in the spectacular dimension of the urban process, as well as the epochal shifts in the ways in which cities are currently "put together" in both a physical and virtual sense.

For Atlanta's boosters, the awarding of the 1996 Centennial Olympic Games seemingly confirmed their boast that Atlanta was truly "the world's next great international city." Indeed, the Atlanta Committee for the Olympic Games relied heavily on off-the-shelf promotional imagery of Atlanta as a "world-class city" to sell the International Olympic Committee on Atlanta for the Centennial Games. The city's selection also raised hopes amongst considerable segments of the population that the Olympics would be a catalyst for ambitious revitalization schemes similar to the $12 billion program then being undertaken in Barcelona. Prospects for a tangible Olympic legacy figured prominently in mustering popular support for, and minimizing public opposition to, the city's bid. However, from the outset, ACOG's model of operations was not the lavishly state-subsidized Barcelona Olympics of 1992, but the highly corporatized Los Angeles Games of 1984, which featured a minimum of new public investment and a maximization of private profit.

Far from producing consensus or unity of purpose, the preparations for the 1996 Olympics have accentuated the cross-cutting cleavages that bind and divide Atlanta's populace. Over the last thirty years, the population of the metropolitan region has dramatically expanded in size and diversity, bringing in both corporate nomads and Rust Belt émigrés, as well as refugees and immigrants from Latin America, Asia, Africa, and Eastern Europe. The intensification of cultural heterogeneity has further complicated a social field already deeply riven by differences of gender, class, and, especially, race. The influx of national and international capital and the restructuring of the world economy have also fundamentally reordered the organization of power in the city and in the metropolitan region as a whole. The region's growth over the last three decades has been rapid, extensive, and highly uneven, concentrated in a broad swath of the majority white exurbs and in isolated pockets elsewhere. Despite numerous efforts to revitalize the core, the central city continues to hemorrhage jobs and residents, leaving isolated nodes of enclaved development amidst a crumbling infrastructure, a shrinking tax base, and an increasingly poor and largely African-American majority population.

My primary focus in this book is on this historic core of the metropolitan area, or, to use a popular spatial metaphor, "the hole in the center of the doughnut."[16] A test bed for federal urban renewal during the 1950s and 1960s and for long a relatively unsupervised playground for private capital, the city of Atlanta provides an object lesson in the internal colonization of the North American urban frontier in the late twentieth century. A close reading of its built environment reveals the changing fashions of "creative destruction" and the social alignments that shape them.

The contemporary Olympic Games are a lineal descendant of the grand expositions and world's fairs of the urban past: not only a spectacle of ritualized warfare and barely sublimated geopolitics, but a grandiose celebration of the commodity form and the triumph of the free market. As the "largest peacetime event in history" (only wars are bigger, one ACOG minion quipped), the 1996 Centennial Olympics provide an unprecedented opportunity for rethinking Atlanta and opening up new dimensions in what Mike Davis has called the "infinite game" of urban redevelopment.[17] With most of the major venues located within a five-kilometer-wide "Olympic Ring" centered on downtown, the Games have focused renewed speculation, of both a literal and a figurative sort, on the future of the central city, which had been increasingly abandoned by the private sector. In so doing, the Olympics have also helped to restructure relationships between and among entities with different levels of interest and influence in the urban core. These include not only white corporate leaders and black politicians, but a welter of city government agencies, quasi-public state authorities, public–private partnerships, an increasingly fragmented business community, and sundry, less empowered "others," such as neighborhood organizations and advocacy groups, not to mention "the public" at large. This book examines the interrelationships of these varied actors and places their multi-sided struggle over downtown redevelopment within a cultural–historical context.

Divided by race, "vision," and questions of turf, weakened by the centrifugal pull of exurban growth and the penetration of outside corporate influences, the Olympic efforts of Atlanta's power structure have focused primarily on creating an appealing stage set for visitors and viewers – an alluring, magical tapestry of what Christine Boyer has elsewhere termed "ornamental nodes" and "scenographic sites"[18] – that hopefully confirms Atlanta's self-ascribed status as a "world-class" city. Atlanta provides a demonstration project of contemporary practices of urban revitalization that are more concerned with the artful design of secure, simulated, and resegregated environments – Jim Crow[19] in twenty-first-century drag – than in confronting the more deep-rooted and intractable issues of poverty, unemployment, crime, and racism. Indeed, in many ways, Atlanta's Olympic preparations constitute no more than a not so ingenious array of facades, props, smoke, and mirrors designed to present the image of a healthy, vital, and integrated city.

Still, however exemplary of general trends it may be, Atlanta also represents a unique conjuncture of universals and particulars, and describes a reality quite unlike either New York or Los Angeles – two cities to which it has often compared itself and which have dominated the literature on the postmodern city in the United States. In this sense, then, this work can be read as a case study in the extensive comparative literature on contemporary urbanism. The aims of this book, though, extend beyond providing another account of the uneven development and theme-parking of a North American city. It also aims to stimulate reflection on the "place," variously conceived, of cities in contemporary American society and how and why "urbanity," even in its most simulated, hyperreal incarnations, continues to exert such an enduring and compelling influence on our cultural imagination. Cities have occupied an ambivalent, contradictory, but always central place within our national consciousness. Urban areas have, by turns, been represented as sites of evil and virtue, savagery and civilization, threat and opportunity, the natural habitat of both the virtuous power elite and the disorderly, threatening mob.[20] These contradictory tendencies have been accentuated not only by the ceaseless transformation of the built environment of metropolitan areas, but by the changing modes of representing and reflecting upon their social realities. Even in their most decentralized manifestations, cities remain key sites and symbols in the perpetually unfolding, highly mythologized discourse about the changing "nature" of American society.

WHATIZITNOT

Although I am a cultural anthropologist, this book is not an ethnography – a monograph in which a neatly bounded group is holistically drawn and quartered in time and space by an omniscient participant-observer. Given the inherent limitations of this narrative form – not the least of which are the arbitrary delimitations of boundaries and contexts – few anthropologists write ethnographies anymore, anyway. Instead, over the last two decades we have been experimenting with a wide variety of narrative styles, ranging from epic analyses of world-systemic scope to introspective monologues probing the depths of epistemic murk.[21] There has even been talk of returning to the public intellectuality of an earlier generation of American anthropologists, such as Ruth Benedict, Margaret Mead, and Jules Henry (although not their explanatory models), and writing for a broader, i.e. non-anthropological, readership. Despite such sentiments, however, few such accounts have appeared in print.[22] This book is intended as a modest attempt at producing a cultural critique that is accessible to a wider audience. Consequently, I have generally avoided making explicit reference to the manifold academic debates that have informed and reformed my critical gaze. Although some of my more hide-bound scholarly brethren might dismiss this work as a mere popularization (indeed, there are few more vile epithets in the secular priesthood of academia than "popularizer"), I prefer to think of it more as a work of applied anthropology.

"Ethnography," however, refers as much to a method of analysis as a manner of representation. Often glossed as "fieldwork" or "participant observation," the ethnographic method is, aside from our attachment to the sometimes troublesome concept of culture, cultural anthropology's most distinctive feature. While this work is not an ethnography in either a narrative or strict methodological sense, my analysis is nonetheless informed by an ethnographic sensibility, by which I mean a quasi-empathic attention to the cultural detail and historical context of a particular place and the peoples attached to it, rendered from the point of view of a non-native participant observer. It is a work that attempts to describe and analyze some of the structures and forces that give form and direction to an otherwise impossibly complex, fragmented, and confusing social reality. In its effort to map the "chaos of contradictory and multiple linkages" that comprise the contemporary metropolis,[23] one might consider this to be a guidebook of sorts, albeit one with lots of footnotes.

LOST IN URBAN SPACE

I find the motif of the guide to be an altogether appropriate one, as anthropologists – along with many other kinds of visitors and residents, not to mention members of every other academic tribe and creed – have often been lost in cities even before they sprawled into vast exopolitan regions. In the course of doing research for this book, I encountered many people (and more than a few anthropologists) who were more than a little mystified and confused by the fact that an anthropologist would be interested in cities, and a contemporary American one at that. Their confusion is, in part, warranted (although that manifested by my anthropological colleagues is not) by the hackneyed ways in which my discipline has often been represented in the popular media.[24] While it is true that during the first half of this century cultural anthropology was largely characterized by the intensive participant observation of relatively small, non-literate populations, this state of affairs changed markedly after 1950.[25]

Nowadays, more anthropologists than ever before are working in cities, although only a relative handful focus on the processes distinctive to them. For many anthropologists, cities are just another place where one does fieldwork, no different, conceptually, from the Highlands of Papua New Guinea or the frozen, irradiated tundra of Lapland. In other words, there is nothing distinctively "urban" about urban anthropology; our theories and methods apply equally everywhere. Other critics have claimed that with the proliferation of megalopoli, terms like urban, suburban, and rural simply do not mean much anymore. Still other naysayers claim that there is little that is "anthropological" about urban anthropology. This criticism is, in part, inspired by the neo-romantic, vision quest mentality that holds that if you have electricity and running water, you are not doing fieldwork. A far more pressing and, to a certain extent, valid concern was that the effort to understand the manifold connections of the parts to the urban whole would draw anthropologists away from the signature methods of intensive participant-observation towards the less holistic manners and customs of other disciplines.

More recently, "the city" and urbanity have experienced something of a minor renaissance as appropriate objects/subjects of inquiry across a wide variety of disciplines, including anthropology. Working in diverse locales and inspired by a wide variety of historical and contemporary intellectual influences, these authors are bound together by a common interest in understanding the interrelationships between the hard, cold, and putatively objective structures of socioeconomic reality and the softer, warmer. and more intersubjective understandings located not only in people's heads, but in their stories, books, films, and even less physically tangible cultural residues. Above all, however, they are committed to using this knowledge to imagine alternatives for a more humane metropolitan future.

One of the most significant challenges that contemporary urban areas pose for those who seek to make more than common sense of them lies not in their vast and varied extents, or with synthesizing incompatible research methodologies, but in the sheer density and diversity of images and interpretations that have been built up over, around, and through them, creating virtual cities that float freely within the placeless world of the mass media. These imaginary cities allow one to visit and "know" a place – in a highly attenuated, selective, and distorted way, to be sure – without *actually* having been there. However, they also exert a powerful influence over how the city is perceived by its inhabitants as well. They do not merely constitute a "consensual hallucination we all agree to have"[26] (indeed, many inhabitants neither consent nor agree about the form, content, and/or significance of these images) but are produced by and through an organized field of social activities that leave very material facts on the ground.

More than a decade ago, in an oft-quoted passage discussing the origins of nationalism, Benedict Anderson noted that "all communities larger than primordial villages of face to face contact (and perhaps even these) are imagined . . . to be distinguished not by their falsity and genuineness, but by the style in which they are imagined."[27] Cities and nations share some stylistic affinities in how they are conjured in the social imagination. "Style" here does not only refer to the particular kind of symbolic motifs, but the institutional/organizational means by which these images are produced, distributed, and consumed by a variety of publics. Anderson argues for the crucial importance of print (especially the newspaper and the novel) in the creation of nationness, as well as the official statist mechanisms of the map, census, and museum to further bind people into entities with a shared sense of time, space, and identity. These same institutions of representation are central to the construction of cityness as well, even as they have been supplemented and supplanted by new technologies of communication – e.g., the telephone, television, the Internet, etc. – in the course of the last century. In constructing my interpretation of Atlanta, I have relied heavily on accounts drawn from the newspapers and other media of varying degrees of permanence (local television news, magazines, scholarly works, promotional brochures, and other forms of what collectors of ephemera call "paper"), in addition to the familiar anthropological stock in trade of interviewing, archival research, and participant-observation.

Yet, while cities may come to stand for or symbolize nations, they are also imagined in a manner quite differently from these larger collectivities. Even in their most decentralized and sprawling manifestations, cities are far more concentrated symbolic locales. Not only are there a surfeit of images about the city, but the landscape itself is composed of an overload of images, most of which are purposefully designed to convey a message (although they inevitably carry many more as they are woven into the warp and weft of millions of discrete life trajectories). Indeed, as will be demonstrated in the following pages, the ability to control and shape this publi-city constitutes a central line of conflict and struggle in Olympic-era Atlanta. Inhabitants of metropolitan areas navigate their lives through a densely layered array of cultural constructs to the point now where the boundary between the real and conjured is fairly fluid indeed. Of course, these representations are not just passively consumed: people adapt, resist, and revise these images and interpretations in crafting their own vernacular responses to them. Despite the pervasive commodification and ever-increasing virtualization of everyday life, the obliteration of locality, of placefulness, is never complete. There always remains some "here" there, if only deep beneath the "urbane disguises,"[28] in the interstices of social activity, in the contradictions of experience, and in the decaying residues of individual and collective memory.

Given the sheer extent and pervasiveness of mediated images of the city, it is not surprising that it has become fashionable to think of a city as a "text" that can be read by an informed observer, with the landscape structured by the reciprocal interplay between the ordering forms of the "pattern languages" employed by planners and urban designers[29] and the creative destruction set in motion by the dynamic incoherences of market forces. The built environment of the city thus can be read for what it tells us about the personality and changing moods of the invisible hand(s) that write the urban text and, by so doing, influence the conditions under which we read it. The text analogy, though useful, has its limits (which I have, perhaps, already exceeded). It gives the impression that there is a purposive order, a scheme of organization, a master narrative, a plot at the very least, all spawned by an identifiable author or authors. Yet, a modern city such as Atlanta is the product of innumerable collaborators, who construct a text that is read by an even greater number of readers, none of whom necessarily share a common language or a way of looking at the world. Such a city is better described as a collage, a palimpsest,[30] a text full of erasures, ink smudges, and indecipherable marginalia, with some pages torn out and others pasted in so carefully as to pass for the original. These days, it seems, most people are content to look at the pictures rather than read the captions or the accompanying text, much less ponder a great deal about the relative merits of the arguments contained within.

As cities are "complex objects which include both realities and their descriptions," scholars, travelers, and residents alike face the occupational hazard of confusing cities with the words (and images) used to describe them.[31] One of my more sage-like colleagues has complained that "anthropologists don't do fieldwork anymore. They just read, and they don't read carefully."[32] He was referring to literal texts, but his comment holds true for those of a more metaphorical kind, as well as for non-anthropological readers. In response to his observation, I have attempted to be a careful reader (and writer) of Atlanta, although I make no claims about my account being particularly comprehensive or definitive in any way. Rather, it is an initial effort at what I hope will evolve into a critical public dialogue about what Atlanta "is" and is not, as well as what it could, and should, be. For far too long, questions of Atlanta's identity have been uttered and answered in an advertiser's monologue, with one, albeit not completely unified, segment of Atlantan society defining the city in terms of its own image and interests, while ignoring, dismissing, or degrading those of other groups.

I begin my account of Atlanta with a critique of the more official authoritative imaginings manifest in popular, scholarly, and entrepreneurial discourse, and along the way introduce some alternative mythologies of the city's past and present. From there, I move on to describing the political, economic, and social contexts of the metropolitan area, looking at the different ways in which the region is divided up and organized into different social topographies that provide contrasting meanings and orientations for Atlanta's diverse inhabitants. The next two chapters explore the forces that have radically restructured and redefined the "whole in the center" over time. I conclude with a chapter that explores Atlanta's Olympic-related development, chronicling the unfolding drama of crises, scandals, and protests, as well as discussing some of the enduring legacies the Olympics will leave for Atlantans.

1

BUILDING THE IMAGINARY CITY

The city as we might imagine it, the soft city of illusion, myth, aspiration, nightmare, is as real, maybe more real, than the hard city one can locate in maps and statistics, in monographs on urban sociology, demography, and architecture.

Jonathan Raban[1]

This imaginary institution of the city defines the scope – the possibilities and their limits – within which at any particular time, we can imagine, think, and experience city life; it defines the aesthetic and intellectual field within which cities will be designed, planned, and engineered.

Kevin Robins[2]

As cities swelled and fragmented in the late nineteenth century, a variety of technologies and forms of representation developed to facilitate comprehension of their principal features and extents. In the course of the twentieth century, the bird's-eye view, the city view book, and the narrative guide, with its thumb-nail descriptions of commercial establishments, history, and "points of interest," have been joined by other cultural productions that purvey a carefully designed vision of the city as a whole. These highly selective, serialized representations are thought to convey something of the "essence" of the place, the unique particularity sedimented over time in this space, even as deep structural forces render the metropolis they describe less coherent and uniquely distinctive. The "visitors' center" also belongs to this family of representative forms, although initially merely as a locus for the distribution of a multitude of informative, ephemeral texts: maps, guides, brochures, and the like. In recent years, however, these physical spaces have themselves become multimediated venues of programmed communication, key nodes in what Sharon Zukin has termed "the critical infrastructure" that shapes the public's hunger for information and other consuming desires.[3] With displays that combine the functions of the billboard, the menu, and the museum, the visitors' center sells a comprehensive abridged vision of the city's past, as well as *the* way around and through the skein of "fine-mesh money screens"[4] that constitute its contemporary landscape.

The new Welcome South Visitors' Center in downtown Atlanta is one such place of contrived spectacle, a venue whose mission it is to represent the city and the region of which it claims to be the capital. The facility is the brainchild of the Atlanta Convention and Visitors Bureau (ACVB), and is funded by the well-advertised beneficence of local corporate patrons, Olympic sponsors, and the tourism departments of seven Southern states. As the city mobilized for the Olympics, market research found that the city had a very ill defined identity. The goal of the Welcome South Visitors' Center is to craft a distinctive image for Atlanta, one that locates it firmly on the cusp between a regional and an international identity. In a snappy display of words and images, Atlanta invites the world to "Come Share Our Dream."

Atlanta has long prided itself as a city of dreams, a place where anything is possible. A dreamy quality pervades the 21,000 square feet of exhibit space. Users of the facility wander through a series of colorful displays on each of the states, pass by an information booth on the region's national parks manned by real live forest rangers, quench their thirst for the real thing at a working Coca-Cola soda fountain, satisfy other consuming desires at a large gift shop peddling Olympic and city souvenirs, before experiencing a feel-good celebration of the "Soul of the South" in still photographs and a twelve-minute film narrated by Johnny Cash. This last portrays a surreally "Sunny South": a region of proud people, abundant joy, warmth, grace, and invincible spirit that has renewed itself time and time again. Aside from a brief and cryptic mention of its "turbulent past" (which exists, it would seem, only to provide challenges for the region's invincible spirit to overcome), the conflicts and contradictions of its history – of slavery, the Civil War, the Klan, Jim Crow, and massive resistance to desegregation – are swept away by a flood tide of sweetness and light and high production values.

A similarly saccharine sensibility is manifest in the display devoted to articulating the definitive Atlanta myth. Sponsored by Bell South, an Olympic sponsor and one of the city's oldest corporate citizens, the exhibit consists of a curved wall approximately thirty feet long featuring a densely layered collage of still and video images of key people, places, and events of Atlanta's past, present, and future. With little explanatory text, the images acquire their meanings through juxtaposition and association. The wall is divided into seven segments, one focused on "history," the others on various features of its contemporary identity, e.g. its centrality in transportation, education, entertainment, telecommunications, and, of course, business. The largest amount of space, however, is devoted to a pantheon of the city's visionary dreamers. In the surfeit of guides and other promotional ephemera that constitute the single largest corpus of information on the city, Atlanta's history is often rendered as the collective biography of its visionary dreamers, of men (indeed, with one notable exception, they have tended to be male) who, infused with the magical enabling powers of the mystical Atlanta Spirit, envisioned and realized the unlikely, the improbable, the impossible. Portraits of nineteenth-century New South promoter Henry Grady, Coca-Cola founder Asa Candler and his successor, Robert Woodruff, *Gone With the Wind* author Margaret Mitchell, and former mayors William Hartsfield and Andrew Young, share pride of place with CNN founder Ted Turner, former president Jimmy Carter, ACOG czar Billy Payne, and, of course, *the* dreamer, Martin Luther King, Jr. King's black-and-white portrait is by far the largest image in this collection and is neighbor to a large color image of two persons in African dress laying flowers on his crypt.

Nowhere is it acknowledged, however, that not all of these dreamers shared the same dream. The profound differences between, say, Grady's vision of Atlanta as the capital of an industrialized, but unrepentantly white-supremacist "New" South and King's dream of a just, equal, and integrated social order, are smoothed over and effaced by their shared ability to envision a future that transcended the mundane restrictions of their respective contemporary "realities." Along with all the other omissions in the memory wall, such a condensation simplifies and sanitizes Atlanta's turbulent past in order to reinforce the image of the city's socially progressive and racially harmonious present and future.

This chapter, by contrast, presents an alternative rendering of the city's histories, placing its emphasis on the conflicts and contradictions of the different mythologies that have been elaborated over the years through a multiplicity of media. These include not only texts of literal sort, such as novels, guidebooks, magazines, films, advertisements, and scholarly works, but media events, monuments, and points of interest which are taken to define, describe, and explain the singular essence of Atlanta. Four major mythological themes dominate these representations of the city's identity: Atlanta as symbol of the antebellum South, as self-proclaimed capital of the New South, as Black Mecca, and as cosmopolitan technopolis, "the world's next great international city." Each theme arose at a particular moment in the city's history, but they do not comprise a chronological sequence. The notion of Atlanta as a city of the idealized Old South, for example, follows rather than precedes that of the city as the capital of the New South. Indeed, in a certain sense, the New South Creed can be considered to be the master myth of Atlanta history, to which the three others are complexly related and ultimately subsumed. Much like the marketplace which it venerates, the idea of the

New South has demonstrated a remarkable resiliency and ability to selectively absorb opposing points of view. In many respects, one of the most significant aspects of the history of imaginary Atlanta is the continuity of the Atlanta Spirit. In the survey that follows, I chart the socioeconomic contexts in which these mythologies emerge and mingle.

ORIGINS, 1837–65

In the perpetual shadows beneath the Central Avenue and Wall Street viaducts, across the railroad tracks from the festival marketplace of Underground Atlanta and the lurid commodity fetishism of the World of Coca-Cola advertiseum,[5] is a relatively small brick building surrounded by a spike-topped, wrought iron fence. Much of the surrounding subterranean space is given over to parking lots for the nearby government office complex and Georgia State University. The structure does not look particularly distinctive or old, and there are no signs on the exterior indicating what it is. The interior, though, has been partially fitted out as a nineteenth-century railroad station of the kind that might once have been found in small towns throughout the South and Midwest. Inside, the lighting is subdued except for a spotlit alcove in the north wall in which lies a worn stone marker approximately three feet high. Inscribed with a few cryptic letters and numbers – "W&A 00" on one side and "W&A 138" on the other – this modest granite obelisk is Atlanta's *omphalos*, its *axis mundi*, the Zero Mile Marker of the Western and Atlantic Railroad.

For over a century, this marker, from which the city's initial boundaries were drawn in 1847, had been surrounded only by a protective byre of railroad ties at the eastern end of the Union Depot train shed (quite familiar, at least in its cinematic incarnation, to the millions of viewers of *Gone With the Wind*). Rebuilt after what some Southerners still refer to as the War Between the States, the depot was demolished in 1930, after the completion of the neo-classical rotunda of the new Union Station in the western part of the railroad gulch. In 1985, the New Georgia Railroad constructed this "historic" station house around the marker as part of its efforts to run a tourist line from downtown to the neo-Confederate shrine and theme park sixteen miles to the east at Stone Mountain.

Although Stone Mountain is advertised as the third most visited theme park in the United States (after Disneyworld/Epcot and Disneyland), most of the more than six million visitors avoid the new railway and continue to make their pilgrimage by private automobile. They come to see the mighty bas relief (the world's largest sculpture, we are told) of the holy trinity of the Confederacy (Robert E. Lee, Jefferson Davis, and Stonewall Jackson), to view the laser show and hear Elvis Presley warble "Dixie," to ride the cable car to the summit and marvel at the view, to hike and gambol in the woods, to attend conferences, and to play golf. Most, apparently, do not care to spend time in downtown Atlanta, or rather, they prefer to drive when they visit the World of Coca-Cola. Owing to lack of passengers, the New Georgia Railroad ceased operations in 1993, leaving only a six-story parking deck and the ghosted station below ground.

During the work week, the fence around the station remains open to allow easy access to the subterranean parking lots that surround it, but on the weekends it is padlocked shut. One can walk around it and peer in through the windows, but cannot enter. It is occasionally used for private receptions, but on the whole it is a dead, mute space, a poorly rendered diorama, a study in unintentional emptiness. In contrast to earlier in this century, only a few contemporary guidebooks mention the site anymore, and many of the commuters that pass by it every day are oblivious to what is contained within. There is something quite appropriate about Atlanta's historic center lying inaccessible and largely forgotten by residents and tour books, as many Atlantans have highly ambivalent or outrightly antagonistic relationships to their pasts. Even more than most American cities, which tend to be a rather forward-looking lot, Atlanta has always had a particularly intense future-orientation and a peculiar fondness for the bulldozer and the wrecking-ball. This is usually attributed to the city's "lack" of history, a state of affairs owing to its youth and its destruction during the Civil War.

The station building is itself what Umberto Eco has called an "absolute fake,"[6] a monument to a conjured past, a simulation without historic precedent; the Union Depot is the only structure to have stood on this site. Although Atlanta owes its existence to the railroad, its two magnificent rail passenger terminals were demolished in the early 1970s. The few visitors arriving by either of the two daily trains that still serve Atlanta must disembark at the small Beaux Arts station a few miles to the north of downtown. Having largely eradicated many of the actual legacies of its past so as to better embrace a limitless future, Atlanta is obliged to create in their places spurious, and often second-rate, reproductions that are something less than compelling or persuasive. Few seem to notice, however, in this city of the always shimmering future.

Properly speaking, even the Zero Mile Marker is something less than an absolutely genuine foundation stone. Contrary to the renditions in numerous guidebooks, and even a number of scholarly accounts, the first zero mile post, or terminus, of the state-chartered Western and Atlantic Railroad was located a quarter of a mile to the west/north-west in 1837. Significantly, the exact location is no longer known, but different interpretations put it anywhere between the Broad Street viaduct and somewhere under the vast bunkered domain of the Georgia World Congress Center.[7] In an effort to avoid the cognitive dissonance that comes with the presence of two points of origin, many popular and scholarly authors have effaced this early shifting of centers and have treated the decisive stroke of 1837 as the founding moment of the city.[8]

The surveying party that hammered in the stake, however, was quite clear that it was merely establishing a railroad juncture and *not* founding a settlement. The chief engineer of the Western and Atlantic Railroad, Colonel Stephen Long, does not occupy a place in Atlanta's pantheon of visionary dreamers. He was of the opinion that the site would never amount to anything more than "a tavern, a blacksmith's shop, a general store, and nothing else."[9] Given the poor soil and the handful of extant white settlers, the area was certainly not an auspicious location for a town, much less a city. The nearest Native American settlement, the village of Standing Peachtree,[10] was seven miles distant, and the pioneering white settlements of Marietta and Decatur were sixteen and six miles away, respectively. Still, the site afforded easy access to nearly grade level routes running to the north, south, east, and west, and was already a crossing point for Indian trails and the crude wagon roads of the few early white pioneers who had settled in the area after the Creek Nation was forced to cede the land to the State of Georgia in 1821. In focusing on the site's then marginality, Colonel Long failed to appreciate the revolutionary potential of railroads and markets to create an artificial network of advantageous and strategic locations.

From 1837 to 1842, the area around the zero mile post was formally known as Terminus. Irish laborers brought in to build the cuts and embankments necessary for the railroad established a shantytown known as Thrasherville, named after the contractor in charge of the project, "Cousin" John Thrasher. The crude settlement was located approximately where the Federal Reserve Bank now stands on Marietta Street. Before any of the railroads reached the terminus, the mile post was moved to its present location in 1842, ostensibly because the original location was disadvantageous for the construction of the train shed, machine shops, warehouses, and other necessary facilities.[11] In the following year, the settlement's name was changed from Terminus to the village of Marthasville, in honor of Martha Lumpkin, the daughter of Georgia's governor.

In 1847, the name of the settlement was changed yet again, to "Atlanta," and the same year it was incorporated as a city, with its boundaries extending in a mile radius from the zero mile post. The name change was an early manifestation of what would later evolve into an obsessive concern for manipulating the city's image. Marthasville was deemed not to be a propitious moniker for the major metropolis some of its more expansively minded citizenry envisioned the place would one day be. The new name was inspired not by the fleet-footed but greed-damned Boeotian goddess Atalanta (although, as W.E.B. DuBois noted, given the lusty commercial obsessions of the early city fathers this would have been most appropriate[12]), but from the feminization of the "Atlantic" in the Western and Atlantic Railroad.[13] From the outset, then, Atlanta enjoyed an explicitly gendered identity, an association that was later reinforced in the fictional personage of Scarlett O'Hara.

At the time, however, Atlanta resembled anything but an idealized notion of southern femininity. In its early years, the city was a rough and rowdy frontier town possessed of far more saloons and bawdy houses than churches and reputable establishments. Work on the railroads was frequently interrupted by nationwide financial panics, with the consequence that a large percentage of the laborers were frequently unemployed. The latter group was largely composed of unmarried workmen, "adventurers," and "a liberal sprinkling of desperate characters,"[14] who drank, whored, and gambled along Murrell's Row (a two-block stretch of Decatur Street from Five Points to Pryor Street, a site now occupied by Georgia State University), and in two encampments on the eastern and western peripheries of the city, known as Slab Town and Snake Nation respectively. In these "two suburban villages of huts," one of the city's earliest mythographers noted, "prevailed almost every species of idle, vicious, and criminal amusement."[15]

Like most frontier towns, the establishment of the city of Atlanta is often rendered as a tale of the triumph of civilization over savagery. However, with the native Creeks and Cherokees having been displaced by treaties and force of arms during the 1820s and 1830s,[16] the role of the savage other was played by the lawless rabble of white laborers who constructed the railroads on which the future prosperity of the settlement was based. As the railroads were completed in the late 1840s and early 1850s, the eminently respectable, God-fearing merchant class began to assert themselves in municipal affairs. The denizens of the poorer regions, together with the "gamblers and drinking faction," loosely organized under the banner of the "Rowdy Party," fought for control of the settlement against the steadily increasing numbers of wealthier and more respectable citizenry, who had formed themselves into the "Moral" or "Orderly Party."[17]

Initially, what one chronicler has referred to as the "looser element" held sway. The city's first mayor, Moses Formwalt, was a Murrell's Row saloon owner and manufacturer of distilling apparatuses.[18] By 1850, however, Orderly Party candidate Jonathan Norcross, a wealthy Yankee-born merchant and saw mill owner, was elected mayor and proceeded to wage a forceful campaign against his political rivals. After the Rowdies mounted a failed attack on his store, Norcross had their leaders arrested and run out of town, while a posse of the mayor's cronies razed the offending habitations of Snake Nation and Slab Town to the ground.[19] While these actions did not purge the town of its giddy multitude, it did effectively end their influence in the governing of the settlement. The political ascendancy of the mercantile class during the 1850s reflected the city's growing importance as a trade center that came with the completion of the rail lines that linked the Gulf and Atlantic coasts with the Ohio Valley. Between 1848 and 1854, the population increased from 500 to 6,000, bringing with it the usual frontier-conquering array of churches, newspapers, and associations for civic betterment. By 1857, Atlanta's growth and strategic location at the confluence of several key regional rail lines led boosters to dub it "the Gate City of the South."[20]

DESTRUCTION AND "RESURGENS," 1865–95

It is tempting to think of what would have happened to Atlanta had it not been destroyed in the course of what Southerners used to call the Great Unpleasantness, for the city's phoenix-like rise from its own ashes is the crucial element of the city myth and the crucible in which the Atlanta Spirit was forged. Some years after the event, former Union General William Tecumseh Sherman noted to an Atlanta journalist that the same forces that led him to destroy the city, namely its strategic role in transportation, would make it a great one in the future.[21] In a rhetorical turn that gives a rather literal twist to Schumpeter's notion of "creative destruction," the sacking of Atlanta is now ritually invoked as point of reference and justification for virtually every municipally sanctioned spasm of demolition and displacement. Having been destroyed once, Atlantans have learned to embrace such tragedy as a necessary, and even desirable, virtue.

Even before the city's destruction, the Civil War had greatly enhanced Atlanta's place on the map. Owing to its centrality within the South's underdeveloped rail network, Atlanta's population doubled between 1861 and 1864 as the city became a key industrial, medical, and logistical center for the Confederacy.[22] Later boosters were to make much of the claim that the city was second only in importance to Richmond.[23] Atlanta's centrality made it a strategic target for Union armies moving slowly down from Tennessee. During the summer of 1864, a series of battles raged around the city's periphery that ravaged the defending Confederate garrison and cut the rail lines that tied it with the rest of the South. Facing a lengthy siege and eventual capture, the Confederate armies abandoned the city in September, blowing up whatever might be of use to Yankee forces and inflicting no small amount of damage upon the city in the process. Ironically, the epic conflagration celebrated in *Gone With the Wind* was the handiwork of Confederate, not Union, matches. Sherman's army completed the task of destruction when they began their march to the sea in November.

An enduring feature of the city myth from the 1870s to the present has been that no other American city has suffered such devastation in war. Indeed, the official historical account of the Atlanta Committee for the Olympic Games explicitly claims that Atlanta is "the only city in the United States *ever* destroyed by the flames of war."[24] While the damage inflicted upon the city was incontestably severe, with only 400 of more than 3,800 buildings left standing, other Southern cities, particularly Richmond, Virginia and Columbia, South Carolina, suffered equivalent or greater destruction. Still, neither of these two cities have made as much of their destruction and resurgence as has Atlanta.

Regardless of whether or not it was the most devastated city in the United States, Atlanta's destruction did clear the way for an even greater rebirth. Under Federal occupation, Atlanta became the headquarters for the military government of Georgia, as well as for the Freedmen's Bureau[25] throughout the region. By the end of 1866, it had doubled its 1860 population (although according to legend, half of these were widows).[26] In 1867, the city was made the state capital, after hoteliers in the then capital of Milledgeville refused to accommodate newly elected African-American delegates to the State Assembly. Despite vocal opposition from disenfranchised Confederati at the time, this decision was reconfirmed by Bourbon Democrat redeemers after the end of Reconstruction in 1877. The city's administrative centrality attracted greater numbers of the opportunistic politician–entrepreneurs known throughout the South as "scalawags" and "carpetbaggers."

One of the most important of the Yankee opportunists was Hannibal Kimball, a representative of the Northern railroad interests who were restoring and acquiring the South's network of rails. As vizier to the legendarily corrupt Reconstruction governor Rufus Bullock, Kimball lavishly dispensed state funds to himself and his cronies, some of whom were otherwise respectable members of the city's native business class.[27] While a little more than a century later his activities would have been celebrated as fine examples of a splendid partnership between the public and private sectors, Kimball was much reviled at the time for making a handsome profit on the sale of his "opera house" building to the newly relocated legislative assembly (replaced by the current gold-domed edifice in 1888) and constructing the South's finest hostelry, the Kimball House, with state-backed railroad bonds.[28] Yet, despite his association with the odious forces of Reconstruction, after a brief hiatus Kimball returned to play a major role in the city's economic affairs well into the 1880s. His eponymous hotel, which burned and was replaced by an even grander structure in 1883, was one of the resurgent city's most prominent symbols of progress until after the turn of the century.[29]

With its economy buoyed by the influx of Northern capital and local sweat equity (much of which was provided by chain-gang labor), the population of Atlanta grew more than fivefold in the thirty years after the Civil War. By 1890, Atlanta was inhabited by slightly more than 65,000 people.[30] Thousands of former slaves streamed into the city after the war, settling mostly in creek bottoms and along the railroad tracks in localities called Mechanicsville, Beaver Slide, Shermantown, and Hell's Half Acre. At the start of the war, African-Americans had accounted for no more than one fifth of Atlanta's population; a decade later they comprised approximately 45 percent of the city's inhabitants. The African-American population almost doubled between 1880 and 1890, but this increase was offset by an even greater rise in the white population. These trends continued through the early twentieth century. By 1900, blacks constituted just under 40 percent of the population and by 1910, only a third.[31] While most worked in the lower echelons of the railroad industry or as common laborers, a small but significant "talented tenth" of teachers, preachers, and entrepreneurs also emerged. The development of this black middle class was largely due to the establishment, between 1866 and 1885, of six universities that made Atlanta an unparalleled center of African-American higher education and helped to forge its later reputation as a "Black Mecca."[32] Black students came from all over the country to avail themselves of a classical liberal arts education that was the antithesis of the vocational training being offered at Booker T. Washington's Tuskegee Institute in Alabama.

Although white boosters prided themselves on the city's racial harmony, Atlanta's emergence as a center of African-American opportunity in the later nineteenth century was rarely, and then only reluctantly, acknowledged by them. Located on high ground to the east and west of the city, the colleges were both spatially and socially isolated from the rest of Atlanta. The New Englanders who comprised most of the faculty were treated as pariahs by other whites and their students subjected to discrimination and intimidation.[33] Tales of African-American entrepreneurship and non-vocational higher education did not exactly fit with the forward-thinking, but still unrelentingly white supremacist notions of what historian Paul Gaston has called the "New South Creed."[34]

Although they could not be said to constitute a formally organized movement in a political sense, the ideologues of the New South all envisioned a new socioeconomic order founded on industry, diversified agriculture, racial harmony (albeit based on black subordination), and the reconciliation of sectional differences between North and South. Contrary to the critical claims of planters and populists, the New South involved neither a wholesale rejection of Southern identity nor the simple parroting of Yankee ways. As Gaston and others have noted, the idea of the New South offered a way of reclaiming regional identity and the honor of the Lost Cause in the face of an ignominious defeat. Despite welcoming Northern capital and ways of doing business, there was plenty of the Old South in the New, especially when it came to race relations and a dependent position within the national economy.

The first use of the term "New South" appears in a *Putnam's Magazine* article written by former Confederate propagandist Edward De Leon in 1870.[35] However, most accounts of Atlanta's history have attributed the term to Henry Woodfin Grady, an Athens (Georgia)-born journalist who wrote for what emerged as the city's (and the region's) leading newspaper, the *Atlanta Constitution*. While he may not have coined the term "New South," Grady proved to be its most eloquent and energetic exponent. In 1880, Grady became managing editor and, with the aid of a loan from Northern industrialist Cyrus Field, part owner of the newspaper. Although Birmingham, Chattanooga, and other cities had their devotees, Grady viewed Atlanta, rebuilt by the union of Northern money and "Southern brains and energy," as the perfect embodiment, and undisputed capital, of the New South.[36] Until his death in 1889 at the relatively young age of thirty-nine, Grady assumed the role of chief apostle of this civic religion, using the newspaper and the lecture circuit to spread the gospel of sectional reconciliation and industrialization to his regional compatriots and Northern businessmen alike. Grady's most famous moment occurred in 1886 at a banquet at Delmonico's Restaurant in New York City, where he delivered what has come to be known as his "New South" speech. Among the crowd of bankers and industrialists of the New England Society of New York was General William Tecumseh Sherman, whom Grady rather good-naturedly admonished "for being a little careless with fire." Then, in an oft-quoted passage, he proceeded to tell his audience that "we have raised a brave and beautiful city; that somehow or other we have caught the sunshine in the bricks and mortar of our homes and have builded therein not one ignoble prejudice or memory."[37]

On the matter of prejudice, Grady was referring to Southern attitudes toward the North rather than towards African-Americans. He was very much aware, however, that the modernizing program of the New South required a solution to the "negro question" as much as sectional reconciliation, industrialization, and scientific, diversified agriculture. New Southerners like Grady were willing to grudgingly allow African-Americans an existence in their realm (indeed, they were quite aware of their much-needed labor power), provided they minded their place, which in the post-Reconstruction era was most emphatically separate from, and subordinate to, that of whites.[38] In regard to race relations, the paternalism of the New South was hardly an improvement on the Old.

During the late 1870s, Atlantans begin promoting an image of their city as the New York or Chicago of the South (the choice, presumably, depending on which group of Northern businessmen they were courting), although it possessed less than a tenth the population of either of these two metropolises. Such was the essence of the fervid and zealous attitude that would become known as "the Atlanta Spirit." Local boosters were aided in their efforts by such national periodicals as *Harper's*, *Putnam's*, and *Scribner's*, which were engaged in their own task of sectional reconciliation. The truest emanations of the Atlanta Spirit, however, were to be found in the book-length accounts produced by local authors. Directories of local commercial establishments and services had appeared in Atlanta as early as 1859. Beginning in the 1870s, these commercial listings were embedded in more systematic journalistic efforts at defining the alluring attributes of Atlanta as a place for business. The first of these, *Atlanta As It Is*, was written by a local physician in 1871.[39] While it was the first text to spell out what were soon to be familiar features of the city myth – its foundation at the zero mile post in 1837 and miraculous rebirth in 1865, its unparalleled location and climate, the progressive business orientation of its diverse and moral populace, etc. – it was later spurned for its relatively uncritical assessment of then Governor Rufus Bullock, who was turned out of office later that year in a financial scandal.

What is generally considered to be the *ur*-text of the Atlanta Spirit first appeared some six years later. Reprinted in 1878 and 1881, *Atlanta Illustrated* was written by Colonel E.Y. Clarke, part owner and publisher of the *Atlanta Constitution,* and was regarded as the city's "official history" until after the turn of the century. All key elements of the city myth are present in Clarke's text, from rapturous descriptions of the healthful climate and perfect environment, to the initial founding stroke of the zero mile post and the miraculous rebirth out of the ashes of the war. For Clarke and subsequent generations of boosters, however, the most crucial and defining aspects of Atlanta were the irrepressible spirit of enterprise that motivated the population and the fundamental social equality that this pecuniary metaphysics created: i.e., "there is no city in this or any other country more free from the domination of *caste*."[40]

Clarke was referring, of course, only to the qualities and opportunities peculiar to Atlantans of European extraction and not to the increasingly caste-like status accorded to African-Americans after the defeat of Reconstruction forces in Georgia. In fact, African-Americans are not mentioned at all in his account, even though they constituted more than 40 percent of the city's population at the time and were served by the only institutions of higher education in the city.[41] This textual invisibility, or at best near invisibility, would become a common feature of later descriptions of the city up through the early twentieth century, a literary manifestation of the increasing racial segregation of the post-Reconstruction era. By the 1890s, African-Americans were barred from mixing with whites in virtually every social venue. As elsewhere in the *fin de siècle* South, Atlanta's public sphere was a blindingly whitish orb.

EXPOSING THE NEW SOUTH

The Atlanta of the New South found its most dramatic expression not in oratory or written accounts, but in a trio of major expositions held in 1881, 1887, and 1895. While Atlanta had regularly hosted commercial fairs, these events were of unprecedented scale, complexity, and ambition. The first was the International Cotton Exposition of 1881, which was envisioned as a showcase both of the state of the art in cotton textile production and of the unique capabilities of Atlanta to support such activities. It was also the first effort to market the city in an explicitly international sense, albeit with less than spectacular results in this regard. Atlanta's selection as the exposition's locale was an example of sectional reconciliation in action, the product of the evangelical zeal of Henry Grady and the New England contacts of former carpetbagger, and now respectable citizen, Hannibal Kimball. The latter's central role in the scandals of the Reconstruction era had been conveniently erased, if not from memory, at least from public mention following his clearance by a grand jury called in 1874 to investigate his alleged wrongdoing.[42]

The centerpiece of the exposition was a building modeled after a state-of-the art cotton factory that, together with the grounds (and no small part of the city itself), had been constructed by chain-gang labor. As an example of the leading edge in textile manufacture, the governors of Georgia and Connecticut were provided with finished suits made from cotton picked on the grounds, ginned, woven, dyed, and fabricated into garments between sunrise and sunset. Whether such gimmickry was responsible is unclear, but a number of textile mills were established in and around Atlanta shortly after the exposition was over.[43] While much celebrated by city boosters, textiles remained only a small, if significant, dimension of Atlanta's nineteenth-century manufacturing sector.[44] The marketing of the cotton produced in the Georgia Piedmont, however, remained at the center of the city's economy. The expansion of the cotton trade during the 1880s and early 1890s proved a major element of the city's increasing prosperity, while the demise of cotton monoculture after the turn of the century was responsible for a vast flow of displaced rural migrants into Atlanta.

The International Cotton Exposition coincided with a renewed national interest in southern themes during the post-Reconstruction era. Before the Civil War, images of the region had been polarized between the abolitionist critiques of the evils of slavery and romanticized renderings of an aristocratic plantation society. Despite the efforts of boosters in the years after the war, the image of the agrarian Old South proved far more compelling than the industrious New South for both national writers and readers. This reinfatuation with antebellum plantation life was stimulated in part by the publication of the first of Joel Chandler Harris's Uncle

Remus tales in 1880. At the time, Harris was assistant editor and Romancer-in-residence of the *Atlanta Constitution* and a friend and colleague of Henry Grady.

In some respects, Harris's appropriations of African-American folktales and dialect set within the racially harmonious world of the plantation seem the complete antithesis of the New South. However, New Southerners were not hostile towards tales of an idyllic antebellum past, particularly if they helped reinforce their paternalistic notions of racial inequality. Moreover, in his editorials and articles for the *Constitution*, Harris was a staunch supporter of Grady's modernizing program, even though in his later *Uncle Remus Magazine* he criticized the negative consequences of industrialism.[45] Although Atlanta did not completely lack authors, poets, and other self-styled cultural producers in the late nineteenth century,[46] Harris was the first and only to achieve a lasting national and international reputation.[47] His celebrity alone, more so than the specific content of his stories, helped provide the extra-local recognition that New South Atlanta craved. Harris's gingerbread Victorian home in the streetcar suburb of West End, known as the Wren's Nest, became one of the city's most celebrated attractions after his death in 1908. Like most other places of civic import, the Wren's Nest was off-limits to African-American patrons, and was only desegregated by court order in 1968, long after the city's other public spaces had been integrated.

The success of the 1881 exposition inspired the city's leading businessmen to sponsor a second major fair some six years later. As with the Cotton Exposition, the stated goal of the Piedmont Exposition was to promote the modernization and industrialization of Southern agriculture, although with a less specifically international orientation. Partly due to the impetus provided by the two expositions, the 1880s were a period of tremendous growth and prosperity for Atlanta as a whole. In the course of the decade, it more than doubled its population and emerged as the largest city in Georgia and the third largest in the Southeast. To commemorate its growth, the city adopted a new official symbol in 1887. Using a talisman that had long been employed by local boosters, the locomotive was dropped from the city seal and replaced by a resplendent phoenix rising from the ashes. The legendary bird of Egyptian mythology was flanked by the city's two dates of origin – 1847 and 1865 – while over its head was the new city motto, "Resurgens."

In the course of the 1890s, a series of city view books were published that further served to project and define an authoritative image of the city for both visitors and residents. The first of these was the anonymous *The Gate City: Atlanta, Historical, Descriptive, and Picturesque*, published in 1890 by the Art Publishing Company of Neenah, Wisconsin. Although E.Y. Clarke's *Atlanta Illustrated* contained several line drawings of noted buildings, *The Gate City* was the first text to make lavish use of photography to provide a coherent and laudatory image of the city for mass

circulation. Indeed, the photographs of Atlanta's parks, civic and commercial buildings, fine suburban homes, and factories speak far more loudly than the relatively
simple and unadorned text, providing dramatic proof of Atlanta's recovery from the
devastation of war and its "cityness" by the standards of its time. With its emphasis on the civic-monumental features of Atlanta, and its utter avoidance of people,
slums, or anything that might take away from the orderly and composed nature of
the urban environment, *The Gate City* is a good example of what Charles Hales has
referred to as the "urban grand style" of photography.[48] However, when compared
to view books of other cities at the time, there is little that is grand or particularly
urban about the settlement represented in its pages.[49]

In contrast to earlier works on the city, *The Gate City* does include views and
brief, if slightly misleading, descriptions of five of the six institutions of African-
American higher education located in Atlanta: Atlanta Baptist Seminary (later
Morehouse College), Spelman Seminary (later College), Atlanta University, Clark
College, and Gammon Theological Seminary (for reasons unknown, mention of
Morris Brown College was omitted). However, they appear at the back of the
book and without any mention of the small but successful middle class that led the
city's African-American population. In keeping with the increasingly segregated
tone of the times, the city's African-American preachers, teachers, and entrepreneurs were celebrated in their own and unrelated text, the Rev. E.F. Carter's *The
Black Side: A Partial History of the Business, Religious, and Educational Side of the Negro
in Atlanta, Ga.*, published in 1894.

As might well be expected, Carter's account of what he refers to as the
"Hamitic population" contrasts markedly in many respects with the narratives
proffered by white authors, particularly in its interpretation of the city's destruction by Sherman and the days of Reconstruction. Rather than an act of brutal
barbarism, the rain of Union shells on Atlanta was seen as "the strokes of the
hammer of liberty, unfastening the fetters of the accursed and inhuman institution
of slavery."[50] Likewise, the reign of the Reconstructionists, during which former
slaves became freemen and statesmen, was viewed as a time of jubilation. Much
like white New South authors, however, Carter also struck a note of accommodation amidst the interracial hostility of the post-Reconstruction era. Writing even
as Jim Crow was beginning to tighten its grip over the not-so-New South, Carter
noted that much of the intense hostility of the Reconstruction period was over:
"The white man is glad that the black man is free and the black man is glad that the
white man is free."[51] Carter, though, was no Booker T. Washington, who in his
opening address to the Cotton States and International Exposition the following
year in Atlanta would urge African-Americans to accept social and political subordination in return for economic opportunity. Rather, much like Atlanta

University professor W.E.B. DuBois, Carter argued for the rights of citizenship for African-Americans.

The 1890s, however, were marked by a steady erosion of the social and political position of African-Americans in Atlanta and throughout the South. The racial paternalism of white society and the subordinate place of African-Americans within the social order of the New South were as emphatically displayed at the 1895 Cotton States and International Exposition as any other feature of the region. The largest of the regional expositions of the period, the fair took its organizational cues from the 1893 Columbian Exposition in Chicago. Displeased by the way in which the region had been represented at the latter event, Atlanta's wealthiest citizens sought to create an event that would rectify the image of the city and region, as well as stimulate economic activity in the throes of a serious global depression.

Amidst the Romanesque revival and Italianate pavilions celebrating manufactures and other manifestations of the modern age,[52] exposition organizers could point proudly to the existence of a Woman's Building and a Negro Building as evidence of their progressive attitude on both gender and race relations. Constructed by an African-American contractor, the Negro Building celebrated the achievements of black Southerners in the postwar period. However, its exhibits were calculated to display the limits as well as the accomplishments of African-Americans. Furthermore, the building's location in the low-lying southeastern corner of the fair site, between the grandstand for Buffalo Bill's Wild West Show and the entertainments of the Midway, also clearly demonstrated the subordinate position of blacks.

The exposition did not merely reflect the position of African-Americans in the New South, it enacted it as well. Black visitors were allowed equal access to all of the public venues, although they were barred from most of the private exhibitions and were excluded from purchasing refreshment at all but the Negro Building.[53] The most telling event of the expo occurred on opening day in Booker T. Washington's speech offering the Negro Building as a gift of the colored people of the South to the world. Prior to his address, Washington had achieved some recognition as the founder of the Tuskegee Institute in Alabama, the institution which had pioneered advanced vocational training for African-Americans. He had been one of three black leaders whom fair organizers had enlisted to help lobby the federal government for financial support for the exposition.[54] As a consequence of his speech that day, which W.E.B. DuBois labeled "the Atlanta Compromise," Washington gained recognition as the country's foremost African-American leader. In urging acceptance of black political and social disenfranchisement in return for educational and economic opportunities, Washington signaled African-American acceptance of the "separate but equal" doctrine that would be given legal sanction in the Supreme

Court's *Plessy vs. Ferguson* decision the following year and in a series of "Jim Crow laws" enacted over the next two decades. Although Washington's message of subordinate reconciliation was eagerly consumed by white Southerners and offered as further proof of their enlightened attitude towards race, it prompted much opposition from African-American intellectuals, most notably from W.E.B. DuBois at Atlanta University.

The expo was a celebration of sectional, as much as racial reconciliation. Considerable numbers of Union and Confederate veterans were among the 800,000 who attended. There was great celebration of national symbols throughout the exposition. The Liberty Bell was brought down from Philadelphia by special train, there were visitations by President Grover Cleveland and soon-to-be president William McKinley, as well as days given over to the celebration of states and cities from around the nation. The exposition celebrated Atlanta's status as capital of a resurgent region that was firmly reintegrated into the national union. However, fair organizers were not content to highlight Atlanta's position within the United States; they were also interested in heightening the prospects for Atlanta's international commercial ties, especially with Latin America.

The internationality of the exposition extended far beyond the desire to stimulate trade. Much like the 1893 Chicago Columbian Exposition and the 1904 Louisiana Purchase Exposition and Olympic World's Fair in St Louis, the 1895 fair featured numerous exhibits that sought to represent the world to Atlantans and other visitors. As if to underscore the sociocultural hierarchy at work, these exhibits were housed not in formal pavilions like those celebrating machinery or manufactures, but in a series of "villages" – Mexican, Japanese, Chinese, African (Dahomey), and German – scattered throughout the fairgrounds, as well as in a "Midway Heights" entertainment zone. The latter featured living dioramas of exotic landscapes, such as the "Streets of Cairo" exhibit, interspersed with thrilling rides like "Shoot the Chute" and a Phoenix (or Ferris) Wheel. Anticipating the worst excesses of contemporary US amusement parks – such as Busch Gardens' "Dark Continent" in Tampa, Florida – by more than three-quarters of a century, these displays of cultural otherness were both wildly popular and deeply dehumanizing. The Chinese had to be literally locked in their village after their arrival at the city's Union Depot provoked a near riot of curious and abusive onlookers.[55] By far the worst treatment, however, was that accorded to America's "domestic" foreigners. Among the Midway's most popular exhibits was one organized by the Rosebud Indian Organization of South Dakota, which featured a re-enactment of the 1890 Wounded Knee massacre by Sioux who had participated in, and survived the government repression of, the Ghost Dance movement.[56]

Unlike the 1881 exposition, that of 1895 did not immediately produce the anticipated wave of new outside investment in Atlanta, nor did it greatly stimulate the city's global linkages. In fact, the economic realities of the fair helped to underscore the weakness, fragility, and contradictions of Atlanta and the underdeveloped region of which it was the capital. Despite the impressive attendance figures, gate receipts did not come close to covering the $3 million cost. Facing bankruptcy halfway through its three-month run, the exposition only barely staved off closure through the personal subvention of the city's leading businessmen who comprised the exposition's board of directors.[57] Despite a third of a century of New South boosterism, the economy of Georgia and the greater Southeast was still overly dependent on the monocrop production of cotton and a series of industrial-extractive activities, such as timbering, quarrying, and kaolin-mining, largely controlled by Northern interests.

THE CAPITAL OF CAPITAL IN THE NEW SOUTH, 1895–1959

Despite the 1895 exposition's lack of financial success, and the generally weak state of the economy, Atlanta did manage to enhance its position as the leading city of the underdeveloped Southeast in the ensuing years. While its efforts to lure more industry remained hamstrung by discriminatory freight rates, Atlanta's robust economic growth after the turn of the century came via the consolidated expansion of transportation, trade, and both commercial and governmental administration. During the first three decades of the twentieth century, Atlanta emerged as an unparalleled regional center for finance, insurance, wholesaling, and conventions, as well as for the location for US Government agencies like the Federal Reserve Bank, the Federal Appeals Court, and a large federal penitentiary.[58] Expansion of these regional command and control functions stimulated the construction of a classic Central Business District that resembled, in miniature to be sure, those of Chicago and New York. Meanwhile, an extensive network of streetcars and, after 1920, the widespread use of automobiles encouraged the expansion of a suburban frontier.

Atlanta's population grew rapidly in the late nineteenth and early twentieth centuries, increasing by some 28 percent between 1890 and 1900 to reach a turn-of-the-century figure of approximately 90,000. The city grew by 42 percent between 1900 and 1910 and an explosive 72 percent between 1920 and 1929. By the onset of the Great Depression, the city of Atlanta had some 285,000 inhabitants, while its immediate metropolitan environs were home to another 75,000.[59] The great majority of these new residents prior to 1920 were poor whites and blacks

fleeing a rural economy devastated by plummeting cotton prices and the depreda-
tions of the boll weevil. They concentrated in the low-lying peripheries of
downtown and near the railroad tracks, in neighborhoods that lacked even the most
basic of municipal services. The resultant living conditions produced crime and
death rates that were among the highest in the nation.[60] In 1917, W.E.B. DuBois
gave an impassioned description of the uneven landscape of booming Atlanta:

> The Atlanta rich have wrung city taxes out of poor blacks and poor whites and then
> squandered wealth to lay mile upon mile of beautiful boulevard through silent and
> empty forests with mile upon mile of nine inch water mains and sewers of the latest
> design, while here and there rise grudgingly the spreading castles of the Suddenly
> Rich; but in the city's heart . . . the children sicken and die because there is no city
> water, 5,000 black children sit in the streets, for there are no seats in the schools.[61]

DuBois's voice was a lonely and solitary one, however. A new wave of city
view books between the turn of the century and the Depression celebrated only the
prosperous features of Atlanta's new urban landscape.[62] The chief iconic feature of
the early twentieth century city was not the decaying Union Depot (demolished in
1930) or the new Terminal Station (completed in 1905), but the emergent business
district just north of the railroad tracks. Known as Five Points, owing to the intersection of the city's five most important streets – Whitehall, Peachtree, Marietta,
Edgewood, and Decatur – it had long been the principal gathering place in a city
that lacked any significant public open space downtown. A small forest of neo-
Gothic, Italianate, and "Chicago-style" office buildings arose to house the
headquarters of major banks and insurance firms, as well as lawyers, accountants,
and other purveyors of professional services. A thicket of upscale hotels followed
to serve the city's growing convention industry, along with theaters and retail
establishments. Owing to its uncontested multifunctional centrality in commerce,
retail, entertainment, and finance, Five Points was touted as the "Times Square, the
Hollywood and Vine, the Singapore of the South."[63] Photographs of its densely
crowded streets and sidewalks figured prominently in guidebooks and city view
books of the era, offering proof of Atlanta's modernity, industriousness, and bustle.[64] As historian Tim Crimmins has noted, Five Points came to constitute a visual
metaphor for the entire city by the third decade of the twentieth century.[65]

FORWARD ATLANTA

Both the city view books and the expositions sought to highlight the city's unique
attributes to prospective visitors and investors. By the 1920s, enhanced competition between American cities for increasingly footloose capital obliged Atlanta to

adopt methods of urban promotion that had been used with great effect in other cities, most notably Los Angeles. Faced with competition from the Florida land boom and a decline in the local construction industry, the Atlanta Chamber of Commerce embarked in 1925 on an ambitious marketing campaign to sell the city to national concerns. The city had been aggressively promoted throughout its brief history, but the "Forward Atlanta" campaign constituted a new level in marketing the city as a commodity using state-of-the-art techniques of advertising.

In the four years of the campaign, more than 125 million impressions of advertisements were placed in specialized trade and financial publications (*Forbes, Barrons*), newspapers (*New York Times*), and general periodicals (*Harper's, Saturday Evening Post*).[66] While the ads differed slightly in emphasis, they all touted Atlanta's strategic location in an increasingly decentralized national economy and its abundant, non-unionized supply of "intelligent, willing, inherently skillful Anglo-Saxon workers" who were "free from the unreasonable attitude which elsewhere has so seriously hampered production and raised costs."[67] As with E.Y. Clarke's account fifty years earlier, and true to the deeply racist spirit of the age, no mention was made of African-American Atlantans, who comprised approximately 35 percent of the city's population and a substantial segment of its labor force.[68]

The Forward Atlanta campaign also subsidized the publication of a book to further disseminate Atlanta's message. Written by the president of the Chamber of Commerce, *Atlanta From the Ashes* was the perfect embodiment of the Atlanta Spirit in action. Indeed, its author, Ivan Allen, Sr, would go on to write *the* book defining the Atlanta Spirit ("Altitude + Attitude") some years later.[69] Somewhat ironically published by the Ruralist Press, Allen's first volume was intended to allow the reader "to place an exact valuation upon Atlanta"[70] by means of a comprehensive survey of the city's economic development. In many ways no more than a contemporary update of Clarke's earlier work, the book provided an elaborated exegesis of the themes in the ads (Atlanta's strategic location, transportation infrastructure, low taxes, intelligent non-unionized Anglo-Saxon labor) mingled with the by now familiar mythistory of an energetic, industrious people raising the city up out of its own ashes into a modern metropolis.

Drawn by cheap labor, low taxes, and centrality of transportation, over 700 businesses established operations in the city between 1926 and 1929. While a few of these were industrial operations, the vast majority involved warehousing, distribution, or branch office space.[71] With its emphasis on office work and the distribution of rather than the production of goods, Atlanta anticipated the service orientation of the post-World War II economy. Together with the establishment of the South's first radio station (WSB, "The Voice of the South") these enterprises helped to reinforce Atlanta's role and image as regional capital. However, the region it controlled was an exceedingly poor one. In many respects, Atlanta was not unlike one of those colonial cities scattered over European-governed territories in Africa and Asia, an outpost through which the wealth of the region was extracted.[72] The economic underdevelopment of rural Georgia and the rest of the Southeastern states placed limits on Atlanta's growth, a state of affairs that was underscored by the devastating effects of the Great Depression on the economy of the city and the region.

THE NOT SO NEW SOUTH: HATEFUL ATLANTA

In Georgia . . . the liberated lower orders of whites have borrowed the worst commercial bounderism of the Yankee and superimposed it on a culture that, at bottom, is but little removed from savagery. Georgia is at once the home of the cotton mill sweater and of the most noisy and vapid Chamber of Commerce, of the Methodist parson turned Savonarola and of the lynching bee. A self-respecting European, going there to live, would not only find intellectual stimulation lacking; he would actually feel a certain insecurity as if the scene were the Balkans or the China Coast. The Leo Frank affair was no isolated phenomenon. It fitted into its frame very snugly. It was a natural expression of Georgian notions of truth and justice . . .

H.L. Mencken, "The Sahara of the Bozart" [73]

As H.L. Mencken rather acerbically noted in 1917, the sociocultural underdevelopment of the New South paralleled, or even exceeded, that of its economy. The rise of Populism as a political force in the 1890s and the early years of the twentieth century only served to accentuate what W.E.B. DuBois later referred to as the "naked and unashamed race hatred of whites."[74] Although the Populist Party would in its waning days make an appeal to black voters, its racial consciousness was ultimately no more enlightened than that of the urban boosters it excoriated.

The regressive racial attitudes of the so-called Progressive Era were a national rather than a regional phenomenon. Indeed, if the New South movement might be partially characterized by the adoption of Yankee business ways by Southerners, we might also talk about a sort of reverse Reconstruction in the decades after 1877, in the course of which Northern attitudes to race underwent a profound "Southernization." This was nowhere better demonstrated than in the national popularity of revisionist accounts of the Civil War and Reconstruction, best typified by Thomas Dixon's novel *The Clansman*, D.W. Griffith's film *Birth of a Nation* (based in part on Dixon's novel), and the so-called Dunning School of Southern historiography, all of which emphasized the corruption, incompetence, and venality of carpetbaggers, scalawags, and, especially, the newly enfranchised African-Americans.[75]

The New South contained within it some of the worst features of the Old South, especially when it came to race. Yet, despite intensifying disenfranchisement, segregation, and the denial of even the most basic of civil rights, the accelerating decline of the rural economy prompted African-Americans to continue to migrate to Atlanta in the 1890s. Despite the steady immigration flow, the percentage of blacks in the overall Atlanta population declined from 42.9 percent to 39.8 percent in 1900, as even more poor white rural migrants moved to the city.[76] While residential segregation had yet to be institutionalized in law, and African-Americans worked and resided in various locations all over the city, they were most intensively concentrated in overcrowded neighborhoods west, south, and east of the urban core.[77] Virtually all public accommodations were segregated, however, and blacks were banned from using such civic facilities as the public library, city parks, and other recreation facilities.

One of the central places of *fin de siècle* Black Atlanta was a section of Decatur Street running east for several blocks from Five Points known as Rusty Row. Home to an array of stores, saloons, brothels, and other places frequented by African-Americans, whites considered the street a sordid zone of immorality and a place of dangerous black male sexuality.[78] It was thus a paramount target in late September 1906 for an armed, drunken mob of 5,000 whites, inflamed by fabricated press accounts of attacks on white women. After laying waste to Rusty Row, the frenzied mob spread throughout the city, assaulting and murdering African-Americans in an indiscriminate orgy of violence that lasted for several days.[79]

The 1906 race riot constituted a major blow to the myth of racial harmony spun by both white and black proponents of the New South Creed. As such, it was excised completely from the more explicitly promotional accounts of the city's history that appeared in the 1920s, even John Hornady's pro-Klan ode *Atlanta: Yesterday, Today, and Tomorrow* (1922). Two decades later, this reticence had vanished and the locally, but anonymously, authored Work Projects Administration guide to the city, *Atlanta: Capital of the Modern South* (1942), provided an account that played up the "justifiable" nature of the riot given the "boldness and insolence of the lower Negro element" and the all-too-familiar blood libel of sexual assaults on white womanhood.[80]

Following the riot, race-based zoning and other more informal means were used to enforce residential and commercial segregation. Decatur Street remained a center of African-American retail and working-class entertainment, but the more successful black entrepreneurs concentrated themselves in a segregated business district east of downtown and two blocks north of Decatur Street on Auburn Avenue. By mid-century, "Sweet Auburn" was known as "the richest Negro Street in the World."[81] Here were located the headquarters for black-owned banks, insurance companies, and, after 1932, the nation's only black daily newspaper, the *Atlanta World*. The concentration of black capital in Sweet Auburn helped to define an entrepreneurial black elite that mediated relations with the white city fathers and bankrolled African-American residential expansion to the city's near westside, adjacent to Atlanta University.[82] The shift to the westside was underscored by the move of Morris Brown College and the Gammon Theological Seminary from their original eastside locales. A second commercial center developed on West Hunter Street (now Martin Luther King Boulevard) and the center of gravity of the African-American community gradually shifted to the westside after mid-century.[83] While not as celebrated a Black Mecca in the 1920s as Harlem, Atlanta could arguably be considered the African-American Medina of the period, or at least its Damascus.

THE KLAN RIDES AGAIN

Shortly after the release of D. W. Griffith's *Birth of a Nation*, an Atlantan salesman and sometime Methodist circuit rider gathered a group of thirty-three followers and resurrected the Ku Klux Klan in a solemn, fiery ceremony on top of Stone Mountain on Thanksgiving eve, 1915.[84] The film provided only a partial inspiration for William Simmons's actions. Xenophobic sentiments were surging through the nation and the previous two years had been marked by an intensification of racist attitudes throughout Georgia brought about by the Leo Frank trial. Frank, the New York-born Jewish manager of an Atlanta pencil factory, had been convicted of murdering Mary Phagan, a young female employee, in a highly dubious trial and was sentenced to death amidst courtroom cries of "Kill the Jew!"[85] The case received national attention as Frank's conviction was twice appealed and upheld, before his death sentence was reviewed and commuted by Georgia's governor.

Enraged by the governor's decision, a mob of several thousand men armed with guns and dynamite marched on his residence, but were repulsed by the state militia.[86] Shortly thereafter, a smaller group that styled itself "the Knights of Mary Phagan" took Frank from his cell at the Georgia State Penitentiary in Milledgeville and lynched him near the Marietta town square. These same Knights, who included a number of the most prominent citizens of Cobb County, formed the nucleus of the group that reconstituted the Klan later that year.[87] Frank's lynching was the culmination of three decades of increasing anti-Semitism in Atlanta, although this tended towards violence of a symbolic rather than a physical kind. Meanwhile, dozens of African-Americans in and around Atlanta shared Frank's fate in uncelebrated and unrelated incidents around the same time.

Relatively few accounts of the city's past dwell on the fact that in 1916 Atlanta was designated as the Imperial City, or national headquarters, of the revived Ku Klux Klan.[88] From its lodgings in a neo-colonial mansion on Peachtree Road and its offices in a prominent downtown office building, Imperial Kleagle E.Y. Clarke, Jr (the son of the author of *Atlanta Illustrated*) engineered a successful recruitment drive that saw Klan chapters established in every Northern state and brought "leaders of commerce and industry, professional men, ministers of the Gospel, statesmen, soldiers, men from every walk of life" into its white-robed fold.[89] The Klan's stated mission to provide a fraternity for native-born Gentile white males found fertile soil in the nationwide xenophobia that had developed in response to intensifying immigration of non-Anglo-Saxon people. By the early 1920s, tens of thousands of Atlantans belonged to the Klan, including a high percentage of city employees and most policemen. Through its multiple business enterprises, such as its Buckhead robe factory, the Klan also pumped millions of dollars into the Atlantan economy. Klan parades through the central business district and the adjacent African-American communities were common occasions through the late 1930s.[90]

The Klan was not the only racial extremist group operating in Atlanta, or the state of Georgia. In June 1930, a trio of Atlantan businessmen and politicians, including the state agricultural commissioner and soon-to-be governor Eugene Talmadge, formed the American Fascisti Association, better known as the Order of Black Shirts.[91] Dedicated to replacing African-American workers with unemployed whites, the order experienced a rapid burst of popularity in the summer of 1930, claiming between 27,000 and 40,000 supporters statewide within a few months, although the dues-paying membership barely exceeded 1,000.[92] Much like the Klan, they held public rallies and engaged in night-riding and other acts of violence, culminating in the murder of a fifteen-year-old black youth. However, public outcry over the murder, combined with internecine power struggles, the opposition of the KKK (who viewed the Black Shirts as under the control of a foreign power and thus un-American) and a less than dire employment situation at the time led to their demise within a few months.

The Depression also served to build some nascent alliances across, as well as along, the divides of race, bringing national attention to the oppressive nature of the city regime. In 1930, Atlanta authorities arrested a racially mixed group of leftist labor organizers working among the unemployed and charged "the Atlanta Six" with violating a century-old slave insurrection law that had been modified in 1868 to stifle the organization of freedmen.[93] Two years later, Atlanta police arrested Angelo Herndon, a young black labor organizer, under the same ordinance, charging him with "inciting an armed insurrection and the seizure of the major part of five Southern States for the establishment of a Soviet Republic independent of the United States."[94] Herndon was convicted by an all-white jury and sentenced to twenty years on a chain gang, but his case attracted national attention and the support of the National Association for the Advancement of Colored People, the American Civil Liberties Union, and the National Bar Association. After five years of rejected appeals, Herndon was freed when the US Supreme Court, which had twice upheld his conviction, finally ruled the insurrection law unconstitutional.

DIXIE REDIVIVUS

Although Atlanta remained resolutely future-oriented, as the title of the "Forward Atlanta" promotion campaign attests, the 1920s and 1930s also witnessed something of a change in its attitude towards the past and the city's place within the South, as well as a changing idea of the South's place within the nation. As if rising to the challenge of Mencken's sarcastic rebuke, the region enjoyed a cultural efflorescence during the 1930s. Writing from the elite confines of Vanderbilt University, the "Nashville Agrarians" delivered a stinging ruralized riposte to the urbanized, industrializing ethos of the New South Creed and, by way of association, to Atlanta as well.[95] The spiritual stepchildren of Henry Grady fared little better in the popular literature and film of the period, which alternated between idealized representations of the antebellum plantation (*So Red the Rose*, etc.) and fictional and documentary accounts of its sordid, debased present (*I Am a Fugitive from a Chain Gang, Tobacco Road, Let Us Now Praise Famous Men*). The writing and reception of Atlanta's own contribution to "media-made Dixie,"[96] *Gone With the Wind*, needs to be understood within this wider context of mass-mediated imagery.

Margaret Mitchell's novel marked the culmination, rather than the beginning, of Atlanta's revised, if still highly attenuated, attention towards its past and its Southern identity. Between 1900 and 1929, as the population tripled and its physical extent sprawled, Atlanta became increasingly incomprehensible to its older residents. Even Peachtree Street was not spared as it underwent conversion from a neighborhood of elite homes, including the Governor's Mansion, into a modern zone of stores, hotels, and theaters. In 1902, the Pioneer Citizens' Society published its *History of Atlanta* to "rescue from oblivion the memory of former incidents, and to render a just tribute of renown to the many great and wonderful transactions of our progenitors."[97] In 1926, a small group of elite citizens, including Mitchell's father and brother, founded the Atlanta Historical Society (AHS) to conserve their collective memory of the city's past. Their primary focus was, quite naturally, the railroad, the Civil War, and the histories of their own families. However, due to its small size and meager financial resources, the early activities of the AHS were limited to little more than the assembly of an archive.

Still, Atlanta had not completely avoided recognizing its past, particularly the Civil War. During the late 1800s and early 1900s, various groups like the Sons and

Daughters of the Confederacy and the Pioneer Citizens' Society had erected several monuments in and around the city. Most of these, such as the obelisk to the Confederate war dead in Oakland Cemetery, commemorated the Lost Cause, but the establishment of a monument to fallen Union General John B. McPherson indicated something of a sectionally reconciling spirit at work as well. Having died in the Battle of Atlanta, McPherson was free of the taint arising from the city's later destruction, and could be unproblematically commemorated for his noble sacrifice. These sites, however, did not figure prominently in textual representations of the city.

In 1921, the finishing touches were placed on an historical monument of a fundamentally different sort, the neo-classical rotunda housing the Cyclorama in Grant Park, just to the southeast of downtown. Some fifty feet high and some four hundred feet in circumference, the circular painting commemorated a dramatic moment in the Battle of Atlanta, when Confederate defenders made a temporary breakthrough of the Union lines. It had been painted in the late 1880s by a traveling troupe of German artists commissioned by Union General and Illinois Senator John Logan as a prop for his vice-presidential campaign. When Logan died soon after its completion, the nine-ton painting passed through several hands before being purchased by a wealthy Atlanta merchant, who donated it to the city in 1898. It was exhibited in a temporary wooden structure adjacent to the city zoo in Grant Park, where it was damaged by the elements. Private contributions funded construction of the new fire-proof facility, but repair and restoration would only come sixteen years later as part of a Work Projects Administration (WPA) effort directed by the artist and AHS founding member Wilbur Kurtz.

The Cyclorama presents a good example of a kind of tableau that enjoyed widespread popularity in the late nineteenth century, a sort of pre-electronic effort at virtual reality. Research for the painting was so accurate that it was claimed that veterans of the battle were able to identify many of the combatants.[98] Visitors to the Cyclorama entered the building through a subterranean tunnel leading to a central reviewing platform that allowed a 360-degree view of the painting while guides gave a narration of the battle. The illusion of reality was greatly enhanced in the course of the 1937 restoration, with the addition of special lighting and a diorama that filled in the space between the painting and the reviewing platform with plaster reproductions of men, animals, and equipment.

The Cyclorama, however, was exceedingly small fare in comparison to what was happening, or at least being envisioned, some sixteen miles to the east at Stone Mountain. Once a sacred site for the Native American inhabitants of the area (and later to New Age cultists and neo-Gnostic seekers of telluric currents[99]), this massive granite monadnock had been a tourist attraction and quarry site for building stone since the mid nineteenth century. As early as 1914, the United Daughters of the Confederacy had deemed the mountain an ideal location for a monument to General Robert E. Lee. In 1915, the UDC negotiated a thirteen-year lease to the massif's north face from the Venable brothers (one of whom would soon go on to become the Imperial Wizard of the Ku Klux Klan) and commissioned sculptor Gutzon Borglum to design and execute the carving of the singular hero of the Confederacy. Borglum, who would later go on to carve Mt Rushmore, had achieved fame as the sculptor of the seated figure of the sixteenth president for the Lincoln Memorial in Washington DC. Overcome by the prospects of such a canvas, Borglum conceived a project that would do justice to both the Lost Cause and the site. On Confederate Memorial Day 1916, the mountain was officially dedicated as a monument to the Confederacy, but work on the carving was delayed by the First World War and by fund-raising difficulties. Little progress on the monument took place until 1923 when a group of Atlanta businessmen, a number of whom were associated with the Ku Klux Klan, formed the Stone Mountain Confederate Monumental Association to finance the project.[100]

In the intervening years, Borglum had sketched out a plan that was, quite literally, pharaonic, and that anticipated some of the monumental monstrosities of Italian and German fascism that would appear in the ensuing decades. He had in mind the creation of nothing less than the "Eighth Wonder of the World," a place of noble splendor that would endure long after Lincoln's Memorial in Washington had crumbled to dust.[101] Whereas the United Daughters of the Confederacy had originally asked for a single profile bust of Robert E. Lee, Borglum envisioned a massive bas relief some 2,000 feet wide featuring more than a thousand marching figures, some more than 100 feet tall.[102] At the core of the frieze was the horseback-mounted trinity of Robert E. Lee, Jefferson Davis, and Stonewall Jackson. Together with four lesser generals who were to be selected by Southern state historians, this central group would be surrounded by representatives of every branch of the Confederate armed forces passing in review. The president of the Daughters of the Confederacy suggested that this epic pantheon of Southern manhood should include some hooded Klan figures as well. This inclusion, however, was vetoed by Borglum.[103]

Despite Borglum's opposition to the inclusion of Klan figures, the artist was sympathetic to and actually deeply involved in the national activities of the Ku Klux Klan.[104] In fact, Borglum's role in internecine Klan politics served to complicate his relationships with the non-Klan members of the Stone Mountain Monumental Association, who had already grown concerned, from a financial point of view, with the scope of his proposed project. The bas relief formed only part of Borglum's total plan. Directly below the carving, a semi-circular "temple of sacred memories in the Breast of a Granite Mountain" was to be carved deep into the rock.[105] Rumors abound that Borglum planned to include a secret Klan altar somewhere in the memorial hall as well.[106] While evidence is sketchy, given Borglum's active participation in Ku Kluxury, this is not inconceivable. Then again, the mountain's significance as a holy place for the KKK was anything but secret. Stone Mountain remained a key site for Klan activities long after the initial convocation in 1915, and Sam Venable had granted the Klan an easement for unrestricted use of the mountain for its activities in 1923. The easement remained in effect until the State of Georgia purchased the property in 1958[107] and cross-burnings regularly took place on the mountain top until 1941, when they were moved to a spot lower down, where they continued, intermittently, until 1979.

If the skyscrapers being raised in the central business district during the 1920s were a concrete manifestation of Atlanta's desire to be the New York of the South, the original plans for Stone Mountain indicate its desire to be known as the Giza of the Confederacy as well. Nothing better represents the two sides of the New South, one looking earnestly forward, the other nostalgically backward, but joined together in an unshakable faith in white supremacy and the eternal greatness of the South. Promoters of the project made much of the fact that, if it were to be somehow erected at the mountain's base, Atlanta's new skyline would only partially obscure the bas relief. In its sheer monumental hubris, the original plan for the Stone Mountain Memorial was a fine representation of, rather than a deviation from, the giddiest and most overreaching aspects of the Atlanta Spirit.

Ultimately, however, financial realities triumphed over nostalgic sentimentality. Although the public response was enthusiastic, problems with the ambitious project's cost dogged it from the outset. In 1925, a series of conflicts between Borglum and the Stone Mountain Monumental Association over aesthetic and financial matters prompted the sculptor to flee the state after destroying all of his working models and drawings. Another sculptor, Augustus Lukeman, was hired to assume the project. Lukeman's plan to build "an American Monument to Surpass the Pyramids" borrowed extensively from Borglum's initial vision.[108] Lukeman's frieze was of more modest, if still epic, proportions – calling for a mere 700 figures instead of the more than 1,000 envisioned by Borglum. The Memorial Hall, however, retained its original Borglumesque scale, being "larger than the famous tombs of the second cataract of the Nile and larger than most of the natural caves of the world."[109] The inner chamber of this Memorial Hall was fronted by six enormous Doric columns, which bore an entablature with an inscription in six ancient and modern languages, identifying it as a memorial to the Confederate nation. In the center of the vast sanctum was to be another immense sculpture of a grieving and heavily veiled female figure symbolizing "memory" and the sacrifices of Southern womanhood. The surrounding walls of the chamber would be inscribed with the names of the Confederate dead. The sanctuary would be approached from the outside by a monumental staircase flanked by large urns in which incense would be burned on ceremonial occasions. The whole would be fronted by a large reflecting pool that would appear to issue forth from the mountain itself. On the edge of the reflecting pool would be the tomb of the Unknown Soldier, "giving the impression that his bier is floating upon a barge into eternity."[110] Despite this grandiose scheme, Lukeman was unsuccessful in stirring up additional support. He was only able to complete Lee's head and the outlines of his horse before the funds (which had never materialized to the extent necessary) and the lease of the cliff face terminated in 1928.[111]

Owing to the Depression and World War II, work on the carving was not resumed until 1964, six years after the Georgia Assembly authorized completion of the sculpture as part of a tourist attraction that would serve as an official memorial to the Confederacy. With its restored antebellum plantation, hotel, campground, golf course, and other leisure facilities, the new Stone Mountain Park owed more to Walt Disney than to Borglum's and Lukeman's Albert Speer-like visions. Still, with the initial legislative authorization for the project coming only two years after the Georgia Assembly had added the Confederate battle emblem to the state flag (1956), Stone Mountain Park must be seen as part of the wider state and regional campaign of massive resistance against desegregation. The irony is that some of the businessmen involved in the efforts to construct the park were also key members of the urban power structure, a collective that was soon to advertise Atlanta as the "City Too Busy To Hate."[112] As with the original effort in the 1920s, the internal contradictions of the New South Creed could be effectively managed if their physical representations were kept spatially separated.

GOING, GOING, GONE WITH THE WIND

Looming even larger than Stone Mountain over everything else in the imagined landscape of Lost Cause Atlanta, however, is Margaret Mitchell's *Gone With the Wind*. Seldom has one single work had such a profound effect on shaping the image of a city, initially for its residents, and secondly and far more enduringly, in the eyes of outsiders. Thanks to the book and the film, Peachtree Street became one of the world's best-known thoroughfares and millions of tourists have flocked to Atlanta over the years looking for Tara. A not insignificant cottage industry has emerged to service their interests with a variety of guides, shrines, and simulations. One of the most popular cultural productions in history (more than 25 million copies were sold in over 27 languages, and over $100 million in film rentals were earned in the pre-video era alone),[113] *Gone With the Wind* illustrates some of the power of mediated fictions to shape social reality in their own image.

Some scholars claim that *Gone With the Wind* has nothing at all to do with the "real" Atlanta.[114] In so far as they argue that Atlanta and its environs did not support a graciously wealthy antebellum plantation culture they are absolutely correct. Untold millions of persons in the United States and around the world have a misleading impression of Atlanta as a city of the Old South, not unlike Charleston and Savannah. However, the widespread image of *Gone With the Wind* as a moonlit and magnolia-scented celebration of the plantation South is due more to producer David O. Selznick's "gentrification" of the novel than to Mitchell's text.[115] As numerous critics have noted, the novel provides a portrait of antebellum culture that is far less than ideal, especially in its inability to deal with the confused conditions of the Reconstruction period.[116] Rather than idealizing the Old South, Mitchell is far more concerned with rendering the necessary, if unfortunate, opportunism, moral turpitude and social turmoil of the New South. Indeed, what is Scarlett O'Hara if not a living embodiment of the Atlanta Spirit, a Henry Grady (or is it a Hannibal Kimball?) in hoop skirts, concerned, above all, with moving forward with little regard for the cherished norms of antebellum society?

Despite the film's misleading projection of an image of the Old South, I wish to argue that *Gone With the Wind* is very much connected up with the "real" Atlanta, although its point of reference is the city of the 1920s and 1930s, rather than that of the 1860s and 1870s. Born in 1900, Margaret Mitchell was descended from some of the city's oldest settlers, and as a child roamed over the still partially extant postwar landscape. She was regaled with eyewitness accounts of the conflict and its aftermath by older members of her family and their friends. As she later confided to a journalist, she was ten years old before she found out that the Confederacy had lost the war.[117] As such, *Gone With the Wind* can be read, in part, as a sort of elite folk history, one that derives its "truth" not from its correspondence with the historical record (although, as I will note below, Mitchell was fastidious about some details), but from the collective, and highly selective, memory of a particular group of people. Written during the city's booming 1920s, it responded to local and national concerns generated by that era. Furthermore, once published and popularized, it generated its own sense of reality, creating very real and material facts on the ground that were eagerly consumed as "history" by both local and national audiences alike.

Mitchell took great pains to be accurate in her representations of the Atlanta landscape. She purposefully located Tara at a point in Clayton County where there was no house and put Aunt Pittypat's Peachtree Street mansion on what was then a vacant lot.[118] Given her fidelity to this kind of detail, Mitchell was especially displeased with the liberties the film's producer took with the representation of Tara.

In the novel, the house is described as a rambling and somewhat less than impressive affair, without the portico of white columns that the pristine version in the film has made emblematic. Producer David O. Selznick did far more than tinker with the novel's representations of the built environment. Driven by the twin desires of making escapist entertainment for Depression audiences and ensuring "that Negroes come out decidedly on the right side of the ledger,"[119] Selznick chose to excise the novel's favorable treatment of the Klan during Reconstruction. However, despite Selznick's stated desire to make a "liberal" race picture, the film's representation of African-Americans hardly varied from the racist stereotypes of happy, simple-minded, dependent slaves that predominated in other plantation movies of the period. The embedded racism went largely unnoticed by the mainstream white media, which were unceasing in their effusive praise for the production. As with the novel, the only meaningful critique of the film was delivered by the country's leftist press.[120]

The enormous success of the novel and the film provided the city with an unprecedented amount of national attention, as well as a noble sense of conjured history that matched its expansive dreams of the future. Within a year of the book's release, the city's tourist flow increased significantly, with tens of thousands of visitors coming to look for Tara and Twelve Oaks. Down in Clayton County, filling station attendants willingly answered tourist queries with directions to a variety of ramshackle mansions they claimed were the "real" Tara.[121] The Atlanta Historical Society averaged one hundred requests a day, and not just from tourists, for directions to the mix of fictional and historical spots mentioned in the book.[122] Attendance at the Cyclorama doubled in 1937, the same year that the WPA restoration was undertaken. In response to repeated requests by visitors after the film was released in 1939, a figure modeled after Clark Gable was added to the diorama, although not in the person of Rhett Butler. Instead, the actor's visage graced the body of a dying Union soldier.

For a city that never cared much for its history, both the book and film provoked a spasmodic interest in marking Atlanta's past and in so doing provided a good indication of the permeable membrane between fiction and reality created by new techniques of communication and representation. In 1937, the Atlanta Convention Bureau prepared maps and brochures of Civil War sites and police were educated to direct visitors to scenes of interest. One hundred temporary wooden markers were placed to identify key sites on the battlefields surrounding the city, with plans for 170 permanent markers "to help develop a historically conscious citizenry."[123] These ambitious plans were never realized, although after the film's premiere in December 1939, city businessmen did finance the installation of thirty-five bronze tablets commemorating important places in the city's past. As part of the festivities surrounding the latter event, an old gas street lamp at the corner of Whitehall (as lower Peachtree was originally called) and Alabama Streets was dedicated as the Eternal Flame of the Confederacy. It received this honor on account of having been hit by the first shell fired on the city during the siege in the summer of 1864. Relocated from its original place underneath the viaducts constructed in the 1920s to the same spot on the raised street level, the lamp was provided with a permanent gas connection and a bronze plaque.[124]

The dedication of the lamppost was only part of the festivities surrounding the film's premiere. From all accounts, the three-day event had more the look and feel of a long-delayed victory celebration for the Confederate army than a film debut. Thousands of Georgians, many dressed in period costume, waited at the airport for the arrival of the cast and producers on a frigid afternoon that December. Thousands more, "more than were in the combined armies of Hood, Johnston, and Sherman,"[125] flanked the parade route from the airport through the poor black neighborhoods on the south side of town and up Peachtree Street to the Georgian Terrace Hotel, where the mayor, governor, and prominent citizens exchanged welcoming comments with the Hollywood celebrities. Noticeably absent from the latter group were the film's African-American cast members, who, in deference to Atlanta's segregated sensibilities, had not been invited to attend the event. The ritual exchange of greetings was followed by a Junior League ball in which the city's elite, dressed in hoop skirts and Confederate grey, enjoyed an evening of "entertainment typical of the Old South."[126] Atlanta debutantes engaged in a tightly fought contest to see who would wear Scarlett's green gown to the ball.[127]

The following day had been declared an official state-wide holiday, and more than one million persons flocked to Atlanta, at a time when the entire population of Georgia was little more than three million. Meanwhile, the Hollywood contingent toured the city and was fêted in elite homes and clubs. That evening, hundreds of Georgia National Guardsmen struggled to keep the crowds at bay outside the Loew's Grand Theater, whose facade had been redecorated to resemble the columned portico of the Wilkses' Twelve Oaks mansion. Inside the theater, the cast and the city's elite were joined by the governors of five Southern states and a troop of moneyed New Yorkers who had helped to finance the picture.

Contemporary newspaper accounts described the screening in sanctified tones.[128] As the film was shown, "great waves of nostalgic Southern fervor engulfed the audience . . . When war was announced, the cheers in the audience drowned out those on the screen."[129] Unlike the author, the audience was not troubled by the slight deviations of the film from the novel. Indeed, they did not notice them, the picture being described as an accurate and dramatic representation: "the only major book in recent years which truly depicts the life of the Old South."[130] The film provided the city with a noble "history" to match the scale of its present and future ambitions.

Gone With the Wind's influence was also soon manifest in the city's architecture. A renaissance of the prototypically Southern Greek Revival style had begun earlier in the 1930s for both domestic and public buildings. However, after the film was released, numerous representations of Tara and Twelve Oaks, some highly stylized, appeared on the landscape in the ensuing decades, including the headquarters for WSB radio and television known as White Columns (1953), and the new Georgia Governor's Mansion (1968). The plantation theme proved an enduringly popular one for the look and menu of the city's restaurants as well. Mammy's Shanty on Peachtree Street lasted from the 1940s well into the early 1970s. In 1967, Aunt Pittypat's Porch restaurant opened where it still exists on International Boulevard, not far from its fictitious Peachtree Street location.

The success of Gone With the Wind made the diminutive Margaret Mitchell into the best-known Atlantan in the world, as well as a local celebrity of unprecedented importance. In 1941, she commissioned the light cruiser USS Atlanta, and when that ship was sunk early in the war, she led a successful local fund-raising campaign to help build its replacement. An active member of the Atlanta Historical Society, she sponsored an annual dinner commemorating the Battle of Atlanta. However, by all accounts, she felt burdened by her fame and never published another piece of work, although many were burned at her request after she was struck by a taxi in 1949. As a noteworthy celebrity, her tragic death drew national attention to the city and initiated her transformation from Atlanta debutante turned journalist/author into a quasi-mythical character. Her grave in the historic Oakland cemetery became an important site of touristic pilgrimage. In 1967, the city renamed the open space at the triangular intersection of Peachtree, Broad, and Carnegie, Margaret Mitchell Square. Indeed, over the years, the spaces associated with Mitchell's life have, to a certain extent, supplanted those places made famous in Gone With the Wind as primary sites of touristic interest.

Margaret Mitchell's Atlanta, however, has fared little better than other material legacies of Atlanta's past. In the years after her death, most of the sites associated with the author's life were demolished by fire, urban redevelopment, or, as in the case of her parents' home, by her own posthumous request.[131] By the early 1990s, only two of her former residences were left standing. One was a neo-Tudor apartment house she had christened The Dump in which she had written the famed work and which was the object of an intense battle between preservationists and developers in the 1980s and early 1990s.[132] The Loew's Grand Theater and the Carnegie Library, where Mitchell had done research for the book, were both demolished in the late 1970s, while Jonesboro Road has been transformed from a sleepy country road into a prototypical commercial strip.

During the 1980s and early 1990s, a series of conjured shrines to the memory of Mitchell and *Gone With the Wind* emerged in Atlanta to satisfy the growing hordes of tourists, particularly those from Europe and Japan. The most extensive of these is the Road to Tara museum in the Georgian Terrace Condominiums, which had served as the hotel for the Hollywood contingent during the premiere festivities. In 1986, native son and media mogul Ted Turner bought the MGM/UA film archive to which *Gone With the Wind* belonged, and staged an elaborate re-premiere in the Fox Theater across the street to celebrate the film's fiftieth anniversary in 1989. The re-premiere stimulated a new burst of interest in the film and the personage of Margaret Mitchell. This was manifested nationally in a sequel to *GWTW* – *Scarlett* – and a made-for-TV movie of Margaret Mitchell's life starring *Beverly Hills 90210* bad girl, Shannen Doherty. In 1994, a local newspaper reporter published the definitive *Gone With the Wind Guide to Margaret Mitchell's Atlanta,* which detailed the primary locales of the author's life combined with a section on where to buy *GWTW* collectibles and advice on "where Scarlett would eat today."[133]

The tendency of real life to imitate fiction came full circle, however, with plans to build a *Gone With the Wind* theme park. In December 1992, promoters sparked a bidding war among three southern suburban counties – Douglas, Henry, and Clayton (the latter the site of the "real" fictional Tara) – for a $50 million extravaganza to be completed in time for the 1996 Olympics. Designed by the same firm responsible for the MCA/Universal Studios entertainment complex in Orlando, the park would feature recreations of Old Atlanta and the Tara and Twelve Oaks plantations, along with a hotel/condominium complex, a golf course, and facilities for recreational vehicles. As with the case of the Disney's America historical theme park in Manassas, Virginia, concerns were raised about how the venue would deal with the issue of slavery. Much like David O. Selznick, the park's developer claimed sensitivity to the "racial issue."[134] Rather than glorify slavery, he argued, the park would emphasize African-American contributions to Southern culture (although it limited these to food and music!) and would focus on the most popular movie ever made instead of trying to represent an historical reality. That the film itself was chock-full of denigratory racist stereotypes seemed not to occur to the developer, nor to anyone else, for that matter.

Interestingly enough, the idea for the theme park received little critical reaction from local black leaders. The head of the regional National Association for the Advancement of Colored People was quoted as saying that as long as it depicted slavery realistically and sensitively "I don't view it any differently from Dollywood."[135] Rather, it was the largely white, official imagineering establishment, led by the Atlanta Convention and Visitors Bureau, that raised public concerns about the possible glamorization of the age of slavery, although no mention was made of the restored antebellum plantation and neo-Confederate ethos at Stone Mountain Park. In the end, it was the silence of national and global capital which spoke the loudest. After almost two years of scouring the world for a financial backer without success, plans for the theme park were put on indefinite hold in the spring of 1995.[136]

EPICENTER OF THE *NEW* NEW SOUTH CREED: THE CITY TOO BUSY TO HATE

Given the current popularity of conjured worlds of thematic entertainment and the close association of the city with the novel and the film, the failure of the effort to build the *Gone With the Wind* theme park might seem surprising. However, the film's Old South imagery has always been something of an anachronism to city boosters trying to project a vision of a modern and bustling city. Although the modernity of the city has been a constant theme of promotional literature since the late nineteenth century, it received even more emphasis in textual representations of Atlanta from the mid twentieth century on. The best known of these accounts was the Work Projects Administration guide to the city, *Atlanta: City of the Modern South,* published in 1942. Sponsored by the Atlanta Board of Education, and written by a number of local but unidentified contributors, the book provides a far more systematic, if multiply biased, treatment of the city than any other previous text. As part of the WPA's "American Guide Series," the book follows a fairly standardized format in describing Atlanta's history and political, economic, and sociocultural organization, as well as its principal points of interest. Based on interviews as well as archival research, it constitutes a crude sort of locally produced historical ethnography that purports to represent something of the essential nature of the city to an outside audience. In 1949, it was reissued largely unchanged, save for a new foreword and a new title, *Atlanta: Capital of the South*, that reflected the postwar boosters' claims that the city was the uncontested center of the region.

The Atlanta that emerges in the pages of both texts is an elaboration of the peculiarly contradictory synthesis first advanced by earlier generations of New South boosters. With its business practices dominated by the "methods and manners of the metropolitan East" and its social life governed by the "more traditionally southern qualities of graciousness and gentility," Atlanta is advertised as combining the best of both worlds.[137] This ideal mixture is also manifest in the city's morphology, with a dense core region of urban bustle surrounded by lush, tree-shrouded suburban domains. Admitting the presence of slums and ethnic "others" (not just African-Americans, but Jews and Greeks) on the one hand takes away from the idyllic imagery, but on the other reconfirms Atlanta's identity as a modern urban place. Atlanta's modernity is further reinforced, contra the imagery projected by *Gone With the Wind*, by its lack of history and freedom from a slavish obedience to the past: "Atlanta seems to harbor no carefully preserved tradition and its ever-changing outline and rapid pace help to further the illusion. Instead, the tradition is more evident as a restless, sometimes overzealous, spirit."[138] The city's history, in other words, is one of constant orientation towards the future.

Atlanta's unique marriage of Northern bustle and Southern charm continued to be emphasized in postwar descriptions and travel accounts. However, during the 1950s an increasing divide began to appear between the city and the state and region of which it claimed to be capital. The crucial difference lay not in Yankee methods and manners of business, but in the matter of race. Atlanta was far from being free of race hatred, as the postwar popularity of the white supremacist Columbians and the Ku Klux Klan attests.[139] Yet, in contrast to virtually every other Deep South newspaper, the *Atlanta Constitution* under editor Ralph McGill adopted an editorial position that was supportive of African-American civil rights. With the court-mandated end to the all-white Democratic primary in 1946, Atlanta's blacks became a key bloc of voters who were actively courted by the city's mayor. Working through extant organizations like the Urban League and the Negro Voters League, the black middle class negotiated a series of understandings with the white power structure that traded black votes (for the mayoral election, annexation, etc.) for a series of largely symbolic gestures (black policemen, areas for residential expansion, etc.).[140] It was far from being a system of balanced reciprocity – African-Americans were definitely the junior partners in this exchange – but it was an improvement on the treatment they received elsewhere in the South.

The anomalous place of Atlanta in the not-so-New South was accentuated by the increasingly acrimonious regional and national debate over desegregation and civil rights in the 1950s. After the United States Supreme Court ruled in 1954 that racial segregation in schools was illegal, the Georgia State Assembly passed a law that would deny state funds to and effectively close any public school attempting to integrate.[141] Two years later, the Assembly added the Confederate battle emblem to the state flag, ostensibly to honor the Confederate war dead, and in 1958 voted to complete the Stone Mountain carving as part of a larger memorial to the Confederacy. In these actions, Georgia legislators were well in keeping with the campaign of massive resistance being practiced in other Southern states.

Amidst this atmosphere of dedicated intolerance, the actions of the city's civic commercial elite seemed downright progressive. In 1959, Mayor William Hartsfield declared Atlanta "a city too busy to hate."[142] This attitude was not so much inspired by a lack of racism on the part of white city leaders, but by the pragmatic recognition that, in the age of television, resistance to school desegregation à la Little Rock and New Orleans would damage the city's image and hinder the attraction of outside capital. Furthermore, a progressive attitude on race would also go a long way to demonstrating that Atlanta was no longer just a provincial Southern capital, but a city of national prominence.

In 1959, the US Supreme Court mandated that the Atlanta school system begin desegregation the following year. Working with the leadership of the black community, the white civic-commercial establishment was able to get a one-year extension on the decree in order to mount an effective campaign to get a "free choice" program for desegregation approved by the state legislature. Given the strength of the opposition to desegregation in that body, the success of these efforts was an indication of the political influence that the corporate elite possessed. When the plan was to be implemented in 1961, civic and business leaders and community groups mounted an energetic effort to ensure that the first desegregation efforts would not be marred by violence and would receive the best possible coverage from the press.[143] Although only token numbers of African-American students were involved in the initial phase of Atlanta's school choice program, when compared with the violent opposition occurring in Little Rock and other Southern cities, the effort had a significant positive impact on the city's image in the national media. Atlanta's successful beginnings to school desegregation led President Kennedy to commend it and glowing portraits of the city soon followed in major national magazines, such as *Life, Good Housekeeping,* and *Look,* with the last deeming Atlanta to be "the leader of the New South."[144] Actually, the *New* New South was more like it, as the white supremacy and Jim Crow-ism that had been explicit in Henry Grady's vision were silently excised in favor of at least a symbolic commitment to equal rights and desegregation.

Although he would have violently opposed school desegregation, Grady would otherwise have been proud of the proactive campaign city leaders mounted to project a positive and progressive image of Atlanta to the nation. In 1961, an aging William Hartsfield was succeeded as mayor by Chamber of Commerce president Ivan Allen, Jr, who narrowly defeated arch-segregationist and local restaurateur Lester Maddox in a nasty, race-baiting campaign. Allen's victory over Maddox, who had led the campaign against school desegregation, was seen as a triumph of progressivism over provinciality. Still, the narrowness of Allen's victory (he received less than half the white vote) indicated that liberal race sentiments were not shared by large segments of the city's white populace, nor by the state as a whole. In 1964, Maddox would go on to be elected governor, while Allen further contributed to Atlanta's, and his own, anomalous image by being the only Southern mayor to testify in favor of the Civil Rights Act in 1963.

Allen's enlightened attitude on civil rights was part of his larger vision of transforming Atlanta from a regional capital into a "national city." This somewhat ambiguous status was defined by the Chamber of Commerce in primarily economic terms: a national city exerted "a powerful economic force far beyond its normal regional functions."[145] This included not only attracting national investment capital and the headquarters of major US corporations, but the development of gargantuan hotel-convention facilities and the attraction of professional sports teams. The importance of the latter was as much symbolic as economic, especially in the era before lucrative television broadcast contracts. A "major league" city was a city of national importance, on a par, conceptually at least, with New York, Chicago, Boston, Los Angeles, and other established urban areas. Allen's strategy relied heavily on the use of federal urban renewal and other public monies to help build the necessary infrastructure to attract new private investment from outside the region.

As Allen reconfigured the city into a publically subsidized support structure for private capital, the Chamber of Commerce revived the Forward Atlanta marketing campaign, first engineered by Allen's father in the 1920s, to sell the new and improved Atlanta to America. As part of Forward Atlanta II, the Chamber hired a major New York advertising firm to create a multimillion-dollar, multi-year campaign that emphasized Atlanta's unparalleled climate for lifestyle and business. Unlike Atlanta's current claim of being the capital of the civil rights movement, little or no emphasis was placed on its non-Southern attitudes towards race and civil rights. With ads appearing in the *New Yorker*, the *Wall Street Journal*, *Fortune*, and other high-end business-oriented publications, Atlanta became one of the best advertised metro areas in the country.[146] The success of the initial campaign convinced the Chamber of Commerce to keep Forward Atlanta as an ongoing feature of its activities. Driven in part by the ad campaign, the Atlanta metropolitan area enjoyed the highest job growth of any urban region in the country during the 1960s.[147]

In addition to the advertising blitz in the print media, the Chamber also bankrolled one of the first "city" magazines in the nation. Whereas the ad campaign was directed primarily at an outside audience, *Atlanta Magazine* was oriented to a local readership, particularly the large number of newcomers arriving in the city each year. Edited by the often outrageous Jim Townsend, and staffed by a stable of young writers who would later achieve national notoriety as novelists (e.g. William Diehl, Anne River Siddons), *Atlanta Magazine* projected an image of the city as bright, alive, vital, striving, and predominantly white. Among its monthly features celebrating the accomplishments of the city was one that highlighted "the young man on the go," the new breed of white, male, twenty- to thirtysomething go-getters who were cheerleading Atlanta's rise to greatness. As house organ of the Chamber of Commerce, the magazine's ability to be something other than an extended advertisement for the vision of Atlanta's white power structure was well-nigh impossible. However, as the city's old-time establishment lost its uncontested grip on power in the latter part of the decade, and even more so after the sale of the magazine in 1972, the monthly did establish a slightly less uncritical, absolutely adulatory voice. Still, the tone of *Atlanta Magazine* has always been more celebrative than investigatory, especially in its current incarnation, which favors "lifestyle reporting" over hard news and controversial stories.

Atlanta's steady growth and careful cultivation of its progressive image during the 1950s and 1960s intensified the imaginary divide between the city and the rest of the state of Georgia, and provided one of the major motifs for literary treatments of Atlanta during this period. It figured as the principal urban backdrop in a number of Flannery O'Connor's stories, including "Everything That Rises Must Converge," and "The Artificial Nigger." The latter, first published in 1955 in the *Kenyon Review*, portrayed Atlanta as a place of threatening otherness for visiting white countryfolk, an incomprehensible, immoral terrain for a rural man, Mr Head, set on showing his young grandson Nelson "everything there is to see in a city so that he would be content to stay at home for the rest of his life."[148] In so doing he hoped to inoculate Nelson against the alluring evils of the city which had attracted the boy's mother there (like many other rural people during World War II), with fatal results. O'Connor's rural/urban dichotomy is a highly racialized one. Before taking the train to the city, twelve-year-old Nelson had never seen a black person. Just as with the real life case of a number of rural counties outside of Atlanta, African-Americans had been run out of the county in which the Heads lived many years before.

Race, though, is only one of the threatening aspects of the city for the Heads. While the boy is initially afflicted with a sense of wonderment, the elder Head is alienated by the industrialized quality of its time and space, the confusion of its street grids, the bustle of its commerce, the bewildering vastness of its department stores, and the pitch-black network of its sewers, which he views, quite literally, as entrances to hell itself. Walking about the city, they inevitably get lost and only find their way back to the train after a series of degrading encounters that initially divide but ultimately bind them together in a shared understanding of the threatening, evil otherness of the city. Hopelessly lost in the white suburbs after wandering through a series of poor black and white neighborhoods, the Heads experience an epiphany of sorts in front of a lawn jockey that provides the title of O'Connor's story. After a day of bewilderment and alienation, the figurine allows the Heads a momentary identification with suburban whites, like whom they understand themselves only in opposition to the urban black world they keep at a distance.

A little more than a decade later, when the Atlanta metro area was in the early stages of pushing beyond the arc of the soon-to-be-finished Perimeter highway, Atlanta native James Dickey re-explored the contrasting moral landscapes of city and region in his 1969 novel and 1972 screenplay, *Deliverance*. This time, however, it is a group of urbanites who travel into a wilderness whose threat lies in both the nature of its terrain and its people. Four white Atlanta businessmen, representing two of those signature occupations of the 1960s boom — advertising and real estate — journey to the north Georgia mountains to canoe a white-water river before it is to be dammed to provide electricity, drinking water, and recreational space for the tens of thousands of newcomers flocking to the city each year. Led by the thrill-seeking Lewis, the men leave their humdrum workaday worlds to venture into the primeval forest, where they find themselves engaged in an epic battle for survival, not only with the raging natural force of the river, but with the threatening venality of the local hill people, who rape one member of the party and who are presumed to have killed another. In the Iron John revenge fantasy that ensues, the urban businessmen are revealed to be every bit as savage as their adversaries, killing one of the attackers outright, then stalking and killing another (a relative of the local sheriff) who may, or may not, have been the guilty party. Safely off the river, they must confront and outwit the forces of local law and order to make good their escape back to the city. Like the Heads, they return with their bodies intact, but their spirits shaken by an encounter with an evil that lies within themselves just as much as in their adversaries.

The film version of *Deliverance* is remembered in popular consciousness far more for its stereotyped representation of inbred backwoods Appalachians than for anything it reveals about Atlanta as a distinctive place. Still, this lack of specificity is itself significant. In *Deliverance*, Atlanta assumes the role of a generic city, a civilized place with expansive suburbs, a proverbial "island in a sea of rednecks." Even though all four businessmen are Southern-born, they find themselves profoundly estranged from their upcountry kin. All four subscribe to the "stunning and stubborn delusion" of "I'm from Atlanta, I'm not from Georgia" that author James Baldwin has rightly identified as one of the keys to understanding the mythology of the city.[149]

Yet, even as *Deliverance* was being written and filmed, the stark contrasts between urban and rural Georgia were becoming slowly attenuated by the steady march of the suburban frontier. The damming of rivers not only ensured water for mushrooming subdivisions and office parks, but provoked an invasion of Atlantans seeking second homes and recreational activities in the north Georgia mountains. In the course of the 1970s and 1980s, the once threatening mountains were partially pacified with outlet malls, state camp grounds, and theme-parked upcountry villages that belonged to other times and places. The old mining town of Dahlonega rediscovered its "Gold Rush days," staged gunfights in the street, and seemed more a creation of the Wild West than the plantation South. Meanwhile, the sleepy former lumbering hamlet of Helen reconfigured itself into a self-conscious parody of a Bavarian Alpine village, complete with half-timbered facades and the obligatory Oktoberfest bash. Even remote Blairsville, near where *Deliverance* was filmed, eventually sported its share of bed and breakfasts and homesteads for urban refugees. By the early 1990s, new highways had brought planned unit developments and commercial strips into the southern reaches of the mountains themselves, and plans for an Outer Perimeter highway promised even more intensive development in the not so distant future.

THE CITY THAT EXPLODED

If cities could be in any way likened to persons, one could generously say that from the late 1960s onward, Atlanta enjoyed a complex personality. If one wished to be less charitable, one could say that the city was outrightly schizophrenic and suffered from delusions of grandeur. Even before fully consolidating Atlanta's status as a national or major league city, the Chamber of Commerce and other business groups embarked on promoting the dubious notion of Atlanta as "the world's next great international city," nothing less than a techno-cosmopolitan capital of the twenty-first century. At the same time, Atlanta developed a reputation as a "Black Mecca,"[150] not only on account of its historically black universities and community entrepreneurs, but for its emergent African-American political establishment, enhanced economic opportunities, and central role in the civil rights movement.

Both of these themes reinforced the exceptional and anomalous position of Atlanta in the wider region: somehow in Georgia, but not really of it. Yet, after more than two decades of rapid growth, the principal divide was no longer between the cosmopolitan metropolis and the rural hinterlands, but between the majority black, poor, sociopolitically liberal, and Democratic urban core and the overwhelmingly white, conservative, and booming Republican suburban and exurban periphery. Despite extensive use of renewal and the construction of a number of glitzy new mixed-use developments, such as John Portman's Peachtree Center, white suburbanites, many of whom arrived from outside Georgia, viewed the urban core in terms not too far removed from those used by Flannery O'Connor's characters. Far from being the center of a prosperous region, the central city was conceptualized by them as debased, dangerous, and all too *different* – the black hole at the center of the doughnut, a place to be avoided if at all possible. Portman and other architects working downtown responded by designing hardened citadels closed off from the street to create little outposts of suburbia downtown. Such divides between city and suburb were, however, rarely manifest in the official imagined constructions of metropolitan Atlanta, which projected blanket generalizations of growth, prosperity, progressivism, and racial harmony in the capital of the *New* New South.

Atlanta's physical and symbolic expansion during the 1960s and 1970s led to the multiplication of mediated representations, as well as a fundamental change in the way(s) in which the city was imagined. The growth of the convention industry led to a profusion of guidebooks of various degrees of officialness written by both local journalists and authors connected with national concerns like *Fodor's*. The former invariably exuded thick gobs of syrupy Atlanta Spirit, knitting the same old familiar yarns about the city's magic marriage of Northern bustle and Southern charm with rapturous descriptions of the climate and the bold new landscape of modernist mixed-use developments that had recolonized downtown. Reading one overly effusive description of the new Marriot Motor Inn (in terms that made it seem on a par with the Ritz) some twenty-five years after the fact, one gets the feeling of just how tenuous and insecure Atlanta's "national" status was in 1969.[151] National travel writers were for the most part far less partisan, at times condescendingly critical of the city's recent achievements. Boosters were, however, oblivious to anything but praise.

With tens of thousands of newcomers moving to Atlanta each year, a specialized genre of publications, brochures, and videos emerged to satisfy the way-finding and home-buying needs of new residents and the relocation industry that served them. As mentioned previously, *Atlanta Magazine* played a key role in articulating a happy, upbeat, and giddily positive image of the city. Numerous lushly illustrated "coffee table books," the linear descendants of nineteenth-century city view books, were published in the 1970s and 1980s as well. Usually authored by local journalists, like Norman Shavin, Bruce Galphin (both associated with the second incarnation of *Atlanta Magazine*) and Celestine Sibley, and featuring photographs by nationally known photographers like Peter Beney, these expensive texts presented an unabashedly celebrative view of Atlanta that confirmed and advanced the myth of the modern, national city in word and image.[152] The photography was firmly in the tradition of the "urban grand" variety and doted on panoramic views of the city's new downtown (and later midtown) skylines, well-composed portraits of its most prominent civic institutions, and glimpses of the sylvan beauty of its most prosperous neighborhoods. Much as *Atlanta in 1890: The Gate City* had done, these books presented a cohesive and putatively comprehensive view of a fragmented, sprawling and often confusing metropolitan landscape.

The gaze of these books, however, was highly selective; focusing only on those features that reinforced the upbeat and positive image of the city. As one photographer noted, they used "only photographs [of] the beautiful, never the ugly or depressing."[153] The weather was always sunny, and there was never a cloud in the sky, unless it helped accentuate the sunset. Even if the authors mentioned, rarely and briefly, the fact that things were not so cheerful everywhere in Atlanta, the photographs never did. This is crucial, for these books were organized far more to be looked at than read. In many cases, the text comprised nothing but a short foreword and brief captions, sometimes at the back of the book. True to the forward-thinking spirit of Atlanta, the books were bent on "celebrating" the present, rather than the past, or as one author noted: "This book is about the 'is' Atlanta, with a few glimpses of the 'was' which remains."[154] Interestingly enough, even as the majority of the most intensive growth was occurring on the peripheries, these books focused most of their attention on the features of the core: the modernist towers of Peachtree Center and the tree-shaded and azalea-filled streets of the city's residential neighborhoods.

Of course, these texts did not purport to be scholarly histories or works of social analysis. Rather, they were unabashedly affectionate celebrations of Atlanta as a special place. As such, they might best be considered advertisements of a very special kind, advertisements for the status quo. They provided proof that things really were okay despite the unrelenting body count on the evening news, and the boarded-up housing projects one glimpsed from the elevated expressway, or any of the other features of the urban wasteland that lay outside the immediate lifeworld of the middle-class readership for whom these volumes were intended. While the authors might claim that the books were for all Atlantans (as long as they could come up with the $40–60 cost), they included little that would allow a poor person to agree, "Yes, this is my city, too." At times, the disjuncture between the perpetually sunny, traffic- and smog-free Atlantas of the view book where the azaleas were always in bloom and the congested, conflicted, unevenly developed maelstrom of a city was so profound as to inspire, if not vertigo, at least distrust of all mediated representations.

Some may argue that, like all advertisements, no one *really* took these books seriously anyway, that we know Atlanta is something other than what they made it out to be. Yet, in 1995 when two Catalan photographers pointed their lenses uncharitably towards the stark and the depressing features of the urban moonscape, the resulting howl of righteous indignation could be heard halfway to Barcelona. Most city view books, while not malevolent in intent, nonetheless reinforce the intense social fragmentation of the urban population and the highly selective understandings people possess about where they live. They do so by asserting that the perspective of the white middle class is not one among many, but a comprehensive, holistic, and inclusive vision.

Advertising, in all fairness, is not supposed to be critical; it is supposed to persuade rather than enlighten (although the latest trend in advertising seems to realize the former by claiming to do the latter). Enlightenment, critique, and the exegesis of historical and contemporary reality are the business of the guild of professional scholarship, which is separated from the realm of popular discourse by firewalls of institutionalized authority and intimidating jargon. Despite the large number of institutions of higher education in Atlanta, this was a rather thinly populated domain until roughly two decades ago. Just as the 1970s and 1980s saw a proliferation of promotional texts, they also witnessed a major surge in the scholarly discourse regarding the city. With several notable exceptions, though, local academics have helped to reinforce rather than challenge the promotional myth-making, city-building establishment.

The first scholarly studies of Atlanta were associated with the *fin de siècle* work of W.E.B. DuBois and others at Atlanta University. Under DuBois's stewardship, Atlanta University became one of the foremost centers of sociological research on African-Americans, as well as the host of an annual conference on "negro problems" between 1896 and 1917. Students in history, sociology, and economics conducted pioneering research on numerous aspects of black life in Atlanta.[155] African-American Atlanta remained a research focus for the faculty and students of the schools that comprised the Atlanta University Center in ensuing decades, although until recently it lacked an institutional mechanism through which it could articulate an alternative vision to that being expressed by the official imagineering establishment. Beginning in 1993, the Southern Center for Studies in Public Policy at Clark-Atlanta University has issued an annual report on the status of Black Atlanta that is intended to sensitize policy-makers to the reality behind the hype of "Mecca-ness."

By contrast, the Georgia Institute of Technology has long enjoyed close relations with the city's official visioning apparatus, especially in the areas of architecture, urban planning, and civil engineering. Redesigning downtown has been the favorite subject of generations of Georgia Tech architecture and planning students, and many of the city's architects have been Tech graduates. Tech faculty members have played key roles in most of the urban redevelopment projects of the past three decades, including preparations for the Olympics. Yet some Tech faculty members have played critical rather than adulatory roles. In the late 1980s and early 1990s, the "Architectural Jihad" group and members of the Atlanta Society of Architects publically challenged the social agenda behind the technopolitan strategies that recolonized downtown in a series of fortified enclaves like Peachtree

Center and the Omni/CNN Center, though with little lasting effect.

Much as with fiction and film, the academic literature on Atlanta history has been relatively modest in quantity. Until the 1970s, the historiography of the city was largely a matter for journalists and gentlemen scholars. While the accounts of the former usually left something to be desired in the way of scholarly integrity, those of the latter were not necessarily amateur. In 1954, Franklin Garrett, a public relations man in the employ of the Coca-Cola Corporation and a long-time president of the Atlanta Historical Society, published the first two volumes of his *Atlanta and Environs*, a chronological compendium of facts and figures that is, in many ways, the "bible" of Atlanta history. Designated recently as the city's official historian by the Atlanta City Council, the nonagenarian Garrett is something of a resource unto himself, a walking compendium of local folklore and cadastral history, "Mr Atlanta History." While richly detailed and the source of a vast amount of information, Garrett's two volumes, along with a third written by the late *Atlanta Journal* columnist Harold Martin, tend to be long on description and short on critical analysis, as well as focused largely on the activities of the city's white movers and shakers. Similar limitations bedevil other popular, if far less detailed, histories written in the 1960s.[156]

The representation of Atlanta's past changed markedly in the 1970s, as a young generation of professional scholars and others began filling in the gaps and silences in the city's historical record. As elsewhere in the country, the impending American Bicentennial and the intellectual ferment of the late 1960s sparked a re-evaluation of the regnant interpretation of Atlanta's past. In 1973, noncommercial community radio station WRFG – Radio Free Georgia – was founded "to highlight the culture and heritage of the Southeast, to provide a broadcast voice for those traditionally denied access to the media, and to offer alternative programming to that carried over the local airwaves."[157] In 1977, WRFG received a grant from the National Endowment for the Humanities to undertake an extensive oral history project that mapped the "segregation of memory" that divided Atlanta's aging black and white working and middle classes.[158] Quite unlike more promotional booster histories, the WRFG project emphasized vernacular accounts of events that had been excluded from the official historical record of the first half of the twentieth century.

A number of young academic historians from local universities served as consultants on the project. In 1975, as part of the preparations for the upcoming Bicentennial, Tim Crimmins of Georgia State University and Dana White of Emory University authored a series of pamphlets describing a variety of "An-other Atlanta(s)" peopled by African-Americans, women, and other "others." Between the mid 1970s and the late 1980s, Crimmins and White, along with several cohorts of their students and a few other colleagues, turned out a substantial body of work that focused on developing a "usable urban history" of both the city's infrastructure and key locales and neighborhoods. Their work was explicitly for popular as well as academic consumption, enabling "Atlantans to read their cities in new ways . . . to see patterns in the historical development of the metropolitan area which they have not noticed before."[159] Chief among these patterns were the linkages between the separate and unequally documented histories of the city's white and black residents, which previous accounts of the city's past had ignored and contemporary efforts of city boosters tried to obscure behind an Atlanta Spirit-filled smokescreen of eternal racial harmony and social progressivism.

In a more general sense, by insisting that Atlanta did indeed have a past, or rather multiples ones, and that they needed to be represented and preserved in some way, the work of the GSU/Emory group fundamentally challenged the relentless future-orientation of city boosters in a manner they could not easily ignore. Their analyses helped animate the historic preservation movement in Atlanta, which, in the 1980s, often put them at odds with downtown business interests adamantly opposed to any kind of restrictions on private property owners. Preservationists, most of whom were white, also found themselves at odds with black politicians, such as Andrew Young, who were opposed to the protection of what to them were unpleasant reminders of a segregated city. By the 1990s, however, a tenuous rapprochement between preservationists and developers emerged as the latter belatedly discovered the value of the "historic" in conjuring much-desired magical and alluring worlds of consumption.

Despite these few contrary and critical voices, the more professional–technical sectors of the academic establishment in Atlanta have tended to work closely with the business community in promoting both a technopolitan vision of downtown redevelopment and the notion of Atlanta as "the capital of the twenty-first century" – the ultimate hi-tech city of the future. All three university complexes located in, or adjacent to, downtown are members of the Georgia Research Alliance (which is intended to promote the city as a center of cutting-edge research in science and technology) and are closely tied in with the city's business establishment. During its late 1960s expansion from a college to a university, Georgia State was reconceived as an "urban observatory," where the methods of the natural sciences could be brought to bear on urban problems. While the terminology has changed, this sense of "urban mission" endures at GSU and, in fact, has been expanded as the university has itself emerged as a major player in the game of downtown revitalization with the goal of becoming the model urban university of the next century. However, it is clear that this notion of "the urban" is defined more in terms of corporations than communities. GSU's president has explicitly called for an even more intimate melding of the academy and business to create synergistic "industries of the mind" that produce new kinds of informational commodities.[160] Faced with tightening budgets, GSU is redirecting resources to programs that are consistent with the university's rearticulated mission and that serve to encourage new kinds of partnerships between the public and private sectors. While academic autonomy has always been somewhat illusory and partial at best, and the drying up of government research dollars necessitates identifying new sources of funds, the proposed closer integration of the academy and business raises questions about the future of the university as a site where critical, contrary, or dissenting perspectives on urban redevelopment can be articulated.

HIGH CULTURE

As venues for the cultivation of new industries of the mind, local colleges and universities play a key role in building up Atlanta's stock of cultural capital. Floating atop a more than one-billion-dollar endowment provided in large measure by the Candlers, the Woodruffs, and other Coca-Cola families, Emory University perhaps best exemplifies the Atlanta alchemy of arts and science. Originally an institution for the provincial elite, in the 1980s Emory embarked on a major effort to buy itself an international reputation by, among other things, dramatically expanding programs, raiding top universities for their talent, and affiliating itself with the Carter Presidential Center.[161] While the university's overall scholarly reputation has yet to catch up with its outlays, bolstered by the nearby presence of the federal Center for Disease Control (CDC), Emory's Schools of Medicine and Public Health have emerged as renowned centers of health and biotech research. City boosters proudly point to the global reach of the CDC's activity as proof of Atlanta's international status.

The arts, too, have been mobilized to legitimize Atlanta's claim to cosmopolitanism, although the city's museums, symphonies, and the like are not as extensive or as highly evolved as its sports stadiums, convention facilities, and golf courses. Nonetheless, largely due to the beneficence of the Woodruff Foundation, from the 1960s onward Atlanta has experienced an expansion of its elite cultural infrastructure. In 1962, when Atlanta was in many ways still a relatively small town, over a hundred of its wealthiest patrons of the arts were tragically killed in a Paris plane crash while returning from a continental grand tour. Six years later, they were commemorated with a large Woodruff-funded arts center in Midtown, the Atlanta Memorial Arts Building. Later renamed the Woodruff Arts Center, after its major patron, the megastructure originally housed the High Museum of Art, as well as the Atlanta College of Art, and facilities for the Atlanta Symphony and the Atlanta Ballet. Until the early 1980s, the building was, literally, Atlanta's one-stop shop for elite culture.

In 1983, the High Museum of Art moved into new quarters on an adjacent site. Inspired by Frank Lloyd Wright's Guggenheim Museum in New York City, Richard Meirer's pristine modernist vision in white porcelain-enameled steel quickly became one of the city's most noted landmarks, another man-made oasis in Mencken's "Sahara of the Bozart." In the early 1990s, two other new museums opened – the Fernbank Natural History Museum in Druid Hills and the Atlanta History Center in Buckhead – while the Woodruff Center underwent a major renovation to soften its bunkered facade.

The original fortress aesthetic of the Arts Center firmly dates the edifice as a product of the late 1960s and reveals a good deal about the nature of the surrounding landscape at the time of its construction. Not all of Atlanta's escape from provinciality came as a result of the official imagineering apparatus and the deliberate seeding of authorized franchises of the culture industry. By the summer of 1966, the area just down the street from the Arts Center was home to the largest "hippie ghetto" in the Southeast. Known variously as "the Hip Strip," "the Neighborhood," and "Tight Squeeze,"[162] Peachtree Street between 10th and 14th Streets quickly became one of Atlanta's most noteworthy attractions for the turned-on, tuned-in progeny of Dixie and wannabe local teenagers, as well as the "straight" citizenry who came to gawk at the self-proclaimed "freaks."

While some Atlantans proudly viewed the Hip Strip as a symbol of unprovincial cosmopolitan urbanity – the truest sign that Atlanta was in a radically different "league" from Birmingham, Charlotte, and Nashville – this attitude was not widely shared by city and state authorities or by area property owners.[163] Georgia governor Lester Maddox regularly threatened to mobilize the National Guard to eradicate the menace posed by the area's barefoot, long-haired, drug-taking denizens. The Atlanta police proved only a little more enlightened, initially allowing the community some autonomy, but intensifying their repression towards the end of the decade. In the summer of 1969, when rumors circulated that the entire hippie community of Chicago was going to move en masse to the "free city" of Atlanta, city authorities responded with what *Time* magazine called "the Great Atlanta Hippie Hunt," a series of raids which culminated in a late-summer police riot in Piedmont Park.[164] The intensified police crackdown, coupled with the fragmentation within the hippie community and the spread of methamphetamine and heroin, served to erode the vitality of the community. By the early 1970s, the more commercial parts of the Hip Strip, like many other similar areas around the country, had been transformed into a combat zone of pornographic bookstores, strip joints, and prostitution. Just to the east of lower Midtown, the three miles of

Ponce De Leon Avenue running to North Highland Avenue became the city's prime white vice corridor, prompting a chorus of moral panic from city and business leaders.[165]

Not all of Midtown, however, was dedicated to the night trades. Many small theaters and arts venues continued to thrive in the neighborhood and the existing stock of early-twentieth-century homes in Midtown and nearby Virginia-Highland attracted the first wave of gay gentrifiers.[166] While the definitive history of Atlanta as "Gay Mecca" has yet to be written, it is nonetheless clear that the immigration of gay and lesbian artists, designers, and other cultural producers is closely related to the florescence of the creative arts in Atlanta within the last two decades. Beginning in the late 1970s, Midtown emerged as the epicenter of an increasingly large and nationally known gay community, even as the state of Georgia maintained some of the strictest anti-sodomy statutes on the books. By the 1980s, the positive image of "Hotlanta" was well established in the gay media. The rainbow flag was a ubiquitous feature on car bumpers and house porches in Midtown, Virginia-Highland, and a number of other intown neighborhoods. The prominence of the gay community in Atlanta further served to reaffirm the divide between city and the remainder of the metropolitan region in the 1980s and 1990s. One did not have to travel too far beyond the Perimeter to encounter institutionalized homophobia, however. In 1993, the Cobb County Commission passed an ordinance condemning the "gay lifestyle" and promoting "family values" and the city of Stone Mountain contemplated a similar measure. As both Cobb County and Stone Mountain were originally scheduled to host Olympic venues, these measures created serious controversies (they will be discussed in greater detail in Chapter 5).

Atlanta's reputation as a place of unprovincial lifestyles from the late 1960s onward was not limited to the hippie and gay/lesbian communities. Despite the projection of propriety and early experiments with prohibition, the spirit of "Snake Nation" had never really been eradicated from the city, only suppressed. Although the Chamber of Commerce did not officially approve, young local journalists helped popularize the notion of Atlanta as a "party town" in the late 1960s and 1970s.[167] Many of the new arrivals were young singles, and a wide variety of bars, discotheques, and related venues developed to meet the demands of the marketplace. The original incarnation of Underground Atlanta first gained fame for its bars and nightclubs, while Peachtree Street between Midtown and Buckhead emerged as a prime strip of watering holes and meat markets for the youthful white middle class doing the "Peachtree Shuffle." Even legendarily staid Cobb County had its share of "swinging singles" apartment complexes in the late 1960s and early 1970s.

The dramatic expansion of the hotel-convention industry also spurred the development of an entertainment sector geared to satisfying the wanton lusts of drunken male conventioneers and traveling salesmen. Displaced from Midtown during the gentrification of the 1980s, the multi-tiered and legally sanctioned industry of upscale strip clubs, lingerie modeling studios, massage parlors, and escort services spread throughout the metropolitan area. According to market research sponsored by the Atlanta Convention and Visitors Bureau, by the early 1990s the adult entertainment industry was one of Atlanta's most distinctive features, far more so than the institutions dedicated to more respectable cultural activities.[168] In their own way, Atlanta's extensive and multi-faceted vice industries were fairly reliable indicators that it had achieved the status of a "national," as opposed to a merely provincial, city.

NOT TOO BUSY TO PARTY, BUT
WAY TOO BUSY TO CARE

By the late 1960s, the city that called itself too busy to hate could just as well be referred to as a city too busy to care. Although the desegregation of schools had begun in 1961, progress was slowed, then reversed, by the voluntary nature of the program and by white flight. By the end of the decade, most of Atlanta's school-children were in de facto segregated institutions and integration became impossible without metropolitan-wide busing. In what became known as the "Second Atlanta Compromise," black leaders agreed not to pursue busing beyond city boundaries in return for greater control over the school system.[169] Public spaces and transportation had been integrated, but through the mechanism of urban renewal the contours of a new and more insidious urban apartheid took root, even as the city acquired a reputation as a center of black opportunity. One third of the city's housing stock, and an even higher percentage of its low-income units, were demolished to make way for expressways, a sports stadium, a civic center, and other public facilities necessary for a national city. Urban renewal increasingly came to be seen as "negro removal" by displaced residents. The search of the black middle class for housing prompted massive white flight from suburban neighborhoods to the south and west of the central city.

In the course of the 1960s, younger African-Americans became increasingly unhappy to work within the old system of negotiated settlements. The Student Nonviolent Coordinating Committee (SNCC) was especially active in Atlanta and was instrumental in organizing community resistance to displacement. In 1966, the Summerhill neighborhood, which was largely obliterated during stadium construction, was the site of the city's first major civil disturbance. Similar episodes occurred again the following year in the black communities of Vine City and Dixie Hills, although none of the three was as severe or violent as the riots taking place in most every other major urban area during this period. Most significant, though, was the relative lack of a violent response to the assassination of Martin Luther King, Jr in 1968. As the site of his funeral and burial, Atlanta was once again thrust into the world media spotlight and city leaders made every effort to project the proper image. In his memoirs, Ivan Allen, Jr noted that he received a call from Coca-Cola president Robert Woodruff offering to pay for whatever was necessary to "do it right."[170] The relative state of calm that reigned in Atlanta during the funeral contrasted greatly with the rioting and looting that occurred elsewhere throughout urban America, and served to reinforce the image of the city as a haven of racial moderation and social progressiveness, even as Atlanta was becoming more, rather than less, racially polarized.

(EF)FACING BLACK MECCA

Atlanta's status as a haven for African-Americans was greatly reinforced by the election of the city's first black mayor, Maynard Jackson, in 1973. This accomplishment was due not to the progressive sentiments of the majority of Atlanta's white population, but rather to their departure from the city in large numbers. By 1970, African-Americans constituted a majority of Atlanta's population for the first time in its history.[171] A scion of a prominent Atlantan family (his maternal grandfather, John Wesley Dobbs, was a major political leader who had coined the sobriquet "Sweet Auburn"), Maynard Jackson was not, however, a product of the *ancien régime* of negotiated settlements. He assumed a confrontationalist posture vis-à-vis the white business community, arguing passionately for a greater distribution of the benefits of growth among African-Americans. In a showdown over the new airport, Jackson succeeded in establishing a minority business enterprise program that became widely regarded as a model for minority set-asides for municipal contracts (until they were struck down by the US Supreme Court in 1989). Together with extensive affirmative action hiring by Atlanta-based corporations like Coca-Cola and Delta Airlines, and an already-established black business community, the set-aside program made Atlanta a nationally known center for African-American economic opportunity in the latter part of the 1970s and the 1980s.

The notion of Atlanta as Black Mecca was much celebrated during the 1980s in the pages of *Ebony, Black Enterprise,* and similar publications, as well as by the *Christian Science Monitor* and white authors, such as Joel Garreau. It referred not only to the success of the city's native-born black middle class, but to the prospects afforded to educated African-Americans around the country. As in the past, a major segment of this grouping was closely associated with the schools of the Atlanta University complex: Clark-Atlanta University, Morehouse, Spellman, and Morris Brown Colleges, and the Interdenominational Seminary. Roughly a quarter of the schools' graduates stayed in the area following graduation and, through associations like the "100 Black Men," helped constitute a close-knit network of contacts and references. Some dubbed the network of black entrepreneurs and politicians that developed during the first two Jackson administrations as "the Morehouse Mafia," on account of the prevalence of alumni in their ranks. One's success was dependent on the degree to which one was plugged into this network of acquaintances.

However, the schools of the Atlanta University complex were far from being an unproblematically unified body. The component institutions were marked by differences in status (with Morehouse and Spelman Colleges occupying the apex of the status hierarchy and Morris Brown the nadir), while the student bodies themselves were divided on the basis of gender, class, skin color, and political orientation. These divides were explored by filmmaker Spike Lee, himself an ex-Morehouse man, in his film *School Daze* (1988). Set at fictional "Mission College," and partially filmed on the grounds of Spelman, Lee's film highlights the conflict between mostly light-skinned professionally and business-minded "wannabes" and a minority of politically activist, more steadfastly Afri-centric students. *School Daze* also drew attention to the less than harmonious relations between the school's largely out-of-town population and the surrounding communities. Lee's portrayal of elitism and fractures within the university community was not well received locally, and his permission to film on location was revoked midway through the shooting. Interestingly enough, despite the presence of a large number of African-American cultural producers and the city being the site for the biannual National Black Arts Festival, Atlanta has not figured prominently as either a setting or a subject for many contemporary African-American writers and filmmakers.

Although the real Atlanta University system possessed numerous connections and relations with the surrounding neighborhoods, which were among Atlanta's poorest and most crime-ridden areas, the divide between the black middle and working classes deepened and widened in the 1970s and 1980s. Despite economic opportunities for the middle class and a continuous black presence at city hall for two decades, Atlanta was far from being a decent place, much less a paradise, for the majority of its African-American residents. By any and every statistical measure, from poverty and unemployment to graduation rates and crime, the quality of life "enjoyed" by the city's African-American majority plummeted during this period.[172] The percentage of black households living in poverty nearly doubled between 1980 and 1990, to more than a third of all households. Over half of the city's children lived in poverty.

Despite the hype in the black and white press, Atlanta was also far from being a secure place for the black middle class. A 1994 study by Clark-Atlanta University found that Atlanta ranked ninth in levels of black entrepreneurship, behind such less well known cities as Columbus, Ohio, Sacramento, California and Richmond, Virginia.[173] Moreover, the majority of black-owned firms were highly dependent on public-sector contracts. Minority set-asides tended to go to established and well-connected African-American firms, like HJR Russell Construction, which enjoyed annual sales of $180 million, and had long ceased to represent the disadvantaged corporations for which the system was designed. In 1995, Maynard Jackson himself was the beneficiary of a minority business enterprise contract for a restaurant concession at Hartsfield Airport. Beginning with Andrew Young's election in 1982, Atlanta's mayors have not made revitalization of the city's poor African-American neighborhoods more than a rhetorical priority of their administrations. Young was especially guilty of articulating a rhetoric of compassion for the poor, while at the same time adhering to the uncompassionate logic of Reaganite trickle-down economics.[174]

Nowhere was the divide between the two black Atlantas more manifest than in the area of crime. Atlanta was nationally renowned for its high crime rate in the late 1960s and early 1970s. Its homicide rate more than doubled between 1965 and 1970, making the city the country's "murder capital."[175] Atlanta has retained the dubious honor of being one of the nation's most violent cities to the present day. The vast majority of these crimes occurred, then as now, in the city's poorest census tracts to the south, east, and west of downtown, areas that are more than 95 percent African-American. However, the high rate of violent crime there, as opposed to, say, in the central business district and the mostly white, gentrified intown neighborhoods, elicited relatively little attention until the end of the 1970s, when it became a matter of national and international interest.

Between 1979 and 1981, twenty-eight black children disappeared and were murdered in a case that became known as the Atlanta Child Murders. City authorities were initially slow to respond. The victims came from Atlanta's poorest communities and the police refused to acknowledge that these crimes constituted anything other than the "normal" level of violence in these areas. It was only after the thirteenth body was discovered and parents of the victims organized and brought in famous celebrities (such as Mohammad Ali, Sammy Davis, Jr, and Dick Gregory) to help their cause that the city responded by inviting in the FBI and, in true Atlanta fashion, undertaking a promotional campaign to forestall any potential harm to the city's image. As the body count mounted, the circus-like atmosphere that surrounded the city intensified. James Baldwin noted of that time, "Atlanta became, for a season, a kind of grotesque Disneyland," as "prophets, soothsayers" and other media ghouls descended upon the city to offer their assistance and feed the hype.[176] Largely forgotten today, the Atlanta Child Murders was one of the first of the hypermediated, necrophiliac courtroom spectacles that have since become such compelling and regular fare on American television.

Given the identity of the victims, initial speculation tagged the crime as the work of the Klan, or other white hate groups. However, in 1981, a young black man, Wayne Williams, was arrested and later found guilty of two of the murders, largely on the basis of circumstantial, but scientific, fiber evidence. Although the authorities were unable to come up with evidence linking Williams with the other twenty-six cases, they nonetheless considered him to be the sole perpetrator of the heinous acts and the case to be closed with his conviction. Critics have charged, with extremely good reason, that Williams was no more than a convenient patsy, whose conviction allowed Atlanta to return to "normal" without further damage to its image. As it was, the city suffered no fall off in business during the murder spree; the greatest danger appeared to be to the already tenuous reputation of the city's African-American administration, rather than to the health of its economy.[177]

With Williams behind bars, matters have most definitely returned to "normal:" rates of violent crime in the city's poorest areas have skyrocketed without inciting even a fraction of the attention generated by the twenty-eight murders between 1979 and 1981. Meanwhile, the killings have been wiped from the city's collective memory; the event has been even more forgotten and obscured than the 1906 race riot, the dominance of the Klan, and other embarrassing reminders of Atlanta's less than progressive and racially harmonious past. In late 1993, lawyers for Wayne Williams tried to get their client a new trial, arguing that police and prosecutors suppressed evidence, including secret tapes of Ku Klux Klan members confessing to some of the killings.[178] Not only were the lawyers unsuccessful in their efforts, but the allegations were virtually ignored by the mainstream Atlanta news media. Forever looking forward, Atlanta cannot be bothered with the distractions of even the recent past.

ATLANTA GOING INTERNATIONAL

Although the city's official imagineering apparatus proudly boasts of Atlanta as birthplace of the civil rights movement, the representation of Atlanta as Black Mecca has always been secondary and subordinate to a more expansive vision. Having achieved, in their minds at least, the status of a "national city" by the end of the 1960s, Atlanta's boosters next set their sights on becoming the "world's next great international city." This provoked a great deal of mirth from critics, as there was very little that was "international" about Atlanta in 1970. The slogan was widely viewed at the time as a joke, a lie, a delusion, a collective hallucination, a sure sign that the denizens of the Commerce Club were hanging out on the Hip Strip and imbibing something stronger than their usual lunchtime bourbon and branch water.

Then again, the original New South boosters had long hoped for an enhanced role for Atlanta in global trade, as the 1881 *International* Cotton Exposition and the 1895 Cotton States and *International* Exposition attest. These events had not, however, stimulated much international commerce. Aside from the Coca-Cola Corporation, which produced, arguably, the world's best-known commodity, few of the city's businesses had transnational operations of significant extent until the 1970s. Nor were there many foreign companies with business activities or investments in Atlanta. The city possessed no port, and, more importantly, the airport had no international flights until 1978.

Atlanta's desires for global connectivity had been historically at odds with the South's deeply rooted xenophobia. In the past, Atlanta businessmen wanted foreign trade passing through their stores and warehouses, but were much less enthusiastic about non-Anglo-Saxon people residing among them. Atlanta's internationalists, however, had a number of things in their favor. First, they never really defined what the term "international city" meant, and whatever it did, it referred to what Atlanta desired to be in the future, rather than what it was in the present, or had been in the past.[179] More importantly, as numerous scholars have noted, the world economy was becoming increasingly globalized in the early 1970s, thanks to the ability of new technologies of transportation and communication to shrink time and space and reconfigure regimes of accumulation.[180] The oil shock of 1973–74 served to further intensify the global redistribution of capital and Atlanta was well positioned to receive its share of petrodollars, Eurodollars, and other dollar-denominated capital surpluses that coursed through the terrestrial bourse looking for a friendly home.

City boosters followed essentially the same strategy that had served them so well nationally in the 1960s. They extensively advertised the city's virtues in the European business press, sank nearly five billion dollars of public funds into building the necessary infrastructure, including an international airport and the Georgia *World* Congress Center (located, fittingly enough, on *International* Boulevard), sent scores of trade missions to the business capitals of Europe and Asia, and to all intents and purposes hung a big sign on the city that said "Y'all Come." Or, as Atlanta native and *Fortune* managing editor John Huey recently put it, boosters made up "the biggest lie they could possibly think of and [ran] around the world telling everybody about it until it [came] true."[181] The election of former Georgia governor Jimmy Carter also highlighted the city's and state's image, as did his nomination of Andrew

Young as his United Nations ambassador. In the 1980s and 1990s, Atlanta became its own *Field of Dreams*: if you build it (up), they will come. Foreign investment flooded in and international business activity surged, along with an influx of Latin American, Asian, African, and Eastern European immigrants and refugees.

During much of the 1970s, however, Atlanta's internationality was best realized in works of fiction. These included not only the giddy promotional advertisements in the *Economist*, *Financial Times*, and the *International Herald Tribune*, but in a novel written by former *Atlanta Magazine* staffer Bill Diehl. Diehl, who would later go on to make a name and a comfortable living for himself with a number of other globe-girdling tales of intrigue like *Thai Horse*, published *Sharky's Machine* in 1978. A somewhat less than inspired film version, starring and directed by Burt Reynolds (who had played Lewis in *Deliverance* and had since then been almost single-handedly responsible for a whole *oeuvre* of good ol' boy "Southerns" filmed, for the most part, in Georgia), followed in 1981. Part gritty urban police drama, part quasi-Orientalist pot-boiler, part homage to the hard-partying Atlanta of the swinging seventies, *Sharky's Machine* gave Atlanta the internationality that it claimed to have a decade before the facts on the ground began to catch up with the promotional bluster.

Set in 1975, it tells the story of the efforts of a dedicated cop and his "machine" of like-minded cronies to solve a murder and, in the process, foil the nefarious plans of an evil international businessman, Victor Delaroza. An American army deserter from World War II, Delaroza has assumed the identity of a mysterious Brazilian who has moved the headquarters of his vast and highly diversified multinational business empire (toys, electronics, oil, arms, real estate, and sundry criminal enterprises) to Atlanta, thanks to foreign investment incentives dreamed up by the former state governor, and now US senator, Donald Hotchins, whose political career Delaroza has masterminded for decades. This Delaroza is something of a Dr No-like character, a decadent sinophile with a bodyguard of silently inscrutable Chinese martial artists and a dragon-sailed junk on Lake Lanier. Not unlike the doyens of the Atlanta Chamber of Commerce and Central Atlanta Progress, Delaroza dreams of national, if not world, dominion: he is secretly bankrolling Hotchins's candidacy for the presidency. Even evil geniuses miscalculate, though. To obviate the problem of a possible future scandal, Delaroza arranges to have the callgirl mistress he shares with Hotchins, the Scheherazade-like Domino, murdered. However, the killing goes awry and, worse yet, leaves a trail of evidence that leads Sharky (who himself has become obsessed with Domino) unwittingly into the heart of Delaroza's plot.

While Delaroza and Sharky seem to have no real-life referents, Diehl appears to have partially modeled the figure of the Kennedyesque Hotchins on the youthful, urbane Carl Sanders, Georgia's governor between 1963 and 1967. Occupying the Governor's Mansion between the race-baiting regimes of Ernest Vandiver and Lester Maddox, Sanders backed programs to attract foreign investment to the state and was often compared by the media to John Kennedy.[182] In addition to being a philanderer, Hotchins is a successful lawyer, businessman, and war hero, who has served two terms in the state house and one as governor, before defeating the senior senator (who, at the time in question, was the patriarchal Dixiecrat Richard Russell) to represent the state in Washington. Hotchins is most definitely *not* Jimmy Carter, who is described as his principal rival for the Democratic presidential nomination. Unlike Carter, Hotchins has charismatic sex appeal and is considered a sure bet to defeat Gerald Ford. This is truly the *New* New South: with a stroke of his pen, Diehl conveniently excises such provincial embarrassments as Lester Maddox and his legislative pack of yellow-dog Democrats from Georgia's political landscape. In fact, there is little in the book that would lead the reader to believe the action is set in the South at all.

Delaroza might be a criminal, but he is an Atlanta-Spirited one, a visionary dreamer who thinks big and has an edifice complex. In some ways, his presidential aspirations for Hotchins seem secondary to his concerns for the completion of the ultimate in indoor theme parks he is building downtown. Delaroza spares no expense in constructing a hyper-real simulation of his beloved Hong Kong inside an office building. Anticipating MGM/Universal's extravaganza in Orlando by several years, the centerpiece of the theme park is a gigantic Pachinko game thrill ride, in which visitors in large silver balls speed through a phantasmagoric landscape complete with giant fire-breathing animatrons acting out the climactic battle of Hong Kong's foundation myth.

Unlike *Gone With the Wind*, *Sharky's Machine* did not go on to become one of the bestselling novels of all time, although it did enjoy respectable sales when it was released. Yet not unlike Margaret Mitchell, Diehl maneuvered a stock set of stereotypical characters (the rogue, yet noble, cop, the courtesan with a heart of gold, the decadent master criminal, etc.) in an Atlanta landscape in a time of transition. Sharky and his crew are homeboys (although they do not speak with Southern accents), and Diehl firmly grounds the action in a local context, providing the most comprehensive fictional rendering of the city since *Gone With the Wind*. Well-known local landmarks and districts are blended in with fictional sites to convey the feel of a small regional city turning into a national metropolis of global reach. Ironically, even though the film version was shot on location in Atlanta, it is precisely this local coloration – along with the simulacrum of Hong Kong – that gets bleached out and excised in the transition to the big screen. The sole concession to Atlanta-ness is multiple shots of the cylindrical Peachtree Plaza Hotel tower, at the time the highest building in the city's attenuated skyline and an iconic symbol of Atlanta's new technopolitan identity. With the local color and international dimensions of the plot removed, what is left is a generically late-seventies urban landscape that could very well be anywhere. In short, it is of a piece with "real-life" efforts to reimagine Atlanta as a city like any other and no place in particular.

Unlike the book, the film version of *Sharky's Machine* did not enjoy even a modicum of financial success. Not widely available on video, it has been relegated to sporadic late-night appearances on the Atlanta-based cable television "superstation," WTBS. Like that other cinematic representation of Atlanta, *Gone With the Wind*, *Sharky's Machine* belongs, appropriately enough, to the extensive film library owned by local media mogul and entrepreneurial visionary extraordinaire Ted Turner.

CITIZEN TED

Richard Edward "Ted" Turner III is firmly enshrined in the ranks of Atlanta's spirited visionary dreamers. Assuming control of his father's failing billboard business in the early 1960s, Turner turned its fortunes around through adroit salesmanship and a preternatural sense of marketing. In the 1970s, he bought an obscure local UHF television station and turned it into the first "superstation" for the evolving national cable television market, WTBS. Part P.T. Barnum, part Commodore Vanderbilt, Turner then pursued and won the prestigious America's Cup yachting race in 1977. In the process he earned the tag "mouth of the South" for his outrageous, self-promoting rhetoric. A worthy heir to Henry Grady, Turner both talked the talk and walked the walk: he delivered on his bold promises. In a major gesture of local corporate citizenship, as well as to provide programming for his station, Turner bought the city's lowly major league baseball and national basketball franchises, the Braves and the Hawks, eventually turning the former into one of the sport's dominant teams (the Hawks, alas, have not been as competitive).

Turner's best-known venture, and the one that has contributed greatly to Atlanta's national and putatively international status, has been the Cable News Network, or CNN. Next to Coca-Cola and *Gone With the Wind*, CNN is probably the best known Atlantan "product" in the world. Widely derided as the "Chicken Noodle Network" when it debuted in June 1980, the 24-hour all-news television network reached more than 145 million households in 210 countries fourteen years later.[183] One of eleven worldwide news and entertainment networks that comprise the Turner Broadcasting System (TBS), CNN advertises itself as "the fullest manifestation of the global direction of modern television" and the "preeminent news source for the world."[184] These claims are not all mere promotional blather, as the network's success has been built on live and (sometimes) unedited coverage of breaking news from around the world, such as the Gulf War. To further its status as the global television news network of record, CNN spun off the less Americentric CNN International in 1991. Segments of the latter's broadcasts have only recently (fall, 1995) become available to viewers in the United States.

The choice of Atlanta as headquarters for a major news network was initially widely ridiculed in the industry, for unlike New York, Washington, or even Los Angeles, the city was simply not a place where news of national, much less world, importance was made. CNN solved this problem by crafting an articulated network of bureaus at key news-making locales around the world and using the miracles of satellite technology to shunt it all through Atlanta. Other networks utilized similar technology to gather and disseminate information, but CNN demonstrated the potential of the technology to undermine existing place hierarchies within the global information order. To city boosters, the presence of CNN put Atlanta on the same symbolic level as New York, London, Washington, Tokyo, and other nodal points of the world political–economic system; it served as "proof" of the city's international reach. Such a claim has a certain kind of (very) limited truth to it. As home to the headquarters of a broadcast network of global extent, Atlanta belongs to a relatively elite fraternity of world cities. But the same technologies that make it possible also make it a somewhat hollow status. With the exception of the 1996 Summer Olympics, Atlanta is still not a place where much world or national news is made on a regular basis. Atlanta is just where CNN happens to be, where Ted Turner is from.

CNN's Atlanta exists more in the placeless world of near-instantaneous communication than anywhere else. For the most part, all viewers get to see are accentless talking heads in a broadcast studio, with line producers in the background hunched over the blue glow of their monitors. The scene could be anywhere. Occupying what was originally an upscale shopping mall, the bunkered mass of the CNN Center is a hive of activity tuned more to the rhythms of the global day than to those of the city in which it is located. The lack of relation to its immediate surroundings was made abundantly clear during the uprisings in the wake of the Rodney King verdict in late April 1992. Even as large angry crowds rioted in the streets just outside CNN Center over the course of two days, CNN's attention remained resolutely focused on LA, with only the briefest of mentions of what was occurring locally. Granted, the disturbances in Atlanta were fairly minor in scale compared to what was happening in Los Angeles – they were confined to a small section of downtown and property damage was minimal – but, together with the contemporaneous disturbances in Las Vegas and a dozen other cities, these local events were of considerable national significance. Indeed, the simultaneous uprisings across the

United States were, in part, made possible by the near-instantaneous diffusion of information provided by media entities like CNN.

The break between CNN and the rest of Atlanta is by no means total. CNN often sends camera crews to the city's streets and malls to get background shots or "person on the street" interviews for soft, non-place-specific news stories. However, the place is never identified; one only knows it is Atlanta if one is already familiar with the city. In this manner, Atlanta's non-distinct identity as "anyplace USA" is reinforced. Its urban landscape becomes a default setting, much in the way the built environment of Los Angeles has become insinuated into popular consciousness as the generic urban backdrop for thousands of films and television shows.

CNN Center itself has become one of Atlanta's more popular tourist attractions. Located on the western peripheries of downtown in the air-rights over the Norfolk Southern Railroad's tracks, CNN Center is part of a megastructure that includes the Omni Coliseum, the Georgia Dome, the Georgia World Congress Center, the Georgia International Plaza, the Omni Hotel, and a layered forest of decked parking. Originally built as a mixed-use development in the 1970s known as the Omni *International* (which, like the phantasmagoric setting of *Sharky's Machine*, featured a simulated international bazaar and an indoor amusement park), CNN Center consists of two fourteen-story office buildings and a 500-room hotel enclosing a large glassed-in atrium. Hundreds of people line up each day to take the CNN studio tour and scores of others take part in the "Talk Back Live" show broadcast from the atrium. Advertised as "A World of News and Entertainment," "In the Center of It All," CNN Center boasts a multiplex cinema, an "international" food court, and stores, in addition to offices and studio space. The largest of the retail establishments is "The Turner Store," which features virtually every kind of Turnerabilia imaginable, and then some. One can even have a special-effects photo taken and appear in a scene from *Gone With the Wind* or one of forty other films from the Turner film library (alas, *Sharky's Machine* is not among them).

As mentioned above, a good deal of Atlanta's symbolic capital as a major city of global importance derives from the fact that it is the headquarters of a worldwide media empire founded by a favorite native son. Consequently, news of the Time-Warner Corporation's acquisition of Turner Broadcasting System in a $7.5-billion stock deal in September 1995 sent Atlanta's civic and corporate elite reeling.[185] Having seen the city's once-dominant major banks swallowed up by out-of-state rivals, resulting in the loss of Atlanta's long-cherished status as a regional financial center to, of all places, Charlotte, North Carolina, boosters feared that the buy-out would endanger the city's status as an emerging center for global communications. Although CNN and the rest of TBS will remain in Atlanta, most local boosters were crestfallen by the networks' absorption into a New York-based media metaconglomerate. It was feared, quite sensibly, that the new entity would feel less corporate citizenship of Atlanta. Yet, true to the giddy zeal of the Atlanta Spirit, a few of the city's cheerleaders viewed this not as a crisis, but as an opportunity to lure Time-Warner – or at least its subsidiary Home Box Office – to Atlanta, and thus bolster the city's status as a center of the new world information order.

However, the global extent of Atlanta-based corporations, whether they be TBS, Coca-Cola, United Parcel Service, or Holiday Inn Worldwide, form only a part of the city's putative internationality. As one of the more official promotional accounts notes: "it boils down to whether the city feels cosmopolitan or not, and how much international activity is going on."[186] To the imagineers at Central Atlanta Progress and the Chamber of Commerce, the activities and investments of foreign corporations are clearly the most important and easily demonstrable criterion of Atlanta's global significance. By these measures, Atlanta has become incontestably more international over the last two decades. During the early 1980s, twenty of the world's largest banks opened up branches in Atlanta, followed by European and, later, Japanese insurance companies and pension funds. Still, as extensive as it is, the influx of foreign capital hardly distinguishes Atlanta from a host of other American cities – not just New York, Los Angeles, and San Francisco, but Boston, Houston, Dallas, and Miami – with equivalent or greater amounts of foreign investment. Perhaps in this manner, foreign investment reaffirms Atlanta's place in the upper tier of the national urban system more than establishing a commanding position in the global urban hierarchy.

The mere presence of even a substantial amount of foreign investment hardly makes a city "cosmopolitan." This highly mystified status of "belonging to the world" accrues from many sources, but is more a function of sociocultural heterogeneity – of the not always harmonious mixing of a diversity of peoples in a variety of settings – than of the promiscuous mingling of global capital. In seeking to refigure itself as a cosmopolis, Atlanta struggles under a dual burden. First, there is the drag weight of the State of Georgia's, and Atlanta's, historic xenophobia. Despite two decades of efforts to attract foreign investment, this legacy is very much alive, as evidenced by the recent, and unsuccessful, efforts of the state legislature to make English the official language of Georgia (as if there was a real danger of it being supplanted by Pashto, Khmer, or Spanish) and the lack of urban signage in foreign languages. Despite a number of cursory, multilingual picturebook guides to the city, Atlanta is virtually incomprehensible to a non-English-speaking visitor or resident. Much to the dismay of Atlanta's internationalists, a recent study of foreign visitors found that they considered the city to be quintessentially American instead of cosmopolitan or international.[187] The globalist hype is so far ahead of the facts on the ground that even the shamelessly boosterish *Atlanta Constitution* has had to concede that the city is not *really* international.[188]

In their earnest attempt to realize internationality, Atlanta's powers that be have literally inscribed globality into the very streetscape of downtown. As part of the "world's next great international city" campaign of the early 1970s, city officials renamed Cain Street, which connected the Omni/Georgia World Congress Center with the expressway, International Boulevard and designated it as the official gateway into downtown. For the next twenty years, it was perhaps better described as "International-style Boulevard": a pedestrian-hostile corridor bereft of street life running along the south bank of John Portman's Peachtree Center/Atlanta Market Center arcology.

Designated as a prime pedestrian corridor for the Olympics, the boulevard has recently received some enhancements than accentuate its "international" character. Exiting the expressway, the traveler passes under a proscenium of flags at the base of the boulevard. At the intersection with Peachtree Street (Atlanta's best-known thoroughfare) is a large asphalt tile mosaic of the world. Unfortunately, the globe's designers did not seem to take into account how quickly the image would be obscured by exhaust, burnt rubber, and assorted road soil. Just a month after its completion in the summer of 1995, the world was barely discernible from ground level. The area around the intersection has been renamed International Square and is advertised as such, by colorful banners and special lighting. Further west, past the Welcome South Visitors' Center, International bisects the central square of the Centennial Olympic Park (itself highly redolent of internationalism, with a symbolic grove of flags of previous Olympic hosts contained within an double row of oaks) before entering the cantonment formed by the Omni/CNN Center, the Georgia World Congress Center, and the Georgia Dome, where it terminates in the new Georgia International Plaza, which possesses, yes, yet another ceremonial thicket of flags. "All that is missing," one downtown critic was heard to quip, "is *It's a Small World After All* blaring from speakers." Yet given downtown's lack of attractions and moribund streetscapes, Disneyland is far more, if not authentic, at least differentiated and diverting. The overall effect of all this literalized "internationality" is the inverse of both globality *and* locality, the ultimate nonplace that belongs to everywhere, yet is located nowhere in particular and which has little to offer but Planet Hollywood, the Hard Rock Café, and other sites of serialized uniqueness.

2

ONE, TWO, MANY ATLANTAS

No place in the South is more thoroughly American than Atlanta. The appearance of its streets is like Boston. In the cosmopolitan character of its population and variety of its business interests it is like New York, while in the busy activity of its people it is like Chicago. It has the summer climate of Jerusalem and the winter climate of Rome, altogether giving the finest climate in which English is spoken.[1]

As the above example indicates, city boosters have often begun their paean to Atlanta with a celebration of its natural setting. Yet in the contemporary period, along with rapturous descriptions of its altitude, weather, and overall high quality of life, one of their most emphatic boasts is that the rolling hills and hollows of the north Georgia Piedmont present no natural barriers to development. To this assertion we might add that there are remarkably few man-made ones, either. Although it is firmly situated in the temperate zone, Atlanta's investment climate is nothing short of equatorial, a greenhouse environment purpose-built to cultivate luxuriant growth. Abundant, cheap, and vacant land, lack of regulation, weak labor unions, the restructuring of the global economy, and a strategic position astride lines of road, rail, and air transportation have made the Atlanta metropolitan region an inviting locale for national and foreign capital. Owing to these and other attributes, it has consistently ranked among the fastest-growing urban areas in the United States since the late 1950s. In the early 1980s, the Chamber of Commerce proudly advertised Atlanta as "a city without limits."

Given Atlanta's loving embrace of full-throttle development and an "unlimited low-density vision of growth,"[2] the Chamber's claim is not without substance. However, the drawing of limits and boundaries is central to understanding the political, economic, and sociocultural processes that restlessly reconfigure Atlanta's landscape. Although boosters speak of Atlanta as if it were an undifferentiated whole, the benefits of growth have been most unevenly distributed across the metropolitan region. New jobs and residents have concentrated in a broad swath of majority-white northern suburbs, but, with the exception of a few privileged enclaves, the predominantly black urban core has languished. Indeed, although the Atlanta metropolitan region led the nation in job growth between 1990 and 1995, unemployment in the central city grew fivefold during that same period.[3] Despite the much-celebrated rise of the black middle class and incessant testimonials to racial harmony, the city of Atlanta has itself become increasingly polarized along the divides of race and class, as well.

There are far more than two Atlantas, however. The modern metropolis is, by definition, a place characterized by a highly differentiated and dispersed sociospatial organization, and Atlanta is no exception. Increased sociocultural diversity, economic restructuring, and shifts in the technologies of transportation, communication, and representation have helped to construct a multitude of selectively imagined Atlantas that coexist, but only infrequently interact with one another. Indeed, since the 1960s the emphasis has been on reinforcing the conceptual and physical divides between different groups of people. In these segregative tendencies, of course, Atlanta is far from unique. Rather it is exemplary of current processes of city-building in the United States and many other countries.

Politicians, bureaucrats, businessmen, planners, developers, marketers, and numerous others have imposed dense strata of spatial divisions upon the landscape that shape and constrain, but in no way completely determine, the beliefs and actions of inhabitants, visitors, and other "users." Indeed, there are a multitude of vernacular landscapes that alternately correspond to, cross-cut, and contradict those created by institutions with varying levels of authority and officialness. A comprehensive accounting of these alternative worlds is a massive undertaking, however, that greatly exceeds the scope of this present study. In the pages that follow, I have limited myself to mapping out the principal political, economic, and sociocultural features of the metropolitan landscape, as well as outlining some of the major ways in which these various parts are interconnected to constitute a whole. I begin with the questions of limits and boundaries.

DELIMITING THE CITY WITHOUT LIMITS

At its most extensive, "Atlanta" refers to both a city and a region, or rather, a series of regions of varying scale and inclusiveness that have changed over time. In its most restricted sense, the term refers to the current municipal entity of 136 square miles in the center of Fulton County that was home to an estimated 424,300 persons in 1995.[4] At the other extreme is the Atlanta Metropolitan Statistical Area as defined by the US Bureau of the Census, which grew from five counties and 1.4 million people in 1970 to embrace twenty counties with almost

3.4 million people twenty-five years later.[5] In that time, Atlanta went from the eighteenth to the ninth most populous metropolitan area in the United States. However, with less than 14 percent of the total metro area population, the city of Atlanta is the smallest urban center of any of the twenty largest MSAs in the country.[6] A number of "lesser" formerly rival Southern cities, such as Memphis, Tennessee, and Charlotte, North Carolina, are, in fact, larger than the city of Atlanta.[7]

Within the metropolitan area, planners identify a central cluster of five "urban core counties" (Fulton, DeKalb, Cobb, Gwinnett, and Clayton), which comprised the entirety of the MSA in 1970 and which still account for nearly three-quarters of the total metro population and almost nine out of every ten jobs.[8] Three of these counties – DeKalb, Cobb, and Gwinnett – have larger populations than the city of Atlanta. The latter two counties accounted for over half the Atlanta region's population growth during the 1980s and fully 40 percent of the new jobs.[9] In 1990, almost three-quarters of all the region's jobs were located outside the city.[10] Although Fulton remains the region's largest county, those portions that lie outside Atlanta's municipal boundaries are approaching the size of the city. Indeed, virtually all of the growth in Fulton's population and employment over the past two decades has occurred outside the city limits, especially in the north.[11] The intensive development of the peripheries has placed a heavy burden on county governments, since Atlanta's suburbs are for the most part unincorporated, with the county responsible for providing utilities, police, fire services, education, and local government. At the same time, county residents have usually been reluctant to approve tax increases to finance the improvement of the essential infrastructures of the suburban good life, such as roads and schools. Together with five "suburban" counties (Cherokee, Rockdale, Fayette, Henry, and Douglas), the urban core constitutes the planning region of the Atlanta Regional Commission (ARC), or the "Atlanta Region" (as distinguished from the larger "metropolitan region").

The ARC came into being in 1972, replacing the Atlanta Region Metropolitan Planning Commission, which had succeeded the original Metropolitan Planning Commission, chartered by the state in 1947. Although these entities drafted plans for the area, their authority was severely restricted, nor did the State of Georgia permit localities to impose impact fees on developers. It was not until 1989 that the Georgia legislature passed the state's first strategic planning ordinance that allowed for the assessment of impact fees, as well as strengthening the role of the ARC as the area's primary comprehensive planning agency. As the area's premier visioning body, the ARC has responsibility for the issues of transportation, environmental services, community service, and job training. Any new highway projects, for example, require ARC approval if they are to be eligible for federal funds. Plans for housing, commercial development, and other specific land-use elements, however, remain the prerogative of individual county and municipal governments, which usually have been loath to place restrictions of any kind on developers. Indeed, the lack of regulation has been an essential part of the region's inviting business climate and a major reason for its rapid growth over the last two decades. The ARC is more an advisory than a regulatory body, since it can only suggest, not require, changes in local land-use plans. Given that the 39-member body is dominated by officials from suburban counties, the ARC only rarely diverges from the initiatives of local governments and developers. Consequently, its ability to manage growth in the ten-county area is effectively quite limited. Following the recession of 1990–91, when the metro area lost 26,000 jobs (most of which were in the city and other parts of Fulton County), growth rates rebounded in the first half of the 1990s. In 1994, the area covered by the ARC grew by 4 percent and added more people – 105,500 – than in any other year in history.[12] In 1995, the ten-county planning region's population stood at slightly more than 2.8 million, roughly the same as the entire metro area in 1990.

As Atlanta's suburban periphery has developed relentlessly, the cutting edge of speculation has shifted to the outer tier of metropolitan counties, such as Paulding, where one developer has secured options on no less than one fifth of the county's total land area,[13] and the longtime Klan stronghold of Forsyth, which as recently as the mid-1980s proclaimed its lack of a single African-American household almost as proudly as its low tax rate. Despite its past association with the Ku Klux Klan (the most recent large Klan rally was in 1987), Forsyth's proximity to the promised lands of north Fulton and Gwinnett has made it one of the most appealing places in the entire metro area for the construction of high-priced luxury housing.[14] Along with the other nine counties that comprise the "exurban fringe" (Barrow, Butts, Carroll, Coweta, Newton, Paulding, Pickens, Spalding, and Walton), Forsyth grew 50 percent or more in population between 1985 and 1993.[15] Congestion and rising real estate prices in the core counties, as well as the proposed construction of an Outer Perimeter Highway some twenty miles beyond the current arc of I-285, will continue to fuel the growth of exurbia into the next millennium. As elsewhere in the metropolitan region, the philosophy of "disjointed incrementalism" rules on Atlanta's exurban frontier.[16]

DISORIENTATIONS

Given the vast and seemingly irresistible sprawl of metropolitan Atlanta, it is impossible to find a single terrestrial vantage point from which to comprehend the whole. Like the line drawings on the plains of Nazca in Peru, the limits and major features of what Rem Koolhaus called the "invisible metropolis"[17] are comprehensible only from a heavenly prospect. An enhanced false color Landsat photograph taken from orbit reveals a very unevenly concentrated pattern of settlement within the twenty-county area. Living forest and farmland are represented in shades of red and yellow, urbanized areas show light blue speckled with white. Most of the five urban core counties glow turquoise and teal with the heat reflected from roads, shopping malls, and the roofs of postmodernized faux French Country and neo-Georgian planned unit developments. The boundaries of this zone are uneven, diffuse and fluid, conforming to a fractal rather than a Euclidean geometry.

To some observers, this new metropolitan geography "resembles a galaxy of stars and planets, held together by mutual gravitational attraction, but with large empty areas between clusters."[18] The image is also reminiscent of a CAT scan of cancerous tissue – a value-laden cliché to be sure and burdened by all sorts of mixed metaphorical entailments – but the comparison is not altogether inappropriate, as the region's growth over the last two decades, and especially the last five years, has been nothing short of metastatic. From a central, fuzzily defined mass, feathery tendrils mark growth corridors defined by expressways and secondary roads (themselves inscribed over earlier corridors of foot, horse, and rail transit along the ridges and through the valleys of the Piedmont), blooming into major nodes where the corridors intersect to form what have been variously termed "edge cities," "technoburbs," or "new downtowns." Out on the fringes, a thousand points of blue light glimmer amidst the crimson and gold, marking where small agricultural towns are being plowed under for tract homes and retail "power centers."[19]

Comprehensiveness of vision, however, comes at the expense of resolution. While it is difficult to tell much from this altitude and level of abstraction, one thing is quite clear. The most intensive development is concentrated in the northern half of the region; south of the center the blots of blue are smaller and more widely spaced. The Landsat cameras do not tell much about the particular qualities of the built environment, though, or what the area looks like, who lives where, the routes they traverse, the networks they define by their transits and relationships, much less the meanings people attribute to space, the degree to which these meanings are recognized by others, or how these qualitative evaluations change over time. As with the many maps in the repertoire of developers and planners, a distinctly human referent is lacking in these satellite photos. It is not an image of the city that we encounter on a daily basis.

A more accessible, but still quite omniscient, image of Atlanta is that experienced by the hundreds of thousands of air travelers flying into or out of Atlanta's Hartsfield International Airport on any given day. The view from the window lends credence to the Atlanta Chamber of Commerce's latest marketing line –

"Among the Trees There Grows A City." Well, maybe not a city in the high industrial sense, with its dense verticalized centrality, but a collage of standardized bits
juxtaposed amidst the rolling hills rendered in multiple shades of green, save where
the scars of new construction have temporarily revealed the fabled red clay of
Georgia. As the plane banks lower, the highways acquire traffic and the abstract patterns formed by curving contours of cul-de-sacs, golf courses, shopping malls, and
office parks become more recognizable as inhabited (and inhabitable) places. On
most days, planes make their final approach from the east, coming in over the granite dome of Stone Mountain and descending over acres of warehouses, trucking
terminals, and the massive Ford plant at Hapeville, before touching down on one
of Hartsfield's 12,000-foot runways.

THE ENIGMA OF ARRIVAL

Save for the ethereal conduits of the Turner Broadcast System (comprising the
CNN, TBS, and TNT networks, among others) that enter into tens of millions of
the nation's (and the world's) households every day, Hartsfield International
Airport is where most Americans' experience of Atlanta begins, and ends. Of the
more than 50 million people who deplane here each year, nearly three-quarters just
catch another plane, as the airport is the major hub of Atlanta-based Delta Air
Lines, as well as for New Age budget carriers like ValueJet and Kiwi International.
The nineteenth-century testament to the city's role as a railroad hub and "Gate City
of the South" has been updated for the air age: "Whether you're going to heaven or
hell, you have to change planes in Atlanta." Just as the rail nexus provided the city's
original *raison d'être*, Hartsfield's nodal role in the invisible continental and global
skein of airways has also been both cause and consequence of Atlanta's emergence
as a national and putatively international center.

The remaining quarter of deplaning passengers, though, flow all the way
through Hartsfield's articulated network of featureless passageways and cross over
the threshold of the city on the other side of baggage claim. A little more than half
of these are residents of the greater metro area. The remainder are domestic conventioneers, business travelers, and other visitors, although Atlanta has recently
become a North American terminus for a plethora of air bridges from Europe and
the Far East. Although Hartsfield does not possess the polyglot multitudes of New
York's JFK, Los Angeles's LAX, or Miami's International, the crowds have become
increasingly diverse in recent years. Atlanta's enhanced global interconnectivity is
manifest in the newly completed Concourse E, which is proudly described as the
largest terminal in the United States dedicated exclusively to international arrivals
and departures. With its paucity of non-English signage, however, the airport is

something less than welcoming to the international visitor.

The current airport is but the latest incarnation of Atlanta's infatuation with transportation in general and with air travel in particular. The city established its first airport in the late 1920s on the site of a race track and crude dirt airstrip owned by Coca-Cola founder Asa Candler. Thanks to the aggressive cheerleading of a then alderman and aviation commissioner (and later mayor) William B. Hartsfield, Atlanta's Candler Field won out over Birmingham as a refueling point on the New York to Miami mail route.[20] Well before the development of mass air travel, Hartsfield presciently realized the need to establish Atlanta's place within an emerging aerial transportation order. During World War II, Candler Field almost doubled in size and became the nation's busiest airport.[21] Under Hartsfield's stewardship, the city built new terminals in 1948 and 1961.[22] Despite expansion, both of these facilities were rapidly made obsolete by the explosive growth of air traffic in the postwar decades and Delta's pioneering role in the creation of the "hub and spoke" system of aerial routes. In the mid 1960s, the Atlanta Region Metropolitan Planning Commission (the immediate predecessor of the current Atlanta Regional Commission) developed the nation's first Airport Systems Plan for a vast midfield complex, although it would take more than a decade to work out the design and financing of the facility.[23]

Named after the city's late visionary ex-mayor, Hartsfield International Airport opened on 21 September 1980. Proudly advertising itself as the largest and one of the busiest airports in the world, Hartsfield is also Atlanta's single largest employer, with over 35,000 jobs.[24] The main terminal is a cavernous T-shaped building divided along its long axis by a service core. In addition to handling ticketing and baggage claim, the "landside" facility serves as the transportation interface with the city. The southern terminus of Atlanta's rapid rail system is located inside. The southern half of the terminal is dedicated exclusively to Delta Air Lines, while twenty-five other carriers share the northern half. In addition to the "T" concourse at the end of the terminal building, five half-mile-long parallel concourses extend eastward linked by a mile-long subterranean "transportation mall" that allows planes to access any gate from any runway. Unlike most other malls, however, nothing in this one is for sale. Aside from a few zones of advertising space at the six station stops, the only things available to the users of this space are three modes of movement. As one descends from a concourse into the mall, an earnestly cheerful voice notes that consumers may walk down the featureless central corridor or use the moving sidewalks that flank it. The more passive, heavily burdened, or less frantic ride the cars of the people-mover system, which offers instructions in a mechanical voice filtered free of any accent or humanity. Whereas the cast-iron train sheds of the nineteenth century were the first purposive structures to celebrate the glories of industrialized speed, movement, and flow,[25] the late-twentieth-century airport as typified by Atlanta's Hartsfield is the fullest realization of the building as a "megamachine."[26]

With its assembly-line qualities and blockhouse feel, the Hartsfield mega-structure is, quite literally, a concrete embodiment of Atlanta's most generically technopolitan fantasies. All function and (until recently) no frills, dedicated to movement and flow to the exclusion of all else, it is a monument to bad modernistic futurism, resembling something beamed off the set of the original *Star Trek* or, better yet, one of those other early 1970s post-apocalyptic science fiction epics, like *Logan's Run* or *Earth II*. The concourses are gray-buff and burgundy-colored nightmares of serial repetition, with identical gates differentiated only by the limited variety of airline logos. Equally standardized concessionaires and rest rooms are interspersed at regular intervals along each concourse. In marked contrast to the nature of transportation offered, there are no soaring spaces in the concourses; even twenty-foot ceilings seem uncomfortably low when laid over a corridor a half mile long. Built before the introduction of moving sidewalks within the concourses themselves, the corridors are clotted with the Brownian motion of bewildered travelers and bleating vehicular droids bearing those unable to walk. At peak times, the concourses and the transportation mall achieve truly Tokyo-like densities of frenetic, desperate movement. Indeed, if levels of urbanity are measured by the density of human flow and the intensity of angst-ridden anomie, the corridors of Hartsfield are easily the most "urban" places in all of Atlanta, far surpassing the streets of downtown on even the busiest of convention days. The people-mover carries more people per year than the city's Metropolitan Atlanta Rapid Transit Authority (MARTA) rapid rail system. Indeed, between its employees and the more than 150,000 passengers who pass through on any given day, Hartsfield is often said to be the second largest "city" in the state of Georgia. At the other extreme, late at night when devoid of traffic, the concourses present some of the most extreme cases of abstract inhuman emptiness to be found anywhere.

Despite the overwhelming effect of standardized homogeneity, the concourses are not all created equal and reflect a social hierarchy of sorts. Concourses A and B, occupied by Atlanta-based Delta, are the widest and best appointed with concessions, bars, and restaurants. Concourse C, which was a major hub for Eastern Airlines before its demise in 1990, is of the same width, but not as well appointed. Now it is occupied by a number of low-budget carriers, such as ValueJet and Kiwi International, which have emerged, phoenix-like, from the ashes of airline deregulation (Kiwi was founded by former Eastern pilots). Concourse D, which is used by a variety of major carriers with other regional hubs (American, United,

Northwest, USAIR) is the runt of the litter, with the narrowest central corridor and fewest amenities.

Concourse E, however, constitutes a major break from the hierarchy of alphabet and distance. Whereas the original concourses had all the allure of twenty-first-century bus stations, the International Concourse, completed in 1994, is all postmodern flash and luxury, with terrazzo floors, stylized neo-Art Deco fixtures, expansive vertical spaces, and diffuse natural light. As befits a postmodern space, the food court and concessions are geared to a slightly more reflexive mode of consumption. These more upmarket motifs are now being retrofitted onto the entire airport, in a more than $150-million renovation project to get the facility in proper shape for the Olympics. The concessions are also being diversified, due not so much to the Olympics as to a shakeup of airport administration following the discovery of rampant corruption in concessions and management. In the main terminal itself, a vast white and brightly lit rotunda, much in the manner of Pittsburgh Airport's "sky mall," has been constructed in what had formerly been empty space between the northern and southern halves of the landside terminal. The new space offers to the masses in motion the state of the art in enmalled food and merchandise.

Passengers exit from the transportation mall into the maw of baggage claim. Once reunited with their luggage, Atlanta arrivals face a choice in gaining access to the city proper. Legions of courtesy vans and buses wait to whisk the traveler to the hotel of their choice, as do an even larger array of taxis driven, as in other North American cities, often by recent immigrants. The MARTA trains offer quick and easy connection with the hotel-convention district in the heart of the central city and the elite nexus of Buckhead, as well as a number of residential neighborhoods to the east and west of the core. But with only two major lines, MARTA's reach is limited to parts of the city and the counties of Fulton and DeKalb. With its poly-centered sprawl, Atlanta is first and foremost an "autopolis"[27] and is really only comprehensible from behind the wheel, or, better yet, from the passenger's seat.

HIGHWAYS TO KNOWHERE

The highway system provides not only the principal paths of movement for people and flows of capital investment, but, as the predominant feature of most local maps and diagrams, the spatial frame through which the metropolitan area is most readily comprehended as a differentiated, yet interrelated whole. Easily the most important sociospatial feature is that provided by the I-285 circumferential highway. Dubbed "the Perimeter" after it was completed in late 1969, because it then more or less defined the outer extent of suburban settlement, I-285 is now the over-crowded main street of the metropolitan area and a frontier of a fundamentally different sort. To many of the mostly white residents of the sylvan outer suburbs, the Perimeter is a stockade, with everything on the inside considered to be the moral equivalent of the inner city: a racialized place of danger and decay, to be avoided at all costs. Denizens of Cobb, Gwinnett, or any of the other outer burbs are frequently heard to boast that they never set foot inside the Perimeter. These antagonistic feelings are reciprocated by many residents of the core, who view these sociopolitically repressive, bland, white bread worlds as the second comings of H.L. Mencken's "Sahara of the Bozart."[28] Meanwhile, the postal service has allowed suburban developers to mine what remains of the symbolic capital of centrality by permitting them to use an "Atlanta" mailing address for their new luxury office parks situated just beyond the Perimeter.

The vernacularly constituted divide between inside and outside the Perimeter has recently received reinforcement of a more official sort. Fueled by the metro area's rapid population growth and the proliferation of faxes and the like, the 404 area code faced the imminent exhaustion of all possible permutations by the end of 1995. A new area code was created, but instead of allocating the new 770 designation to new phone numbers throughout the metropolitan area, the Public Service Commission (PSC) decided to use, with a few exceptions, the line of the Perimeter as the boundary between the 404 and 770 codes. The commission explained its decision by noting that the Perimeter constituted an already popularly recognized boundary and that the "overlay" strategy, as the other option was called, was potentially confusing as callers would not be able to tell "where" something was, only "when" it was established. This was an interesting decision given the oft-stated tendency of the telephone and other technologies of "instantaneous artificial adjacency"[29] to annihilate space through time. In choosing to emphasize a spatial rather than a temporal horizon, the PSC also moved away from the tendencies towards the conceptual fudging of the lines between Atlanta the city and Atlanta the metropolitan area.

Like spokes on a wheel, three arterial highways cross the vaguely heart-shaped Perimeter at the major compass headings and converge in a 200-acre interchange just south of the central business district. I-20 connects Atlanta with Birmingham to the west and Savannah to the east and, at the same time, divides the metro area into northern and southern halves. Coming from the southeast and southwest, respectively, I-75 and I-85 converge just north of the airport to form the Downtown Connector. Twelve lanes wide, this somewhat ironically named expressway cleaves an emphatic divide through the city's impoverished southern reaches before curving around the eastern side of the central core and dividing again some miles north of downtown at the Brookwood Interchange. I-75 then trends northwestward, crossing the Chattahoochee River into Cobb County on its way to the city of Marietta and the adjacent Lockheed factory, the carpet mill towns of Dalton and Rome and, ultimately, the Tennessee and Ohio River valleys. I-85 veers in a northeasterly direction through DeKalb and Gwinnett counties, following the old Seaboard Airline Railroad route through the textile belt of the Upper Piedmont to the booming Carolinian cities of Greenville/Spartanburg, Charlotte, and the "research triangle" formed by Raleigh, Durham, and Chapel Hill. Close to the Brookwood Interchange, the recently completed Georgia 400 tollway strikes northward from I-85 through the "new downtown" of Buckhead to the upscale residential and commercial enclaves of north Fulton County beyond.

The expressways provide the principal axes of growth in the region, with investment concentrating around their intersections with each other and major state highways. The commercial and residential real estate industries use the six distinct legs of I-20, I-75, and I-85 to divide the area outside the Perimeter into six primary zones: North-Central, South-East, etc. These cardinal regions, while important for commercial reasons, do not constitute compelling districts within vernacular geographies of the social imagination, however. Instead, counties, municipalities, and neighborhoods provide a nested hierarchy of the most popularly employed place designations.

ATLANTA IN BLACK AND WHITE

Local mythographers like to claim that Atlanta is a paragon of racial harmony, although this assertion is belied by how, and where, people live. Nearly a century after W.E.B. DuBois decried the oppressiveness of the color line, the veil of race remains the paramount feature of Atlanta's landscape. In addition to being paths of development, some highways also serve as borders in a highly race-conscious region. There is considerable evidence to indicate that I-20 West was planned in the 1950s as a racial buffer between existing white and emerging black suburbs on the city's westside.[30] Some Atlantans continue to refer to I-20 as the major dividing line between white northern and black southern Atlanta. By the late 1960s, however, this color line had been effectively breached on the westside by middle-class African-Americans seeking desirable housing.[31] The area around Greenbriar Mall, almost exclusively white in the early 1960s, was predominantly black less than a decade later.

Despite their city's self-description as being "too busy to hate," white Atlantans have proven no more accepting of residential integration than whites in most other US metropolitan areas. More than two decades after the passage of the Fair Housing Act of 1968, the northern parts of the city of Atlanta and its suburbs remain, for the most part, "off limits" to all but the wealthiest African-Americans. To this day,

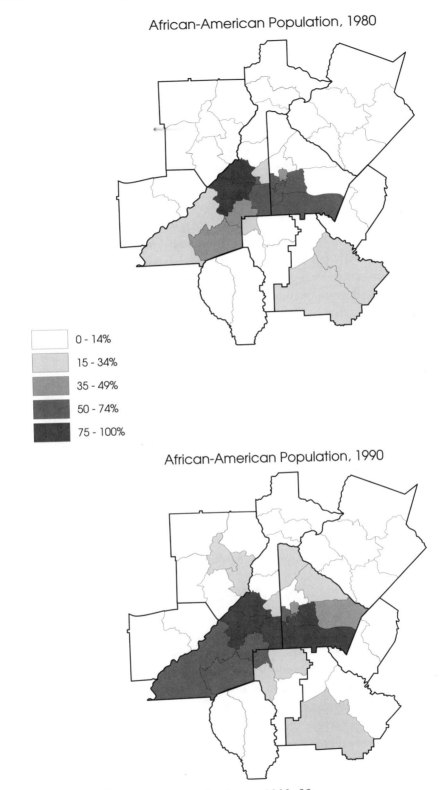

African-American Population, 1980

	0 - 14%
	15 - 34%
	35 - 49%
	50 - 74%
	75 - 100%

African-American Population, 1990

Map 2: Distribution of African-American Population, 1980–90

African-Americans constitute little more than 15 percent of the population in parts of northern DeKalb and Cobb, and in most other areas, a great deal less.[32] As the accompanying map demonstrates, most of the region's African-American population lives in a modern-day "black belt" reaching across southern Fulton County through the city of Atlanta into northern Clayton and southern DeKalb counties.

African-Americans suburbanized as intensely as whites in the 1970s and 1980s. In 1970, over 80 percent of Atlanta's metro black population still lived inside the city boundaries, but in 1990, only 39 percent did.[33] Slightly more than 60 percent of the metro area's African-American population now live in the suburbs, but they constitute only a third of the total suburban population. While the African-American populations of northside counties like Cobb and Gwinnett have grown markedly during recent years, these counties remain overwhelmingly white, with high degrees of residential segregation. In fact, contrary to journalistic accounts of Atlanta as a racially harmonious and integrated paradise, levels of residential segregation inside the city and without remain among the highest of any American metropolitan area.[34] While the African-American poor and working class have moved to the suburbs, Atlanta's much-celebrated black middle class has led the exodus from the core. The departure of many of the city's most affluent African-Americans has helped to contribute to extreme income inequality between the city's white and black populations. In 1990, for example, the white median income was $61,691, while for African-Americans it was $22,372.[35]

WHITE MONEY = WHITE POWER

Atlanta's highly racialized topography is vividly manifest in the political landscape of the metropolitan region. Aside from dominating the administration of the city of Atlanta, African-Americans have significant representation only on the county commissions of Fulton and DeKalb. The growth of the white population of north Fulton in the 1980s deeply eroded African-American, and Democratic, influence in Fulton County. The growing power of north Fulton whites in county politics was manifest in the election of Republican lawyer Mitch Skandalakis as county commission chairman in 1993. An exponent of an anti-tax, anti-government ideology, Skandalakis is also a somewhat less than adroit dealer of the race card. In 1994, he was linked to the circulation of racist political advertisements defaming one of his principal African-American opponents on the commission, Gordon Joyner. Disagreements between the city and the rest of Fulton County almost invariably have either an explicit or implicit racial dimension.

Racial polarization is even more evident at the level of the State Assembly and US Congress. Up until the latest round of court-mandated redistricting in late

1995, four US Congressional districts fell entirely within the metropolitan area (the 4th, 5th, 6th, and 7th), while four others (the 3rd, 9th, 10th, and 11th) lay partially in it. White Republicans held six of these eight districts, while the 5th and 11th districts were held by black Democrats. The lattermost district, which had only been created in 1992, reached from the southeastern part of the metro area to the outskirts of Savannah. In 1995, the US Supreme Court ruled that the 11th District, which was represented by Cynthia McKinney, needed to be revised. When a special session of the State Assembly proved unable to complete this task – although it did manage to wipe out black majorities in eleven State House and Senate districts – the decision was passed to a panel of three US district judges.

In addition to the 11th District, the judicial triad found the 2nd District, in the southwestern corner of the state, to be an example of "unconstitutional racial gerrymandering."[36] Both districts were extensively redrawn – the new 11th encompassed a completely different set of counties – and five other districts were modified to varying extents. The 4th District, which formerly comprised the majority-white domains of Gwinnett, Rockdale, and northern DeKalb, now unifies the latter with the majority-black southern half of the county, along with a diversely populated chunk of northwestern Gwinnett. The remainder of the latter county and Rockdale now form part of the 11th, which also included the fast-growing exurban county of Barrow and ten primarily rural counties. Four other districts, however, were untouched or minimally affected by the plan. One of these was the 6th District, represented by House Speaker Newt Gingrich. Georgia's rightwing Robespierre received a large piece of northwest Gwinnett that more than compensated for the loss of the wealthy, white, and conservative DeKalb suburb of Dunwoody. Together with north Fulton and much of Cobb County, the far from arbitrary boundaries of the 6th give Gingrich one of the most secure Republican districts in the entire country. Under the new plan, only former Student Non-Violent Coordinating Committee activist and ex-Atlanta city councilman John Lewis's 5th District, comprising the City of Atlanta, south Fulton, and a slice of northwest Clayton, has a majority-black population.

In opposing the redistricting plan, black Democrats found rare common ground with the three white Republican congressmen whose districts were also substantially redrawn. Both groups viewed the map as overly favorable to white Democrats, as it spread African-American voters, who had been concentrated in three districts, over six. A similar coupling of strange bedfellows stymied the Georgia Assembly's efforts to redraw the electoral map in the summer of 1995, thus prompting the courts to put forth their redistricting plan. Although both groups plan to appeal, it is likely that the new map will survive the challenge in the courts. In addition, in December 1995 the US Justice Department announced that it was looking into the recent re-drawing of State Assembly electoral districts as possibly being prejudicial to the interests of minority voters.[37] While white Democrats still maintain a tenuous hold on the governorship and the State Assembly, the future of the party in Georgia remains unclear. Governor Zell Miller is prohibited by law from running for a third term, and only defeated Republican millionaire businessman Guy Milner in the last election by the narrowest of margins. In Georgia, as elsewhere in the country, party affiliation has become powerfully associated with race. More than a century after the end of Reconstruction, most conservative white Democrats are either converting to Republicanism (like the 7th District's Bob Barr and the 9th District's Nathan Deal), or retiring (as is the case with Senator Sam Nunn).

VARIEGATING THE MIX

For much of its history, Atlanta's ethno-racial landscape was rendered exclusively in the polar shades of American-born black and white. Until recently, neither Atlanta nor Georgia was ever a major center for overseas immigration. At its height in 1860, the foreign-born constituted no more than 6 percent of the population, and most of them were Irish, German, and English.[38] After the Civil War, urban boosters throughout the South tried to attract only Anglo-Saxon immigrants, and Atlanta was no exception. Despite this, small but significant numbers of German and Russian Jews and Greeks settled in Atlanta between 1865 and 1915.[39] They resided in distinctive areas in the southern, and especially, southeastern parts of the city near the State Capitol.[40] For the most part, they enjoyed a prosperous, but tenuous existence. Although few in number, Atlanta's Jews played a key role in the city's commercial life during its resurgence. However, xenophobia, nativism, and the rise of the Ku Klux Klan made Atlanta a much less than hospitable place for immigrants and American-born persons of non-Anglo-Saxon origin – as well as for African-Americans – after the turn of the century. The reform of national immigration laws in the early 1920s also served to lessen what was never more than a modest flow into Atlanta. By 1940, only 1.4 percent of Atlanta's population was foreign-born, and this figure was little changed a decade later.[41]

Major changes were underway in the 1950s, though, as the region's population grew by an average annual rate of over 3 percent. By 1960, the foreign-born had increased to 3.2 percent of the metro region's population. The sixties boom continued to diversify the population. In the wake of the Cuban Revolution of 1959, several thousand Cubans settled in Atlanta; by the end of the 1960s, Cubans accounted for roughly three-quarters of the metropolitan area's Hispanics.[42] This began to change in the 1970s, although there were still officially only 20,000 Hispanics in the metro area in 1980, with most of them living near the deindustrializing city of Chamblee in northern DeKalb, in the Hone Park neighborhood north of Georgia Tech, and in the southern reaches of the Grant Park area just to the southeast of downtown. Other major immigrant groups came from Western Europe, and South and East Asia. In 1980, however, there were still fewer than 10,000 Asians living in the entire metropolitan area.[43]

Beginning in the early 1980s, the ethno-racial landscape of Atlanta changed markedly. Second- and third-generation immigrants from the Northeast, the Midwest, and elsewhere in the US introduced a more variegated range of cultural identities to the area. Far more importantly from the standpoint of sociocultural diversity, however, Atlanta emerged for the first time as a destination for a significant flow of immigrants and refugees from Asia, Latin America, Africa, and Eastern Europe. Several factors were responsible for this situation. First, private relief agencies designated Atlanta as a favored location for the resettlement of Southeast Asian refugees. During the 1980s, approximately 10,000 Vietnamese, Cambodians, Laotians, and Hmong arrived in Atlanta. Almost two-thirds of these refugees resided in the cities of Doraville, Chamblee, Clarkston, and other areas of northern DeKalb County.[44] These industrial and, in some cases, deindustrializing locales were particularly appealing for their availability of low-rent housing and opportunities for employment. Such was also the case with other centers of refugee resettlement in urban areas of Cobb County and in the Riverdale area of Clayton County. Refugees settled in the western part of Gwinnett County too. As these refugees normalized their immigration status, they were able to sponsor the arrival of close relatives and most of the above-mentioned areas have become distinctive ethnic centers. In the late 1980s and early 1990s, relief agencies added to the cultural mix, by resettling refugees from Afghanistan, Ethiopia, Eritrea, Somalia, and Eastern Europe in the same communities. Already one of the major locales for Atlanta's Hispanic population, the stretch of Buford Highway near the cities of Doraville and Chamblee became known as "Atlanta's *Real* International Boulevard" in the late 1980s.

In sheer volume, however, refugees were greatly outnumbered by legal and illegal immigrants. The Atlanta area's booming economy served as a magnet for both people living overseas and the foreign-born already living in other parts of the United States. In the early 1980s, Mexican laborers displaced by the collapse of the Texan construction industry flocked to Atlanta, and large numbers were attracted by the expansion of the poultry and textile industries on the peripheries of the metropolitan area.[45] While Mexicans are by far the largest single group of Hispanics in Atlanta, immigrants from virtually every nation in Central and South America followed. As in other areas of the US, the Caribbean, the Middle East, and West Africa also were major source areas of immigration. Asians constituted the fastest-growing, and perhaps most visible, group of immigrants. Economic opportunities provided by the region's boom attracted thousands of entrepreneurially minded Koreans, Chinese, and Indians to Atlanta in the 1980s. In 1980, there was only one Korean-owned business in the metropolitan area; by 1994, it was estimated that there were three hundred.[46] As was common in other American cities, many of the latter establishments were grocery stores in poor African-American neighborhoods in the central city and in DeKalb County.

An accurate accounting of exactly how many immigrants and refugees now live in Atlanta is a difficult undertaking. According to the 1990 census, there were 115,642 foreign-born persons in the metropolitan area, with all but 15,604 living outside the city of Atlanta.[47] In both areas, the foreign-born accounted for 4 percent of their respective populations. Asians comprised the largest group, constituting some 36 percent of the legal flow. Latin America was the second largest source area, with 21 percent coming from Mexico and the Caribbean and 6 percent from South America. Europe (including the former Soviet Union) accounted for 15 percent of immigrants/refugees, followed by Africa (8 percent), and Oceania (6 percent).[48]

It is widely agreed by researchers that the census drastically undercounted the immigrant population at the time. Even so, it revealed that Atlanta's enumerated Asian and Hispanic populations grew by 292 percent and 138 percent, respectively, during the 1980s. Not all of these persons were immigrants, however, as only 45 percent of Hispanics and 77 percent of Asians were foreign-born. While a good number of the American-born were children of immigrants, these figures also included Asian- and Hispanic-Americans who had arrived as part of the extensive internal migration during the decade. A number of accounts, including various ethnic and cultural associations, fail to note this difference and discuss Atlanta's Asians and Hispanics as if they are all immigrants or reside in immigrant households.[49]

Atlanta's immigrant/refugee population continued to grow rapidly during the first half of the 1990s. Yet the overall size and composition of this segment of the population remains a matter of much speculation and debate. Estimates provided by various cultural associations and popular published accounts are often without any clear empirical substantiation. However, a group of researchers at Georgia State University's Center for Applied Research in Anthropology has combined field research, interviews, and statistics compiled by a variety of sources – ranging from the Immigration and Naturalization Service to cultural associations, consulates, and county boards of education – to produce a "best guess." The results are summarized in the accompanying table. While only rough estimates, these

Hispanic:		Middle East/SW Asia:	
Mexican	82,000	Lebanese	7,000
Puerto Rican	12,000	Afghan	1,300
Colombian	8,000	Iranian	1,000
Cuban	6,000	Turkish	2,000
Other	10,400	Other	3,000
TOTAL	118,400	TOTAL	15,300

Caribbean (excluding Cuba):		African:	
Jamaican	20,000	Ethiopian/Eritrean	4,600
Trinidad and Tobago	6,600	Nigerian	3,500
Haiti	3,000	Somalian	1,500
Other	13,000	Other	10,000
TOTAL	42,600	TOTAL	19,600

South, East, and Southeast Asian:		European:	
Chinese	20,000	Greek	8,700
Korean	18,500	Russian	3,500
Indian/Pakistani	15,000	Bosnian	2,000
Vietnamese	10,200	Other	12,000
Laotian	8,200	TOTAL	26,200
Cambodian	6,200		
Hmong	1,000	TOTAL:	310,600
Thai	1,400		
Japanese	5,000		
Filipino	3,000		
TOTAL	88,500		

Estimate of Refugee/Immigrant Population, 1995

figures provide some important correctives to popular perceptions that conceptualize immigrants only in terms of two broad categories of "Hispanics" and "Asians." As they tend to be dispersed over the metropolitan landscape, rather than concentrated in specific locales, Anglophone Afro-Caribbeans, sub-Saharan Africans, and Europeans may be superficially "blended in" into existing dichotomous categories of black and white.

The overwhelming majority of Atlanta's immigrants and refugees are concentrated in the five urban core counties, although there have been some spatial shifts in distribution over the last five years. In 1990, 40 percent resided in DeKalb County, with 18 percent each in Cobb and Gwinnett, 14 percent in Fulton, and

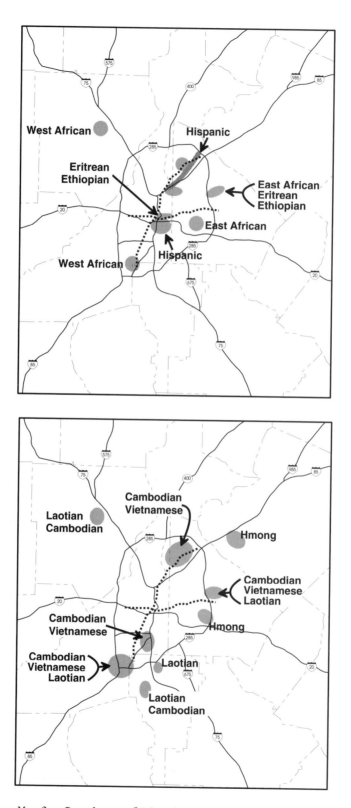

Map 3: Distribution of Selected Immigrant / Refugee Groups

10 percent in Clayton.[50] By 1995, however, only 30 percent of the region's immigrant/refugee population lived in DeKalb and 16 percent in Cobb, while Gwinnett (21 percent) Fulton (16 percent), and Clayton (13 percent) counties all registered increases.[51] There was also an increase in the number of immigrants and refugees living in once-peripheral counties like Cherokee, Douglas, Henry, and Rockdale. While DeKalb's immigrant/refugee population remained the largest in absolute numbers in 1995 and its Buford Highway corridor the best-known "ethnic" area, the county had been eclipsed by Clayton in terms of the ratio of the foreign-born to the overall population. It was estimated that 17 percent of Clayton County's population were immigrants or refugees in 1995, compared with 13.5 percent of DeKalb's, and 13 percent of Gwinnett's.[52]

Sprawl has served to make immigrants as well as non-immigrant Asians and Hispanics less visible than their numbers would otherwise indicate. Like much of the region's population, the overwhelming majority live outside the city of Atlanta. Consequently, one does not find the traditional urban ethnic neighborhoods along the lines of, say, New York City's or San Francisco's Chinatown. Instead, much as in Los Angeles, one encounters the diversity spread out over suburban strip malls and apartment complexes, with different ethnic groups sharing the same neighborhoods or juxtaposed with one another. Still, as communities are first and foremost states of mind, the sprawled aspect of the landscape has not stopped members from conceptualizing their communities as distinct spatial domains. Many Korean merchants in Chamblee/Doraville, for example, offer their customers maps of a "Koreatown" that is centered on the intersection of I-85 and the Perimeter. However, these representations of place and claims to space most often go unrecognized by the numerically dominant white and black populations of the metropolitan area. For most non-Koreans, the area of Koreatown is better known as Spaghetti Junction, after the roller coaster-like array of ramps comprising what is officially known as the Tom Moreland Interchange.[53] Despite city boosters' rhetoric of "internationality," and the fact that they constituted nearly 10 percent of the Atlanta Regional Commission (ARC) region's population, Atlanta's immigrants and refugees remained marginalized from the area's social and political life in the mid 1990s.

SUBURBAN ALCHEMY: FROM GOLDEN CRESCENT TO PLATINUM TRIANGLE

Toponymy is crucial to understanding the organization of both the vernacular and "official" landscapes of Atlanta. The most authoritative place-namers are not government functionaries, but real estate developers, journalists, travel writers, and other operatives who form part of the "critical infrastructure" of contemporary urban life.[54] In the 1970s, place entrepreneurs began to refer to the top end of the Perimeter between I-75 and I-85 as the "Golden Crescent" on account of the intense commercial and residential development (not to mention greatly enhanced property values) occurring in the vicinity of these arterial highways' intersections with the Perimeter. With the dramatic growth of Cumberland/Galleria (at I-75 and I-285) and Perimeter Center (Ga 400 and I-285) areas during the 1980s, the Golden Crescent was transmuted into the "Platinum Triangle." These terms, in turn, were picked up by the media, especially the business press, and found their way into popular usage.

Radiating around the new corporate campuses and shopping malls were hundreds of square miles of forested suburban subdivisions. The names of some of these residential developments call attention to their Southern provenance. There are a multitude of Plantations, although not so many Confederate-themed streets as one might expect. However, there are a number of places with a *Gone With the Wind* theme: Tara Woods, Tara Estates (where one could live at the corner of Scarlett O'Hara Drive and Rhett Road), Scarlett Oaks, Ashley Crossing, Ashley Downs (in fact, there are more Ashley Places than Scarletts; poor Melanie, however, is not represented at all in the toponymy). Most of these developments are of 1960s or early 1970s vintage. The vast majority of subdivisions and planned unit developments built more recently conjure up a generically Southern pastoral image rather than the Lost Cause of *Gone With the Wind*. The landscape is littered with an overabundance of Traces, Chases, Parks, Villages, Forests, Woods, Hollows, Landings, Crossings, Walks, Farms, Mills, and Estates. Nonetheless, some developments inspire alternative imagined geographies. A few places recall the landscapes of New as well as merry old England. For homesick Yankees, there are a Boston Common and a Stonington, while for Anglophiles, medievalists, Celtic enthusiasts, and assorted neo-Druids, there are a Sherwood Forest, a Camelot Club, a Celtic Club, a Druid Hills,[55] even a Stonehenge.

The medievalizing ethos is not limited to place names. Following a national trend, developers built a dozen gated "suburban fortresses" during the first half of the 1990s.[56] These privatized domains varied in size from a score to several thousand homes, and offered amenities ranging from tennis courts and swimming pools to 24-hour security patrols with dogs and Jack Nicklaus-designed golf courses. Average home prices ranged from $400,000 to more than $3 million, but increasingly, developers have priced a number of units in the $200,000 range, which puts them within the reach of non-elite, if still upper-middle-class, home buyers. While a few were located in Cobb and Gwinnett counties, the greatest number of guarded and gated communities were located in the Ga 400 corridor of north Fulton.

Among the most upmarket is the Country Club of the South, which is home to a number of sports and entertainment celebrities like football player Andre Rison and singer Bobby Brown. Although these two celebrities are African-American, the upscale developments, like most housing in the Atlanta area, tend more toward racial segregation than integration. One of the more recent planned communities in southwest Fulton County, the Landings at Cascade, is specifically marketed towards Atlanta's black upper middle class.

The order of gated communities extends far beyond closing the communities off to public traffic. Residents subject themselves to a rigid code that regiments virtually every aspect of how their house and grounds can look, even the sort of vehicles they may own. While such restrictions are hardly exclusive to gated communities (indeed, they are to be found even in more traditional suburban neighborhoods around the country), they contribute to the overall programmed feel of these domains. In this regard, they have much in common with the festival markets and newly minted historic districts that have recolonized the inner urban frontier in Atlanta and elsewhere. The preferred architectural style for many of these developments is an eclectic mixing of motifs, with high gabled roofs that accentuate the facade and provide the high-ceilinged spaces necessary for enormous "great rooms." The overall visual effect of all these enormous houses massed so close together on tiny plots is at once both sterile and ludicrous, nothing more than an upmarket, interior-obsessed Levittown, glorified playhomes for *nouveaux riches* baby-boomers. Not all of the developments go for the generically continental luxury look, however. One gated community in Gwinnett County, Sweetbottom Plantation, features reproductions of "classic" homes in Charleston, New Orleans, and other Southern cities. Prospective home-builders must have their designs certified as "authentic" by a panel of architectural experts before they can start construction.

Despite their hardened features, gated communities sell the perception, rather than the actuality, of security. In fact, owing to their great concentrations of wealth, they may even serve as magnets for certain kinds of crime. One comparative study of adjacent gated and non-gated communities in north Fulton County during 1994 found that the former experienced ten times as many burglaries and three times as many thefts by taking as the latter.[57] The communities are far better at offering and delivering a sense of exclusion and exclusivity, an environment free of potentially threatening social others, than freedom from crime.

The rise in gated communities is just part of the wave of upscale suburbanization that has significantly altered the landscape of privilege in Atlanta. In 1980, fully three-quarters of the elite market segment of "executive housing" (homes in excess of $300,000) were located in either Buckhead (41 percent) or Sandy Springs/Dunwoody (31 percent).[58] The former, located in the northeastern corner of Atlanta, had been the preferred locale for the city's elite since the 1920s. The Sandy Springs/Dunwoody area, which straddled the Fulton/DeKalb line along the northeastern arc of the Perimeter, emerged as a posh neighborhood in the late 1960s and 1970s following the construction of the nearby Perimeter Center office park and mall. By 1990, the two areas' combined market share had dropped to 52 percent. Five years later, Buckhead possessed only 23 percent of elite homes and Sandy Springs/Dunwoody's share had been reduced to 20 percent. This decline in market share reflected the extent of construction in the outer suburbs, rather than the abandonment or down-classing of housing in Buckhead and Sandy Springs/Dunwoody. Between 1980 and 1995, north Fulton increased its share of upper-crust homes from 3 to 15 percent. In fact, due largely to high land prices, virtually all new home construction in north Fulton has been oriented to an upper-income market, with little or no affordable apartments or houses built.[59] Consequently, the malls and corporate campuses of north Fulton are dependent on hordes of commuters to staff their low-paying commercial and office service jobs. Rapid population growth and a dependence on imported servile labor has overwhelmed north Fulton's Third World road network. Continued growth, when combined with the steadfast refusal of the county commission to upgrade the county's roads only promises to exacerbate an already horrendous traffic situation. The reluctance of the Fulton county commission to levy taxes to upgrade the road network in the northern part of its domain has led individual municipalities like Alpharetta to undertake their own projects.

The development of north Fulton County was made possible by the construction of the Georgia 400 multi-lane highway in the 1970s, which linked the once relatively inexpensive farmland near Alpharetta with the Perimeter. In the late 1960s, Atlanta-based developers Mack Taylor, Harvey Mathis, and Michael Gearon acquired 550 acres of farmland in Dunwoody, in the extreme northwestern corner of DeKalb County near the intersection of Ga 400 and I-285. Fresh from their success in creating the metro area's first suburban office park off I-85 in North Druid Hills (Executive Park), the trio of developers unveiled plans for a nine-building complex of offices known as Perimeter Center linked to the first metro area shopping mall designed from the outset as an enclosed pedestrian space – Perimeter Mall. The vast retail/office complex was ideally located to service the nearby emerging elite communities of Sandy Springs, Roswell, and Dunwoody. Extensive residential development led three of Atlanta's leading hospitals to establish themselves in a medical megalopolis dubbed "Pill Hill" just to the south of the I-285/Ga 400 intersection. Spurred on by the Georgia Department of Transportation's plans to extend Ga 400 southward from the Perimeter to Buckhead, more partnerships of local developers and national money built a series of office complexes, hotels,

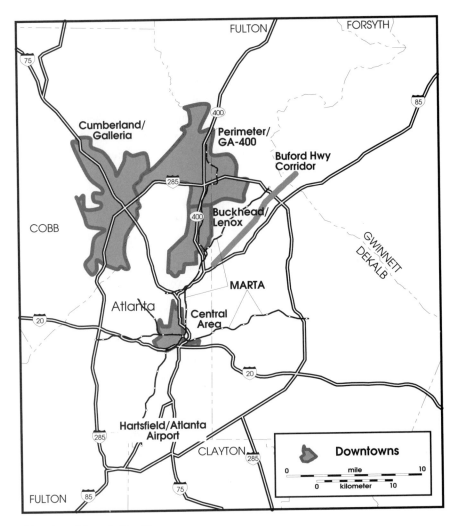

Map 4: Atlanta's New Downtowns

and secondary retail establishments spreading over a twenty-square-mile area of north Fulton and DeKalb.

The first of these outsiders was Texan Gerald Hines, developer of Houston's Galleria retail/office/hotel complex. Hines's Ravina project, which he began in 1981, was modest in comparison to the Galleria, but was revolutionary in its effects on the area. Unlike Perimeter Center, which was comprised of low- to mid-rise structures, Hines's plans for Ravina consisted of a series of 15–18-story office buildings and a hotel spread out over a 42-acre parcel. Although DeKalb County initially refused to rezone the area for high-rise development, Hines worked his magic to get the rezoning approved in the summer of 1982.[60] During the remainder of the 1980s, developers were able to get even higher density high-rise complexes approved, culminating in the concourse at Landmark Center, a prototypical postmodern high-rise corporate campus in a lavishly landscaped, park-like setting. By the early 1990s, the Perimeter Center area had more office space – twenty million square feet – and more corporate headquarters – including United Parcel Service and Holiday Inn Worldwide – than any other market in the metro area, including downtown. With its northward extent lined with luxurious golf courses and residential developments, Ga 400 is the bisector of the Platinum Triangle.

COBBOPHILIA/PHOBIA

The western leg of the triangle is formed by the I-75 corridor in Cobb County. First suburbanized in the early to mid 1960s, East Cobb is now home to hordes of resettling upper-middle-class Yankee transplants. As in north Fulton, just over half of Cobb's population was born outside of Georgia.[61] Yet, unlike its eastern neighbor, most of Cobb manages to still display a characteristically Southern face, albeit one with some modern touches. Much of the county forms the core of House Speaker Newt Gingrich's 6th Congressional District. Gingrich has described Cobb "as sort of a Norman Rockwell world with fiber optic computers and jet air-planes."[62] The county's largest city is Marietta, which was founded almost two decades before Atlanta was established. Eclipsed by the rapid growth of its upstart neighbor in the post-Civil War period, Marietta's economy boomed during and after World War II. In 1943, Bell Aircraft Corporation started construction of a B-29 bomber plant, which was taken over by Lockheed and greatly expanded during the Cold War defense boom which has only recently ended. Adjacent to the Lockheed facility, the military constructed Rickenbacker Field, now known as Dobbins Air Force Base. Like most other military facilities in both the Atlanta area and the state of Georgia, Dobbins has regularly escaped the wave of post-Cold War base closures.

Thanks largely to Lockheed and Dobbins, Cobb has greatly benefited from government largesse over the years, a fact that its anti-federalist politicians, such as Gingrich, have failed to acknowledge. In 1992, only two other counties received more federal monies than Cobb.[63] Spurred on by a defense-related industrial core in Marietta during the 1950s, Cobb became the second suburban boom county (after DeKalb) in the following decade. Even after the 1990–91 recession and the end of the Cold War prompted the layoff of 10,000 workers, Lockheed remains the county's largest employer, with over 12,000 on its payroll. Despite the importance of Lockheed, however, Cobb's economic landscape is decidedly post-industrial.

Nearly three-quarters of the county's current workforce are employed in insurance, electronics, computers, and trade.[64]

Until the early 1980s, Cobb's most famous landmark was the Big Chicken, a giant pullet looming over a Kentucky Fried Chicken franchise at the corner of Cobb Parkway (US 41) and Roswell Road. In a familiar evolutionary scenario, the strip malls, shopping centers, and split-level subdivisions built along the I-75 corridor in the 1960s gave way to office complexes and more upscale planned unit developments in the 1980s. In 1982, Texan developer Trammell Crow built its Galleria Town Center mixed-use complex next to the early-1970s-vintage Cumberland Mall near the Intersection of I-75 and the Perimeter. The 85-acre office/hotel/retail complex was briefly home to the ill-fated merger of RJR–Nabisco between 1987 and 1989. It was followed by a series of other glitzy office parks built by tag teams of local and national developers. By 1990, the edge city known as Cumberland/Galleria possessed 16 million square feet of office space in a variety of corporate campuses scattered over some twenty square miles.[65] Commercial construction was paced by upmarket residential development. In addition, the number of African-Americans and other ethnic minorities living in the county tripled between 1980 and 1990, although they still constitute approximately only 10 percent of the county population. Most of Cobb's new minority residents settled in and around the aging, but still economically thriving, city of Smyrna, just south of Dobbins Air Force Base.[66]

Despite the modernization of its landscape and the influx of non-Georgians and immigrants, Cobb retains its long-held image as a hotbed of cultural intolerance and sociopolitical conservativism – a state of mind that one *Atlanta Constitution* reporter termed "Cobbservatism."[67] In 1915, a group of the county's most esteemed citizens formed the mob that abducted Leo Frank from the State Prison in Milledgeville and lynched him in the Marietta town square. During the 1920s and 1930s, Cobb was a center of activity for the resurgent Ku Klux Klan. Long the home of segregationist provocateur and former governor Lester Maddox and National States Rights Party leader (and convicted church-bomber) J.B. Stoner, Cobb was the preferred destination of white Atlantans fleeing school desegregation in the 1960s.

In the late 1960s, Cobb joined Gwinnett County in refusing to be part of the Metropolitan Atlanta Rapid Transit Authority. Residents feared that MARTA would provide easy access for criminally minded urban black youth. As one former mayor of Marietta noted in 1975, Cobb residents "want to keep [the Chattahoochee river] as a moat. They wish they could build forts across there to keep people from coming up here."[68] In a similar vein, one former Cobb commissioner only half-jokingly proposed to "stock the Chattahoochee with piranha."[69] In 1968, on the initiative of one of Cobb's representatives, the State Assembly passed legislation creating the

10-foot-wide "city" of Chattahoochee Plantation along the western bank of the river. As Georgia law prevented one city from jumping over another in an annexation, the law prevented Atlanta from annexing any part of Cobb in the future.[70] More than twenty years later, the racist anti-Atlanta ethos is still in full effect. In 1995, one of Cobb County's state legislators created a major ruckus by claiming that the buses of Cobb County Transit served mostly to bring "bands of urban Atlanta [read black] teenagers" to the county's malls, who were "not there to try on suits."[71] He later withdrew his comment, as well as his effort to wrest control of the bus line from county officials, but the racist sentiment behind the outburst is not as easily eradicated.

In the 1970s and early 1980s, Cobbites re-elected John Birch Society head Larry McDonald five times as their representative in the US House. When he died in the crash of Korean Airlines flight 007 in 1983, they renamed a section of I-75 in his memory and later elected Newt Gringrich to take his place. In 1982, the Kennesaw city council protested a firearms ban in a Massachusetts municipality by mandating that "every head of household residing in the city limits of the City of Kennesaw is required to maintain a firearm, together with ammunition thereof."[72] More recently, Kennesaw State College has been plagued by reports of racist and anti-Semitic harassment of students and faculty. In the spring of 1995, two former Jewish faculty members lodged formal complaints against KSC with the Equal Employment Opportunity Commission, claiming that they had been fired because of their faith.[73] The college has close ties to Gingrich and his rightwing revolution; it was the initial site for the House Speaker's controversial series of "educational seminars" that plugged corporate sponsors, and is the home institution of former Gingrich crony Christina Jefferies, who was forced to resign as historian of the House of Representatives for remarks that were construed as pro-Nazi. Kennesaw is also home to Wild Man's Civil War Surplus, a one-stop shop for not only Confederate memorabilia, but a wide assortment of white supremacist literature and racist knickknacks.

Perhaps the most widely known manifestation of Cobbservatism, however, took place during 1993–94. In August 1993, after the performance of a play that featured homosexual characters (*Lips Together Teeth Apart*), the all-white, male, and ostensibly straight Cobb County Commission rescinded its financial support for the local theater group and passed a resolution condemning "the gay lifestyle" as incompatible with community values. The resultant protest by gay rights groups was national in scope and directed not only at Cobb, but at the Atlanta Committee for the Olympic Games (ACOG), which had planned to use the Cobb Galleria Center as a venue for the opening rounds of the volleyball competition in 1996. Neither gay advocacy groups nor ACOG – which feared the prospect of nationwide protests by the former – were successful in getting the Commission to rescind the ordinance. Before a reluctant ACOG could act to formally pull volleyball out of Cobb, an unrepentant county commission pre-empted any punitive actions by denying ACOG use of the Galleria facility. Reactions from county residents were split down the middle, but a slight majority claimed that the resolution did not reflect the community standards of metropolitan Atlanta.[74]

GWINNETT: AMONG THE TREES THERE GROWS ANOTHER ORANGE COUNTY

While Cobb County had easily the most defined identity of all Atlanta suburbs, Gwinnett County experienced the most extensive growth within the metropolitan region during the 1980s and 1990s. While it lacked a dominant edge city like Cumberland/Galleria in Cobb and Perimeter Center in DeKalb/north Fulton, Gwinnett had a series of less cohesive growth nodes. One of these, the Spaghetti Junction area, it shares with DeKalb County. So named for the crazed tangle of nine-story-tall ramps and bridges formed by the intersection of 1-85 and I-285, it is officially called the Tom Moreland Interchange, in honor of a former state Department of Transportation czar. Prior to an expansion in the 1980s, the interchange was popularly known as Malfunction Junction, owing to the demented confusion of its traffic patterns. The interchange itself is located in DeKalb County, and is surrounded by a dense network of retail stores, small office buildings, and wholesale outlets. Without a major mall to anchor it, the Junction is not "recognizable as a place unto itself," however.[75] Beyond the Perimeter, I-85 is paralleled by a virtually unbroken corridor of business and hi-tech industrial parks which stretches more than five miles eastward into Gwinnett to the city of Norcross. Here, and along Georgia Highway 316, are located key office, production, and distribution facilities for such Japanese companies as Hitachi Home Electronics, Panasonic, Mitsubishi, Oki Telecom, Fuji Film, and Ricoh. Forty percent of all Japanese businesses in Georgia (which is second only to California in numbers of Japanese companies) are located in this area of northern Gwinnett.[76] A considerable number of expatriate Japanese executives and their families live in nearby residential areas.

Fueled by robust job growth, Gwinnett's population increased from less than 73,000 in 1970 to 167,000 in 1980 to 356,500 in 1990. In 1995, Atlanta Regional Commission (ARC) planners estimated that 438,400 persons lived in Gwinnett and anticipated that the county could be twice as populous as the city of Atlanta by the year 2020.[77] As in the pale-skinned pastures of Cobb and north Fulton, more than 80 percent of Gwinnettians are white, with more than half the total population born outside the state of Georgia.[78] Nonetheless, with 13 percent of its population composed of immigrants, refugees, and their American-born children, Gwinnett is considerably more ethnically diverse than either Cobb or Fulton, and only slightly less so than DeKalb, Georgia's most culturally heterogeneous county. By contrast, African-Americans constitute only 4 percent of Gwinnett's population, even though their numbers have increased fourfold over the last decade. Rapid growth has strained the county's infrastructure, from schools to roads and other basic services, to breaking point. Urbanization has also brought with it some of the problems associated with the urban core, particularly crime. In 1993, the *Atlanta Constitution* noted with a mixed sense of smugness and alarm that nationally known gangs like the Crips, Bloods, FOLKS, La Raza, and others were appearing amongst Gwinnett's minority youth.[79]

Transportation is the key to Gwinnett's continued growth, and, lacking a system of mass transit, this revolves around developing an enhanced automotive infrastructure. The county has embarked on an ambitious road-building and upgrading program, but the single most important road project – the Outer Perimeter Highway – is metropolitan in scope. The battle over whether to build the highway reveals not only Gwinnett's enhanced position in the metro region, but the limitations of the ARC as a planning body. Plans for an "outer loop" go back to 1971, when it was first proposed by state legislators from suburban counties looking for an economic development engine for their home districts. Shelved by the ARC in 1973, plans for a federally subsidized, $2-billion, 215-mile meta-beltway were revived by the Georgia Department of Transportation in the late 1980s. Under its 1989 mandate as chief transportation visioning body for the region, the ARC conducted a feasibility study of the proposed highway, which had risen in cost to an estimated $5 billion by the early 1990s. In 1993, the ARC's in-house transportation planners found little justification for the loop and recommended scrapping all but a northern segment between I-75 in Bartow County and I-85 in Gwinnett. They found the Outer Loop to have "very serious potentially negative environmental, community, air quality, and overall regional growth and development impacts; it is very costly; and has marginal transportation benefits."[80] Despite this evaluation, the ARC's transportation committee overruled the study and voted to build the highway between I-75 and I-20 in Rockdale County, although the ARC's environmental and land-use committees voted to kill the project entirely. With the ARC internally divided, prospects for the Outer Perimeter seemed dim. Nonetheless, intensive last-minute lobbying by DOT officials and developers led the full ARC board to approve plans for building an 88.5-mile northern arc from I-75 to Ga 316 and recommend further study of a second section continuing to I-20. This vote, which broke down neatly on urban/suburban lines, cleared the way for the Outer Loop's eligibility for federal funds.

Supporters of the Outer Perimeter like to argue that it would serve as a bypass for traffic just passing through metro Atlanta and would relieve congestion on the overburdened I-285. As ARC's own study showed, however, such claims were disingenuous. The real motive force behind the Outer Perimeter is the strategic economic impact it will have on the areas it traverses from Bartow to Gwinnett counties, especially the latter. As with the Perimeter before it, the Outer Loop will attract new investment, create new "centers," and vastly inflate land values throughout its corridor. Such developments will only deepen and intensify the boom in Gwinnett County. No matter the final extent of the highway, Gwinnett stands to benefit the most from its construction. Indeed, critics point out that the hidden agenda of Loop supporters is to "create a second urban center, rivaling Atlanta, and focused on Gwinnett County" that would serve as an "unofficial capital" for a greatly expanded metropolitan region.[81] One of the project's leading boosters, DOT Commissioner Wayne Shackleford, is a former Gwinnett real estate developer who has also been pushing for the construction of a second metropolitan airport in the county. Opposition from local residents shelved the latter plan, but it seems there is nothing, short of a national depression, that stands in the way of Gwinnett becoming a doppelgänger of Orange County, California: a hi-tech- and real-estate-driven, majority-white and politically conservative exopolis.

When they are unable to influence the ARC, Gwinnett leaders prefer to ignore it. Since 1989, the Gwinnett County Commission has approved three large-scale projects that the ARC had deemed "not in the best interest of the state."[82] The latest of these is a planned 375-acre retail–residential–industrial park complex adjoining the existing Gwinnett Place Mall at I-85 in the small city of Duluth. Despite the ARC's objection that it would worsen the area's already horrendous traffic, Gwinnett leaders approved the project, which would add another million square feet of retail space and 1,200 apartments, along with a half million square feet of hi-tech industrial space. This proposed development would go a long way to putting the Gwinnett Place Mall area on a par with Perimeter Center and Cumberland/ Galleria, and giving the county its own quasi-urban nodal nonplace. Once known as Atlanta's "quintessential bedroom community," Gwinnett is becoming more an employment center, and is spurring the rapid development of more moderately priced housing in once-rural neighboring counties like Barrow and Forsyth.[83]

THE SOUTHERN CRESCENT

The decision to build only the northeastern quadrant of the Outer Perimeter reveals the political and economic dominance of north metro development interests within the ARC. However, there is still the possibility that additional segments will be built, which explains the support that southern county officials on the

ARC board have manifested for the project. The spectacular growth of the northern end of I-285 during the 1980s obscured the substantial boom occurring along its southern periphery. By the end of the decade, developers referred to a broad swath of Clayton, Henry, Fayette, Douglas, Coweta, and Rockdale counties as the "Southern Crescent."[84] The boom in residential construction continued throughout the first half of the 1990s, as the region attracted value- and lifestyle-conscious middle-class households displeased by the high-priced congestion of Cobb, north Fulton, and Gwinnett. Blessed with cheap land and easy access to existing interstate highways, the southeastern counties of Henry and Rockdale (which would benefit greatly by the second section of the Outer Perimeter) grew especially rapidly. Further to the southwest, Fayette County emerged as the county with the highest per capita income in the region, a status that was in large measure due to upscale enclaves like Peachtree City.[85] Home to thousands of well-paid employees of Delta Airlines and knit together by fifty miles of golf cart tracks, Peachtree City is the metro area's largest colony in the exurban wilderness.

Still, despite a number of luxury residential enclaves, the Southern Crescent has not yet received the numbers of people necessary to fuel the high-end retail and commercial development that the Platinum Triangle has experienced. Once predominantly agricultural, the Crescent's economy is now dominated by distribution and manufacturing. More than one out of three jobs in Clayton County, admittedly the most urbanized of the Crescent counties, is associated with either Hartsfield Airport or trucking.[86] Not all economic activity in the Southern Crescent is so mundane, however. In the early 1990s, a housewife living on a farm outside the small Rockdale County city of Conyers began claiming to receive regular visitations by an image of the Virgin Mary. During 1992 and 1993, the monthly events drew tens of thousands of domestic and foreign onlookers – fueling a substantial carnivalesque cottage industry to service both the spiritual and more temporal needs of the pilgrims – before the visitations abruptly ceased. For their part, Olympic officials envision that the nearby equestrian venue will effect a not too dissimilar, but longer lasting, economic miracle on the local economy.

Even more than their compatriots in the northern suburbs, residents of the southern arc have been reluctant to approve tax increases necessary for improving the basic infrastructures (roads, sewers, schools, etc.) to support the growth. If only the northeastern segments of the Outer Perimeter are built, as is possible, the southern counties could well find themselves even further removed from the shifting center of gravity of the metropolitan region. As in the northern part of the metropolitan area, the fastest rates of residential and employment growth in the Southern Crescent have been in the outlying counties. In closer-in counties like Clayton, the changes have not been so much in the overall increase in the population, as in its diversity. With Hartsfield International Airport located in its northwestern corner, Clayton was the first of the southern counties to be included within the Atlanta metropolitan area, in 1970. Despite this association, the county south of the airport maintained a distinctly rural regional ethos befitting the "home" of the fictional Tara (Margaret Mitchell located the O'Hara mansion near the city of Jonesboro) for at least another decade. Despite the creation of an international trade zone and the construction of numerous hotels, the area around the airport has not attracted the familiar edge city mix of office and retail development.

As recently as the early 1980s, Clayton was more than 90 percent white and had more Baptist churches per capita than any other county in the metro area.[87] By 1995, however, 17 percent of Clayton's total population of approximately 202,000 lived in immigrant or refugee households and 34 different languages were spoken by students in its schools.[88] In the early 1980s, the areas around Riverdale, south of the airport, became a major site for settling Southeast Asian refugees, particularly Cambodian, Laotian, and Hmong. Other Asian and Latin American immigrants settled in the area as well. Now Riverdale boasts an elaborate Hindu temple and a Buddhist shrine, along with a considerable number of ethnic groceries, restaurants, and other shops. As with similarly diverse DeKalb County to the east of Atlanta, Clayton civic and business leaders have rhetorically embraced "cultural diversity," at least as an economy-generating tool. However, despite a series of fairs and festivals celebrating cultural diversity, as elsewhere in the metro region, immigrants and refugees have a limited voice in the county's political and social life.

BETWIXT AND BETWEEN: DEKALB DIVIDED

Lying both inside and outside the Perimeter, DeKalb was the first metro area county other than Fulton to experience significant industrialization and suburban-ization. By the mid twentieth century, a nearly continuous corridor of white middle-class residential development spread eastward from the upscale neighbor-hood of Druid Hills (part of which lay in the city of Atlanta) through the city of Decatur (which, like Marietta in Cobb County, was founded before Atlanta) on to the 1940s-vintage neo-Tudor subdivision of Avondale Estates and the small town Klan idyll of Stone Mountain. During and immediately after World War II, the adjoining cities of Chamblee and Doraville in the northeastern part of the county attracted new factories, warehouses, and other kinds of industrial development. In 1947, General Motors opened a large assembly plant in Doraville to supplement its Lakewood Heights facility, which it had opened in the late 1920s (located betweeen downtown and the airport, the Lakewood area was annexed by the city in 1952). Although the Lakewood plant closed in 1989, the Doraville GM factory has been recently retooled to make minivans, and the city remains one of the few stable, manufacturing-oriented, working-class areas in the metropolitan region.

During the late 1950s and 1960s, DeKalb benefited greatly from federally subsidized highway construction – large segments of I-85, I-20, and I-285 pass through the county – and the residential and commercial activity centers that these roadways generated. In the late 1960s, the area around Dunwoody in the extreme northwestern section of DeKalb emerged as the first upscale residential neighborhood outside of the city of Atlanta. Located just to the north of Perimeter Center, Dunwoody has become known as a refuge for socially and politically conservative (and Christian) white upper-middle-class émigrés from Atlanta. Beginning in the early 1980s, however, DeKalb has undergone a fragmentation and polarization that mirror the centrifugal processes occurring in the metropolitan area as a whole.

Along with Cobb County, DeKalb was one of the primary beneficiaries of white flight from the city of Atlanta in the late 1960s and 1970s. Since 1985, however, the county has lost more whites than all but one county in the nation and gained more African-Americans than all but one county in the South.[89] The result has been a deeply racialized and class-stratified landscape. The southern half of the county is nearly 80 percent African-American, the northern half is almost 80 percent white. Whites dominate DeKalb's political establishment, control its school system, and possess most of its wealth. Recently, though, the county has emerged, along with south Fulton, as a bastion of the metro area's black middle class. The southeastern quadrant of DeKalb between I-285 and the Rockdale County line is filled with upscale subdivisions developed and inhabited by well-to-do African-Americans. Ironically, some of the suburbs just to the south of the Confederate memorial and theme park at Stone Mountain are now majority-black middle-class neighborhoods.

Even with the arrival of the black middle class, south DeKalb has yet to experience the commercial development that has occurred in the northern half. Unlike other expressway interchanges, the intersection of I-285 and I-20 has not generated the sprawled array of upscale malls, hotels, and office complexes that one finds in northern DeKalb, Gwinnett, and Cobb. In fact, most of the shopping centers of southwest DeKalb, which were originally developed as white middle-class areas in the 1950s and 1960s, have experienced disinvestment and "downmarketing." These shifts in the commercial sector paralleled changes in the region's racial and class demographics. While Atlanta's black middle class has moved into new developments further to the east, the city's African-American poor and working class have moved into split-level subdivisions vacated by whites moving on up to the exurbs. Most of DeKalb's white flight has been from the area west of the Perimeter and south of Decatur. South DeKalb has a poverty rate nearly a third higher than that of the county as a whole, and most of the households living in poverty are located in the southwestern quadrant.[90]

DeKalb's large numbers of immigrants and refugees occupy a social and spatial position that is, literally, in between the county's whites and blacks, although they are far from being a uniform population. According to the 1990 census, slightly more than a quarter of the metro area's Asian and Hispanic households lived below the poverty line, compared to nearly a third of black households and slightly less than 5 percent of whites. As noted earlier, the largest number of Hispanics and Asians resides in the northern part of DeKalb, concentrating in the Chamblee/Doraville area along the Buford Highway corridor and around the city of Clarkston, just to the east of the Perimeter. While Chamblee/Doraville is larger in absolute terms and better known, Clarkston is more ethnically diverse than any city in the state. Owing largely to the efforts of refugee resettlement agencies, approximately 20 percent of the city's residents are either Asian-, African-, or European-born.[91] While Clarkston's population is comprised of a wide variety of groups, its commercial profile is far more limited. Almost a third of the city's businesses are owned by Vietnamese, while elsewhere in Chamblee/Doraville, commercial activities are dominated by Korean, Chinese, and Indian families. While there are significant numbers of second- and third-generation middle-class Hispanic professionals in the metro area, many of the recent Mexican and other Latin American immigrants are concentrated on the lower end of the economic spectrum.

With the heterogeneity of the county's population and Atlanta's claim to internationality, a few of DeKalb's Anglo-owned commercial establishments have embraced diversity. By far the best known and most important of these is Your [sic] DeKalb Farmers' Market, A World Market, which is located just to the east of downtown Decatur. Its name is misleading, for it is not a farmers' market in the traditional sense of the term, i.e. a place where local agricultural producers sell the fruits (and vegetables) of their own labor from individual stalls or from a truck in the parking lot. Rather, it is a warehouse-sized operation owned by a single entrepreneur, Robert Blazer. While he does not have his picture up in Atlanta's pantheon of visionary dreamers, Blazer is clearly of that ilk, although his particular vision is perhaps a little too "New Age" for the downtown establishment to handle. In a glossy brochure, Blazer himself sets out his globalist creed:

> We declare the world is designed to work. We are responsible for what does not work. We make the difference. No matter how technologically advanced we become, we can not escape our fundamental relationships with food and each other. The possibility of these relationships is the world market. In this context the world works for everyone *free of scarcity and suffering* [emphasis added]. We commit ourselves to the possibility this world market is for future generations of this planet.

If we can imagine as real a world that works for everyone free of scarcity and suffering, then it is possible. Each of us has in us that which makes the difference. DARE WE BE OURSELVES?

This is a bit excessive for what is essentially nothing more than a very large grocery store, but it is well in keeping with the proud Atlantan tradition of over-the-top hyperbole. That it bears little relation to *the* world and the DeKalb Farmers' Market as it is actually constituted should not be surprising. Much like Atlanta's claim to be "the world's *next* great international city," Your DeKalb Farmers' Market offers up a prospectus for an idealized future more than a description of the present; it is very much a work in progress. Along with mangoes, yucca, and snapping turtles, the Farmers' Market sells Blazer's EST-tinged vision of what the world ought to be.[92] To hear him talk about it, Blazer is as much driven by desires to educate and enlighten as to make a profit: "when people of different cultures interact with each other, fear is eliminated . . . I'm interested in helping people eliminate some of the fear they have toward the unknown."[93]

The market's worldliness is constituted on a number of levels. As with many other global venues in Atlanta (International Boulevard, International Square, the Georgia World Congress Center, the Georgia International Plaza, the World of Coca-Cola, the Carter Center, even Underground Atlanta), the market emphatically declares its internationality with lots of flags. The market's ubiquitous icon, found on shopping bags, placards, and the like, is an Atlanta-centric projection of the globe surrounded by a halo of flags (Russia, India, France, China, the United States, Britain, Japan, and Italy). Inside, a veritable United Nations of official banners hangs down from the ceiling of the 140,000-square-foot space, each with an identifying label. The display manifests a selective, rather than a comprehensive-world-view, however. The flags of Iran and Iraq, for example, were removed after protests by veterans' groups around the time of the Gulf War.[94]

The selection of merchandise is extensive and calculated to satisfy the diverse demands of multicultural appetites. The market boasts one of Atlanta's widest assortments of produce, baked goods, meats, cheeses, and beer and wine from around the world. However, the market's worldliness is as much constituted by its multiethnic workforce as by its array of goods. Blazer employs over 450 employees from over 40 different countries, most of whom are recent immigrants or refugees who live in adjacent communities. The largest number of immigrants are from the Indian subcontinent, the largest group of refugees are Vietnamese. In addition to reinforcing the market's image of exotic otherness, the reliance on immigrant/refugee labor hired through individual referrals rather than service agencies provides management with a low-cost and tractable labor force "who speak little or no

English, have few support systems in place in the area, and have little or no political organization and clout."[95] The happy image of a world market "free of scarcity and suffering" (yet one that continues to work on the hallowed principles of buy cheap and sell dear) conveniently obscures the absolute and often oppressive conditions of employment at *your* DeKalb Farmers' Market.[96] As if to add insult to indignity, each worker is as clearly labeled as the flags overhead or any of the items for sale, as all must wear a large tag bearing their name and the languages they speak. The overall effect of this packaging is to reduce employees to the status of objects, necessary props for the stage set of the world market.

Although much of the spectacle of the DeKalb Farmers' Market seems to be contrived with a white middle-class market in mind, the clientele is quite diverse. Although exact figures on customer ethnic diversity are lacking (perhaps to complete the effect of objectified ethnicity management should require customers to wear name tags, too), extensive informal observation suggests that approximately one third of the 75,000 people who pass through its doors each week are foreign-born. Parking-lot surveys of license plates reveal that customers are drawn from all over the metropolitan region, as well as from as far away as Savannah, Georgia and the Carolinas. In fact, between the staff and the clientele, the DeKalb Farmers' Market is one of the most diversely populated places in the Atlanta metropolitan region, one of the few locales in which the crowds look like those in other "international cities" like San Francisco, Los Angeles, New York, and Chicago. Still, relations between staff and customers tend to be of a cursory and superficial nature, while interaction between the customers also is rather limited and not always harmonious. On peak weekend days, for example, the vast space is filled with jostling throngs of people who have radically different notions of decorum, queuing, and behaving in crowds. The resultant tumult, which often spills over into the parking lot, does little to promote intercultural understanding, although it does contribute to a refreshing bazaar-like atmosphere of un-Atlantan foreignness.

Several miles to the north of the Farmers' Market, and twelve miles from downtown Atlanta, the DeKalb Chamber of Commerce is laying the groundwork for a model "International Village" that promises to exceed Blazer's establishment in imagineered internationality. In 1992, the Chamber unveiled plans for a multicultural community in the heart of the Buford Highway corridor that would "provide an opportunity for immigrants and refugees, of various cultures to live, work and socialize together," as well as provide a unique educational and tourist attraction.[97] In addition to apartments, stores, and restaurants clad in the appropriate multicultural veneer (e.g. vaguely pagoda-like roofs, etc.), the village will house a community center for the provision of social services for the corridor's large immigrant/refugee population. The center also provides a location for staging festivals promoting intercultural understanding. Plans for having "alternative trans-portation," such as rickshaws, have also been discussed by the project's enthusiastic Anglo boosters.[98] Over the course of the last few years, however, the initial plans have been scaled back considerably and slowed by the opposition of the white community in the neighboring working-class city of Doraville. Current plans down-play the residential aspect and emphasize the community center and lots of retail space; the village is more of a "world in a shopping mall"[99] than a living community.

With its sanitized representation of diversity, the International Village is the epitome of commodified ethnicity, what writer Jeff Yang has presciently called "mallticulturalism."[100] Despite the community center, the emphasis of the project is very much on presenting a homogenized spectacle of cultural otherness to be consumed by non-immigrant visitors. Yet, even with its overwhelming Disneyfied ethos, the International Village is in one way more genuinely "international" than the DeKalb Farmers' Market, or for that matter downtown's World of Coca-Cola. Rather than being the property of a single Anglo entrepreneur lording it over a dis-empowered immigrant workforce, or of a transnational corporate colossus, the Village will be the product of an international public–private partnership. Although much of the infrastructure for the project, including the community center, is to be financed with public funds, a substantial amount of local and overseas Asian capi-tal is poised to invest in the project.[101]

SPACES IN MOTION

Both the DeKalb Farmers' Market and the proposed International Village are good examples of the quasi-public domains of commodified spectacle that have become such ubiquitous features of the contemporary metropolitan landscape. They offer up sanitized and secure simulations of diversity and substitute impersonal relations of market exchange for non-spurious intercultural communication and social interac-tion. They are matched in the urban core by the festival marketplace of Underground Atlanta and the corporate showpiece of the World of Coca-Cola, which will be discussed in the following chapters. Over the past several years, a large body of literature has described, analyzed and criticized these kinds of privatized dio-ramas that have insidiously taken the place of public space.[102] Few of these accounts, however, have dealt very much with the liminal places that have been created "in-between" everywhere else. While Sharon Zukin has characterized the entire urban landscape as a "liminal" space on account of its implacable shapeshifting,[103] I am using the term here to refer to a particular kind of institutionalized site or setting dedi-cated to constant, or at least rhythmic, movement, what Manuel Castells has termed (in a somewhat different context) "spaces of flows."[104] The Hartsfield Terminal megastructure is a good example of this kind of interstitial space, a place dedicated to mediating between different kinds of flows (of persons, goods, planes, and other vehicles). So, too, are the stations, subways, and buses of the Metropolitan Atlanta Rapid Transit Authority, which I shall talk about in the next two chapters. Atlanta's roads and highways also constitute a particular form of social space that is among the most "public" of domains in Atlanta. This is not so much a comment on their "openness" – they are actually rather closed, constrained, and inhuman systems – as a criticism of the utter lack of places in Atlanta where persons of different backgrounds can mix and mingle in relations of social equivalence.

Along with local television (which, thanks to cable, is not really all that local anymore), driving is one of the few collective experiences that bring Atlantans of diverse backgrounds into contact with one another on a daily basis. Admittedly, it is far from being a completely inclusive activity, as there are hundreds of thousands of people in the Atlanta area who cannot afford to, or who are otherwise unable to drive, on account of age, infirmity, or disposition. Given the sprawl of Atlanta, these non-drivers are reduced to the status of second-class citizens, wholly dependent on the goodwill of others or the vagaries of the mass transit system. Like Los Angelenos, Houstonians, and inhabitants of other wide-open autopolises, Atlantans are zealous celebrants of the car cult, and have been since the early part of this century. Ford Motor Company opened up one its first factories outside Detroit in Atlanta in 1909 (it has since been converted into loft apartments), and despite poor roads, the city enjoyed one of the highest per capita levels of automobile ownership in the nation during the 1920s.[105] Atlantans invest a great deal of money and themselves into their cars – frequently pushing their credit limits to the wall – in the belief that you are what you drive, and for the simple reason that so many of them spend so much time in them.

Driving is also a great equalizer. No matter what car one owns, all who drive are subjected to the second nature of the traffic system, which is as unyielding and capricious as the weather itself. For the great majority of the metro area's residents, the morning (6:45–9:00) and evening (4:00–7:00) rush hours are defining moments of the working day, mass events that subject hundreds of thousands of otherwise unconnected people to collective rituals of frustration and misery. To inform commuters of the inevitable accidents and delays, Atlanta radio stations (or, rather, their sponsors) support the nation's (and no doubt the world's) largest armada of eye-in-the-sky traffic helicopters, while a large assortment of local and nationally syndicated vitriolic radio shock jocks try to keep drivers from venting their anger on each other. Meanwhile, the largest per capita assemblage of billboards in the world has been erected along the roadsides to allow advertisers to take advantage of the captive market produced by hundreds of thousands of motorists stuck in traffic.

Much like the Hartsfield megastructure, with which they share a certain kinship, Atlanta's multi-lane highways are highly mechanized, resolutely inhuman spaces of flow and movement. They promise to be even more so after 1996, when high-occupancy vehicle (HOV) lanes and a new "intelligent" traffic monitoring and control system, said to be the most advanced in the United States, will be completed in time to aid in the epic task of moving the Olympic hordes. HOV lanes are a common enough feature of the nation's highway system, but the new Advanced Transportation Management System (ATMS) will allow the Georgia Department of Transportation to keep watch over 160 miles of highway and roadway within the Perimeter. More than four hundred cameras and an unspecified number of sensors will allow the DOT to collect information that will allow it to time street lights, monitor road conditions, and direct vehicles to avoid traffic jams.[106]

While no one likes to be stuck in traffic, the ATMS poses a potential dual threat to individual autonomy and privacy. The collection of roadway data will be used to computer-design optimum traffic patterns that may dictate, rather than merely suggest, the routes that travelers may take. Secondly, and perhaps far more alarmingly, the ATMS gives the Georgia DOT the potential to collect all kinds of information about specific vehicles and individual travel patterns that it may pass along or sell to a wide variety of governmental or marketing entities. The DOT refuses to draft policies regarding the use or misuse of information it will collect through the system because it steadfastly claims that its actions do not impinge on individual privacy, or as one DOT spokesman tellingly noted, "We're not interested in privacy issues." At the same time, however, it also promises to "work very closely with enforcement agencies."[107] Given the imperious attitude the DOT has assumed in the past with regard to ignoring or outrightly crushing community opposition to its road-building projects, there seems to be considerable cause for skepticism over the good faith in which it claims to be operating.

At present, however, Atlanta's highways are anything but controlled spaces, and it remains to be seen if even these extreme panoptic strategies will be effective mechanisms of social control. Current levels of traffic are considerably in excess of planned volume and continue to increase every year. Traffic enforcement is minimal and the twelve-laned expanses of the Downtown Connector and the Perimeter present Hobbesian spectacles of the first order, pitting vehicle against vehicle and God against all. Massive tractor trailers blithely ignore regulations banning them from the Downtown Connector unless they have a central city destination. The advent of HOV lanes promises to worsen the Darwinian struggle for survival on Atlanta's highways. Rather than simply utilizing the left-hand lanes that were originally designed, but never used, for high-occupancy traffic, DOT engineers are instead shaving a foot off existing lanes and shoulders to create a new lane. If the

DOT's first experiment with HOV lanes on I-20 is any guide, most Atlanta drivers will continue to refuse to carpool, thus creating the prospect of even higher levels of high-speed traffic in the same number of perilously narrow lanes.

As social spaces, highways have curiously contradictory qualities. Even though they are among the most generic features of the contemporary American landscape, built to common US DOT specs, a unique conjuncture of factors, from seasonal weather to employment patterns and local driving styles, conspire to imprint a city's roadways with a stamp of unmistakable particularity. Each state may have its own peculiar sachet of driving laws and regulations, but each locality has its own distinctive and unwritten rules of the road. Although Los Angeles, Houston, New York and a host of other cities may have more vehicles and/or more miles of roadway, Atlanta drivers enjoy the fastest average speed of any major metropolitan area in the nation. On one section of the Perimeter, average speeds hover in the neighborhood of 90 miles per hour. When speed is combined with a mix of driving styles (slightly more than 40 percent of the metro area population was born outside of Georgia), road etiquette (use of the horn is considered an incitement to violence rather than an act of communication), sheer volume of traffic, and a state law that allows possession of a loaded handgun in the vehicle (as long as it is in plain sight), the state of play on Atlanta's highways is accurately characterized by a bumper sticker seen one especially wild morning on the Downtown Connector: Driving is War.

The situation is little better on the net of secondary and tertiary surface streets that criss-cross the metropolitan area. Outside of the roughly two-mile-wide urban core there is nothing even remotely resembling a grid. Major roads tend to follow the contours of the topography, tracing former wagon routes along ridge tops and valley bottoms, curving frequently and conforming to no easily visualized pattern. Residential and commercial development over the last four decades has greatly overloaded their capacity to handle traffic. Upgrading of roadways, and parking, has proved futile, as traffic expands to exceed the available space. Lanes disappear, roads end with surprising suddenness, and signage is both inadequate and confusing. An essential part of becoming an Atlantan is developing an intuitive knowledge of the maze of roads, of learning the necessary shortcuts through subdivisions, of being able to anticipate, improvise, avoid. One learns one's way around not so much by consulting a map as by getting lost and finding one's way home, by designating landmarks in an unexceptional suburban landscape, e.g. Cobb's Big Chicken.

Inside the city of Atlanta, confusion is further compounded by frequent changes in street names, especially on the major north–south one-way pairs in the core. The abrupt name changes are another legacy of the highly racialized nature of the urban terrain. In much the same manner as the metro area as a whole, the city is divided into a white north side and black south side, with Ponce De Leon Avenue the divider. Between 1913 and 1923, the city zoned residential neighborhoods by race, separating them with railroad corridors and industrial buffer zones where possible. Even after racial zoning ordinances were struck down as unconstitutional in the 1920s, restrictive covenants and other less formal (but no less effective) means were used to maintain the discriminative integrity of white and black areas. African-Americans were, for most of the twentieth century, spatially confined to a belt of neighborhoods ringing the central business district on the south, east, and west, which were, in turn, circumscribed by a cordon of railroad tracks and a zone of warehouses and factories. Outside this "Central Area" lay the streetcar suburbs and automobilized subdivisions built between 1890 and 1929. Beginning in the early twentieth century, white residents of northern neighborhoods had the names of the principal streets in their communities changed so as to not live on the same street as black residents living south of the divide. Thus, in the city's eastern residential neighborhoods, Monroe Drive becomes Boulevard and Briarcliff Road turns into Moreland Avenue south of Ponce De Leon Avenue, while in the core, Courtland Street turns into Washington Street south of Decatur Street.

There are additional ways in which Atlanta's street names reflect its conflicted past. For much of its first century of existence, the city's streets were named after pioneer citizens (e.g. Cain, Ivy, Mitchell), Confederate Civil War heros (Nathan Bedford Forrest), and local flora (Pine, Linden, and, most famously, Peachtree), among others. Beginning in the 1970s, a number of thoroughfares were renamed to commemorate prominent local African-Americans and heroes of the civil rights movement. The first of these was Martin Luther King Drive, which was originally known as Hunter Street. King's associate, the Reverend Ralph David Abernathy, has been similarly honored, as has John Wesley Dobbs, a leader in the black community of the 1920s and the maternal grandfather of Atlanta's first black mayor, Maynard Jackson. All three of these renamed thoroughfares pass through predominantly or historically African-American areas of the city. Other renamings display a certain amount of just irony: to wit, the boulevard now named after legendarily liberal *Atlanta Constitution* editor Ralph McGill (known disparagingly as "Rastus McGill" to his unenlightened white Atlantan contemporaries) was originally named after the Confederate General and original Ku Klux Klan founder Nathan Bedford Forrest. Other new street names reflect contemporary corporate landmarks (Coca-Cola Way, Peachtree Center Avenue) or the city's global aspirations (International Boulevard). In 1992, one city official even proposed selling the rights to rename streets and public spaces to corporations willing to pay for revitalizing them in time for the Olympics (of this, more in Chapter 5).

Some of Atlanta's thoroughfares constitute not just paths of movement or boundaries between areas, but icons in their own right. The best-known of the former is Peachtree Street, which runs more than nine miles from the center of downtown northward to the elite enclave of Buckhead, where it turns into Peachtree Road. Atlanta boasts a veritable orchard of Peachtrees. There are over a hundred thoroughfares with Peachtree in their name, in addition to a bounty of buildings (the Peachtree Center mixed-use complex), suburban municipalities (Peachtree Corners, Peachtree City), and other places (e.g. the DeKalb–Peachtree Airport). Thanks to *Gone With the Wind*, for many around the world "Peachtree Street" symbolizes Atlanta. The sentiment is not limited to outsiders, as is evidenced by two of the better-known popular accounts of the city written by local authors in the 1960s: Celestine Sibley's *Peachtree Street, U.S.A.* and William Willeford's *Peachtree Street, Atlanta*. In the post-Civil War period, Peachtree Street developed its mystique as an elite residential address. Beginning in the 1920s, its residential status was supplanted by prestige retail, office, and entertainment uses. After the building boom of the 1960s to 1990s, the section of Peachtree Street downtown is the only one in Atlanta that is the concrete canyon usually associated with twentieth-century cities. Given its length and the diversity of terrain it passes through, Peachtree Street is not so much a singular district as a linear spine or bridge between the city's isolated nodes of development.

Some streets constitute districts in their own right. One of these is Sweet Auburn Avenue, once called "the richest Negro Street in the World."[108] Between the 1920s and the late 1950s, Auburn Avenue was the social and commercial heart of Black Atlanta. Running east from the downtown white business district, Sweet Auburn was home to the most prominent black businesses, such as Citizens Trust Bank and Atlanta Life Insurance Company, the Atlanta *Daily World* (the only black-owned daily in the country for a time), and two of the largest churches in the city: Big Bethel AME and Ebenezer Baptist. The latter was the pulpit of Martin Luther King, Jr and Sr. The junior King's birth home is also located on Auburn Avenue, as is the Martin Luther King Jr Center for Non-violent Social Change. The birth home and the King Center constitute the core of the federally designated Martin Luther King, Jr Historic Site, which lies within a much larger city-designated Sweet Auburn Urban Conservation District, which actually covers several streets in addition to Auburn Avenue. Beginning in the 1920s, however, the residential locus of the black middle class shifted to the westside near Atlanta University, and a rival commercial district developed on what is now Martin Luther King, Jr Drive. The killing blow to the district came in the early 1960s, when the Avenue was brutally bisected by the Downtown Connector. Despite a great deal of rhetorical concern from city officials, revitalization efforts have been unsuccessful, with the sole exception of the King Historic District. However, even the latter has been a center of controversy recently, which will be detailed below. First, we need to delineate the wider framework in which Sweet Auburn, Peachtree Street, and other elements of the city are situated.

CIRCUMNAVIGATING THE CENTER

No matter what the denizens of the outer suburbs might think, the world within the Perimeter is far from being an undifferentiated whole. The area inside I-285 comprises most of the city of Atlanta (only the extreme western parts lie outside) and the western third of DeKalb County, including the city of Decatur and the Buford Highway corridor. When it was incorporated in 1847, the city's initial boundaries, much like those of Abbasid Baghdad, described a perfect circle. Such a manner of delimiting boundaries was a common practice in mid-nineteenth-century Georgia, as a number of nearby municipalities originally had circular extents. A few, such as Clarkston, maintain these boundaries to the present day. Until the 1870s, Atlanta's municipal extent included everything within a one-mile radius of the Zero Mile Post located in the Union Railroad Depot. Twice in the nineteenth century this radius was extended, first by a half-mile, then by a quarter-mile. For the purposes of political administration, the city was subdivided into first five, then six, eight, and eventually ten wards as it expanded.

After 1890, the city grew piecemeal by periodically annexing its expanding suburban fringe. Its rapid and extensive growth in the first third of the twentieth century overwhelmed the somewhat arbitrary street numbering system. In 1926, the city planning commission used the intersection of Edgewood and Pryor Streets (just one block east of Five Points) as the zero point for dividing the city into four cardinal quadrants: Northeast, Northwest, Southeast, Southwest.[109] This revision helped to rationalize postal deliveries and the provision of basic utilities somewhat, even as the city continued to expand its spatial extent through the end of the decade. It attained its current jigsaw-like shape in 1952, after the "Plan of Improvement" tripled the city's area and brought both the elite white residential area of Buckhead and large undeveloped sections to the south and west onto city tax rolls. Aside from the annexation of Ben Hill (1953) and a few other unincorporated areas to the southwest (1967), subsequent efforts at annexation have encountered effective opposition from both suburban residents and state legislators. Atlanta politicians, however, still regularly toy with the idea of annexing the lily-white and cash-rich provinces of north Fulton County, much to the abject horror of the fine citizens of Roswell, Sandy Springs, and Alpharetta and their representatives on the Fulton County Commission.

Within the municipal boundaries of the city of Atlanta, there are many cross-cutting and overlapping layers of spatial organization that, at best, imperfectly correspond with vernacular categories: police zones, city council districts, census tracts, zip codes, school catchment areas, etc. If all of these strata were to be laid upon a map of the city, the resulting image would be absolutely unreadable. Some reduction, then, is clearly in order if we are to be able to visualize the city at all.

Prior to interstate construction, railroad tracks, rather than highways, were the principal structuring features of Atlanta's morphology. More than a dozen railroads passed through the city by the first decade of the twentieth century and they overlaid a crazy quilt of tracks upon the urban landscape. In the early 1950s, planners of the state-chartered Metropolitan Planning Commission and the Central Atlanta Improvement Association (CAIA), an organization of major downtown property owners, used a two-mile-wide cordon of railroad tracks to distinguish a "Central Area" from the rest of the city. While it was assembled from the trackage of a number of railroads and formed an arbitrary boundary, the railroad cordon did have the virtue of encompassing virtually all of Atlanta's street grid and did mark the limits of the pre-World War II urbanized area. Although Atlanta's landscape has been profoundly changed since the 1950s, the successor organization to the CAIA, Central Atlanta Progress, Inc. (CAP), continues to use the railroad cordon as its defining outer boundary of the Central Area. In 1971, CAP planners used the lines of the Downtown Connector and I-20 to subdivide the Central Area into a rather compact central business district, and an "inner ring" of mixed industrial, residential, commercial, and recreational uses. One of the principal limitations of this spatial scheme is that it left a good deal of the city literally "off the map." The omissions included not only the poor African-American areas to the south and west of the city, but the most affluent majority white areas in the northernmost reaches of Atlanta as well. However, it did in part describe reality, in that CAP and, for that matter, the city have frequently acted as if there was little relation between the core and the inner ring, much less between the Central Area and the rest of the city. As much as the metropolitan area as a whole, the city of Atlanta is at its core a deeply fragmented reality.

NEIGHBORHOODS BY THE NUMBERS

However, even fragmentation presupposes unities, or at least units, of some kind. The fragments of which cities are composed are most commonly referred to as "neighborhoods," but these units are notoriously ambiguous entities. This slipperiness is manifest in the Atlanta City Code, which defines a neighborhood as "a geographic area either with distinguishing characteristics or in which the residents have a sense of identity and a commonality of perceived interest, or both. Factors that may contribute to neighborhood identity include shared development history, architecture, social and economic relationships, physical boundaries," as well as "organizations dedicated to neighborhood preservation and improvement."[110] In 1993, the city's Bureau of Planning recognized over 200 discrete neighborhoods of varying size, an increase of several dozen from the 1970s. These communities are organized into twenty-four neighborhood planning units, or NPUs. When first devised in the early 1970s, the NPU system was intended to provide community input into planning decisions. However, over the past two decades the mechanisms for rendering meaningful input have been gutted by city administrations eager to provide an inviting investment climate, and the NPUs remain artifacts that hardly function as impersonalized interest groups, much less *gemeinschaftsen* in the spirit of Ferdinand Tönnies. Nonetheless, the city continues to use them as basic units of urban structure. Meanwhile, some of the more gentrified areas, such as Virginia-Highland, have developed quite effective neighborhood organizations that have been able to constrain unwanted commercial development.

In 1991, the Bureau of Planning further subdivided the city into six irregularly sized "study areas" of four NPUs each: Northside, Northeast, Northwest, Westside, Intown South, and Southside. This system of classification both coincided with, and cross-cut, vernacular categories of spatial organization. The Northside, for example, was largely coterminous with the upscale area of Buckhead, but also included the less exclusive area covered by NPU D, which included a large railroad yard complex and significant areas without any distinctive neighborhood identity. The Northeast area, by contrast, took in a number of areas with separate place identities, including the old central business district or Downtown, the 1980s boom area of Midtown, and the gentrified eastside neighborhoods popularly known as Intown. The last is not to be confused with the Bureau of Planning's Intown South, which comprises an east–west belt of poor neighborhoods and public housing projects south of downtown and the old Georgia Railroad corridor (now owned by CSX), running from the Atlanta University area in the west to the East Lake Meadows housing project (otherwise known as Little Vietnam, for its high rates of violent crime) in the east.

The Southside study area has the largest chunks of undeveloped land in the city, along with some of the more recent (late 1960s), and largest, public housing projects, like Carver Homes. Southside is also home to the forbidding bulk of the federal penitentiary (one of the largest in the US penal system), the Lakewood Fairgrounds, and the now vacant Lakewood General Motors plant. The area is also sometimes referred to by planners at the Atlanta Economic Development Corporation (AEDC) as Southtowne. The Northwest is the smallest district in both area and population; its landscape is dominated by large public housing projects such as the Perry and Bankhead Homes, as well as a mix of industrial uses, landfills, and the city's overburdened principal sewage treatment plant. The Westside study area which, along with the Southside, was largely annexed by the city in 1952, has a few poor neighborhoods and little industry, but is best known for its "Black Enterprise"[111] neighborhoods, like Collier Heights and Cascade Heights.

Despite some limitations, the Bureau of Planning's study areas do provide a handy way of talking about some of the sociospatial divides of Atlanta's landscape. In 1990, 65 percent of the city's population was African-American, 33 percent was white, and the remainder was other racial minorities: Native American, Asian, Pacific Islander. Nearly two-thirds of the Northeast area's population was white, as was almost 90 percent of the Northside's.[112] Most of the minority population of these areas were concentrated in a few neighborhoods, like Lindbergh-Morosgo in the Northside and the Old Fourth Ward and Home Park in the Northeast. Together, these two areas were home to some 90 percent of the city's white residents, while the four other areas accounted for virtually the same percentage of Atlanta's "minority" (sic) majority population, which for the most part was coterminous with "African-American." The Westside and Northwest areas were 97 and 98 percent minority, respectively, and their racial composition was virtually unchanged from 1980. The minority populations of the Southside and Intown South increased from 79 percent to 83 percent and from 86 percent to 88 percent between 1980 and 1990.

While the Northside and the Northeast remain majority white, the percentage of minorities rose from 6 to 12 percent and from 31 to 37 percent, respectively, between 1980 and 1990.[113] The latter two areas led the city in population and job growth, while the Southside and Northwest dropped precipitously in both categories. The most striking disparity between areas was in income. The median income of households in the Northeast and Northside areas is two to three times as high as household income in the other districts, even the Westside. Poverty rates are mirror images at the geographical poles. Fewer than 6 percent of the population lives below the poverty line in the Northside area, but no more than that lives *above* the poverty line in large sections of the Northwest, Intown South, and Southside study areas.[114] The latter three areas are also characterized by the lowest rates of school attendance and graduation in the city, as well as the highest levels of unemployment, single-parent households, teenage pregnancies, and violent crime.

LANDSCAPES OF DISEMPOWERMENT

Atlanta's poorest communities to the south, east, and west of the core have been collectively referred to by a number of terms over the years. One can track the changing phases of federal urban policy in the different labels that have applied to these areas. In the 1940s, they were called "blighted areas" threatening to infect more "mature," residential neighborhoods. The presence of blight and incompatible uses made these communities ripe for "urban renewal" in the 1960s. As part of the urban renewal process, some of these areas were renamed. For example, the poor black community of Buttermilk Bottom located just to the east of downtown, was razed and renamed "Bedford-Pine." Between 1967 and 1973, a large swath of neighborhoods south of I-20 (Mechanicsville, Pittsburgh, Summerhill, Peoplestown, Grant Park, and Reynoldstown) were known collectively as the "Model Cities area," after the urban renewal program of that name. Following the failure of the Model Cities program, no new concerted project was forthcoming for two decades. In 1994, the Model Cities area (minus Grant Park, which had partly gentrified in the interim) was packaged with other poor black neighborhoods to its south, east, and west to form an "Empowerment Zone." Covering approximately nine square miles, the zone encompassed a total of thirty neighborhoods in which over half of the population lived below the poverty line and nearly a fifth were unemployed. The zone also comprised one of Atlanta's most prolific killing fields, in 1993, with more than one quarter of all of the city's reported crime occurring in the zone, as well as one third of the homicides and half of the rapes reported to police.[115] Approximately 40 percent of the zone population lived in substandard public housing (much of which had been built in the early 1940s), and of these 95 percent lived in poverty.

The boundaries of the Empowerment Zone are arbitrary delimitations, however, set to meet specific criteria dictated by the US Department of Housing and Urban Development (HUD) and the machinations of local politics. Grant Park was excluded, for example, because it had undergone partial gentrification and its residents no longer identified with the inhabitants of adjacent areas. However, some areas that did meet the criteria, such as Techwood/Clark Howell housing projects just to the northwest of downtown, were excluded from the zone because they have been penciled-in for transformation into privatized, mixed-income housing. In the meantime, their inhabitants have been relocated to other public housing projects or given "Section VIII" vouchers to find accommodation in the private housing market. Similar plans have been proposed by developer Thomas Cousins for the East Lake Meadows housing project, which lies outside the boundaries of the zone. The outcome of these two projects is in some ways more significant than the Empowerment Zone project itself, as privatization has been bandied about as the solution to the notoriously mismanaged Atlanta Housing Authority.

As the city Bureau of Planning figures suggest, the actual landscape of poverty in Atlanta pays little heed to municipal boundaries. As noted earlier in this chapter, the growth of the Atlanta region has been characterized as much by the suburbanization of poverty as of affluence. The boundaries of The Atlanta Project (TAP) – an effort started by former president Jimmy Carter to jumpstart grassroots

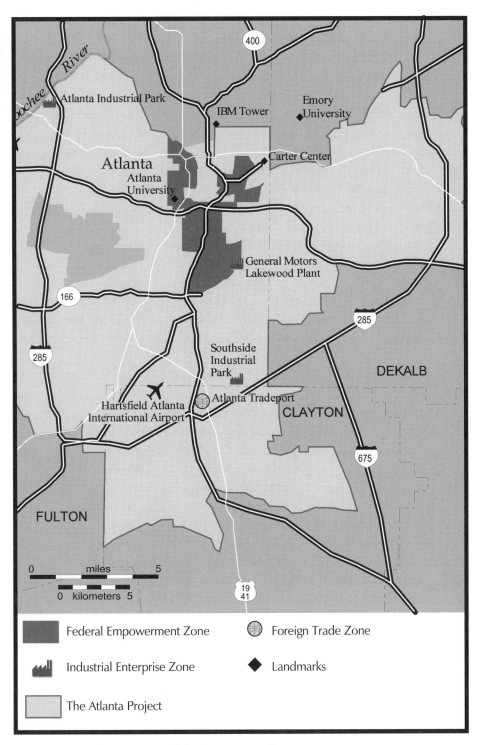

Map 5: The Atlanta Project and the Empowerment Zone

redevelopment of poverty-stricken communities – links the poorest parts of the city with similar areas in Fulton, Clayton, and DeKalb Counties. Rather than following existing municipal or neighborhood boundaries, the TAP area is divided up into twenty "clusters" defined by high school catchment areas. A number of criteria were used to determine inclusion within the TAP area, including low income, number of single-parent households and rates of teenage pregnancies. Atlanta-based corporations were enlisted as sponsors of particular clusters, contributing not only money, but volunteers to assist in neighborhood empowerment. Corporate sponsorship has been perhaps TAP's most effective public relations stratagem quite apart from its effects on the target clusters, allowing corporations to "prove" their commitment to Atlanta's poor.

Despite the close association of TAP with the personage of Jimmy Carter in the media (local newspapers always referred to it as "Jimmy Carter's Atlanta Project"), the globe-trotting ex-president played a minor role in the direction and management of TAP activities. Instead, from its inception in 1992 to late 1994, the reins of TAP lay in the hands of a racially balanced six-member secretariat headed by Dan Sweat, long-time business leader and president of Central Atlanta Progress between 1972 and 1991. A 23-member advisory board drew heavily upon recognized leaders of the business community, as well as public institutions and non-profit agencies. Despite a great deal of laudatory media hoopla in its first year, TAP has been somewhat less than successful in empowering communities. Within a year of the project's start, all three of the secretariat's original African-American members had resigned their posts, with one alleging a pervasive sense of racial arrogance and insensitivity within the organization.[116] Despite a pledge to empower the grassroots, TAP's approach has been far more top-down than bottom-up. A 1995 audit of the project's efforts found it had strayed far from its founding principles, with TAP employees making decisions that originally were intended for neighborhood residents. TAP was also criticized for not encouraging collaboration with non-profits, charities and other groups active in the communities.[117] Community participation in the project was low, reflecting both a distrust of the powers behind the organization and the fact that the clusters were arbitrary designations that did not conform to the social networks of the target communities.

BUCKHEAD: THE OTHER EXTREME

Although it lies within the boundaries of Atlanta, many residents of Buckhead define it as a world apart from the rest of the city. In many ways they are correct. Traveling north from downtown on Peachtree Street, one encounters signs welcoming the driver to the "Buckhead Community," as if it were a separate municipality. The signs were erected by the Buckhead Coalition, a group of major property and business owners headed by former (1969–73) Atlanta mayor Sam Massell that acts, in many ways, as a shadow government. By virtue of that office, Massell now enjoys the unofficial sobriquet of "Mayor of Buckhead." Although Buckhead falls within the domain of Atlanta's Bureau of Planning, the Coalition has developed its own master plan for the area. While Buckhead is very much a "state of mind,"[118] it also possesses some physical limits. Bounded on the north and east by the city limits, on the west by the Chattahoochee river, and on the south by the Peachtree Creek (site of a famous Civil War battle) and the diverging lines of I-75 and I-85, Buckhead occupies the entire northern quadrant of Atlanta.

Home to approximately 70,000 people, nearly two-thirds of whom were born outside of Georgia, Buckhead is also 91 percent white. The average family income is $113,186 (compared to an average of $44,514 for the city as a whole) and its poverty rate is less than a quarter of the rest of the city's. Differences in race and income are paralleled in educational attainment. Fewer than 2 percent of Buckhead residents have less than a 9th Grade education (compared to 11 percent of city residents), while 59 percent have graduated from college (27 percent in the city).[119] With over 10 million square feet of office space (most of it "Class A" and built within the last fifteen years), more than 5 million square feet of retail space (including two of the South's most upmarket malls and more than 1,000 specialty stores) and 4,000 hotel rooms (in luxury establishments like the Ritz Carlton and the Hotel Nikko), Buckhead is an unparalleled zone of urban wealth and privilege.

The area has had an elite cachet since the 1920s, when the densely wooded streets west of Peachtree Road became the premiere residential area for families made rich by real estate speculation, textiles, and, especially, Coca-Cola. Prior to the advent of the automobile, Buckhead Village had been a small agricultural settlement that took its name from a mounted stag's head on the wall of a tavern that once stood on what is now the intersection of Peachtree and Roswell Roads. By the onset of the Great Depression, this unincorporated section of Fulton County had the highest per capita income of any area south of Philadelphia.[120] A secondary wave of more modest homes and apartment houses for the city's upper middle classes followed, as did a low-rise commercial district. The wave turned into a flood following the city's annexation of Buckhead in 1952, as a number of the city's major downtown developers assembled large tracts of land for subdivisions, commercial strips, and shopping malls.

During the 1960s, Buckhead's low-rise mid-century commercial core was overwhelmed by the congestion generated by the hierarchical system of strip, community, regional, and super-regional shopping centers. Chief among these temples of consumption were Lenox Square Mall (1959), located just to the north of downtown

Buckhead on Peachtree Road, and Phipps Plaza (1969) across the street. Originally built as open-air shopping centers, they were both eventually enclosed and have undergone successive waves of "enhancement." Both malls underwent major renovations in the 1990s, adding domes, skylights, and additional levels of luxury shopping. With three major anchor stores apiece (Macy's, Rich's, and Neiman Marcus at Lenox; Parisian, Lord & Taylor, Saks Fifth Avenue, and, it is rumored, Bloomingdale's, at Phipps) the two represent the densest concentration of upscale shopping in the southeast. In 1992, Lenox Mall alone attracted 14 million visitors, 6 million of whom were from outside the metropolitan region. These figures led one guidebook to the city to call Lenox Mall Atlanta's most popular tourist attraction.[121]

In the latter part of the 1960s, local developers in league with national partners built the first office buildings and mixed-use developments along Peachtree and Piedmont Roads between the core of Buckhead Village and Lenox Square. Retail and especially commercial development continued unabated during the 1970s. No fewer than seventeen new office complexes were constructed between 1970 and 1982, more than doubling the leasable space.[122] Even more prestige office space was added in the 1980s, as Buckhead attracted a large percentage of the metro area's hot FIRE (Finance, Insurance, and Real Estate) sector. The culmination of these efforts was the black mirrored glass Atlanta Financial Center, which was built on pilings over the depressed cut of Georgia 400. As with Cumberland-Galleria and Perimeter Center, the growth of the upscale office market was accompanied by the construction of luxury hotels, apartments, and condominiums.

Not all of Buckhead's growth in the 1980s came from new construction; the area also enhanced its position as the city's center for reflexive consumption through the extensive adaptive reuse of existing building stock. Between the growth corridors along Peachtree and Piedmont Roads, the bungalows of Buckhead's residential development of the 1940s and 1950s underwent mass conversion into boutiques, restaurants, and other outposts of high-end retail. Meanwhile the low-rise prewar commercial core of Buckhead Village, itself a casualty of the first wave of enmalling in the 1960s, was reincarnated as a dedicated entertainment zone, with the densest network of restaurants, bars and discotheques to be found anywhere in the metro area. Buckhead is the home of Atlanta's swankiest eateries, the principal locus of the college-age to post-40s singles scene. The heady mix of high-rise skylines, high-end retail, upscale entertainment, and luxury residences has led more than one observer to conclude that Buckhead is "the closest thing to a true 24-hour urban center in Atlanta" and thus the area's truest "new downtown."[123]

Such a claim, however, confuses ostentation with urbanity, for there is little that is traditionally urban about the built environment of Buckhead. In this regard, the absence of a pedestrian streetscape is even more glaring than Buckhead's lack of social diversity (although the latter is just as important). Outside of the malls and the central entertainment zone, Buckhead is one of the most pedestrian-hostile areas in the entire city. The streetscape is entirely oriented to the automobile. In some cases, it is literally impossible to walk directly between adjacent complexes, which are oriented to their parking lots rather than to each other. What sidewalks exist are invariably empty, save for the ones linking the Lenox Square Mall with its MARTA station. Appropriately enough, future plans for improving the circulation of consumers through Buckhead focus on a Disneylike "people-mover" rather than enhancing its pedestrian streetscape. Even more telling, however, is the complete and utter absence of a large, non-commercial open space, such as a park or square.

INTOWN: AT PLAY IN THE FIELDS
OF GENTRIFICATION

Geographers Neil Smith and Peter Williams have written of the "Manhattanization" of much of the contemporary urban landscape.[124] By this term they refer not only to the proliferation of dense vertical urban cores, but to the inexorable gentrification of former working-class areas and the emergence of new zones of intensified cultural consumption. Since the 1970s, several parts of Atlanta have undergone gentrification, but there has also been another, more literal, kind of metaphorical Manhattanization at work as well. Whether it is due to the large number of New Yorkers who have moved to Atlanta in recent years, or merely the salience of New York City in the national urban imagination, is unclear, but there has been a marked tendency for Atlantans to refer to parts of the city in terms of Manhattan's cultural geography. As early as the 1880s, Atlanta boosters referred to their city as the New York of the South. They were referring more to its bustle and attitude toward business than features of its built environment, however. In 1962, an Atlanta newspaper identified the environs near the Atlanta College of Art in Midtown (then known as Uptown) as "Atlanta's Greenwich Village," on account of its quasi-bohemian population. As will be detailed elsewhere in this volume, Midtown has subsequently been transformed into the moral equivalent of New York's Battery Park City – a petrified forest of postmodern residential and office towers – although no one refers to the area as such. In the latter part of the 1960s, proud Atlantans took to calling John Portman's Peachtree Center mixed-use complex Rockefeller Center South.

The latest *locale fixée* is "SoHo," New York City's loft-living, art-dealing district of converted nineteenth-century factories and warehouses. To hear the current crop of real estate agents tell it, Atlanta's Intown is home to both its

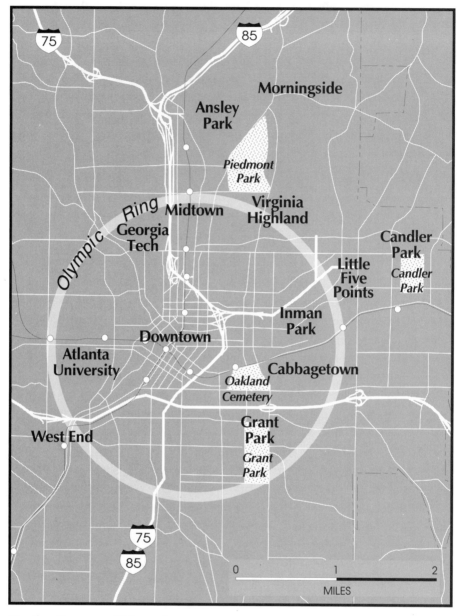

Map 6:   Downtown, Midtown, Intown

"SoHo" and "East Village" (which would presumably make Buckhead its "Upper East Side"). The association is, on the face of it, a curious one since the two neighborhoods to which they refer – Virginia-Highland and Little Five Points, respectively – are heavily wooded residential areas, with limited zones of low-rise commercial development. Technically speaking, Little Five Points is not so much a neighborhood (it does not appear on the city's "official" list) as a district of the imagination situated between the Edwardian mansions of Inman Park (Atlanta's first planned suburb) and the later Craftsman-style bungalows of Candler Park. The first commercial district outside of downtown (hence the name, modeled after downtown's Five Points business district), Little Five Points thrived during the first four decades of this century, but declined as the homes in the surrounding neighborhoods were subdivided into rooming houses for Atlanta's white poor and working classes. Virginia-Highland underwent a similar class transformation in the early 1960s. Like their New York referents, both Virginia-Highland and Little Five Points have undergone considerable gentrification over the last two decades.

Virginia-Highland's distant claim to SoHo-ness arises from the large concentration of art galleries, trendy clothing boutiques, New Age bookstores, hair salons, bars, restaurants, and coffee houses that line its main drag, North Highland Avenue. The coffee houses are a recent development, however, and a good number are outlets of national chains like Starbuck's and Caribou Coffee. Little Five Points' resemblance to New York's East Village is a little more substantive. While it lacks a Tompkins Square Park, the small pedestrian plaza near the intersection of Moreland and Euclid Avenues is the epicenter of a diverse array of divey bars, used clothing stores, piercing parlors, and a lively street scene featuring Rastas, skinheads, homeless persons, and slumming suburban teenagers. Like its metaphorical New York counterpart, Little Five Points is currently undergoing an upscaling of its adjacent residential neighborhoods and a smothering of its more radical, nonconformist edges.

Virginia-Highland and Little Five Points constitute the core areas of Intown, a patchwork belt of gentrified residential neighborhoods on the east side of the city that stretch southward from I-85 to just beyond I-20. While neither as blindingly white nor as ostentatiously wealthy as Buckhead, the census tracts that comprise the Intown neighborhoods have both very limited minority populations and median incomes nearly twice that of the remainder of the city. As indicated above, they differ from Buckhead more in lifestyle quotient than in race and class. As with many other such pecuniary definitions of space, it is subject to variable definition. At first, the term was limited to Inman Park and Virginia-Highland. By the early 1980s, the *Atlanta Constitution* had expanded the extent of Intown to include most of the residential neighborhoods east of the central business district and the Downtown Connector, including such poor, mostly African-American neighborhoods as the Old Fourth Ward, Reynoldstown, Edgewood, Kirkwood, and East Lake, as well as such established white middle-class areas as Morningside/Lenox Park and Druid Hills, the latter of *Driving Miss Daisy* fame. More than a decade later, the majority black communities between Intown and downtown have yet to experience much in the way of "revitalization," although gentrification has spread southward across the Georgia Railroad tracks and I-20 to the former white working-class neighborhoods of Cabbagetown and Grant Park.

Cabbagetown originated as a mill village outside the then city limits of Atlanta in the 1880s. Located just to the east of Oakland Cemetery, the city's first burial ground, the site was initially used for a foundry and rolling mill during and after the Civil War. Now a city and nationally-designated historic district, Cabbagetown consists of the nine-building complex that housed the Fulton Bag and Cotton Mill and eighteen blocks of narrow "shotgun" houses and cottages for the mill's Appalachian workforce. The mill closed in the early 1970s, putting most of Cabbagetown's residents out of work. The neighborhood's close proximity to downtown, and historic housing stock, made it ripe for revitalization. By 1995, roughly 40 percent of the village was inhabited by upwardly mobile urban gentry. The mill complex itself has long been eyed for "adaptive reuse" as housing. In 1994, one of the city's major developers unveiled plans to convert the mill into hundreds of units of loft housing, along with associated retail and studio space. At the time of writing, however, the redevelopment of this little self-contained "mini-SoHo" has been stymied by the unwillingness of local bankers to finance the project.

In contrast to Cabbagetown, and much like Inman Park and Candler Park, Grant Park originated as an area of middle-class homes. In 1883, one of the city's early land barons, Colonel Lemuel P. Grant, donated eighty-eight acres of his holdings for a public park, the city's first, southeast of downtown. Forty-four additional acres were purchased by the city in 1890, and extensive residential development of the surrounding area began soon after. Unlike other public spaces in Jim Crow Atlanta, the green fields of Grant Park were never made off-limits to the city's African-American population.[125] In the 1920s and 1930s, the neighborhood's original white middle-class population gave way to a working-class one. After World War II, Grant Park experienced a good deal of white flight and the neighborhood acquired a significant African-American population. In the 1960s, the southern reaches of the neighborhood, between the park and the federal penitentiary, became one of the centers of the city's small but emerging Hispanic population. Drawn by the area's inexpensive stock of historic homes, the white middle class returned to Grant Park in the late 1970s and early 1980s, but in contrast to the communities north of I-20, it remains a racially and ethnically mixed neighborhood.

Beginning in the mid 1980s, new frontiers of gentrification also appeared on the westside, in the disused factory and warehouse lofts of Castleberry Hill southwest of the CBD and along the Marietta Street industrial corridor.[126] However, gentrification has yet to come to the interstitial area west of Intown and east of downtown known as the Old Fourth Ward. The southern half of the Old Fourth Ward is dominated by Sweet Auburn Avenue and the Martin Luther King, Jr Historic District. Despite the historic importance and symbolic centrality of these two areas in Atlanta's mythology, neither experienced much in the way of redevelopment during the 1970s and 1980s. This lack of attention changed after Atlanta was selected to host the 1996 Olympic Games. However, plans for enhancing the King Center and its surrounding neighborhood have been the source of great conflict rather than broad consensus, and reveal some of the essential contradictions both in Atlanta's image and in the processes of urban redevelopment more generally.

I HAVE A DREAM-LAND

Only a few months after King's assassination, his widow Coretta Scott King founded the Martin Luther King Jr Center for Non-Violent Social Change, Inc. to serve as a living legacy by carrying on his work. In 1971, King's body was reinterred in a crypt in the grounds of the King Center, located next to the Ebenezer Baptist Church where he and his father had preached (and where his mother a few years later was murdered by a deranged psychopath). Over the next ten years, a memorial plaza, fountain, and the Freedom Hall administrative/archive/exhibit space were added to the complex. Between 1974 and 1976, much of the grave site and the surrounding neighborhood were added to the National Register of Historic Places and placed within two of the city's first historic preservation zones: the Martin Luther King, Jr and Sweet Auburn Historic Districts. In 1976, Coretta Scott King successfully lobbied on behalf of the city for federal funds to construct a Martin Luther King, Jr Community Center across the street from Ebenezer Baptist Church. The following year, the MLK Historic District was designated a National Historic Landmark, and in 1980 became a federally protected Preservation District.[127] In 1991, the King Center invited the National Park Service to set up interpretive displays about King's life in Freedom Hall and to conduct tours of the birth home. Attracting more than three million visitors annually, the MLK Historic Site is one of the most popular locales within the National Park Service system.

Despite its symbolic centrality and popularity, the King Historic Site has been the center of great multi-sided conflict between the King family, the city, and neighborhood businesses and residents. After more than two decades of African-American mayors (including seven years by former King lieutenant Andrew Young) and various and sundry preservation ordinances, neither city hall nor the downtown business community has done much to encourage the revitalization of Sweet Auburn. Prior to 1995, new investment and construction were limited to the grounds of the King Center itself and the western end of Auburn Avenue, where the African-American Panoramic Experience Museum (APEX) and Auburn Avenue Research Library are located. At the local level, the efforts of the Sweet Auburn Improvement Association were undermined by internecine feuding amongst its members. Meanwhile, most of the efforts of the King Center have been directed outside the community in which it is located, much to the dismay of its neighbors.

Simmering discontent and discord between and among the National Park Service, the city, the Sweet Auburn community, and the King Center boiled over into outright war during the winter of 1994–95. The flash point of disagreement was provided by Park Service plans to build a new visitors' center to accommodate the expected increased hordes of visitors in the summer of 1996. When it was revealed that plans for the visitors' center included a small museum on King's life, and it was to be located on the site of the city-owned MLK Community Center, the conflict quickly evolved into battle over who, literally, *owned* King's legacy and, more specifically, the ability to interpret it and represent it to the public.

The Park Service's visitors' center is part of an $11.8-million enhancement of the King Historic Site that includes more green space and parking, as well as a new sanctuary for Ebenezer Baptist Church to be built after 1996.[128] Designed by the same firm responsible for the Holocaust Museum in Washington DC, the visitors' center will have exhibits on both the history of the Sweet Auburn neighborhood and King's life. The latter will feature six circular displays, with the shape of the circles increasingly breaking open, "in keeping with the way King exploded racial and social shackles."[129] The displays will be divided by a simulated two-lane highway – Freedom's Road – that commemorates the multitude of protest marches King organized and led. The plan would also demolish a number of vacant factory buildings and warehouses, two blocks to the north of the center which had been a locus for drugs and prostitution.

The NPS plan was vigorously opposed by the King family, which had its own plans for a hi-tech "edutainment" civil rights theme park to be located on the Community Center site. The motive force behind this vision of a Disneylike interactive venue was King's youngest son, Dexter. A Morehouse graduate and former music producer, Dexter King assumed effective control of the King estate in 1993 and quickly embarked on an aggressive enforcement of the copyright protection of his father's intellectual property, including his speeches and images. In summer 1994, Dexter King unveiled his plans for the $100-million, for-profit, virtual-reality "King Dream" facility, modeled on the Universal/MGM Studios venue at

Disney World. Through the use of holography and other virtual-reality technologies, visitors would be able to encounter the Ku Klux Klan, fire hoses, and police dogs, as well as enjoy a "Southern-style" eatery and gift shop. The proceeds from the venue would go to enhancing the activities of the King Center.[130]

The King family was upset not only by the denial of their desired piece of real estate, which the city had conveyed over to the Park Service, but what they saw as the latter's "usurpation" of their ownership of Martin Luther King's legacy.[131] The late summer and fall of 1994 was marked by an increasingly hostile exchange of letters and legal documents that culminated in the King family banning the Park Service from conducting tours of the tomb and birth home in December. The Park Service responded by suspending its annual half-million-dollar operating subsidy for the center. Following the banishment, the King family intensified its vitriolic assault on the Park Service, accusing it of plotting to take over the King Center, and vilifying it in the strongest terms possible. When *Atlanta Constitution* editorial page editor Cynthia Tucker accused the King family of undermining Martin Luther King's legacy through the shameless pursuit of profit, the Rev. Bernice King labeled her a tool of "Satan himself."[132] A series of scathing editorials and cartoons followed, lambasting the King family as greedy hypocritical profiteers who were sullying rather than honoring King's legacy. Since King was now a national treasure, the newspaper argued, he and his works no longer belonged to the King family, but to the nation as a whole.[133]

Even after vowing that profits from the theme park would be used to endow a fund to build housing for the homeless and other community redevelopment projects, the King family found they had few allies. The city, neighborhood businesses and residents, even Ebenezer Church, all favored the Park Service plan. The conflict got uglier during the week surrounding the national holiday celebrating King's birth. The King Center took out a series of newspaper ads accusing the media of distorting the position of the King family and aiding and abetting the dark designs of the NPS, which, it argued among other things, was unqualified to interpret "people's history."[134] The *Constitution* responded with an exposé of the Center's finances, which revealed a pattern of disorganization and financial improprieties, as well as raising serious questions about the integrity of Dexter King and his closest advisors.[135]

The call and response of accusations and recriminations continued into the spring, before a series of grueling negotiations mediated by US Congressman John Lewis resulted in a rapprochement between the King Center and the National Park Service. In a face-saving gesture to the King family, public details of the reconciliation agreement were sketchy. With contributions drying up, lacking allies and, most importantly, financing for the theme park, the King Center agreed to allow the Park Service to return and abandoned its opposition to the visitors' center, in return for the restoration of the modest half-million-dollar annual operating subsidy. In the final analysis, the only thing the King Center ended up with was a diminished reputation, at a time when the movement to roll back civil rights was gaining momentum across the nation.

The King Center controversy highlights a good deal about how the process of mythologization works and how the central social conflicts these days are being played out over issues of image and representation. As the visitors' center is far from being completed at the time of writing, it is impossible to adequately assess the qualities of the federally sponsored interpretation of King's life. Yet, the King family raised quite valid questions about the ability of the Park Service (or, rather, its design firm) to render an interpretation of King's life and legacy. One wonders, for example, about the degree to which the "radicalism" of King's final years will be addressed, or how the issue of governmental surveillance will be dealt with, or whether questions will be raised about possible government involvement in his assassination. It is highly unlikely that the National Park Service will wish to deal with any of these issues, especially the last.

Of course, there is no guarantee that a virtual reality edutainment theme park envisioned by a son who has previously displayed little interest in pursuing his father's commitment to realizing equality for all Americans would represent "people's history" any better either. Indeed, one wonders if the message might get lost in the medium somewhere amidst all the hi-tech conjuring tricks. Many of the project's critics argued that this form of commodified spectacularization by itself subverts King's legacy. However, it might just as well be argued that with the post-Second Reconstruction urban renewal of our national collective memory, a close encounter with a holographic lynch mob or a virtual snarling doberman is just what is necessary to penetrate the callused brainbox of even the most disaffected vidiot. However, questions of the form and substance of interpretation were noticeably lacking in the discourse of the local and national media, both of whom preferred to concentrate on what they saw as the King family's efforts to "cash in" on MLK. As relatives of the sanctified one, the family were held to a higher standard of behavior than lesser mortals. No one in the media, for example, had raised a peep about the hypocrisy of Olympic organizers (including former King lieutenant Andrew Young) shamelessly bandying about the figure of King while simultaneously holding to the line that they had no moral or legal obligations to use the Games to improve the living conditions of the city's poor.[136] Perversely, it was only when the family sought to play by the rules of the almighty marketplace in which we all must live that it was castigated as being motivated by baser motives of profit.

CAN'T STOP THE FREAKNIK

The King Center controversy focused on the question, to whom does control over the representation/interpretation of Martin Luther King, Jr belong? In a similar vein, the matter of Black College Spring Break, or Freaknik as it is more popularly known, raised the question of to whom the city of Atlanta belonged. Myths serve not only as promotional notions, but as legitimations, authorizations, and claims to space. If Atlanta was indeed a, or the, Black Mecca, it followed that African-Americans around the United States, and not just in Atlanta, enjoyed particular claims upon the city, claims that became manifested in a pilgrimage of a very specific sort. In a matter of a few short years, Freaknik grew dramatically in size and emerged as the flashpoint of a series of racially charged conflicts between and among the city's African-American political establishment, the media, and an urban population divided not only by race, but by class, generation, and lifestyle. The ongoing battle over Freaknik not only illuminates how mythologies are inscribed in the landscape, but highlights the contested nature of "public" space in contemporary urban society.

Freaknik began innocuously enough in 1983, when a group of several dozen Atlanta University students from the Washington DC area hosted a dance party/picnic instead of returning home for spring break. They called the event "Freaknik," a reference to a popular song of the 1970s, "The Return of the Freak."[137] True to the late adolescent rites of spring, a freak, in the argot of this particular subculture, referred to someone zealously interested in sex. Over the next decade, the event gradually grew in size, moving from the Atlanta University campus to a number of the city's parks, and eventually to its streets, sidewalks, expressways, and shopping malls. Thanks to word of mouth and mention in the television sitcom "A Different World," by the early 1990s Freaknik had evolved into a full-fledged "Black College Spring Break" involving tens of thousands of students from historically black colleges across the nation. Another factor contributing to the surge of Freaknikers was the banishment of the annual black "Greek Week" celebrations from Virginia Beach, Virginia after 1989's celebrations had resulted in riotous violence between police and revelers.

At first glance, Atlanta was an unlikely destination for spring break celebrants, as it lacked the beaches and resort-like atmosphere of Virginia Beach or Daytona. However, as the third busiest convention city in the United States, Atlanta had worked hard at cultivating an image of itself as a place that welcomed visitors. Moreover, what Atlanta possessed, and what Freaknik reinforced, was the city's status as a historically significant place and center of contemporary opportunity for young African-Americans.

The event generated relatively little notice until 1993, when, during the last week of April, an estimated 100,000 students came to Atlanta, some 40,000 more than had been expected. Downtown and Midtown Atlanta, especially the area around Piedmont Park, turned into one massive street party as thousands of cars cruised and parked on the city's roads and expressways in a free-flowing bacchanale, with celebrants dancing, drinking, and exuberantly coupling in the streets. The crowds and resultant traffic jams paralyzed parts of the city over the weekend and caught both civic authorities and residents equally by surprise. City police threw up their hands at enforcement of traffic violations, although they exhibited a rather heavy-handed display of force towards the relatively peaceable crowds in Piedmont Park. The mostly white and middle-class residents of adjacent neighborhoods overwhelmed by Freaknikers, were outraged by their inability to get to or leave their homes and the conversion of their yards into open-air urinals and trash receptacles. The revelers, for the most part, were quite pleased, with many vowing to return, not only to party, but to live.

As a convention city, Atlanta is no stranger to focused gatherings of up to 100,000 people. However, these were for the most part white middle-class businessmen who did their drinking and pursuit of other pleasures within the regularized confines of the hospitality industry and legally sanctioned night trades. Unlike the highly programmed world of the Comdex computer show, or even the SuperBowl, Freaknik was a spontaneous, disorganized vernacular appropriation of the landscape by mostly middle-class African-American youth making good their claim on Atlanta. Participants and supporters, and initially even a segment of the white business community, saw the three days of partying as no different from the other events the city hosted, a mass gathering that provided a lucrative source of revenue to local businesses (estimated at somewhere between $12 and 15 million in 1993, and some $50 million in 1995). If the city could host the 1996 Olympics, proponents argued, they could certainly host Freaknik. Most residents of Midtown and other neighborhoods affected by the festivities vehemently disagreed, as did owners of businesses not patronized by the visitors. Critics who demanded that the city government take steps to prevent the chaos, confusion, and disruption were quickly branded as racists by Freaknik supporters. The city, for its part, argued for the need for greater organization of the festivities to minimize the inconvenience to residents of the Piedmont Park neighborhood. However, with no central or formal body organizing the event, there was really no one to organize with. Besides, the whole point of the festivities was the suspension of everyday rules of behavior: Freaknik was a Dionysian bacchanale like Mardi Gras, the ultimate block party, not a trade show.

Tensions and conflict worsened in 1994, when 200,000 black twentysomethings visited over a five-day period in late April. Only four months into his first term as mayor, Bill Campbell (a former city councilman and protégé of Maynard Jackson) was distracted by an infrastructure crisis, the slow state of preparations for the Olympics, and the threat of a police "sick-out" during the festivities, and had failed to prepare adequately for the event. In a belated effort at control, the city offered to co-sponsor Freaknik, but this had little effect on the revelers' behavior. Once again, police made little effort at enforcing traffic and intoxication laws and much of the central city was effectively paralyzed for the better part of the weekend. The crowds were considerably rowdier than the previous year, especially at night, when a number of shootings and other violent incidents were reported. Whites stuck in Freaknik traffic complained not only of inconvenience, but intimidation by revelers. After the festivities ended, enraged Midtown residents threatened to stage a similar party outside Mayor Campbell's Inman Park home. They recanted when threatened with the full force of the law, thus sparing the city the ugly spectacle of middle-aged white folk dancing naked in the street and being carted off to jail to the sounds of bad seventies disco and rock and roll. The local newspapers, however, dropped their pre-event guarded support for Freaknik and joined the chorus of criticism, openly wondering if the city was capable of handling an Olympic crowd of twice that size for more than three weeks.[138]

Chastened, the mayor agreed to crack down and take in the welcome mat for Freaknik '95. He was joined by city council president Marvin Arrington, who criticized Freaknik as "an ugly display of terroristic behavior." Despite the opposition of Atlanta's two leading African-American elected officials, other city council members and civil rights leaders took the side of the Freaknikers, castigating their critics as racists and profiling the mayor and Arrington as Uncle Toms pandering to the city's white minority. They argued, with great conviction, but little evidence, that if the Freaknikers were white, the city would welcome them with open arms.

It is highly unlikely that racism alone provided the impetus behind the opposition of Midtown residents and others to Freaknik – a couple of hundred thousand drunken college students celebrating the rites of spring and clotting major traffic arteries constitute the same kind of disruptive juggernaut regardless of the color of their skin. Moreover, many revelers – like tourists anywhere – exhibited little regard for the impact that their activities had on the local populace. Nonetheless, the proponents of Freaknik had a very valid point to make. It is undeniable that a large number of whites, both in Atlanta and in the United States as a whole, demonized black youth as a class and that the spectacle of thousands of young African-Americans partying in their streets filled them with a dread that no crowd of drunken white fratboys ever could. In the 1970s and 1980s, "crime" and "danger" had become euphemistic codewords for blackness and the racialization of space, i.e. "Underground Atlanta is a very dangerous place." These perceptions had been reinforced by the mini-riot that had taken place downtown in April 1992 following the acquittal of the Los Angeles police officers charged with the beating of black motorist Rodney King. For supporters of Freaknik, the opposition of their critics was not an isolated instance, but inseparable from the wider drama of institutionalized and pervasive racism.

The rhetorical war between supporters and opponents of Freaknik escalated dramatically during the winter of 1994–95. At first, Mayor Campbell vowed to close off the city to Freaknikers, despite the physical impossibility of doing so. Over time, this position softened to a promise that violations of the law, such as public drinking, lewdness, and parking on the expressways, would not be tolerated. A traffic plan was unveiled that blocked off the previously most affected neighborhoods to all but residential traffic and channeled cruising onto certain designated streets. Supporters of the event draped themselves in the mantle of the civil rights movement and claimed that the actions of the mayor were akin to the water cannon and police dogs employed by Birmingham police captain Bull Connor. The city's actions, they argued, were a suppression of the students' basic civil rights. Atlanta University student organizations attempted to emphasize the connection to the civil rights movement by trying to rename the event "Freedom Fest" and organizing a series of related events on campus. Administrators from the city's black universities supported the students, castigating the mayor for his confrontationalist attitude.

As the event neared in April 1995, tensions escalated to fever pitch. On the one side were the mostly white, upper-middle-class Midtown residents and downtown business interests who viewed the event like a coming plague of carnivorous locusts. On the other extreme were Atlanta's black college students, civil rights leaders (with whom the mayor had in the past enjoyed a tenuous accord), and a majority of the city council. In the middle, despised by both extremes, were Bill Campbell and his recently appointed police chief, Beverly Harvard (herself African-American), who kept to the line that Freaknikers were welcome as long as they abided by the law. The resultant deranged, circus-like atmosphere harked back to the surrealistic spectacular of the late 1970s Atlanta Child Murders. Local newspapers anticipated the worst, and right-wing radio shock jocks stoked the fire with outrageously racist remarks. They were not alone in their civic irresponsibility. As the event neared, one city council member went public with the accusation that she had proof (never produced) that city police planned to kill a number of revelers to "back up the mayor."[139] It seemed, at times, that certain persons actually desired to provoke bloodshed. The governor put a couple of thousand National Guardsmen on alert, and an elite state riot squad was assembled and put at the discretion of the Atlanta police department. Downtown businesses let their employees off early on

Thursday afternoon and untold thousands of people left town.

Fortunately, Freaknik '95 failed to live up to the apocalyptic hype, although it was far from peaceful. Virtually the entire Atlanta police force was deployed and checkpoints and barricades were set up at key intersections throughout the central city. The mayor's efforts at yanking back the welcome mat were partially success-ful. The estimated 100,000 Freaknikers who arrived were only half the previous year's crowd and the restrictive traffic plan succeeded in channeling cruising to a number of designated streets and out of most residential neighborhoods. Forced out of their cars, and away from Piedmont Park, revelers enjoyed a pedestrian festival that migrated from the Atlanta University Center campus to the streets around Underground Atlanta. Late Friday evening, as Underground attempted to close, the festive mood turned ugly as the crowd threw rocks and bottles at police and looted a number of stores, before dissipating without further incident. Small-scale looting took place the following night at a southside suburban mall, but the feared massively violent confrontation never materialized. By Sunday, most of the revel-ers were leaving town, bored and intensely displeased with what they saw as a lack of appreciation of their presence and their dollars. Yet, according to a survey, more than half vowed to return in 1996.[140]

The mayor was quick to claim victory over the forces of disorder. At a post-event press conference, he and the police chief boasted about the success of their traffic plan, then clucked like outraged parents about the pervasiveness of "lewd" behavior amongst the celebrants.[141] Freaknik was thus not only an inconvenience to the city, but a threat to its already precarious moral order. At the same time, a majority of the city council vowed to work with student groups to organize a big-ger Freedom Fest in 1996. Some months later, after tensions had cooled, Campbell named a 21-member task force to brainstorm ways of making Freaknik better organized and less disruptive. Headed by Spelman College president (and anthro-pologist) Johnetta Cole, the biracial group included other university officials, business leaders, and student groups.[142] At the time of writing, it is unclear whether this public–private task force will be successful in transforming a free-form celebration into a far more focused, and less controversial gathering, or whether the city and Freaknikers will abide by its recommendations.

Some sort of formalization of the festivities is very likely. With the Olympics set to begin less than three months later, a good deal of global media attention will already be focused on Atlanta. An overly repressive response from the city would greatly undermine its much-celebrated status as capital of the human rights move-ment, but the spectacle of bacchanalian excess is not the face the powers that be wish to put before the world, either. Instead, the creation of a sanctioned and spa-tially delimited event, perhaps focused more on civil rights themes than on

Dionysian revelry, would allow for more effective policing of unauthorized, and illegal, behavior. Security officials might well take advantage of Freaknik/Freedom Fest to tune up their extensive apparatus of surveillance and control, in much the same way that Olympic sports venues are being pre-tested by hosting a number of pre-Olympic athletic competitions. In any event, by the spring of 1996, it will be quite apparent to most Atlantans that the chaos, confusion, and disruption caused by the Olympics will exceed the levels produced by all the Freakniks in history.

If Freaknik raised the question of "to whom does Atlanta belong?" it did not provide an easy or mutually agreed answer. Rather, it underscored the contested ownership of urban space and the salience of race in shaping the struggle. The power of the event to polarize the city along racial lines was both amazing (from a "detached" social scientist's perspective) and troubling (from the point of view of a "liberal" white resident) to behold. To be white and voice a public criticism of Freaknik invariably led one to be called a racist by many African-Americans (although certainly not all African-Americans supported Freaknik, especially those whose neighborhoods were swamped with revelers), as if there were no possibility of any other rationale motivating the critique (the logic being that, whether they admit it or not, all whites are racists, and, by extension, that all black critics are "Uncle Toms"). Far more disturbing, however, was the way in which irresponsible, publicity-hungry public officials and an overly sensationalistic local media stoked the fires of unrest, as if to purposefully provoke a conflagration. While I do not mean to imply that either the former or the latter actively wished for a riot and bloodshed, such an outcome would certainly have the effect of legitimizing a future tightening of the nets of surveillance and control that would otherwise not meet with popular approval.

The ongoing conflict over Freaknik effectively dispels the notion that Atlanta is the "city too busy to hate" or, as Andrew Young and others like to contend, some sort of paragon of racial harmony. In many ways, the public furor over Freaknik is not so much about the event itself, but a manifestation of the racial and class divides that have deepened and widened over the last thirty years, not only within the city, but between the city and the rest of the metropolitan area – an altogether sorry state of affairs that both the region's business community and its political establishment have cravenly failed to acknowledge in their single-minded devotion to creating an appealing business climate. The specificities of these uneven developments form the subject of the next two chapters.

3

CITY OF HYPE, 1837–1975

Unique, brilliant Atlanta! Breaker of precedents in city building, with no mighty water courses or vast mineral treasures at her door to guarantee success; beautiful Atlanta, standing at the gateway to the New South with vatic fire in her eyes and the aureole of prophecy upon her brow and the spirit of dauntless optimism guiding an indomitable industry, and she has made a city which has defied urban adage and municipal proverb, a city which is Southern, but no longer sectional, Georgian, but national, too.

Dr Carter Helm Jones[1]

As noted in Chapter 1, Atlanta has its origins in the fortuitous coincidence between an irrepressible spirit of boosterism, the necessities of nineteenth-century railway construction, and the idiosyncrasies of topography. As such, it developed as an "accidental city" with what can generously be described as "a *laissez-faire* approach to planning."[2] As historian Tim Crimmins has noted, railroads formed the foundations of Atlanta's built environment.[3] The rail lines were built parallel to the main wagon roads of the earliest settlers, converging in a large triangular interchange a third of a mile to the west of the Zero Mile Post. In the late 1840s and early 1850s, competing owners platted out three separate street grids oriented to the tracks and wagon roads rather than to each other, an early indication of what was to be an enduring lack of coordination between private speculators. In a belated effort to order subsequent development, city officials framed the three contrasting plats within a master street grid oriented to the cardinal points in 1853. While this somewhat rationalized the shape of later real estate development, in the core the end result was not increased order, but a confusing mix of odd-shaped blocks and even odder intersections divided in half by an east–west grade-level rail corridor – known variously as "the Sewer of Smoke," or, simply, "the gulch."

While the ravages of the Civil War destroyed roughly 3,000 of the city's buildings, Atlanta's confused street pattern remained largely intact. With the exception of some significant chunks obliterated by highway construction and urban renewal in the 1960s, the four juxtaposed street grids remain a source of disorientation for pedestrian and driver alike. Much of what has passed for planning downtown over the last century and a half has dealt with how to minimize friction and maximize flow (as well as profit) within the constraints of this morphological legacy.

In the present day, city boosters like to waggishly refer to Sherman's destruction of the city in the fall of 1864 as Atlanta's first instance of urban renewal. The comparison is highly misleading. Unlike the 1960s, the post-Civil War period did not see land taken away from one set of users and conveyed to another, at a publically subsidized cost, for a completely different use. Despite the important role played by Northern money in the reconstruction of the Atlantan economy, real estate speculation remained, with few exceptions, the exclusive province of a handful of local industrialists and property men until the 1920s.[4] Both before and after the Civil War, much of the land around the growing settlement was acquired by a handful of individuals associated in one capacity or another with the different railroads. Richard Peters, the first superintendent of the Georgia Railroad, bought 405 acres just to the north of the city limits in the mid 1850s.[5] Together with former Georgia Railroad conductor George Adair, Peters became one of Atlanta's most powerful land barons during the Reconstruction period. Soon after the Civil War, Adair founded a real estate brokerage firm that dominated the real estate market into the twentieth century and allowed him "to some extent, to direct . . . trading activities."[6] In the late 1860s, Peters and Adair acquired the Atlanta Street Railway Company, and, in 1871, opened the city's first horse-car line to the suburb of West End, where Adair had extensive property holdings. In the following year, the street railway was extended northward to Peters's large parcel, some of which had been brought within municipal boundaries.[7] In the mid 1880s, Peters and Adair entered into an unsuccessful effort with former carpetbagger Hannibal Kimball to develop part of this area as the subdivision of Peters Park. An archetypical Victorian garden suburb with curvilinear streets and lavishly landscaped grounds, Peters Park failed to stimulate much interest at the time from the city's elite, who preferred either to retain their Peachtree Street mansions, or to move to rival streetcar magnate/developer Joel Hurt's streetcar suburb of Inman Park.[8] However, much of the land was subdivided and developed in a less cohesive fashion after the mid 1890s.[9]

Peters and Adair were not the only ex-railroad men to get involved in real estate speculation and other kinds of economic enterprise. Maine native Lemuel P. Grant came to Atlanta as chief engineer of the Atlanta and West Point Railroad in the early 1850s and remained to supervise the construction of its Civil War fortifications, all the while acquiring large tracts of land on the city's southeast side and, together with George Adair in West End.[10] All three were active in the city's nascent banking industry, as well. Indeed, most of the city's elite had rather diversified financial interests, ranging from finance, guano, and cotton, in the case of Hugh T. Inman, to merchandise in the cases of John Ryan and Edward Marsh. Real estate, however, was a key component of all of their portfolios. As one account of Atlanta's wealthiest men in the 1880s noted, "almost every one on the list has been a heavy investor in Atlanta dirt – and a steady holder . . ."[11]

Between 1865 and 1890, a compact, low-rise central district of residences, factories, warehouses, and stores was developed around the Union Depot, as the consolidation of railway lines solidified the city's position as "the Gate City of the South." The commercial zone was, in turn, surrounded by residential neighborhoods which clearly mapped out a social hierarchy in space. The city's growing white middle class occupied the ridge neighborhoods to the north and south of the railway depot and the new State Capitol. Atlanta's six black colleges and universities also occupied high ground to the east and west, although outside of the city's original limits. The vast majority of Atlanta's population – the black and white poor – resided in creek bottoms, along the railroad tracks, and other undesirable low-lying areas, like Beaver's Slide, Tanyard Branch, and Buttermilk Bottom. As the city's population grew more than fivefold between 1865 and 1890, and doubled again in each of the three subsequent decades, these neighborhoods became extremely overcrowded. Bereft of even the most basic municipal services, the areas presented substandard living conditions on a par with the worst neighborhoods of New York and Chicago.[12]

As the city's topography was quite hilly, Atlanta's rich and poor often lived in close proximity to one another. Towards the end of the nineteenth century, however, African-Americans were increasingly segregated in "close-in" neighborhoods to east and west, as well as the "far" south of the urban core, while thanks to an extensive network of streetcars, white residential areas were expanding in all directions. This settlement pattern was further reinforced in the 1920s by low-density (and race-based) zoning and the widespread use of the automobile. Atlanta, in this sense, may be said to have been born suburbanized. In the 1880s, the establishment of a horse-car system stimulated the suburbanization of the formerly rural village of West End, located some two miles to the southwest of the Union Depot. In 1885, Lemuel P. Grant donated 140 acres in southeast Atlanta for a landscaped park that would serve as a catalyst for the development of single family homes. Both the green space and the surrounding neighborhood were referred to as Grant Park. In 1887, some of the northside's major property owners, including Richard Peters and George Adair, established the Piedmont Driving Club and exposition grounds for the similar purpose of using a park to catalyze residential development. Although this occurred, the park itself remained rather undeveloped until after 1910, when the crumbling exposition buildings were torn down and the grounds relandscaped in partial accordance with a master plan drawn up by Olmsted Brothers.[13] Between 1900 and 1920, the residential neighborhoods to the south, west, and north of the park were home to nearly three-quarters of Atlanta's most elite families.[14]

The evolution of suburban areas between the 1890s and 1920s was made possible by the parallel development of the Five Points business district just to the north of the railroad tracks. The area took its name from the intersection of the city's five most important streets – Whitehall, Peachtree, Marietta, Edgewood, and Decatur – which occurred at the cusp of the three original grids. As a crossroads of traffic, as well as the location of the city's main water source until the late 1880s, Five Points was the city's principal public gathering place. In 1892, insurance and streetcar magnate Joel Hurt built the city's first skyscraper one block east of the intersection and so pioneered the transformation of the area into a high-rise office district. At the same time, in a syndicate with Coca-Cola founder Asa Candler and financier/industrialist Samuel Inman, he undertook construction of the streetcar suburb of Inman Park and commissioned Frederick Law Olmsted to design the green spaces of the neighborhood of Druid Hills (later to be celebrated in the film *Driving Miss Daisy*).

Celebrated by historians as Atlanta's first modern developer, what differentiated Hurt from contemporaries like George Adair and Richard Peters was his partnership with outside capital, his employment of nationally known architects, like Daniel Burnham and Frederick Law Olmsted, and his linked development of urban office space and suburban residences.[15] Hurt was joined in his speculative urban and suburban ventures by the handful of other local industrialists and propertymen who dominated the local economy and monopolized Atlanta real estate, including Asa Candler, who ploughed some of his considerable profits realized from the purchase and sale of the Coca-Cola Corporation into the construction of downtown office buildings and suburban single family homes. When financial problems stymied Hurt's efforts to develop Druid Hills, control of the project passed to his partner, Samuel Inman.

The growth of the Five Points business district after the turn of the century was fueled by Atlanta's increasing importance as a banking and insurance center for the Southeast, although these activities did not immediately supplant its existing role as a node of trade and distribution for the regional cotton-based economy. Conventions also became a significant source of income in the early twentieth century and numerous hotels were constructed in the area. Five Points was also the main transfer point in the city's streetcar system, and around the office core there developed a high-intensity zone of shops and theaters. As early as 1929, however, old-time residents were already complaining that office development and the intensive use of automobiles had made Five Points "no longer a place for people to congregate," but to "rush away from."[16] Major satellite commercial areas developed at Little Five Points in Inman Park and along Tenth Street near Piedmont Park.

During the boom years of the 1920s, the central area expanded as local investors in partnership with national real estate syndicates bankrolled the development of an Upper Peachtree Shopping District in what had been until then an elite residential zone just north of the Five Points area.[17] Further north of the enlarged Central Business District was the area known as Uptown, which featured clusters of hotels, theaters, and luxury apartment buildings strung out along the Peachtree Street ridge south and west of Piedmont Park, amidst a heavy concentration of automobile dealerships, neighborhood retailers, and middle-class homes. In response to the commercialization of Uptown, Atlanta's upper and middle classes moved northward up Peachtree Street towards the elite enclave of Buckhead and eastward to Druid Hills. Between 1900 and 1936, developers built no fewer than thirty-six "garden-type" subdivisions in the hills around Atlanta. All but eight of these suburbs were located north of the city.[18]

All thirty-six garden suburbs were for whites only, yet even within the constraints of the Jim Crow system changes were also occurring in black residential patterns. In 1920, African-American entrepreneur Heman Perry purchased 300 acres on the city's near westside, to build housing for Atlanta's emerging black middle classes. African-Americans had lived on the westside since right after the Civil War, but many of the neighborhoods, such as Beaver's Slide and White's Alley, were exceedingly impoverished and lacked even the basics of municipal services.[19] In the first decade of the twentieth century, however, the area just to the north of Atlanta University emerged as an enclave for African-American Atlanta's "Talented Tenth."[20] Chief among these residents was Alonzo Herndon, founder of the Atlanta Life Insurance Company, and the paramount black entrepreneur in the city. Herndon's grand white-columned mansion still crowns a hill overlooking the downtown, although the surrounding neighborhood has decayed to a great extent.

Whereas the Northeast Lot, as it was known, was intended for the black elite, Perry's vision for the area to the north was for African-Americans of much more modest means. The founder of Standard Life Insurance Company, Perry controlled a small but diversified financial empire of thirteen affiliated businesses, which included a bank, a realty firm, and a construction company. Through Standard Life, Perry granted the mortgage loans that white-owned banks refused to issue to blacks, thus allowing them to buy homes sold by his realty company and built by his construction firm. Standard Life's deposits also formed the capital for

Perry's bank, the still-extant Citizen's Trust Company.[21] Although Perry's highly leveraged financial empire collapsed after 1925, the westside continued to be a residential mecca for blacks through the 1930s. To the east of the Atlanta University area, Hunter Street emerged as a major African-American commercial district that competed with the more established Sweet Auburn Avenue in the Old Fourth Ward to the east of downtown.

RACE, TRAFFIC, AND PLANNING

Aside from the availability of investment capital, there was little to limit the activities of Atlanta's white entrepreneurs in the early twentieth century, save the street grid and the railroad gulch that divided the northern and southern parts of town. The built environment was the product of pure unrestrained speculation: zoning and urban design restrictions were non-existent, and there was not a single public open space within the urban core.[22] In what is widely regarded as the first "plan" for central Atlanta, local architect Haralson Bleckley proposed in 1909 to roof the "sewer of smoke" with a City Beautiful plaza and office tower that would link the new Terminal Station with the State Capitol. While Bleckley's plan captured the public's imagination, like many of the schemes that were to follow in the ensuing decades it failed to influence the direction of private capital investment, which was moving inexorably north up Peachtree, away from the railway tracks and the nineteenth-century city that lay to the south.

Although Bleckley's plan was officially rejected by the state road commission in 1917, increased traffic congestion brought on by the spread of automobiles led the city, with the hearty encouragement of major property owners who dominated the new city planning commission, to construct a series of viaducts over the gulch in the 1920s. Together with two earlier bridges over the tracks (built in 1892 and 1906), these structures effectively buried the commercial heart of nineteenth-century Atlanta, while leaving the remainder of the east–west railway corridor largely intact. By displacing large numbers of small shops and businesses, the viaducts created a subterranean dead zone that emphasized rather than ameliorated the divide between the northern and southern halves of the city.[23]

While automobiles posed a significant problem, the primary driving force behind Atlanta's first efforts at municipal planning, as in other Southern cities, came from the desire to control African-American spatial mobility.[24] The first segregation ordinance designating city blocks by race was passed by the city council in 1913. After the US Supreme Court subsequently ruled that such measures were unconstitutional, the city adopted a comprehensive zoning plan in which racial designations were embedded within property usage classifications, with white and "colored" residential districts separated by industrial and commercial buffer zones. Although the zoning ordinance was similarly struck down by the US Supreme Court in 1924, a system of de facto race-based zoning remained in use through the 1960s.[25] While there were a number of poor white neighborhoods close-in to downtown, such as Tech Flats and Lighting near the Georgia Institute of Technology and the mill village of Cabbagetown on the eastside, African-American neighborhoods predominated to the west, south, and east of downtown and were, in turn, circumscribed by a railroad/industrial cordon and an outer ring of white working- and middle-class areas. For the most part overcrowded and under-served, many of the close-in neighborhoods were defined as "blighted" in the 1930s and 1940s and slated for large-scale urban renewal after 1950.

In May 1917, a blaze that began in an old warehouse swept through the densely packed hovels of the Old Fourth Ward and, spurred by a southerly wind, quickly spread to the white middle-class neighborhoods to the north. By the time the conflagration had been checked by the following morning – individual homes and gas lines continued to burn for a week – approximately 2,000 homes on 300 acres in the northeast quadrant of the city had burned to the ground. More than 10,000 persons, most of them African-American, were left homeless by what was known as the "big fire."[26] The two-mile swath of destruction also provided the race-conscious municipal government with an opportunity to create an enhanced buffer zone between black and white residential areas. Shortly after the fire, city officials unveiled plans to build a wide parkway through the center of the devastated region. The Grand Boulevard was intended to serve as a bulwark against the eastward expansion of African-American neighborhoods.[27] Although the roadway was never built, city officials devised further measures to limit black residential expansion on the eastside, and, though the devastated neighborhoods were rebuilt, the center of gravity of black settlement in the city passed to the westside in the 1920s.

From its inception, the urban planning apparatus was quite clearly a tool of the larger white business interests. Fifteen of the twenty-four appointees to the first city planning commission, for example, were members of the Chamber of Commerce. That body, however, was composed of both small businessmen and representatives of larger concerns and was soon replaced by a mayorally appointed board of six "publically minded citizens," all of whom were connected in one way or another with major real estate development, construction, transportation, and banking firms.[28] Although charged with more comprehensive responsibilities, such as housing and urban design, the new commission limited its activities to viaduct construction, parking regulation, and zoning ordinances which, aside from reinforcing segregation, encouraged the development of detached single family homes outside the urban core.

Private companies engaged in their own planning studies also. When its electric street-railway network was threatened by the emergence of "jitney-buses" in the early 1920s, the Georgia Power Company – which had just recently bought out Joel Hurt to consolidate all street railways under its ownership – commissioned a study that examined the costs and consequences of the growing competition between streetcars and jitney-buses. The Beeler Report, as it was known, argued forcefully for the superiority of the street-railway and served as the justification for a municipal ordinance prohibiting jitneys within city limits. Among its other recommendations was a plan for a subterranean people-mover under the streets of downtown, not unlike the one that would be built four decades later in the transportation mall at Hartsfield International Airport.[29] The Georgia Power Company exhibited little interest in Beeler's idea for moving sidewalks; it was too busy enjoying the total monopoly it received over mass transit in the city of Atlanta as a result of the ordinance.[30] Shortly thereafter, Georgia Power initiated its own jitney service to the growing fringe of suburban communities outside of the city. Within slightly more than a decade, however, even mighty Georgia Power was unable to stem the competition from privately owned automobiles.

The collapse of the local and national economy after 1929 pushed major property owners and businesses into a closer alliance with the state, as they attempted to stabilize their sizeable and precarious investment in the Central Business District through lobbying for federally subsidized slum clearance of adjacent blighted neighborhoods. Thanks largely to the efforts of businessman Charles Palmer's connections to the Roosevelt administration, Atlanta received two of the earliest federal public housing projects in the country to replace two of the more dilapidated residential areas on the near westside of town.[31] The first of these, Techwood Homes (named for the Georgia Tech campus just to the north) was for low-income whites, while University Homes (near Atlanta University) was for African-Americans. The ward-based city government – non-activist by inclination, virtually bankrupt, and beset by corruption – played a very minor role in these efforts, allowing private interests to set the municipal agenda even when it came to the exercise of eminent domain.[32] Slum clearance accentuated a divide between different segments of the city's ruling class, as a number of old and distinguished families owned a substantial amount of property in the designated areas. Nonetheless, as with viaduct construction, Palmer and his allies were able to assert the collective interests of large downtown property owners and businesses over more fragmented opposition.[33]

Control over slum clearance was vested in the city's first quasi-public entity, the Atlanta Housing Authority, which enjoyed the status of being the city's primary redevelopment agency until the 1960s. As with the city planning commission, the board of the Atlanta Housing Authority was composed largely of members of what Blaine Brownell has called "the civic-commercial elite."[34] This latter group consisted of the leaders of the utilities (Atlanta Gas Light and Georgia Power), the major banks (Trust Company of Georgia, Citizens & Southern, First National, and National Bank of Georgia), the newspapers (the then separately owned *Journal* and *Constitution*), the major department stores (Rich's and Davison's), real estate and construction firms, and the city's best-known enterprise, the Coca-Cola Corporation. For the next thirty years, leaders of these corporations essentially "ran the city as a benevolent oligarchy with a practically telepathic link to city hall."[35]

There was, however, nothing paranormal in the relationship between city government and the downtown establishment. Without a base in the city's decaying ward-based patronage system, reformist mayor William Hartsfield was particularly dependent on the goodwill and financial largesse of the major downtown business interests after his election in 1937. Hartsfield relied heavily on the advice of business leaders, especially Coca-Cola president Robert Woodruff, to set city policy throughout his 24-year tenure as mayor. While there was considerable competition between different segments of the elite, especially between the two newspapers and Rich's and Davison's (which anchored the Whitehall-Broad and Upper Peachtree Shopping Districts, respectively), it was constrained by their common interests in keeping the center central in what was already by then a significantly suburbanized landscape. With its close relationship between city hall and the business elite, Atlanta presents an early instance of the public–private partnership that came to dominate urban redevelopment in the latter half of the twentieth century.[36]

Efforts at traffic control and slum clearance emphasized the diverging interests of large and small downtown businesses. To further their interests outside the Chamber of Commerce, major downtown property owners established the Central Atlanta Improvement Association (CAIA) in 1941 (later known as the Central Atlanta Association [CAA], and after 1966, as Central Atlanta Progress [CAP]). While similar associations arose in virtually every major US city in the ensuing decades, the CAIA was one of the nation's first. Its principal function was to provide an independent body that could plan for the future and leverage public subsidies for private investment. In 1944, the CAIA, along with the Georgia Department of Transportation, commissioned the Lochner Company of Chicago to prepare a comprehensive traffic study and plan for highway construction to jump-start postwar economic development. Preceeding the Federal Highway Act by a decade, Lochner's 1946 report envisioned Atlanta as the central city in an interstate highway system linking the major cities of the Southeast. The report also called for rationalizing the often quirky street grid and regulating parking to facilitate the flow of traffic into and out of the Central Business District (CBD).[37]

The initial phase of road construction, a connector from the northern suburbs to the outskirts of the CBD, was financed by $60 million in city and county bonds in the late 1940s and early 1950s. After 1956, 90 percent of the costs for an even more expansive highway system through and around the CBD itself were paid for with federal highway funds. Atlanta's new expressways allowed the city to maintain its centrality in long-distance surface transportation after the demise of the railroads, even as it sowed the seeds of future decentralization by opening up the rural hinterland for more extensive suburban expansion. At the same time, the city-owned airport located nine miles to the south of the CBD in the town of Hapeville had already become a major hub for the nation's growing air traffic. Mayor Hartsfield's early recognition of the significance of, and his support for, aviation provided the foundation for a good deal of Atlanta's subsequent economic development.

The Lochner Plan proved as much an exercise in social as traffic engineering, and marked an end to the brief period of business support for low-income housing close-in to downtown. Between 1936 and 1942, nine federally funded housing projects had been constructed on the immediate periphery of the CBD. Most of these housed African-American residents. After the war, a gentlemen's agreement between the city, the Atlanta Housing Authority, and the Central Atlanta Improvement Association ensured that virtually all new public housing was built miles away from the center in the south and west.[38] In the minds of the CAIA, the greatest threat to the center was posed not by automobilized suburbanization – which, they thought, could be managed by annexation and ensuring easy vehicular access to downtown – but by the dangers of adjacent blighted residential neighborhoods. Described as breeding grounds for crime and a multitude of other social evils (not the least of which was their negative effect on nearby property values), these neighborhoods were, for the most part, inhabited by African-Americans. The "scientific" language of national planning discourse allowed the racialized aspects of previous land use to be rearticulated in a neutral guise. There is abundant evidence to indicate that highway construction was explicitly intended by CAA and the city as a means of reinforcing existing patterns of racial segregation and limiting African-American spatial mobility.[39]

Anticipating what was to become a familiar pattern in most US cities, what was initially called the Central Expressway, now known as the I-75/85 Downtown Connector, was directed around the northern and eastern edge of the CBD, burning a *cordon sanitaire* between it and the black residential neighborhoods and public housing projects to the east. In so doing, it brutally bisected Sweet Auburn on its way to the southern edge of the CBD, where it met up with the east–west expressway (now I-20) in a massive interchange just south of the State Capitol building. Coupled with the existing wide railroad corridor and industrial zone on the west, highway construction decisively walled off downtown behind an embrasure of infrastructure.

The Lochner Report coincided neatly with emerging federal postwar policy towards cities, with most of the neighborhoods bordering on the expressway corridor soon to be designated as urban renewal zones (although the first round of demolition would not take place until 1958–61). Expansion of the city's physical extent, and its white population, however, were just as important to the civic-commercial elite as providing easy vehicular access to the center. In 1949, the CAA, working through Hartsfield, orchestrated a successful annexation referendum, the "Plan of Improvement." When the scheme went into effect in January 1952, it tripled the city's area and added 100,000 mostly white, middle-class voters and taxpayers to the rolls. Among the areas brought within the city's boundaries was Buckhead, an upscale northern enclave that was home to many of Atlanta's power elite, as well as other white middle-class suburbs to the northeast and west. The plan also opened up extensive areas to the south and west of downtown for future black residential expansion, although this was to be "contained" – unsuccessfully as it turned out – within a frontier defined by already existing white suburbs.

The Plan of Improvement, though, did little to stem the steady exodus, after 1960, of white working- and middle-class families from the southside, westside, and Uptown to subdivisions in first DeKalb and, later, Cobb counties. White flight was reinforced by "block-busting" as middle-class African-American families displaced by urban renewal moved into many of these neighborhoods. Unlike in other Sunbelt cities, such as Houston, Memphis, and Jacksonville, subsequent efforts at annexation in the 1960s and 1970s were effectively opposed by suburban constituencies. Contrary to later Chamber of Commerce puffery that claimed Atlanta to be a "city without limits," by 1952 Atlanta had acquired what were to become most definitive and inflexible boundaries.

As important as the Lochner Report and the Plan of Improvement were in shaping the field of play, neither provided a new game plan or comprehensive scheme for redevelopment of the city and the surrounding counties of Fulton and DeKalb. This responsibility fell to the Metropolitan Planning Commission (MPC), which had been created by the Georgia General Assembly in 1947. In 1950, the Commission undertook a two-year program to develop the region's first master planning study. In 1952, it released a draft report, *Up Ahead: A Regional Land-use Plan for Metropolitan Atlanta*, followed two years later by a revised version, entitled *Now for Tomorrow*. While there were some significant differences between the two documents, they shared a common vision of a dispersed suburban hinterland linked to the city's "Golden Heart" by a vast web of free-flowing arterial highways far more extensive than those projected by the Lochner Plan.[40] With its sprawling, low density, metro Atlanta was "a prime example of the New City in the making."[41] Reflecting the influence of both Ebenezer Howard and Le Corbusier, the plans envisioned garden cities à la Radburn, New Jersey as the model for the emerging suburban frontier, while close-in blighted areas would be razed for a variety of purposes, ranging from mixed-income housing to a site for a world's fair promoting the peaceful uses of the atom.[42]

The principal difference between the two reports lay in their treatment of the race issue. The first report had specified seven "negro expansion areas" on the outer edges of the metro area, as well as the elimination of most of the African-American neighborhoods on the peripheries of the Central Business District. Subsequently, the MPC decided that their plans should not designate future land uses on the basis of race, as it "would not serve the best interests of the community."[43] Erasure from published policy did not mean elimination from actual practice, however. Most of the designated locales were used as sites for public housing projects built in the late 1950s and 1960s. While there was no explicit mention of "race" in the second report, only "disadvantaged groups," most of the areas slated for renewal were African-American neighborhoods. By contrast, "mature" residential neighborhoods, which were almost exclusively white, were to be protected from blighting influences, such as heavy traffic, incompatible uses, and undesirable populations. Less than a decade later, though, many of the mature neighborhoods to the east of downtown (including Inman Park, Virginia-Highlands and Morningside) had been blighted and were themselves slated to be demolished for additional expressway construction.

The MPC plan's most specific visions, however, were lavished on downtown: "the most important square mile in the Southeast."[44] Executed in a style Jane Jacobs later called "the Radiant Garden City Beautiful,"[45] the center was envisioned as a neatly zoned site of civic, commercial, and cultural functions bounded by the curve of the planned, but as yet uncompleted Downtown Connector. While it anticipated some northward expansion of the CBD into the existing Upper Peachtree Shopping District, the MPC vision was in many respects a modernist update of the 1906 Bleckley Plaza plan. Its primary focus was on the extensive redevelopment of the nineteenth-century core, turning the railroad gulch into an east–west axis of growth that would connect Five Points and the Whitehall-Broad Shopping District with an expanded zone of governmental offices around the State Capitol to the east.

Rather than Bleckley's City Beautiful plaza surrounded by neo-classical and Italianate edifices, the railroad corridor south of Decatur Street would be roofed with a landscaped pedestrian promenade raised above street level and flanked by Corbusier-ian glass boxes housing offices, hotels, and shops. On its western end, near the main railroad station, the walkway was anchored by a large mixed-use development, including a wholesale merchandise mart, built in the air-rights over the triangular intersection of the three major railroad corridors. The eastern end of the promenade terminated in a university–cultural center, which was to include a fine arts center and a large convention hall, in addition to greatly expanded facilities for what was then the Atlanta Division of the University of Georgia (now Georgia State University). This dedicated zone of culture would be bordered on the south by an expanded district of city, county, state, and federal office buildings linked together by a large parklike mall. The whole was to be surrounded by hundreds of acres of decked parking and peripheral surface lots.

The MPC plan was not so much a blueprint for downtown development as a rough, and only partially suggestive, guide. Its direct influence was greatest on the public sector. In the latter part of the 1950s, the city, county, and state governments constructed new office buildings immediately south and west of the Capitol building, while in the 1960s, a somewhat less than grand university campus was indeed built in the area designated for the university–cultural complex. However, the city-financed convention hall (the Atlanta Civic Center) was built on urban renewal land on the other side of the expressway, and the privately funded fine arts center (originally known as the Memorial Arts Center, now named for primary benefactor Robert Woodruff) arose some two miles north in the furthest reaches of Uptown. Much like the Bleckley Plaza plan before it, the MPC plan was a speculative, non-binding vision that failed to halt the northward march of private capital up Peachtree Street and beyond in the 1960s. There was no institutional mechanism for translating the vision into a policy for land use and urban design, or, most importantly, for funding the proposed development. Still, the plan introduced a wide array of "gadgets"[46] – extensive air-rights development, enclaved mixed-use complexes, grade separation of traffic, and the conversion of peripheral space into vast parking reservoirs – that would be employed by private developers in somewhat different configurations and locations in the late 1960s and early 1970s.

Both the Lochner Company and the Metropolitan Planning Commission, however, greatly underestimated the scale and intensity of suburbanization that was to come. Indeed, the Lochner Plan envisioned a metro population of only 400,000 in 1970 (less than would live in the incredibly shrinking central city alone by that time), while for its part the MPC projected 900,000 by 1980.[47] Although the Commission correctly recognized that metro Atlanta comprised a new urban form as compared to the cities of the Northeast and Midwest, it failed to appreciate the truly revolutionary potential of the suburban fringe to appropriate the central, legitimate functions of the historic core. In the early 1950s, it was completely inconceivable that sleepy towns like Vinings or Alpharetta could ever compete with the CBD for prestigious corporate office space or retail establishments.

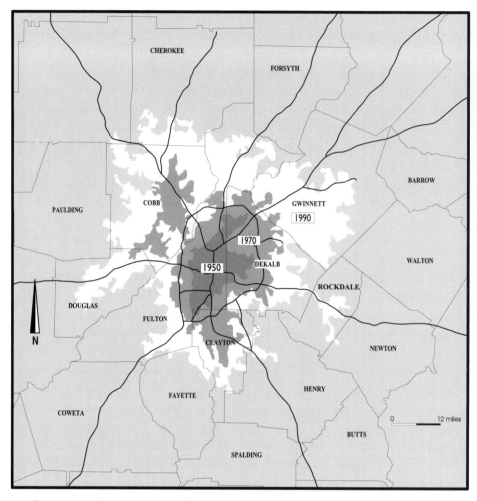

Map 7: Metropolitan Expansion, 1950–90

Besides, the city of Atlanta grew robustly in the 1950s, expanding some 47 percent (partly due to annexation), to reach an even half-million by the end of the decade.[48] However, the suburban portion of the metro area grew at an even faster rate, first exceeding the city in absolute numbers in 1961.[49] Subsequent political, economic, and social developments ensured that this unevenness between core and periphery would only intensify in the ensuing decades.

BUILDING A "NATIONAL CITY"

As the metropolitan region continued to exceed nationwide rates of economic and population growth in the 1960s, its landscape was massively restructured.

Out on the suburban fringes, bulldozers cleared thousands of acres for roads, strip malls, and split-level subdivisions with names like Storybook Estates and Sherwood Forest. The most extensive activity, however, was still occurring in the center. In 1961, Hartsfield was succeeded as mayor by Ivan Allan, Jr, who defeated arch-segregationist Lester Maddox in a close election. The immediate past president of the Chamber of Commerce and a member of the CAA's inner circle, Allen personified the civic–business partnership that had evolved during the Hartsfield era. The son of the former president of the Chamber of Commerce who, literally, wrote the book on the Atlanta Spirit, Allen was a second-generation scion of the "community power structure."[50] He brought with him a vision of making Atlanta a "national" city. This somewhat ambiguous status (defined by the Chamber of Commerce as a city "exerting a powerful economic force far beyond its normal regional functions"[51]) was to be attained by the continuation of the public–private partnership that had already made the Atlanta metro area the largest urban area in the Southeast. Allen's strategy relied heavily on extensive use of federal urban renewal and other public monies to build the necessary infrastructure to attract new private investment, which included stadiums, convention facilities, and a mass transit system focused on downtown.

As in virtually every other American city, however, urban renewal as practiced in Atlanta was nothing other than regressive. Between 1956 and 1966, expressway construction and urban renewal resulted in the demolition of 21,000 housing units (approximately one third of the city's housing stock, and a considerably larger percentage of its low-income units) and the displacement of some 67,000 people, or one in every seven Atlantans.[52] Most of those displaced were poor African-Americans, although a few low-income white neighborhoods were directly or indirectly affected as well. Initial African-American support for renewal was obtained by promises of new public housing and the availability of additional westside land to be developed by black real estate interests.[53] Still, as noted earlier, virtually all of the replacement housing built by public and private initiative was located at a considerable distance from the CBD. Moreover, the rate of replacement housing construction lagged considerably behind the pace of demolition and did not begin to make up for the number of low-income units that were destroyed.

A total of fourteen urban renewal areas covering more than 900 acres were designated between 1958 and 1968, ringing the CBD in a giant "U." Those immediately to the south and east of the center lay in the path of the planned expressway juncture and were demolished first, even before clear plans for redevelopment had been formulated. In the vision of the Metropolitan Planning Commission, the Rawson-Washington area just to the south of the expressway interchange, for example, was originally penciled in for middle-class housing. However, when housing proved unappealing to private developers (who were in the midst of aggressively subdividing the hinterland for that very same purpose), the site was used for the construction of Atlanta-Fulton County Stadium instead.

How the stadium was built reveals quite nicely how the power structure got things done in its prime. After the land had been assembled and extant structures demolished by the Atlanta Housing Authority (AHA), the president of C & S Bank, Mills Lane, bankrolled the construction of the facility (which still lacked a professional team) with the proviso that the mayor would appoint certain leading corporate citizens, including himself, to key positions in the newly reconstituted Stadium Authority.[54] After the stadium was constructed in 1965, the bank was reimbursed via a city/county bond issue and the AHA compensated with land elsewhere in the city. Atlanta's transformation into a "major league city" was completed the following year, when a professional baseball team, the Braves, was lured from Milwaukee and a National Football League franchise, the Falcons, was obtained via expansion. The new status was far from being merely symbolic, as the teams constituted significant economic enterprises in their own right. Professional sports put Atlanta "on the map" in more ways than one.[55]

Although the stadium was built on land already cleared, the construction of parking had a ripple effect, displacing more than 10,000 of the adjoining Summerhill neighborhood's approximately 12,500 residents, who were among the city's poorest.[56] In the summer of 1966, anger with "negro removal" and the slow pace of replacement housing construction sparked a number of civil disturbances in the area around the stadium. Mayor Allen responded with the construction of a small number of public housing units in Peoplestown and the inclusion of the entire southside of the city in the federally funded Model Cities program. Model Cities, however, added little in the way of new low-income housing and did little to improve the areas. In fact, thanks to displaced residents crowding into still extant neighborhoods further to the south, conditions in the Model Cities zone deteriorated further.[57] In other words, the city's poor ended up paying the steepest cost for the stadium.

Flanking the curve of the Downtown Connector on the northern and eastern edge of the CBD, the Butler Street urban renewal area was razed at the same time as Rawson-Washington and redeveloped as a dedicated convention district. A city-financed civic center was built on the north or outer bank of the expressway, while to the south a cluster of large national chain motels (Hyatt, Marriott, Ramada, Holiday Inn) arose on written-down land inside the CBD proper.[58] North and east of Butler Street, the old Buttermilk Bottom ghetto was bulldozed and renamed Bedford-Pine. Thus symbolically cleansed, it was to be redeveloped for mixed-income housing originally intended for the Rawson-Washington area. Effective community opposition and changing federal policy, however, stymied plans for Bedford-Pine until the 1980s.

As the example of Bedford-Pine suggests, the hegemonic power of the downtown business elite was being challenged in the late 1960s. The emergence of Atlanta as a majority black city, the defeat of the business community's candidate for mayor in 1969, and effective opposition to new expressway construction all signalled an end to the status quo. The construction of the stadium and the civic center constitute the high-water mark of the old regime; subsequent projects would no longer be decided by a select group of white oligarchs sitting around a table at the Commerce Club.

The commercial elite responded to the challenge of the new era in a number of ways. The Central Atlanta Association reconstituted itself as a non-profit corporation known as Central Atlanta Progress, Inc., or CAP, in 1966, and merged with the Uptown (later the Midtown) Businessmen's Association a year later. This alliance marked a significant expansion of the Central Area outside the boundaries of the traditional CBD into a neighborhood formerly known for residences, entertainment, and some retail. Whereas CAA exercised a good deal of its influence through informal linkages with the city establishment, CAP was intended as a formal action-oriented player in all aspects of the redevelopment process, from research and planning to funding of selected projects. Towards the late 1960s, CAP and the Chamber of Commerce also pioneered a rapprochement with the city's black business elite, and later, in the early 1970s, with the emergent African-American political establishment. After plans for a rapid rail system were rejected by popular referendum in 1969, major white and black business leaders formed the Action Forum to build elite biracial consensus for the Metropolitan Atlanta Rapid Transit Authority (MARTA) and urban redevelopment, more generally. It would take some take, however, for this new "governing coalition" to consolidate itself.[59]

The fate of MARTA provides a nice case in point of the changing balance of power and the enlarged scope of the redevelopment process in the late 1960s. It was easily the most complicated, ambitious, and costly element of Allen's vision of Atlanta as a national city. It not only required generating consensus between the city, the business community, the four adjacent metropolitan counties (Cobb, Gwinnett, Fulton, and DeKalb), the federal government, and the all-powerful Georgia Department of Transportation, but went against Atlantans' longstanding infatuation with the automobile. Moreover, decades of automobilized suburbanization had created residential densities that fell below the threshold of what would make traditional heavy rail systems cost-effective.[60] Thanks to heavy lobbying on the part of the CAA, the state chartered MARTA in 1965. CAA/CAP consultants played a key role in developing the original MARTA plan, which envisioned a system of underground and elevated rapid rail lines linking the centers of Cobb, Gwinnett, Clayton, and DeKalb counties with a central downtown nexus at Five Points. Together with several new expressways, MARTA was originally envisioned as ensuring suburbanites easy access to the core and thus maintaining the centrality of downtown within a rapidly expanding "horizontal city."

Put to a public referendum in 1968, MARTA's first incarnation was decisively rejected by both city and suburban voters, albeit for different reasons. The white downtown business interests that dominated the MARTA board made no effort to involve the public in the planning process, and planners had done little to make the system serve the needs and interests of the city's emerging African-American majority. With "negro removal" still ongoing, African-American business and community leaders were of no mind to tolerate yet another situation in which the poorest segment of the urban population bore the highest burden to realize benefits that would accrue to the city as whole. The opposition of white suburbanites was motivated by prospects of higher taxes and no small amount of racism; they viewed MARTA not as a means of commuting downtown, but as a mechanism for bringing "crime" (read: black youth) into the heart of their lily-white enclaves.[61] Over the next three years, CAP, the Chamber of Commerce, and the Action Forum courted black business and community leaders to support a slimmed-down and more community-sensitive MARTA plan, with more stations in African-American neighborhoods east and west of downtown, as well as provisions for minority set-asides in contracts and hiring. In late 1971, the second MARTA referendum was narrowly approved by city, Fulton, and DeKalb voters, but was rejected in Cobb and Gwinnett.

Following its approval, the MARTA system became the main fact around which future planning was organized. Even in its scaled-down version, it was the single largest public works project in Atlanta's history, costing some 2 billion in 1971 dollars. The north–south line began at the airport, some eleven miles south of downtown, and traced an existing surface rail corridor to the southern edge of the CBD at Garnett Street, where it plunged underground and burrowed up the length of the Peachtree Street ridge before resurfacing north of Midtown and veering northeastward to the super-regional Lenox Square shopping mall and its terminus in the industrial suburb of Doraville in DeKalb County. A spur line was also planned to link downtown Buckhead and the Georgia 400 highway corridor in north Fulton County with the system. The east–west line also followed another existing rail corridor for much of its length, linking the black suburbs around Hightower Road with the largely white suburbs near Stone Mountain. The two lines crossed in a central station just south of Five Points.

MARTA planners viewed the system as a means of limiting automobile-generated sprawl and redressing the reigning *laissez-faire* attitude towards land-use and development controls.[62] By concentrating growth around certain designated transit stations, system planners hoped to create new economic development opportunities in the central area, while preserving "healthy" intown neighborhoods, and limiting commercial strip development elsewhere. These goals were first elaborated in the city Bureau of Planning's *Urban Framework Plan* of 1973, which became the basis of all subsequent city comprehensive development plans. Five kinds of nodal classification were proposed: urban high intensity, regional mixed-use, commuter transit, neighborhood mixed-use and residential. All but one of the urban high-intensity zones were located in the Central Area.

Over the next seven years, the city, working closely with the urban design team at CAP, undertook a series of transportation station area development studies to plot development around the nine Central Area MARTA stations (Garnett Street, Five Points, Peachtree Center, Civic Center, North Avenue, Tenth Street, Arts Center, Georgia State, and the Omni). Each station would be surrounded by a public plaza and a circular zone of high-intensity, pedestrian-friendly development some 1,000 to 2,000 feet in diameter. These, in turn, would be surrounded by a transition zone that would serve as a buffer between the high-intensity new development and the less intensive uses in the surrounding neighborhood, which would be preserved as much as possible. Every effort would be made, though, to encourage pedestrian, rather than automotive, linkages throughout the area.

Despite these well-meant and ambitious intentions, MARTA has failed to realize many of the aims of its planners. Lacking lines into the boom counties of Cobb and Gwinnett, MARTA has been spectacularly unsuccessful in checking automobilized sprawl, which has increased exponentially since the early 1970s. However, even if Cobb and Gwinnett had been drawn into the system as originally envisioned, it is unlikely that their patterns of development would have been much different from what they are today. Many Atlantans, even those living within the area covered by MARTA, have been loath to abandon their cars and seem outrightly hostile to the notion of public transit. Part of this disenchantment seems to lie with the inconvenience of a system designed for a commuter population that in large measure has moved further out and away. Race, however, also seems to play a role. Racialized designations are not limited to discrete districts or areas, but have been extended to the channels of mass transit. Many whites view MARTA, especially the bus system, as an African-American domain. This attitude is nowhere better illustrated than in the sadly popular racist sobriquet that claims that MARTA really stands for "Moving Africans Rapidly Through Atlanta" and in the fears of Cobbites and Gwinnettians that rapid rail would bring hordes of criminally intentioned black youth into their white suburban idylls.

MARTA-related efforts to establish more rational and restrictive land-use policies were also successfully parried and softened by development interests in the course of the 1970s. When new mixed-use zoning ordinances were passed in 1982, they proved to be far more of an encouragement than a restriction to developers. Where the stations have been successful in seeding redevelopment, as in Midtown, it has been impossible to limit the transformation of the area outside the core high-intensity zone, as inflated land values create irresistible pressures to alter land-use in what were once considered to be "preservation zones." More often than not, Central Area stations have failed to stimulate high-intensity development. Despite the provision of plazas, few of the MARTA stations have become public gathering places. In fact, the station plaza that has been most successful as a place of public assembly, that outside the Five Points station, has been popularly deemed to constitute a problem due to the large number of African-American (and presumably gang-identified) young people who frequent the area.

With its emphasis on nodes, rather than on linkages between them, the MARTA system helped to reinforce the increasingly archipelagic character of the Central Area during the 1970s and 1980s. In addition, the slow, delay-plagued construction of the system, which began in 1976, caused considerable disruption of downtown traffic patterns, especially in the Five Points area. The changes in the built environment, however, paled before that which was occurring in the corridors of power, where a new mayor was calling for a major change in the city's power structure.

RECENTERING THE CENTER

The effects of MARTA, however, would not begin to be felt until active construction began in the late 1970s and the completion of its first phase in the early 1980s. Meanwhile, beginning in the 1960s, the CBD inside the "Chinese wall" of the Downtown Dis-connector underwent a profound restructuring that in many ways foreshadowed the decentralizing tendencies at work in the metropolitan region as a whole. Most of the projects that refigured downtown were privately financed, although they were located and designed with a view to where MARTA stations would be, and thus received a substantial, but unacknowledged public subsidy.

While the Butler Street parcel straddled the expressway, only one urban renewal area was entirely located within downtown itself: a stretch of Decatur Street running east along the railroad gulch from Five Points formerly known as Rusty Row. From the early twentieth century, numerous accounts emphasized the area's depraved and iniquitous nature, but in addition to its seedy bars, pawn shops, and prostitutes, Decatur Street was a popular place of entertainment for working-class African-Americans and the location of the only theatrical outlet for black entertainers such as Bessie Smith, Ethel Waters, and Ma Rainey.[63] In 1966, virtually the entire renewal area was designated for a new campus for the newly renamed Georgia State University.

The Decatur Street area was already home to two other civic institutions dedicated to different forms of social control. Atlanta police headquarters had long been located at the eastern end of the Decatur Street corridor, and received a new building in the early 1960s. Just to the north and east of the police station, hard up against the embankment of the expressway, was Grady Memorial Hospital, the city's and Fulton County's central receiving hospital for the poor and the indigent, the city's first publically supported hospital when it opened in 1892. The present-day structure housing Grady dates from 1958, when the city and Fulton County financed the construction of an enormous then state-of-the art structure, rendered in that generically modern style favored for Goffmanesque "total institutions" (hospitals, prisons, and mental asylums) of the period. Looming like a battlement over the moat of the Connector, the western side of Grady was "enhanced" with a postmodernized Art Deco facade between 1992 and 1995. The original structure, however, is still quite apparent to the hundreds of thousands of drivers who pass by on the expressway each day.

Built between 1966 and 1969, and raised up from street level on a series of "platforms" linked by pedestrian skyways, the new Georgia State campus harked back to the 1954 plans for a university–cultural center and was of a piece with other contemporary street-killing downtown projects, like John Portman's Peachtree Center (described below). Together with Grady Hospital, GSU was intended to anchor the eastern edge of the CBD by linking the government district with Five Points and the new convention area. Very little linkage occurred, however. The fortress mentality of the campus's design (the turreted Urban Life building, for example, bears more than a passing resemblance to a medieval castle) isolated the campus from the urban fabric. Moreover, the university's white administration evinced little desire to interface with the community, until the 1990s.

Further to the west of the GSU platform, the remainder of the "center" was not holding. The establishment of the first major suburban malls in the late 1950s, especially Lenox Square in Buckhead, steadily eroded the hegemony of the downtown retail corridor that ran through the Five Points business district along Peachtree Street. Both Rich's and Davison's department stores, which anchored the Whitehall-Broad and Upper Peachtree shopping districts, respectively, built suburban branches in the 1960s while plausibly maintaining a public commitment to their flagship downtown establishments. Rich's was the larger of the two, having expanded twice since the 1940s, and was much more of an Atlanta institution. The store's giant Christmas tree, for example, was the focal point of public Yuletide celebrations. However, as the racial composition of the city's population shifted during the 1960s, the Whitehall-Broad area became the principal shopping area for low-income African-American Atlantans. To the south of Rich's, the former whole-sale trade and manufacturing district became the scene of increasing disinvestment with the declining importance of rail traffic and the demolition of the city's two principal rail stations in the early 1970s. Aside from the government district to the east, the landscape of the southern CBD was steadily transformed into what geographers call a "zone of discard:"[64] a liminal zone of parking lots, abandoned buildings, and liquor stores catering to the street trade.

To the north of Whitehall-Broad, the Five Points area was completing the transition to a "9 to 5" office zone that had begun in the 1920s. Between 1961 and 1969, major local banks and insurance companies demolished many of the city's first-generation skyscrapers and other historic structures (such as Atlanta's first skyscraper – the Equitable Building – and the Peachtree Shopping Arcade) to build shiny new headquarters towers around the Five Points intersection and northwest down Marietta Street towards the Federal Reserve Bank. By the early 1970s, a total of thirty-six new buildings had been constructed downtown, more than doubling the amount of office space.[65] This construction, in turn, stimulated demand for more parking, and owners of old buildings in nearby areas found it increasingly profitable to tear down their structures for garages and surface lots. To ease the visual blight caused by mass demolition, the city and CAP sponsored the painting of murals by local artists – "the Urban Walls Project" – on the raw surfaces of adjacent buildings in the early 1970s. Only a handful of these murals exists two decades later.

By recycling prime real estate into new office construction, local banks and insurance companies were making a major financial and symbolic investment in the continued centrality of Five Points. At the same time, however, they were helping to undermine their own efforts by pouring vast sums into residential, retail, and, eventually, office park development in the suburbs. In these endeavors they were joined, and eventually exceeded, by national money center banks, insurance companies, pension funds, real estate investment trusts, and the first trickle of foreign capital, from Canada. While it would take a decade or more for the effects of this peripheral urbanization to be felt in the center, the CBD was undergoing its own radical expansion and decentralization.

Though most financial institutions remained in the vicinity of Five Points, two of downtown's most venerable institutions – C & S Bank, and Life of Georgia – built separate new headquarters a mile "uptown" near one of the proposed MARTA stations at the corner of North Avenue and Peachtree Street in 1969. The developments continued the northward reorientation of downtown initiated by the first phase of Peachtree Center two years earlier. Contemporary accounts anticipated that North Avenue would be the undisputed core of the CBD by 1985.[66] While the area did attract some further high-rise development, such as the Southern Bell Center (now BellSouth Center) and the NationsBank Plaza (the city's and the Southeast's tallest building), this status was not realized for a variety of reasons. In the late 1970s, Atlanta's long-embattled preservationist community waged their first successful battle with developers seeking to demolish the moorish "Fabulous" Fox Theater. Bell South's headquarters tower was redesigned to cantilever over the adjacent North Avenue MARTA station.[67] More importantly, however, the North Avenue node was physically separated from the rest of downtown by the deep divide of the Downtown Connector, which was widened to twelve lanes during the 1980s. Unlike the 1920s, when investment capital followed a handful of pioneers north up Peachtree, few other developers and corporate tenants followed the lead of Life of Georgia and C&S Bank, preferring instead to build their own speculative growth nodes away from the high-priced congestion of Five Points and the "danger" of the low-income shopping district that lay directly to the south.

MXD MADNESS

Eager to convey the impression of a modern city on the move, in the late 1960s and early 1970s a new generation of Atlanta developers increasingly eschewed single buildings in favor of massive, enclaved complexes combining various magic mixes of office, hotel, retail, entertainment, and convention space. Before the real estate market meltdown induced by the post-1973 recession, competing consortiums of local, national, and foreign investors bankrolled no less than four of these million-square-foot (or larger) mixed-use developments, or MXDs, within a third of a mile of Five Points. Fed by an abundant supply of investment capital, unencumbered by any meaningful zoning and/or design restrictions, and in the absence of a comprehensive development plan, private developers were free to indulge their own speculative visions without restraint, coordination, or concern for the consequences.

The ur-MXD was Peachtree Center, which was designed, developed, and managed by John Calvin Portman, an Atlanta native, Georgia Tech grad, and popularizer of the "atrium" hotel that Fredric Jameson has taken as the hyperspatial totem of late capitalism.[68] Peachtree Center was the test-bed for the design philosophy that would later create similar inwardly focused enclaved projects in San Francisco (Embarcadero Center), Detroit (Renaissance Center), Los Angeles (Bonaventure Hotel) and elsewhere. The first component was the 22-story Merchandise Mart, begun in 1959 and completed in 1962. While his autobiographical hagiography attributes to Portman the notion of creating this "bold, new dedicated forum for wholesale trade," the idea for the Mart goes back at least to the 1954 MPC plan, which had envisioned it for the triangular air-rights parcel just west of Five Points.[69] Rather than contribute to the redevelopment of the southern CBD, Portman broke with the MPC plan and located his Merchandise Mart a quarter of a mile up Peachtree Street from Five Points in a neighborhood then dominated by low-rise retail stores, theaters, and hotels that had been built in the 1920s boom. The first building in the city with over a million square feet of space (since then, more than doubled to cover much of a city block), the Mart was only the fourth major commercial structure built downtown since the onset of the Depression. As large as it was, the structure was only a modest beginning for what Portman envisioned as nothing less than the core of a wholly new downtown.

Backed by local developer Ben Massell (who had built much of the Upper Peachtree Shopping District in the 1920s) and Texan developer Trammel Crow, Portman began assembling more than ten acres of land between Cain (now International Boulevard), Baker, Ellis, and Williams Streets.[70] The first phase of Peachtree Center proper opened across the street from the Mart in 1965. With its four 25- to 35-story slab-like towers clustered around a multi-level plaza and open-air mall, it was quickly dubbed Rockefeller Center South by local boosters still trying for that New York of the South image.[71] More than the stadium or the civic center, Peachtree Center came to symbolize Atlanta's newfound image as a national metropolis, providing a prototypically modern skyline that figured prominently in promotional images of the city. The network of office buildings quickly became *the* prestige business address in Atlanta, attracting former Five Points denizens, federal offices, and new corporate migrants alike. It also embodied Atlanta's increasing importance as a national center of wholesale trade, as Portman added marts for the apparel, electronics, and gift industries in ensuing decades.

With the civic center located just across the expressway, and the expansion of the mart complex, Peachtree Center also became the focal point of an expanded hotel-convention district that eventually overshadowed the cluster of motor hotels built in the Butler Street urban renewal zone just to the east. In 1967, Portman completed the first of his soon to be (in)famous atrium hotels, the Hyatt Regency, topping it off with a blue-domed, flying-saucer-like, revolving restaurant that provided a god's-eye view of the emergent metropolis (it has since been hemmed in by subsequent high-rise development). The Hyatt was followed by two additional 1,000-plus-room atriumed hotels: the cylindrical 70-story Westin Peachtree Plaza (when completed in 1976, the world's tallest) and the Marriott Marquis. The Marriott, completed in 1985, is particularly noteworthy for its vast, curvilinear atrium, which provides an upwards view akin to that from inside the belly of some monstrous animal.

The whole complex, which would eventually comprise some twenty buildings spread over twelve city blocks by 1992, was knit together by a warren of enclosed skyways built in the publically owned air-rights over city streets. In its present incarnation, Peachtree Center constitutes a pure example of what Trevor Boddy has called an "analogous city" – a hermetic realm wherein office workers, tourists, and conventioneers circulate in an ageographic space uncontaminated by the "congestion" and "danger" of the streets.[72] Devoid of reference to its local cultural–historical context except, perhaps, the It's Atlanta giftshop peddling ephemera in the shopping mall, Peachtree Center is the apotheosis of contemporary Atlanta's generic urbanism and sense of placelessness – one might as well be anywhere . . . else.

While most national and international architectural critics were unimpressed by Portman's creation, both city boosters and many Atlantans were absolutely smitten. The local success of Peachtree Center made Portman the most visible and the most powerful developer working downtown, attributes that were only further solidified by his presidency of Central Atlanta Progress between 1969 and 1971. But he was most certainly not alone. His principal rival, suburban home developer Tom Cousins, assembled a diverse group of backers that included David Rockefeller, Greek shipping magnate Stavros Niarchos, the Ford Foundation, and his own coterie of Texans, to build a similar kind of mixed-use megastructure in the air-rights parcel originally envisioned in the MPC plan for the Merchandise Mart.[73] Rather aptly known as the Omni, the complex attempted to out-Portman Portman, combining a sports arena with a luxury hotel, offices, an upscale atriumed shopping center, an "international bazaar," an ice-skating rink (perhaps making its own claim to being Rockefeller Center South), and what was billed as the world's first enmalled entertainment/theme park, The World of Sid and Marty Krofft.[74] The project's first phase, a city/Fulton County-financed sports/concert arena called the Omni Coliseum, was completed in 1972. However, beset by construction delays and cost overruns, the $100-million Omni International office/retail/hotel/entertainment complex did not open until late 1975, smack in the midst of a deepening recession and a moribund real estate market.

While the arena soon became a successful venue for concerts, as well as home to the National Basketball Association Hawks and National Hockey League Flames (both partially owned by Cousins), the Omni International was an unmitigated debacle of the first order: at the time nothing less than "one of the worst real estate disasters in history."[75] Thanks to overruns that nearly doubled its cost, the complex could not come close to servicing its debt even if fully leased, which it most certainly was not. The much-heralded theme park/ fantasy world closed after less than a year, due to abysmal attendance, while the office space and mall suffered from high vacancy and low sales. The Omni's problems stemmed from not only a phenomenally overbuilt market, but a seeming lack of awareness by its developers of Atlanta's intensely racialized geography. Completed just as the intended prime market segment for the mall – the city's white middle and upper middle classes – were concluding a two-decade-long exodus to the paler pastures of the northside and DeKalb and Cobb counties, the Omni had to compete not only with established upscale retail nodes in Buckhead, but with the perception that it was in a "black" area.

Twice threatened with foreclosure by principal mortgage-holder Morgan Guaranty Trust, Cousins managed to hold on to the Omni by some crafty debt restructuring. In 1987, the complex was sold to Ted Turner, who retrofitted the odd space into the new home for his expanding Cable News Network and renamed the bunker-like complex CNN Center. Chastened by this debacle, the well-financed and even better connected Cousins shifted his attention from downtown back to the suburbs, where he focused his attention on building highly profitable corporate campuses, shopping malls, and residential enclaves. In the late 1980s he returned to the core, where, in league with the Dutch Institutional Holding Company and NationsBank, he built two of the city's new corporate trophy buildings on Peachtree Street – One Ninety One Peachtree and NationsBank Plaza.

Despite the Omni's bad fortunes, the complex remained at the center of a major node of development thanks to massive direct state investment. Indeed, Cousins's Omni, much more than Portman's Peachtree Center, represented a new stage in the evolution of Atlanta's public–private partnership. In the case of the Omni, the public partner was not only the City of Atlanta, but Fulton County and the State of Georgia. Public investment took the form of the Atlanta–Fulton County Recreation Authority-owned arena, a station on the not yet completed east–west MARTA line (initially known as Techwood Station), and a massive state-owned convention facility – the Georgia World Congress Center, or GWCC. The location of the latter was not simply fortuitous, as Cousins had expended a great deal of his considerable political–economic juice to outplay a rival developer – a crony of then Georgia Governor Jimmy Carter – who had gambled on the GWCC being built on an eastern site near the existing Civic Center to anchor his competing mixed-use development, a hotel/office/retail complex called the Atlanta Center, Ltd. To win over the state site selection committee, Cousins not only subsidized the architectural plans for the facility, but donated the land and guaranteed the costs for the first phase of its construction.[76]

Built and managed by a bond-issuing, property-condemning state authority free from public oversight, the GWCC was linked to the Omni proper by a series of pedestrian bridges and parking decks. The first phase of the GWCC, the equivalent of a 50-story building lying on its side (the world's largest single room on one level, according to the promotional literature), opened in 1977. Subsequent expansions of the facility have added more than half a million square feet of exhibition space, which are reserved well into the next millennium for a wide variety of exhibitions, trade shows, and other kinds of corporate conclaves. In the late 1980s, the City of Atlanta, Fulton County, and the State of Georgia combined forces to bail out an initially all-private venture to build a $158-million, 72,000-seat domed stadium immediately to the west of the GWCC. As with the Atlanta-Fulton County Stadium two decades earlier, the construction of the Georgia Dome necessitated the razing of part of the poor inner-city neighborhood of Vine City, as well as a large homeless encampment. Although it was designed by the same architectural firm responsible for both the GWCC and the Omni/CNN Center, with its playfully garish white and red-orange exterior, the Dome does not really seem to be of a piece with the dun-colored brutalist bunkers of the three other megastructures. The recent construction of yet another parking deck topped with a plaza knits together the four separate units into a large, if still pedestrian-hostile, arcology.

The two other mixed-use developments planned for downtown in the late 1960s and completed in the early 1970s – the Peachtree Summit and Atlanta Center, Ltd – fared even worse than the Omni. Of the three towers envisioned to rise up from the south bank of the Downtown Connector atop a proposed but as yet uncompleted MARTA station, only the triangular Summit building was built. Along with another speculative office tower – 101 Marietta Street – built in the go-go years of the early 1970s, the Peachtree Summit was vacant for much of the decade until it was acquired by the General Accounting Office for federal office space. The equally ill-fated Atlanta Center project – a joint venture of local investors, the Hilton Corporation, US insurance companies, and Kuwaiti petrodollars – not only gambled wrong on the location of the GWCC, but was built, quite literally, in the shadow of the expanding Peachtree Center complex. Two decades later, the Atlanta Center's separate origins are still apparent in its lack of skyway connection with adjacent "Portman-teaus"[77] that comprise the heart of the hotel-convention district. Several other large mixed-use developments were proposed for the downtown area in the late 1960s, including one near Five Points, but were never built.

The MXD madness of the late 1960s and early 1970s created approximately five million square feet of new "Class A" office space within the confines of the old Central Business District, in addition to the four million square feet represented by the new financial citadels in the Five Points core and several other solo structures.[78] When all of these new structures were completed by 1976, the space glut dramatically lowered property values and rents throughout the CBD and badly burned local lenders already reeling from the effects of suburban overbuilding and the deepening national recession. Also hard hit were owners of older "Class B" buildings, who found it difficult to compete with the bargain rents being offered for prime space in new structures. The allure of Peachtree Center sucked upscale retail activity and pedestrian movement north up Peachtree. With human activity drawn up and then inside, Five Points' historic "congestion" was increasingly replaced by desolation and the perception of danger by the end of the 1970s.

EXCEPTIONS TO THE RULE

In the shadow of the abovementioned mega-projects were two much more modest efforts to revitalize the historic core. The first of these involved the adaptive reuse of the forgotten spaces created by the construction of viaducts over the railroad gulch in the 1920s. As early as 1966, the well-intentioned but largely ceremonial Atlanta Civic Design Commission had proposed the revitalization of the subterranean area it called the Terminus Historic District. The idea provoked little interest from either the city or the downtown establishment, who were more concerned, as we have seen, with the wholesale eradication of the city's existing landscape and its replacement with large, mirrored glass filing cabinets and mutant simulations of Rockefeller Center.

Inspired by the Civic Design Commission's idea, two ex-Georgia Tech fraternity brothers opened an 1890s-themed complex of bars, shops, and restaurants known as Underground Atlanta in 1969. Preceding Boston's much-celebrated Faneuil Hall Marketplace and Seattle's Pike Place Market (often touted as the first of their ilk) by seven years, Underground was one of the earliest attempts to create a dedicated zone of cultural consumption in the obsolescent spaces of the urban American landscape. With its gas lamps, preserved nineteenth-century structures, and attempts to evoke a sense of place, however conjured and fake, Underground was, to a certain extent at least, the antithesis of the rampant aspatial modernism raging above ground. Still, its highly sanitized representation of Atlanta's past left a good deal to be desired, especially regarding the issue of race. Indeed, there is something not entirely coincidental or innocent in the playful recreation of the Jim Crow era at the same time that the "real" Atlanta was making the transition to a majority black city. Indeed, for a time in the early 1970s, ex-governor Lester Maddox operated a store in Underground where he sold autographed ax handles to those seeking souvenirs of the good old days of segregation.

For several years, Underground was unquestionably the pre-eminent entertainment spot in the entire metropolitan area, its popularity in no small measure due to the fact that some of the booming suburban counties still refused to sell alcohol by the drink. By the mid 1970s, however, competition from new entertainment zones in Buckhead and the suburbs and the perception that it was in a dangerous (read "black") area lessened its popularity considerably. Disruptions and displacement by MARTA construction provided the killing blows, however. When MARTA and the CSX Railroad were unable to come to terms over the use of railroad property, the east–west rail line had to be redirected through the northern half of the city-designated Historic Atlanta Zone. Approximately one third of Underground Atlanta's original space was condemned and demolished for the east–west line and the central Five Points station.[79] Tenant turnover accelerated and cheesy gift stores proliferated to the exclusion of other venues. In 1979, Underground's obituary was written by no less an authority than *People* magazine, which called it one of the ten worst tourist traps in the United States. Within two years, the last enterprise had closed for good.

Just to the north of Underground, another private effort to create public space was underway. In 1971, the Robert Woodruff Foundation (the Coca-Cola president and Hartsfield crony was the city's major philanthropic benefactor) purchased and "anonymously" donated a two-block area just east of the Five Points intersection for a Central City Park. Occupied by a number of local retail establishments that were in the process of relocating to the suburbs or Peachtree Center, the two-acre site had originally been proposed for yet another million-square-foot office/hotel/shopping mall to be built by New York developer Harry Helmsley. Intended as a place where Five Points office workers could stroll, have lunch, and marvel at the surrounding monuments of urban modernism, it was the first major public open space downtown had ever had (two smaller parks had been built in more peripheral areas during the 1940s). With characteristic Atlantan hyperbole, local boosters likened it to New York's Central Park. This pastoral imagery was soon spoiled when many of the newly planted trees withered and died, their roots choked by the still-extant foundations of the buildings that formerly stood on the site.

Soon after opening in 1973, the park attracted not only office workers and tourists, but the urban poor and the homeless, the latter then called "bums" and "vagrants." Most of the workers and tourists were white, most of the poor and homeless were black. As in the case of Underground, the racial divide helped create a perception amongst white users, and the city, that the area was "dangerous." The presence of "undesirables" in the park was ritually invoked by journalists and white residents as both a cause and a symbol of downtown's irreversible decline (not to mention a reason to move to the suburbs). The city's reaction was to remodel the park to make it less amenable to street people, rather than to redress the utter lack of city facilities for the homeless (shelters are provided by either private organizations or Fulton County). As Atlanta's homeless population increased markedly in the 1980s, this "space war" only escalated in intensity (it will be described in detail in Chapter 4).

Despite their somewhat different natures, both Underground and Central City Park were of a piece with the "disjointed incrementalism" that characterized the redevelopment of downtown and the metropolitan area as a whole. That is, even these putatively "public" spaces "just happened" in accordance with market forces, chance, and countless uncoordinated decisions.[80] Beginning in the late 1960s, however, this *laissez-faire* approach to planning was already undergoing change. However, in keeping with past tendencies of growth, these efforts would be overwhelmingly envisioned and driven by the private business interests represented by Central Atlanta Progress, rather than the city government.

THE CENTRAL AREA STUDY

A number of coincident developments prompted a revised attitude towards planning in Atlanta. First, the vast influx of federal monies in the 1960s via Urban Renewal, Model Cities, and Community Development programs necessitated the development of a more formalized capacity within city government for putting these funds to use. These needs resulted in the enhancement of the Bureau of Planning and the drafting of the city's first comprehensive land-use plan, "Planning Atlanta", in 1970. Although the city's Bureau of Planning assumed responsibility for articulating a vision of "ultimate development" for all sectors of the city, it ceded responsibility for the central core to a joint study it conducted with Central Atlanta Progress.

The Central Atlanta Study (CAS) was begun in the late 1960s and released in 1971. It embodied, in large measure, the implicit tenets than had driven development since the 1950s. Financed in part by a grant from the Urban Mass Transportation Administration of the US Department of Transportation, the principal focus of the CAS plan was the preservation of the "strategic importance" of the CBD within a sprawling "horizontal city."[81] This goal was to be accomplished primarily through the expansion of existing expressways and the construction of new freeways and toll roads, as well as development of a mass transit system centered on downtown. The enhancement of the transportation net, it was argued, was necessary not only to allow the core to remain the unchallenged premiere office market in the metro area (a premise invalidated and abandoned only a decade later) but to permit the expansion of the hotel-convention industry, which was seen (accurately as it turns out) as the primary engine of the core's future economic growth.

One of the more notable features of the CAS was its more expansive definition of the "center." At the core was an enlarged Central Business District bounded by the expressways on the east and south and by the Southern Railroad tracks on the west. On the north, however, the CBD extended beyond the moat of the Downtown Connector to embrace the new node of development pioneered by

C & S Bank and Life of Georgia at North Avenue and Peachtree Street. Surrounding the CBD was an eighteen-square-mile "inner ring" of industrial sites and residential neighborhoods defined by a roughly circular cordon of railroad tracks that marked the limits of the street grid and pre-World War II urbanization. With the exception of the northeast quadrant, which included the upscale residential areas of Ansley Park (site of the Georgia Governor's Mansion until 1966) and Uptown, most of the inner ring consisted of areas designated as urban renewal zones in the 1950s and 1960s. According to CAS planners, the inner ring was "perhaps the strategically most important area,"[82] as it provided the needed *lebensraum* for the future expansion of unspecified core functions. The designation of the inner ring as a unrestricted free-fire zone for expansion merely formalized the buffer-zone strategy that had emerged during the urban renewal era.

The CAS plan for the vastly augmented network of freeways and tollways had been drawn up by the Georgia Department of Transportation in the early 1960s. The highways, it was argued, were vitally necessary to "stabilize" connections between the central area and the ever-expanding periphery. Although the I-285 Perimeter highway had been completed just a year before, DOT and CAS planners suggested an outer loop be constructed some ten to fifteen miles beyond the Perimeter. They also envisioned a tollway curving southeastward from Cobb County through downtown and then northeastward to Stone Mountain. Another north–south express tollway (I-485) was planned to run through the neighborhoods just east of the inner ring, from Buckhead to Jonesboro. With the eager support of CAP, the DOT had already bought up and razed considerable sections of the area immediately south of Ponce De Leon Avenue in preparation for the Stone Mountain Tollway and its intersection with I-485. That these stabilization strategies would profoundly destabilize several large residential neighborhoods (a number of them as yet "unblighted"), and ultimately the vitality of the core itself, went unacknowledged by planners. However, unlike the areas razed in the name of urban renewal and the first phase of highway construction in the early 1960s, the affected neighborhoods were majority white, relatively affluent, and, as will be discussed further below, able to mount effective resistance against the planned highways.

The Central Area Study was far more concerned with expanding expressways and the boundaries within which the free play of market forces could operate than detailing specific projects of urban design, with one major exception. The second section of the report was taken up with extensive drawings and explanations of John Portman's plans for the redesign of the Peachtree Street corridor that would take advantage of the disruption (and the federal funds) associated with construction of the as yet unapproved rapid rail system. Owing more to Paolo Soleri than Le Corbusier, Portman's plan called for nothing short of the complete pedestrian enmalling of Peachtree Street from Five Points to Peachtree Center, and its conversion into a "multi-level activity spine" flanked by a Manhattan-like canyon of modernist slab towers. A Disneylike people-mover would whisk travelers above the throngs of pedestrians, while automobile and subway traffic would be shunted below ground in a series of grade-separated tunnels.

A second and far less elaborate pedestrian corridor was envisioned to link the proposed air-rights development west of downtown to the emerging Georgia State University node on the east, intersecting with the Peachtree activity spine in a large plaza at Five Points. As far as the gadgets employed went (air-rights development, grade separation of pedestrian and vehicular traffic, large filing cabinets masquerading as buildings) Portman's plan was akin to the Metropolitan Planning Commission's high modern (1954) vision for downtown. However, whereas the MPC plan placed the main axis of redevelopment along the east–west railway gulch that divided the CBD, Portman articulated a vision of Atlanta as a linear city extending northward along the Peachtree ridge towards the emerging luxury nexus of Buckhead.

Part of this spatial reorientation was driven by simple economics, land around the formerly low-rise commercial district being less expensive and less complicated to assemble than air-rights parcels in the gulch area. However, low land costs alone do not explain the direction of redevelopment, as property in the southern CBD was also rapidly declining in value as suburban malls captured the retail trade oriented to middle-class whites. Rather, the northward thrust also corresponded to ongoing shifts in the city's racialized topography. Even as Atlanta was proudly proclaiming itself "too busy to hate," it was actively creating a stealthier and more insidious form of urban apartheid. Near the center of the city's bus network, the Broad and Peachtree Street shopping corridors south of Five Points were reoriented to a low-income, largely African-American clientele. Portman's "new downtown" dedicated to office workers and the increasing torrent of conventioneers, tourists, and other visitors was thus located at greatest remove from this "black area."

Fortunately, cooler heads prevailed when it came to dealing with Portman's vision. Even as president of CAP, Portman was unable to convince city officials to float some $183 million in bonds needed to finance the project, along with $80 million from state and federal urban development and highway funds. Less than 20 per cent of the estimated $326-million cost of the project – a massive underestimate as it later turned out – would be borne by private capital.[83] Still, while the more ambitious enmalling plans were rejected, certain key features of Portman's vision, especially the idea of a noded "linear city" stretching north on Peachtree, were incorporated into subsequent "official" development plans drawn up by both the city and CAP.

The Central Area Study concluded with a number of issues that merited further study. Chief among them was "the pressing and perplexing problem of housing."[84] While recognizing that more low-income housing was necessary, CAP planners were adamant that it be located outside the Central Area (where was not specified, Alabama perhaps?) and out of their area of responsibility. Instead, the CAS report argued for the provision of state-subsidized incentives, such as written-down land costs and tax abatements, to make the construction of moderate- and upper-income housing competitive with suburban areas. No specific areas within the Central Area were mentioned, although the authors clearly had in mind the Bedford-Pine renewal parcel, which had been awarded to a for-profit CAP subsidiary, called Park Central Communities, for residential redevelopment in 1969. The hoped-for incentives, however, were not manifested until the mid 1980s.

REVENGE OF THE NEIGHBORHOODS

In addition to the expansion of the field of play, the 1970s were marked by a major reformulation of the tacit rules of engagement between city government and the business community, as well as the emergence of a new set of players. Opposition to urban renewal and expressway construction activated a series of neighborhood organizations that successfully lobbied for a change in the city charter that made both the mayor and the city council more responsive to community interests. In 1969, Ivan Allen's vice-mayor, Sam Massell, riding a wave of African-American support, defeated the business community's candidate and became the city's first Jewish chief executive. Although he was both a businessman and the son of a prominent developer (Ben Massell), Massell's faith and liberal proclivities distanced him from the older, and more conservative Protestant establishment. Once in office, Massell created an Office of Affirmative Action and appointed unprecedented numbers of blacks to positions in his administration. Despite these moves, however, Massell shared the world-view of the white business community more than that of the city's African-American majority.[85] Although he was considered to be "pro-labor," Massell nonetheless crushed a strike by sanitation workers. As white flight intensified during his tenure in office, Massell adopted an essentially race-baiting strategy during his ill-fated 1973 re-election campaign. Arguing that black control of city hall would be the death of the city, and running under the slogan "Atlanta is Too Young to Die," Massell lost handily to his vice-mayor, a young, charismatic African-American lawyer named Maynard Jackson.[86]

Although a scion of one of Black Atlanta's most influential families, the outspoken Jackson was viewed as a maverick by the older generation of African-American community leaders comfortable with negotiating alliances with the white elite.[87] Building on popular resentment of the status quo, Jackson opposed the construction of new expressways and moved to involve local communities in the planning process. Jackson's newly created Department of Neighborhood Planning divided the city's approximately two hundred neighborhoods into twenty-four Neighborhood Planning Units (NPUs) to advise and consent to land-use and planning decisions affecting their localities. While the NPUs lacked the power to veto undesirable development, they did mandate an unprecedented level of community involvement in the planning process.

Together with his advocacy of programs to stimulate minority business involvement in the city's economic growth, Jackson's combative rhetoric and assertive actions provoked the wrath of CAP and the wider white business community. Less than a year after Jackson's election in 1973, CAP conducted an in-house survey of white business leaders. A summary of the survey's results, known as the Brockey Letter (after its author), was leaked to, and published by, the *Atlanta Constitution* (whose editor was especially disenchanted with the mayor). Brockey wrote that a majority of business leaders found Jackson to be "anti-white," and were contemplating a massive defection to the suburbs, "for other than economic or management reasons."[88] Soon afterwards, the national recession ended the city's decade-long boom. When the economy rebounded in the latter part of the 1970s, the recovery came to the periphery and the nodal regions of the core, like Peachtree Center and the Omni, rather than to the central city as a whole. Attracted by easy access, cheap land, the lack of land-use restrictions, and freedom from the "problems" of the urban core (not the least of which was the mayor himself), established firms and new companies alike chose sites in new office parks located in DeKalb, Cobb, and north Fulton counties.

Along with his emphasis on affirmative action and minority set-asides, Jackson's commitment to historic preservation did little for his reputation within the business community. Still, the city's position on preservation remained far more rhetorical than actual. Developers continued to enjoy an essentially free hand to swing the wrecking-ball virtually anywhere in the city. An Urban Design Commission (UDC) was created in May 1975 and was charged with an ambitious list of responsibilities, among them the preparation and maintenance of a register of Atlanta's historic structures and districts. Despite these heavy responsibilities, however, the UDC had no more power than the Civic Design Commission it replaced.[89] Although there was opposition, the Commission was obliged to go along with plans to demolish a substantial section of Underground Atlanta (which, along with Druid Hills and the Martin Luther King birth home was one of the city's first three Historic Districts) for the construction of MARTA's Five Points station, after MARTA and the railroad were unable to agree as to the use of railroad property. Later in the decade, however, the UDC helped private preservation groups in preventing Southern Bell's planned demolition of the elaborate, neo-Moorish Fox Theater in the emerging growth node in lower Midtown. Despite the Fox victory and the creation of a new category of significant zones – Urban Conservation and Development Districts – victories for preservationists in Atlanta were few and far between, increasingly so after the election of Andrew Young as mayor in 1981.

Even before Young's election, Jackson had begun to work out a rapprochement with private capital. The focal point of primary conflict and ultimate reconciliation was the construction of a new $400-million international airport complex that had been first envisioned during the Ivan Allen administration. While MARTA construction had involved some guidelines to encourage the participation of minority-owned companies, the airport was the crucible in which the Minority Business Enterprise (MBE) program was formed. As a result of Jackson's insistence, 25 percent (later increased to 35 per cent under Andrew Young) of the construction and operating contracts for the facility were reserved for minority firms. While heralded at the time as a major victory on the road to redressing economic inequality, the MBE program benefited only a relatively small segment of the city's African-American community, namely those with connections to the political establishment. Most recipients of government contracts for the airport, and later big ticket projects like Underground and the Georgia Dome, were cronies of Jackson or city council members.

Following the airport compromise, Jackson distanced himself from the neighborhood movement and attempted to build stronger bridges with the business community through regular meetings ("poundcake summits") and traveling with them on junkets to promote Atlanta to the world. In another gesture to make amends to private capital, Jackson created the quasi-public Atlanta Economic Development Corporation (AEDC) to act as the city's main redevelopment agency, a status formerly bestowed upon the city's first quasi-public entity, the Atlanta Housing Authority. The AEDC billed itself as a behind-the-scenes "process broker" dedicated to packaging the increasingly complex array of creative financing tools and incentives that were becoming available. Initially concerned with stimulating industrial parks near outlying public housing projects and the airport, the AEDC also came to play an important role in the redevelopment of the CBD in the 1980s (Underground) and 1990s (the Federal Center).

As the above examples indicate, by the mid to late 1970s, the city of Atlanta was definitely reaping the whirlwind of two decades of intensive renewal and redevelopment that had hollowed out the urban core from within. When the recovery from the post-1973 recession came at the end of the decade, it largely bypassed downtown in favor of the suburban periphery. Despite considerable public and private investment, the central city continued to hemorrhage jobs and (mostly white) residents throughout the 1970s, leaving an archipelago of inwardly focused enclaves amidst a sea of parking lots and an increasingly poor and African-American population. Chapter 4 charts the further restructuring of the built environment as various public and private sector players moved to reconstitute their partnership across the divides of race, turf, and vision.

4

PLUGGING THE WHOLE IN THE CENTER, 1975–95

If Atlanta could suck as hard as it could blow, it would be a seaport.[1]

Atlanta is the most over-grasping, boastful, insecure, adolescent city in America, bar none. It is also the most successful, remarkable, creative, envied city in the country from the point of view of economic development . . . [yet] Atlanta has to decide what it wants to be when it grows up.[2]

On a sunny morning in late September 1992, several dozen of the Atlanta real estate industry's best and brightest gathered on the forty-fifth floor of John Portman's just completed One Peachtree Center to listen to a panel of distinguished corporate sachems discuss "The Future of Downtown." Despite the city's selection in 1990 as the site of the 1996 Centennial Olympic Games, much had happened in the previous two years to dampen the optimism of even the most Atlanta-Spirited downtown booster. The lingering effects of the 1991 recession and the laying on of millions of square feet of new "Class A" office space (of which One Peachtree Center was a prime example) had reduced property values by half from their inflated late-1980s peaks and increased office vacancies to nearly a third of downtown's available space.[3] In less than two years, eight of the city's ten major banks had decamped from their 1960s-vintage headquarters along Marietta Street for glitzy new trophy buildings near Peachtree Center or in Midtown. They were joined in their exodus by a slew of the city's leading law, architecture, and accounting firms, as well as the service trades that fed off such corporate patronage. Many of these firms had moved to Buckhead or suburban nodes at Cumberland/Galleria and Perimeter Center. Between 1970 and 1990, the city of Atlanta's share of metropolitan employment dropped from 55 percent to 29 percent, while that of the Central Business District fell from 15 percent to 7.5 percent of the regional total.[4]

The area south of Five Points presented an even more dire situation. Despite the reopening of Underground Atlanta in 1989 and the presence of a host of city, county, state and federal offices, the southern Central Business District had continued its freefall into a "zone of discard"[5] in the early 1990s. In 1991, Rich's Department Store, once lower downtown's most stalwart presence and a genuine Atlanta institution, closed the doors of its massive flagship facility. While there were islands of activity scattered about – the dedicated carceral zone emerging around the Garnett Street MARTA station, a still bustling low-income retail corridor along lower Peachtree, an isolated atoll of pioneer lofts along Mitchell Street and another on Castleberry Hill – most of the rest of the district was comprised of decaying buildings and parking lots, a textbook example of what Gary McDonogh has called "the geography of emptiness."[6] The southern CBD's emptiness was reciprocally related to its mediated invisibility: many of the guidebooks to the city no longer included it on maps of downtown.

Even as some of its more problematic areas were being "disappeared," other aspects of downtown were all too visible in the local news media. Ever since Atlanta's transition to a majority African-American city in 1970, downtown, especially the area around Five Points, had acquired a reputation as a place of danger and criminal activity far in excess of what the crime statistics warranted.[7] While Atlanta prided itself on being "a city too busy to hate," Atlantans were certainly not too preoccupied to fear a whole range of implicitly racialized urban dangers. Fears of crime and the "perception" of danger allowed white suburbanites and city planners alike to cloak discriminations made on the basis of race in a more neutral, rational, and ostensibly unprejudiced guise. In the early 1990s, however, the usually implicit connections between danger, race, and crime were becoming more explicitly rendered. In late April 1992, a crowd of African-American youth, splitting off from a larger group protesting the verdict in the Rodney King police brutality trial, had spilled angrily through the streets around Five Points and Underground Atlanta, looting stores and assaulting passers-by. The disturbances, which continued over a span of three days, only reconfirmed white perceptions of downtown as a place of racially tinged danger and disorder, not to mention the wisdom of disinvestment.

The forty-fifth floor of One Peachtree Center provided a commanding view of the area in question. Like much of the rest of the building at the time, the floor was unleased and lacked interior partition walls. The overwhelmingly white, male crowd wandered about, taking in the view and talking shop. The air was exceptionally clear and beyond the pointy pyramidal spires of upper and lower Midtown, one could make out the discrete clusters of exopolitan skylines on the northern horizon that marked the various "edge cities" – Cumberland-Galleria, Buckhead, Perimeter Center – that had snared much of the private capital, jobs, and people that had poured into Atlanta over the previous two decades. Significantly, the dais and the chairs for the morning's presentation had been set up in the southwest corner of the floor, looking away from the competition and facing the twin aediculea atop Burgee and Johnson's One Ninety One Peachtree Building, which had been recently completed by Portman's arch-rival, developer Thomas Cousins.

Aside from its commanding vantage, One Peachtree Center was a particularly appropriate choice from which to contemplate the problems and prospects of the once and future downtown. For over two decades, John Portman had been the city's single most influential player in the downtown redevelopment game, a man who had realized nothing less than the creation of the first of Atlanta's many "new downtowns" around his Peachtree Center mixed-use complex. He had long envisioned a mega-office tower as the crowning achievement to what was once proudly billed as Rockefeller Center South, and began construction of the sixty-story, 1.4 million square foot blue glass and granite tower in 1989. He mortgaged much of Peachtree Center and went deep into personal hock to finance the completely speculative $374-million structure, only to see it come on-line into the backwash of a local office glut and the back end of a double dip nationwide recession. Over-extended, and faced with the prospect of bankruptcy in 1990, Portman was obliged to seek restructuring of his more than $2-billion debt, a process that would eventually take more than five years and strip him of most of his once extensive holdings, including all of Peachtree Center and the adjacent complex of trade marts, the Atlanta Market Center, Ltd. While he was able to retain ownership of One Peachtree Center, in 1995 Portman was obliged to rename it SunTrust Plaza in honor of its largest single tenant, SunTrust Bank (formerly known as Trust Company of Georgia, or, more informally, "the Bank of Coca-Cola").

Portman's problems, or, more generally, those induced by civically irresponsible orgies of speculative over-building and the absence of comprehensive planning, were not the chief items on the morning's agenda, however. Indeed, aside from one speaker's oblique reference to "the downbeat and overly negative portrayals" of the real estate industry in the local media (which, to hear him tell it, seemed the primary cause of the depressed market itself) there was no explicit mention of the effect that the declining fortunes of downtown's largest developer would have on its present or future. Rather, the main concern of the panel, which included representatives from the Atlanta Committee for the Olympic Games (ACOG), Central Atlanta Progress, Inc. (CAP), and the quasi-public Atlanta Economic Development Corporation (AEDC), was the city's preparations for the upcoming 1996 Centennial Olympics.

Along with a number of other civic and business leaders, most of the speakers had recently returned from their month-long stay in Barcelona – where they had been honored guests at the Olympic Games – with the mildly horrifying awareness of Atlanta's lack of "traditional urbanity." While they recognized that they could never "out-Barcelona Barcelona" (whatever that might mean), some enhancement of the public character of the city was deemed vitally necessary. Indeed, bold talk of a very concrete Olympic legacy had done much to build support and stifle local opposition during the bid process for the Centennial Olympic Games.[8] However, with ACOG adamant in its commitment to keeping its dollars "inside the fence" of the venues themselves, and the city as yet to announce its plans (the creation of the Corporation for Olympic Development in Atlanta, or CODA, was not announced until a few weeks later), it was unclear what, if anything, would happen "outside the fence." This state of affairs was deeply troubling to the assembled multitude, for there was considerable consensus that the Olympics provided a critical opportunity for downtown revitalization. As one audience member mumbled gravely to another: "We miss this, we're SOL [shit outta luck]."

From the point of view of the speakers, the Olympics did not so much create a new set of problems as highlight a set of already existing ones. With a truly remarkable sense of amnesia as to the relatively free play of market forces that had creatively destroyed downtown, and rather uncreatively redeveloped it into an archipelago of fortified fantasy islands over the previous two decades, the panelists reiterated a common set of "problems" to be fixed. Chief among the demons was not street-killing megastructures, mass corporate defections, or speculative over-building, but rather the negative perception of the central area as a dangerous, urban jungle inhabited by a "predatory" homeless population and crack-addled, graffiti-painting youth gangs who lived in nearby public housing projects and slum neighborhoods. The panelists talked at great length of the need to "bring people back downtown," implying that the homeless and the residents of surrounding neighborhoods, both of whom were predominantly African-American, were not quite people, or, at the very least, not the kind of people who should be there. Still, the "people" they had in mind were not so much defined by race (indeed the "R" word was never explicitly mentioned in the entirety of the ninety-minute session) as by consumption patterns. Free-spending tourists, conventioneers on expense accounts, suburban office workers, and aspiring urban gentry (none of whom in this "mecca" for the black middle class were necessarily white) were to be lured downtown through the miraculous synergy of enhanced marketing and policing, cosmetic streetscape improvements, new arts and entertainment zones, and middle- and upper-income housing. These neo-Rouse-ian tactics of "making place" were embodied in CAP's most recent playbook for downtown, the Central Area Study II, which had been released in 1988. However, with a few exceptions, these recolonization efforts had yet to be realized some four years later. The Olympics provided a major potential catalyst to finally get things done.

Although the speakers were of a common mind as to what they would like to see happen, they remained more than a little bit uncertain as to whether it could be accomplished. As one member of the panel lamented, there was no longer any all-powerful "player" operating downtown. "Who's got the power?" to make Olympic redevelopment happen, he asked. This was a curious query coming from the then president of Central Atlanta Progress, historically one of the city's most powerful institutions. However, he was not being completely disingenuous. The urban power structure was in the midst of a restructuring as profound as that affecting the built environment or the metro economy as a whole; indeed, these multiple restructurings were related.

According to political scientist Clarence Stone, a biracial "urban regime" had emerged in the course of the 1970s and 1980s that united Atlanta's largely white corporate elite with its newly empowered African-American political establishment in a bond of mutual pecuniary advantage: a mixed and often quite contentious public–private partnership of white money and black power.[9] However, by the early 1990s, the wheels were beginning to come off this "growth machine"[10] that had driven the city, or rather the metropolitan area, to the heights of prosperity. Despite a deep and resounding regional boom, the city's population, its tax rolls, its schools, its infrastructure, and its place in the metropolitan economy continued to decline, while demands for services, unemployment, and the percentage of the population living under the poverty line registered steady increases.[11] Preoccupied by internecine turf battles between the city council and the mayor (Maynard Jackson had recently returned to office after a nine-year hiatus) and beset by accusations of corruption and incompetence, the city government's ability to get things done was held in low regard by the private sector. This low esteem extended to the city's principal quasi-public redevelopment entity, the Atlanta Economic Development Corporation.

For its part, the other half of the much-vaunted civic–business partnership was not faring too much better, either. The absorption of major local banks by aggressive North Carolina institutions in the late 1980s and early 1990s (e.g. Citizens & Southern by NationsBank, First National by Wachovia, and Georgia Federal by First Union) had effectively shattered Atlanta's title as undisputed financial capital of the Southeast and raised questions about the kind of corporate citizens these new institutions would prove to be.[12] The financial troubles of John Portman and the death or retirement of some of the business community's most influential leaders also created something of a temporary crisis of leadership. The growth of new development nodes in Midtown and Buckhead further eroded the integrity of the "urban" power structure already challenged by the delirious growth of the peripheries. The state of flux in the business community was nowhere better represented than in the game of musical presidents atop the summit of CAP, which, after the long reign of Dan Sweat (1973–88), had gone through three top executives in four years.

Atlanta's emergence as a "national city" in the 1960s and its explosive growth and incremental internationalization since then had greatly expanded not only the field of play, but the number and kinds of players as well. Aside from the city government and an increasingly fragmented business community, the roster included a welter of county commissions, state agencies, regional planning bodies, quasi-public bond-peddling authorities, business associations, philanthropies, and a whole sub-roster of public–private task forces, alliances, and partnerships, not to mention a cast of sundry, less empowered "others," such as historic preservationists, community development corporations, and neighborhood groups. At the top of the heap were arranged various tag-teams of local developers and deep-pocketed institutional investors whose interests often spanned the length and breadth of the metro area.

The key word in this increasingly cluttered landscape of the somewhat less than all-powerful, was "partnerships." Atlanta had long been known for its entrepreneurial mode of governance and its embrace of public–private partnerships that transcended the divide of race. The speakers that morning reiterated a call for new partnerships between the private sector and government to coordinate downtown redevelopment. By "government" the speakers meant not so much the city and its quasi-public entities like the Atlanta Economic Development Corporation, which had fallen into disrepute, but various institutional manifestations of the State of Georgia. These included not only such veteran players as the pharaonic Georgia Department of Transportation, but quasi-public entities like the Georgia World Congress Center Authority, and educational institutions such as the Georgia Institute of Technology (better known as Georgia Tech) and Georgia State University. Indeed, the latter two institutions figured prominently in CAP's plans to attract emerging "industries of the mind"[13] downtown. The Olympics also opened up the prospect of attracting new partners from overseas to aid in the process of downtown revitalization.

GOING INTERNATIONAL

As early as the late 1970s, the development game was no longer merely a domestic matter of negotiating an arrangement between white corporate money and black political power. "Atlanta International" was not only a public relations slogan, but gradually began to describe the sources of investment capital. Two of the major mixed-use developments of the late 1960s and early 1970s – the Omni International (now CNN Center) and the Atlanta Center, Ltd (now the Hilton

Hotel and Tower) – were built with significant European and Kuwaiti investment, respectively. Although local banks were still smarting from the post-1973 recession- and over-building-induced collapse of the real estate market, foreign and national money center banks found Atlanta a quite appealing investment, thanks to the relative cheapness of land and more than $5 billion of public investment in the new international airport, MARTA, and other infrastructural improvements (including widened expressways and the Georgia World Congress Center). Between 1975 and 1984, the number of foreign, mostly European, companies with offices in Atlanta increased from 150 to 780, with 240 of these being the US headquarters for these firms.[14] Included in this number were branches of the world's twenty largest banks, making Atlanta Miami's only rival as the international financial center of the Southeast.

By 1984, foreign companies had invested over $3 billion in their metro Atlanta operations. One third of the total foreign presence in the Atlanta economy (and an even greater share of real estate investment) came from Canadian companies, followed by British and Dutch interests ($500 million each), Japanese ($400 million) and Germans ($109 million).[15] Two major members of the downtown power structure, Life of Georgia and the National Bank of Georgia, were purchased by Dutch and Saudi interests, respectively. Interest in Atlanta was not limited to foreign concerns, however. The same conditions that made Atlanta real estate so appealing to foreign investors also attracted the "patient money" of US pension funds and insurance companies, such as Equitable Life Assurance and Metropolitan Life, as well as real estate investment trusts, or REITs. Foreign investment in the metro economy exploded after 1985, with the number of foreign companies increasing tenfold in no more in a few years.[16] While a good deal of this investment was in distribution and office facilities, a significant chunk was directed towards real estate speculation.

Although Maynard Jackson had been an enthusiastic promoter of the city to outside investors, the influx of national and global investment capital was greatly stimulated by the election of former UN ambassador Andrew Young as mayor in November 1981. Whereas Maynard Jackson's relationship with the business community was marked by constant conflict and reluctant cooperation, that of his successor was quite different. Although elected without the support of the business community, Andrew Young quickly moved to forge a spirit of cooperation not only with local but with global interests as well. In these efforts, Young was joined by other key black political leaders, including Fulton County Commission chairman Michael Lomax, city council president Marvin Arrington, and council Finance Committee chair Ira Jackson. Utilizing connections made while United Nations ambassador, Young traveled so widely, at corporate expense, trying to attract foreign investment to Atlanta that he was jokingly known as an "absentee mayor."

Despite his political stature gained as a lieutenant to Martin Luther King and as a progressive US ambassador to the UN under Jimmy Carter, Young embraced an unashamedly Reaganite vision of trickle-down economics. The mayor gutted neighborhood participation in the planning process, which had already been weakened during the latter stages of the Jackson administration, and fought a successful battle against historic preservationists who sought to place restrictions on developers, particularly in the Midtown area.[17]

Encouraged by a pro-growth mayor and fueled by the arrival of US insurance companies and big Eurodollar investors, such as the Dutch Institutional Holding Company, and the completion of significant stretches of MARTA's north–south and east–west lines, Atlanta's economy and real estate market boomed between 1982 and 1987. By the latter year, seventy major metro area commercial properties were wholly foreign-owned, with Dutch, British, Canadian, and German firms accounting for three-quarters of these. Korean, Indian, Saudi, and Taiwanese capital also entered the market in smaller, but still significant, amounts.[18] In 1987, the Japanese made their long-awaited and hoped-for entry into Atlanta real estate with Sumitomo's $300-million purchase of the neo-Gothic One Atlantic Center in upper Midtown, which, owing to its principal tenant, was better known as the IBM Building. Over the next two years, Japanese banks, insurance companies, and pension funds poured nearly a billion dollars into Central Area real estate alone. A former president of the Atlanta Economic Development Corporation wistfully envisioned that by the turn of the century, 50 percent of the Class-A buildings in the metro area would be foreign-owned, with Japanese companies accounting for half of these.[19] While Japanese investment in Atlanta real estate slowed considerably after 1990, the European presence, led by Dutch, German, and Swedish concerns, has intensified. Foreign capital also helped fuel the transmutation of the Golden Crescent along the top end of the Perimeter into the Platinum Triangle during the 1980s, although development there and in Buckhead was primarily the province of domestic capital.

THE NEW DOWNTOWN DOWNTOWN

Much of the growth that occurred in the central city after the mid 1970s took place in the vicinity of Peachtree Center. After the demise of his Central Area Study plan for downtown, Portman used his mixed-use development as a test bed for concepts he later would work out more systematically in projects in other cities. The mall at Peachtree Center provides a good example of the (de)evolution of his design philosophy. The mall began as a sunken garden court and pedestrian promenade along Peachtree Street in 1973. Subsequent renovations in 1979 and 1986 enclosed the garden court and cut the mall off from the street, creating an even more hermetic realm. A vast network of skyways, including one advertised as the world's longest, linked the mall with the Peachtree Plaza Hotel (1976), the Apparel Mart (1979), the Marriott Marquis Hotel and the twin Marquis One and Two Towers (1985–89), the Inforum (1989), and the Gift Mart and One Peachtree Center (both 1992). The growth of the complex vastly inflated the appeal of the Peachtree Street corridor. In 1982, Georgia-Pacific completed its new headquarters tower a few blocks to the south. In the ensuing decade, a new Ritz Carlton Hotel and One Ninety One Peachtree sprouted in the intervening space, creating Atlanta's only Manhattan-like urban canyon.

A few efforts were made to link the Peachtree Center area with the old downtown a third of a mile to the south around Five Points. In 1975, the newly constituted Urban Design Commission (UDC) had proposed building a new Atlanta-Fulton County library on the northern edge of the recently created Central City Park. In addition to connecting the new and the old downtowns, the UDC plan for the library was part of an early and ambitious effort at conjuring a distinctive simulation of quasi-City Beautiful urbanity that was the antithesis of Portman's megalomaniacal modernism arising around Peachtree Center. Under the UDC plan, the five-cornered site where Peachtree Street curved to follow the ridge would be converted into a zone where myth and history would mingle promiscuously. The old site of the Carnegie Library would be converted into a History of Atlanta Park that would feature the building's partially preserved Beaux Arts facade and a below-ground location for the Cyclorama.[20] The latter, an enormous panoramic mural commemorating the Battle of Atlanta, was housed in decaying quarters in Grant Park, near the zoo. Next to the library site, the triangular corner formed by the intersection of Forsyth and Peachtree Streets had already been renamed Margaret Mitchell Square in 1967. Just to the east, the Loew's Grand Theater, where *Gone With the Wind* premiered, was to be restored to its 1930s splendor from its current incarnation as a martial arts film venue.

The Civil War ethos of the UDC plan, however, found little favor with either the business community or the Jackson administration, both of whom desired to promote the image of Atlanta as a modern international city. The Carnegie Library was soon demolished to make way for Marcel Breuer's concrete Rubik's cube design for the new library, while the Loew's Grand met a similar fate after a mysterious fire damaged part of it in 1979. The site was subsequently purchased by the Georgia-Pacific Corporation, which built its new headquarters tower on the site. Along with a neighboring structure built by a Canadian–American joint venture, the 55-story rose granite edifice was much heralded at the time (1982) as proof that downtown "wasn't dead." The Georgia Power Company echoed that chorus by building a black glass monolith (quickly dubbed the "Darth Vader" building)[21] on a 29-acre site that had been originally part of the Bedford-Pine urban renewal zone. Unfortunately, both of these projects were isolated structures that stood apart from their surrounding environment. The Georgia Power building, for example, was separated from the rest of downtown by the twelve-lane cut of the Downtown Connector and some of the most forbidding surface streetscapes in the entire city. Despite encouragement from the city, the enthusiasm of private capital did not extend south of Five Points. Ambitious plans for the south CBD, including a quarter-mile-long pedestrian bridge/arcade linking Rich's and the Omni, as well as a 45-acre mixed-use complex south of the department store, failed to find favor with investors.[22]

Not all downtown activity in the early 1980s was in new construction. Some years after the idea had caught on elsewhere in North America, Atlantan developers finally began experimenting with recycling rather than razing historic structures. Taking advantage of tax breaks for renovation, property owners invested some $70 million in the rehabilitation of turn-of-the-century buildings in the area of Five Points they called Fairlie-Poplar. However, for reasons that will be detailed below, these efforts were unsuccessful. The only major development outside the expansion of the World Congress Center and Peachtree Center took place northwest of downtown where Coca-Cola was quietly adding to its externally understated corporate campus just west of Georgia Tech. The peripheral location of Atlanta's most important corporate citizen might seem a bit curious, as most of the city's other major businesses were at least initially located in the center. Instead, Coke's offset location underscored its dominance in the local corporate landscape. Rather than being mixed up in the center with all the rest, Coke executives were able to enjoy a nicely framed and contemplative view of both the downtown and the emerging Midtown skylines.

MIDTOWN

Efforts to redevelop downtown in the 1980s were undermined by what was taking place a mile up Peachtree Street in the area once known as Uptown. With the emergence of Buckhead in the early 1970s, the area bordered on the west by the Downtown Connector, on the east by Piedmont Park, on the south by North Avenue and on the north by 17th Street, was transformed into Midtown. Once a zone of elite homes and apartment buildings, large sections became heavily commercialized in the 1930s, sending the upper and upper middle classes moving northward to Brookwood Hills, Peachtree Hills, and other residential neighborhoods in the Buckhead area. During the 1950s, many of Midtown's large homes were converted into apartments and rooming houses that provided inexpensive accommodation for the ambitious sons and daughters of Dixie who were flocking to the city. In 1962, one local newspaper had taken to referring to the area as "Atlanta's Own Greenwich Village"[23] on account of its considerable population of students from the Atlanta College of Art, along with a host of bohemian fellow-travelers attracted by cheap rents, and the neighborhood's many theaters and other cultural establishments. Midtown's image as the cultural cutting edge of Atlanta was reinforced by the opening of the Atlanta Memorial Arts Center in 1963. As described in Chapter 2, however, the area soon became the center of a "high culture" of another sort. By 1966, the area between 10th and 14th Streets was known as the premier hippie ghetto in the Southeast. Within a few years, though, much of the Hip Strip had become a red-light district of strip joints and porno houses.

The conversion of Midtown into a zone of "unsavory" influences prompted a predictable response from property owners, who formed a businessmen's association in 1966 that merged with Central Atlanta Progress a year later. Together, they strategized to "take back" the neighborhood. The first attempt at recolonizing the Hip Strip was the Colony Square "micropolis" at Peachtree and 14th, which was proposed in 1967 and built between 1970 and 1974. The $75-million project, financed by a syndicate of local and outside investors, consisted of the familiar enclaved melange of offices, shops, a luxury hotel, and yet another ice rink.[24] Unlike its cousin MXDs downtown, Colony Square also included high-priced apartments and condominiums in its mix. Still, the complex failed to overcome the challenge of its surroundings and filed for bankruptcy in 1975. Since then, the complex has undergone a number of renovations under a series of owners, none of which has succeeded in realizing the project's initial vision as a New Age town center. Unfazed by Colony Square's less than auspicious debut, and encouraged by cheap land and plans to establish three MARTA stations in the area (at North Avenue, Tenth Street, and the Arts Center), a handful of young local developers in league with national and foreign backers assembled large parcels nearby during the 1970s and waited for MARTA to come. Meanwhile, a number of small real estate developers – many of whom were gay – were quietly gentrifying the old homes that line the tree-shaded streets near Piedmont Park and in other parts of Midtown with less commercial potential.

With the encouragement of CAP, the city cooperated by cracking down on drug dealing, porn shops and prostitution and, after the new zoning ordinance was passed in 1982, defining areas around the three MARTA stations as Special Public Interest zones. As first envisioned in the Urban Framework Plan of a decade earlier, an SPI designation encouraged high-density, mixed-use development in an area formerly zoned for low-rise, low-density residential and/or commercial uses.

Midtown property values rose markedly, even outside the SPI zones themselves, as developers assembled the necessary parcels for large-scale development. While SPI zoning was supposed to encourage pedestrian activities, public spaces, and the look and feel of an urban environment, these did not quite occur. Indeed, SPI could very well stand for "special private interest" zoning, for all the good that it did in Midtown. As with downtown development in the late 1960s, there was no effort to coordinate, much less restrict, the activities of competing developers, who aimed to build essentially the same kind of inwardly focused, street-killing projects with some updated architectural flourishes. Along the way, they destroyed a considerable number of historic buildings that housed not only porn shops and prostitution, but a large number of avant-garde theaters, clubs, and other outposts of genuinely urban culture that thrived in the area in the late 1970s and early 1980s.

Although politicians and corporate leaders talked abstractly about the desirability of historic preservation, the Young administration refused to interfere with the ability of owners to do what they wanted with their property, even though developers were enjoying, via MARTA construction, a massive enhancement of their land values.[25] The mayor himself led the charge against preservationists and arts groups that sought to maintain historic structures, or "hunks of junk," as he described them. When his opponents criticized him for destroying the city's character, he replied that "Atlanta has no character, we are building it now."[26]

Yet it was not the absence of character, along with a desire not to hinder the free flow of private capital, that prompted the hostility of Young and other African-American leaders towards historic preservation. Rather, part of their negative attitude lay in the character of the past that was to be preserved. Like a number of other local black leaders, Young argued that many of Atlanta's historic buildings were inimically bound up with the history of racialized inequality and that to preserve them was to somehow preserve and legitimate the memories of those times along with those spaces. This was particularly an issue for structures from which African-Americans were for a long time excluded, such as downtown's Carnegie Library, or where they had been obliged to put up with separate and inferior accommodations, i.e. virtually every public building and space in the city. Seen in this light, historic preservation was thus primarily the preservation of the bricks and mortar of a Jim Crow city. Such an argument, though, does not explain the Young administration's lack of active interest in preserving buildings and areas associated with the proud history of Black Atlanta, such as the Sweet Auburn business district and the area around the Atlanta University Center. Indeed, despite the designation of the former as one of the city's earliest Historic Districts, both of these areas decayed markedly during the 1980s. Nor does unwillingness to preserve the physical remainders of Jim Crow explain the city government's complicity in a redevelopment process that was actively resegregating Atlanta in a far more stealthy and insidious manner.

The speculative frenzy raging on the publicly fertilized greenfields of Midtown was the perfect embodiment of the updated Atlanta Spirit in action. All too predictably, though, none of the projects ever ended up realizing the "build out" potential of their models. Most were only in their first phase, when, again much like the first wave of MXD madness a decade before, the Midtown market (as well as that of the entire metro area) imploded thanks to over-building and a national recession in the late 1980s. In 1989, Australian developer L.J. Hooker filed for bankruptcy and its massive Gateway Atlanta mixed-use project around the Tenth Street MARTA station was taken over by creditors (in this particular case the Bank of Nova Scotia), leaving only Michael Graves's neo-Egyptoid Ten Peachtree Place building looming over eleven acres of vacant lots that had formerly consti-tuted the commercial heart of the hippie ghetto. One block to the east on Peachtree, across the street from the apartment building in which Margaret Mitchell had written *Gone With the Wind*, Texan-based developer Trammell Crow had completed only one of its three planned towers (now the headquarters of First Union Bank). Along the 14th Street corridor, Dallas-based Prentiss Properties had finished only one quarter of its Atlantic Center project (the neo-Gothic IBM Building), while next door, the Landmarks Group (developer of the high-rise Concourse at Perimeter Center) had completed only two-thirds of its Promenade complex. The resultant juxtaposition of shiny towers and vacant lots seemed a pathetic manifestation of the Corbusier-ian notion of "skyscrapers in a park," and only accentuated the inbetweenness of the liminal landscape.

The *reductio ad absurdum* of Midtown development, however, was still to come. In 1991, while other developers were making the rounds in bankruptcy court and new office towers were experiencing more than 20 percent vacancy, a Swedish developer, G. Lars Gullstedt, revealed plans for a "European-style" 11-million-square-foot "mini-city" between the North Avenue and Tenth Street MARTA stations.[27] As Midtown land prices had been bid up during the 1980s boom, Gullstedt had spent an estimated $100 million to acquire eleven blocks around the Biltmore Hotel, once the city's finest hostelry.[28] The area around the Biltmore and nearby Crawford Long Hospital had largely been abandoned and had become a prime cruising ground for male prostitution. Thus, plans for redeveloping the area received an enthusiastic welcome from city boosters. Acting in their capacity as "uncritical cheerleaders for the property men,"[29] local newspapers lauded Gullstedt as a "wheeler-dealer visionary,"[30] and local politicians were even giddier. The project, Atlantans were assured, would fuse the old CBD and Midtown into one large, more impressive downtown area.

Aside from the all-too-obvious observation that the last thing a glutted market needed in a recession was an *additional* 11 million square feet of completely speculative space (in a city built on dreams pragmatic logic is not always appreciated), the city and the media also missed the clear implication that the GLC Park Plaza, as the complex was called, was yet another hermetic enclave that would do little to knit together the urban fabric. As it turned out, this problem was moot. Before beginning the Park Plaza, Gullstedt had already started on a separate, and itself rather ambitious, development some blocks further north, the 53-story GLC Grand tower. The massive postmodernized-Art Deco hotel/office/condo facility had just been completed in the spring of 1993 when Gullstedt declared bankruptcy, a victim of the collapsing Swedish real estate market.[31] His demise added Sweden's Gota Bank to the long list of Canadian, Japanese, European, and American creditors that sat with the detritus of some Midtown developer's failed vision and prompted even the normally Pollyanna-ish business press to question Midtown's future.[32]

By the fall of 1995, however, prospects for the northern half of Midtown had improved considerably with the construction of several new luxury apartment complexes, the adaptive reuse of a number of vacant office buildings for loft-style housing, and the Federal Reserve Bank's decision to move its downtown Marietta Street headquarters to a new facility on the L.J. Hooker parcel north of Tenth Street. Coupled with the buyout of Bank South by NationsBank, the Federal Reserve Bank's move will completely empty the Marietta Street corridor – once known as the Wall Street of the South – of financial institutions by 1998. Prospects for much of the Gullstedt property remain grim, although plans have recently been unveiled to redevelop the long-vacant Biltmore Hotel into a mixed residential, retail, and commercial complex. The construction of more than a thousand new apartments in Midtown competes directly with downtown boosters' efforts to build new housing there. Indeed, these recent developments signify the failure of CAP's strategy during the 1980s to build linkages between its two poles of the central area.

A NEW GAME PLAN

The GLC Park Plaza plan was particularly appealing to city boosters because it promised to fill in some of the gaps between isolated nodes of development. As early as the mid 1980s, it was apparent even to Central Atlanta Progress that the existing pattern of archipelagic enclaves was lacking a "sense of the urbane" (sic). The dearth of middle- and upper-income housing downtown, first noted in the 1971 Central Area Study, remained particularly troublesome. Although a few apartment buildings had been constructed in the 1960s, private developers had generally left residences out of the mix in their mixed-use developments. One notable exception was in the Bedford-Pine renewal area, where a for-profit CAP subsidiary, Park Central Communities, Inc., had been granted the rights for residential development as early as 1969. Its plans to build middle- and upper-income housing on the 78-acre tract were effectively opposed for over a decade by neighborhood groups concerned over "negro removal" and lack of low-income housing. By the mid 1980s, these long-awaited plans for downtown housing were finally forging ahead, thanks to the demise of neighborhood associations, reduced federal oversight, and generous tax abatements and tax-free bonds sold by the state-chartered Urban Residential Finance Authority.[33]

Beginning in the early 1980s, CAP sponsored a number of studies to deal with the questions of linking nodes and encouraged middle- and upper-income intown housing. Not surprisingly, Bedford-Pine figured prominently in these studies, one of which called for the bridging of the Downtown Connector by an enormous park-like platform to physically link Bedford-Pine and the Civic Center with the CBD and the area around the North Avenue MARTA station. Along with an above-ground downtown people-mover, the platform was to be funded through the issue of city bonds.[34] A separate study, commissioned by the city council, explored the possibilities for encouraging housing in the south CBD, in the Special Public Interest zone around the Garnett Street MARTA station (one stop south of Five Points).[35] Although CAP acknowledged the desirability of housing in the southern CBD, it deemed the Garnett Street area to be one of the least appealing areas for it.[36]

With no subsequent interest from the private sector, the city stealthily built a new municipal jail just to the east of the Garnett MARTA station in the early 1990s. Together with the adjoining Pre-Trial Detention Center and a facility for juvenile offenders, the Atlanta City Detention Center occupies an entire block. Looking more like a postmodern office building than a prison, the facility was carefully designed so as not to scare off any possible future private investment in the surrounding area. To this end, as well as to provide a "meditative space" for passersby, the jail's designers included a Memorial Plaza dedicated to victims of violent crime and firefighters, police officers, and corrections officers who had lost their lives in the line of duty. Located adjacent to the main entrance along Peachtree Street, the plaza includes a nine-foot-tall conical bronze sculpture surmounted by a living pine tree. The sculpture was intended to symbolize "the human desire to rise heaven-ward above the suffering of everyday life," while the tree symbolizes "the family's healing power, the sheltering and cooperative qualities of community."[37] The desire for transcendence, family, and community also figures in the adjacent circular black granite "Ceremonial Space," which is inscribed with a twisting light-colored path meant to symbolize life's journeys and the pain of loss. Six polished granite panels bearing the names of the honored dead line the eastern wall of the plaza. Completing the installation are a number of concrete "Carpets" scattered amidst the sidewalk pavers bearing symbols of the passage of time and several engraved bronze plaques bearing snippets of poetry from Georgia writers.

It is unclear what public the plaza's designers had in mind when putting the project together. Since it is located just to the north of the busy battlement of the east–west expressway (I-20), there are very few pedestrians in the carceral district around the Detention Center, apart from customers of the many bail bond establishments that line Peachtree Street for several blocks, and people coming to visit the incarcerated inhabitants of the facility. Otherwise, the plaza is devoid of users and is just another one of downtown's empty places. However, despite the failure of Special Public Interest zoning to stimulate housing, the city has not given up entirely on the Garnett Street area. Rather, it has recently become the site of the relocated inter-city bus station (displaced from the Atlanta Market Center by Olympic-related development), as well as a transfer point for a number of city bus routes. Still, these new uses are not likely to enhance the area's appeal to private investors; in fact they will probably only reinforce the negative image of the district. Nor has the city given up on plans for housing in the south CBD. In 1995, it finally succeeded in attracting a private developer to build the apartment/retail complex just west of city hall. The complex's name – City Plaza – is most appropriate since the city donated the land and arranged for the Urban Residential Finance Authority to float the bonds needed to build the 164 apartments and 20,000 square feet of retail space.

IN SEARCH OF THE USER-FRIENDLY, 24-HOUR CITY

A renewed interest in urban design also marked CAPs efforts in the mid 1980s. This reflected not only the changing tastes of local place entrepreneurs, but a paradigm shift in what Christine Boyer has termed the "pattern language" employed by architects and urban designers nationwide.[38] More like advertising than architecture, this new language provided formulas for the creation of new signature spaces set apart from the remainder of the urban landscape. In Atlanta, these included not just historical buildings and districts, but the streets themselves. Beginning in 1985, CAP organized design competitions for three of the city's principal streetscapes: Peachtree Street, Auburn Avenue, and International Boulevard. While Peachtree and Auburn were historic pedestrian, as well as vehicular, thoroughfares that had been drastically altered by automobilized redevelopment, International Boulevard presented a different kind of design challenge.

Originally known as Cain Street, International Boulevard had been renamed in the early 1970s as part of Atlanta's campaign to promote itself as "the World's Next Great International City." Flanking the southern glacis of Peachtree Center,

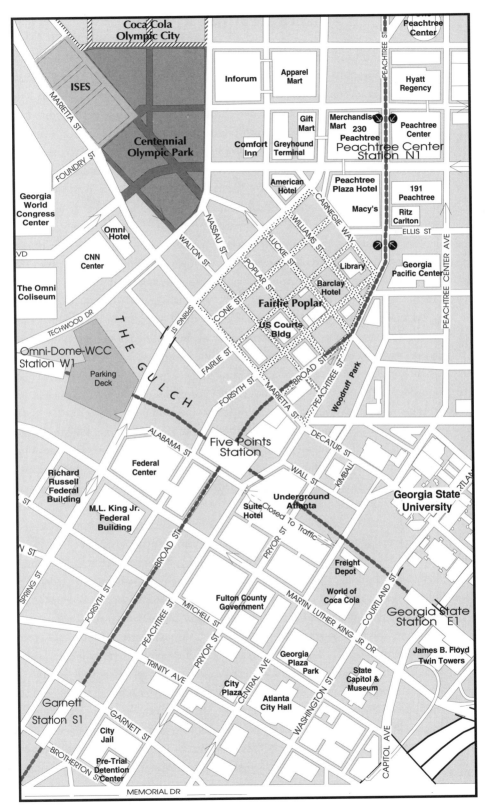

Map 8: The Heart of Atlanta

the boulevard had been designated by traffic engineers as the principal conduit of automobile traffic moving from the Downtown Connector to the Georgia World Congress Center/Omni area. Lacking street-level activities of any kind, International Boulevard was one of the most pedestrian-unfriendly corridors in the entire city. Planners sought to transform it into the central gateway to the new downtown, with twin neo-classical towers greeting motorists as they exited the expressway onto a boulevard flanked by sidewalks full of pedestrians and cafés that terminated in a major public open space at the "front door" of the Georgia World Congress Center.[39] With all the neo-classical flourishes and other things civic, the overall design motif could be called "City Beautiful Lite."

Few could argue with the need to enhance International's desolate streetscape, but the financing of the plan proved to be another matter. As with the park plaza over the Downtown Connector, CAP planners suggested that streetscape improvements be financed by yet another city bond issue and/or federal Community Development Block grants and Urban Development Action grants. That the private sector (principally the Portman companies, whose enclaved development had gone a long way towards destroying the street in the first place) bore a responsibility, or at the very least an interest, in contributing to these "public" improvements was not considered. With a bond referendum widely considered to be political suicide and the bond-issuing capacity of the Downtown Development Authority tied up in mega-projects like Underground Atlanta and the Georgia Dome, the streetscape plans languished on the shelf, only to be curiously recycled a few years later during Atlanta's Olympic bid. The initial plans for the Olympic Village, for example, bore an uncanny resemblance to the twin towers standing guard at the entrance to the International Boulevard gateway.[40]

The flurry of housing and streetscape studies formed the groundwork for another major master planning effort, known as Central Area Study II, during 1986–87. Just as the original CAS reflected the Portmaniac excesses of late modernist city building, CAS-II reflected the postmodern turn towards fabricated placefulness that took hold in the high Reagan era. Unlike its predecessor, CAS-II was concerned not so much with transportation and new construction, but with softening the hard edges of the urban surface "through better maintenance, marketing, and design."[41] The "shared vision" it articulated (without telling us who it was that shared it) for Atlanta was one of a safe, clean, and "user-friendly city."[42]

The notion of a user-friendly city reveals a good deal about the technopolitan notions of CAP's imagineers. The term "user-friendly" is most often encountered in the realm of computers, where it refers to an interface carefully designed not to intimidate or confuse the operator: no information required other than that provided; just plug and play. What makes the interface friendly is that all the complicated choices have been decided upon and worked out for the user by the designer in a simple, persuasive, and clearly rendered manner. CAP's characterization of the urban population as users, rather than as residents, inhabitants, citizens, or, God forbid, voters, is an interesting and ideologically loaded one. On one level, it implies that the city is more oriented to the visitor than to the resident which, given the dedication of most of the new downtown to the hotel-convention industry, is not too far off the empirical mark. On another level, it conveys the notion that the line between residents and visitors is no longer a meaningful one, that even natives are strangers who need a guide to navigate the landscape of spectacular consumption. The notion also assumes that all users have the same needs and same socioeconomic identity, or that certain groups are excluded outright from the category of desired users. CAP had no wish, for example, to make downtown Atlanta any friendlier to the homeless. Indeed, as we will see below, a prime concern of CAP planners was to make the city far less amenable to these undesirable users, who are not really users at all, since they exist outside the nexus of cash and credit relations that constitute our contemporary "community of money."[43] The users CAP has in mind are first and foremost well-heeled visitors and aspiring urban gentry.

The outer boundaries of the Central Area in CAS-II remained as they had been in 1971: an eighteen-square-mile area defined by a cordon of railroad tracks. Nonetheless, there were some changes. Planners no longer differentiated between an "inner ring" and a central business district. The former went unrecognized and the latter had been expanded into a "commercial core" comprising Downtown, Midtown, and the area surrounding the Atlanta University Center known as West End. The inclusion of the West End marks the first time that a distinctly African-American district of Atlanta had been joined, in vision, if not in actuality, to the urban core. Despite this symbolic union, the low-rise, low-density West End neighborhood was functionally different from, and not directly contiguous with, the other two high-rise, high-density zones. By contrast, the much closer-in and historic Sweet Auburn neighborhood, which had been brutally bisected by the Downtown Connector, was not included in the commercial core. Nor did CAS-II discuss, even in the most general terms, projects that would physically link the area around the Atlanta University complex with the rest of the Central Area. Not surprisingly, no major developments have subsequently occurred in this area, although a certain amount of gentrification by mostly African-American middle-class households has occurred in the West End since the early 1980s. For all practical purposes, the West End remains both socially and spatially separated from the rest of the commercial core.

If the boundaries of CAS-II's commercial core were over-extended, the outer boundaries of the Central Area in the late 1980s were arbitrary and overly restrictive. By continuing to use the railroad cordon as the boundary, CAP left the principal areas of gentrification and neighborhood revitalization during the 1970s and 1980s – the "intown" neighborhoods of Morningside, Virginia-Highland, Poncey-Highland, Inman Park, and Candler Park – outside the Central Area. These were the neighborhoods that CAP and the Georgia Department of Transportation had intended to raze for additional expressways in the late 1960s and early 1970s. While CAS-II authors recognized the significance of subsequent development, they did not address themselves to the question of how these neighborhoods were to be linked with the area inside the cordon. For what was advertised as the city's "most comprehensive planning effort to date," this seems a curious omission.

Gentrification, though, was very much on the minds of CAS-II planners, and the intown neighborhoods, with their tracts of much-desired Craftsman-style bungalows, tree-shaded, pedestrian-friendly streets, and lively shopping and entertainment districts, were in direct competition with CAP's efforts to bring "people back downtown." Indeed, for the not insignificant numbers of weekend suburban slummers, these intown areas were coterminous with the inner city, and there was no desire or need to venture further "in." Far more than pedestrian-friendly streetscapes, the development of middle- and upper-income housing was the key element in CAP's efforts to redevelop the central area into a "24-hour city." CAS-II called for no less than 10,000 units of market-rate housing in the Central Area. To realize this end in an era of diminished federal support, new coordinating authorities and new sources of financing would be required. CAS-II outlined a whole ensemble of nifty financing tools, from bonds issued by the state-chartered Urban Residential Finance Authority, to public loan guarantees, housing enterprise zones, tax increment financing, tax credits, and creative use of federal Community Development Block Grants (CDBG) and Urban Development Action Grants (UDAG) monies.

The city quickly complied with some of the CAS-II suggestions, designating eleven housing enterprise zones between 1988 and 1990, six of which were located in Bedford-Pine alone. The resulting gated communities have been relatively successful in attracting residents and making profits for their developers, which include the usual cast of corporate characters involved in the airport, Underground, and later Olympic construction, but have not done much to revitalize the wider area. They remain isolated enclaves that, aside from their spectacular views of the downtown/Midtown skyline, might as well be in Cobb County. Although occupancy rates are high, the townhomes could not even support an adjacent upscale shopping center. Designed by the Miami firm Arquitectonica (perhaps best known for its playful postmodern buildings featured in the opening credits to *Miami Vice*), and partially subsidized by CDBG and UDAG funds, the Rio shopping complex went bankrupt within two years of opening. It has since reopened with a new collection of shops oriented to the surrounding, mostly African-American communities.

Together with housing, the other most important goal of CAS-II was to improve the image of the Central Area and remove perceptions of danger and crime. To these ends, the report proposed a coordinated marketing effort (to be led by the Atlanta Convention and Visitors Bureau), more police precincts, more uniformed and undercover officers on the street, and coordinated communications with private security forces. The city's homeless population was targeted for particular attention, although the report recognized they were a needy group more likely to be victims than perpetrators. They were, nonetheless, a group that was perceived as dangerous by the public at large and perceptions create their own reality. Consequently, a "safeguard zone" was proposed for the entire downtown area, in which a zero-tolerance policy towards homeless "behaviors" such as drunkenness, panhandling, sleeping, loitering, urinating/defecating in public, and traversing parking lots would be enforced.[44]

Shortly after CAS-II was released, Atlanta police conducted a massive sweep to get homeless people off the streets during the 1988 Democratic Convention. Whereas major conventions usually prompted roundups of the homeless, the one accompanying the convention was particularly intense and long-lasting. When Mayor Young balked at the idea of establishing a permanent "safeguard zone," CAP renamed it a "hospitality zone" and the criminalization of homeless behavior proceeded apace. If anything, city policy since 1990 has exceeded the CAS-II recommendations, with the homeless increasingly viewed as a "predatory" rather than a needy population by not only developers, office workers, and police, but otherwise "liberal" newspaper reporters. In the fall of 1994, the *Constitution*'s editorial page editor went so far as to blame the corporate exodus from Five Points in the early 1990s mostly on the presence of vagrants,[45] conveniently overlooking the wider economic forces at play and the fact that the homeless tend to flow to the interstices of the urban landscape that have already been vacated by other users.

CAS-II authors were not completely heartless to the homeless, however. As part of their general public safety recommendations, they called for a shift from emergency services (such as soup kitchens, shelters, and the like) to preventative measures and comprehensive services to get people off the streets and into homes and jobs. These goals were to be accomplished by the collaborative efforts of the City, Fulton County, the Atlanta Regional Commission, and the United Way, which would provide job training and medical services, increase access to public housing (there are literally thousands of vacant units in AHA-owned buildings at the time of writing), and the like. Yet no role for CAP was specified, nor was a mechanism for realizing these goals. No mention was made, either, of how these plans related to efforts to exclude the homeless from the hotel-convention district.

Among its other recommendations, CAS-II noted the possibility of using low-income tax credits to build Single Room Occupancy (SRO) hotels and housing for the poor within the Central Area. The report did not discuss exactly where such facilities would be located, but the mention of the need to construct low-income housing in the Central Area stood in stark contrast with the strictly exclusionary policies of the first Central Area Study. In addition to low-income tax credits, CAS-II also called for the creation of Community Development Corporations (CDCs) to assist in the construction of affordable housing and the rehabilitation of the large number of decaying public housing projects in the former inner ring. Financing for these developments was to be acquired through federal channels (for the rehabilitation of public housing) and from the creation of a State Housing Trust Fund, to be financed through a tax on real estate transactions. Despite these stated goals, low-income housing was much less of a priority than that for middle- and upper-income populations. As will be discussed below, a number of new public–private or wholly private programs (the Atlanta Project, the Atlanta Neighborhood Development Partnership, the Empowerment Zone) were developed in the early 1990s to address the problems of low-income neighborhoods, especially housing.

CAS-II also marked a somewhat revised attitude towards historic preservation by CAP. Much of the CAS-II report was produced during a period of what could only be characterized as an outright state of war between the mayor and the city's beleaguered preservationist community. In 1987 alone, several historic apartment buildings had been demolished in Midtown and upper downtown. Although CAP did not wish to place undue restrictions upon potential downtown developers, its planners also realized that the preservation/rehabilitation of historic structures was an important way of creating pleasing streetscapes that would lure people back downtown. The trick was to find a way of linking or, rather, subsuming preservation "to more widely held goals of building a vital downtown."[46] To this end CAP, along with the National Trust for Historic Preservation, helped sponsor a mediation effort to work out a new consensus between government, business, and preservationist leaders. After ten months of contentious negotiations, during which it was demonstrated that a large percentage of Atlanta landmarks had been demolished for parking lots rather than for tax-enhancing development,[47] a new historic preservation ordinance was arrived at.

The new ordinance provided stringent protection for buildings and districts designated as "landmarks" and reduced protection for structures and areas considered to be "historic." Both designations were the province of an Urban Design Commission (UDC) that had been enlarged to include representatives from the real estate, development, and legal professions. Once the UDC's designations were approved by the city council, landmarks could be demolished only if they posed a threat to public safety or if preservation was economically unfeasible[48] and the owner could submit evidence of plans and financing for a replacement building. The city also had two months to find other buyers to prevent demolition. "Historic" buildings could be demolished if the developer had plans and financing in hand for construction. Certain areas of the city lacking the criteria for landmark or historic status could be designated as Conservation Districts, although this label was advisory and lacked any protections whatsoever.

Given the previous antagonism and hostility of the city and the business community towards their interests, the new ordinance constituted a considerable victory for Atlanta's preservationists. Opposition from property owners was overcome with the prospects for certain financial incentives, such as tax abatements, with the proviso that if the city did not develop a viable incentive package within one year, all landmarks will be reclassified as "historic" and receive reduced protection. The Georgia legislature and the city council subsequently passed legislation providing for tax abatements and freezing taxes at pre-rehabilitation levels. By 1991, thirty-four of thirty-eight proposed buildings had been designated as landmarks and eight as historic sites.[49] Despite the passage of the ordinance and the tacit recognition by CAP of the value of historic structures, preservationists still often face an uphill battle in Atlanta.

UNDERGROUND REDUX

Although CAS-II talked about the importance of reviving the southern CBD, especially around the Garnett Street MARTA station and the cluster of government buildings, public authorities provided few incentives and private developers exhibited even less interest. The sole exception was the effort to revitalize Underground Atlanta, which had closed in 1982. The demise of the original Underground was a major blow to the CAP's strategy to anchor the southern terminus of the triangular "Heart of Atlanta." Plans for its revitalization were underway even before the last venue closed. The city and CAP invited the American City Corporation, a subsidiary of the Rouse Corporation, to devise a plan to redevelop the space as a "festival marketplace."

The revitalization of Underground proved to be a phenomenally complicated undertaking, involving, among other things, the acquisition of 150 separate parcels of land from reluctant owners.[50] Legions of lawyers devised a labyrinthine financial arrangement, whereby the city acquired the land (save for five parcels bought directly by the Underground Festival, Inc. (UFI), the private for-profit company formed in 1985 to develop the complex and headed by a former CAP president) and conveyed the property to the quasi-public Downtown Development Authority (DDA), which sold $85 million worth of revenue bonds to build the complex and repay the city for the land.[51] By working through the DDA, the city avoided the need for a public bond referendum. The balance of the $142 million that was needed for construction was provided by loans from the city and the Atlanta Economic Development Corporation, from UFI, and from CDBG and UDAG. Indeed, the city ultimately loaned $17 million of its CDBG and UDAG funds to the Underground complex, which was to be paid back starting in 1995.[52]

After completion, the city leased the complex and land back from the DDA, and rented the commercial portions of Underground to UFI. In turn, UFI contracted with a joint venture of the Rouse Corporation and two minority partners, both of whom were cronies of the political establishment, to manage the facility. As with the airport (indeed many in the cast of characters were the same), a significant proportion (25 per cent) of construction contracts was set aside for minority firms. The Atlanta Economic Development Corporation also provided low-interest loans to first-time minority entrepreneurs. For its part, the city's main corporate patron, the Coca-Cola Corporation, evinced its support for the project by constructing its World of Coca-Cola museum-cum-theme park on a adjoining parcel of land. Much as the stadium project epitomized the workings of the downtown power structure in the early 1960s, the revived Underground symbolized the successful workings of the biracial governing coalition that crystallized during Andrew Young's tenure as mayor in the 1980s.

As in its earlier incarnation, Underground's main feature was a reconstructed 1890s streetscape beneath the viaducts, with bars, shops, and restaurants, but unlike its predecessor it had an above-ground retail component as well, along with a small for-profit museum, Atlanta Heritage Row. Expectations were that the above-ground plaza would knit together adjacent activity nodes: Five Points and Central City Park lay just a block to the north, on the west was the central MARTA station, to the southwest Rich's Department Store. Across the street to the south was the new Fulton County Office Building (known as the "Taj Mahal" for its extravagant cost), while the State Capitol and related office buildings bordered the eastern edge.

Underground Town Center opened with great fanfare on 15 June 1989, with one million people visiting in the first four days.[53] Management tried its best to make it a popular center of civic life, by scheduling such ceremonial events as the dropping of a large illuminated peach on New Year's Eve and the display of Rich's Department Store's Christmas tree in the complex's open plaza. In September 1990, thousands gathered to witness the announcement of the city's selection as the site for the Centennial Olympic Games. One of ACOG's first acts was to open a promotional space called The Olympic Experience that told the compelling story of how Billy

Payne's "crazy dream" became a reality. Despite these earnest attempts at inculcating placefulness, the complex has not attracted the expected volume of business and has experienced a high turnover of tenants, including most of the first-time minority entrepreneurs. In the course of its first five years of operation, the complex lost some $28 million, with little prospect for a turnaround in the offing.[54]

The reasons for Underground's lack of success are multiple. In hindsight, UFI's estimates of expected revenue are now widely deemed to have been overly optimistic.[55] Among other things, they were based on the assumption that the complex could thrive on the basis of tourist dollars alone. The unreality of revenue estimates was compounded by the loss of more than 7,400 workers in the adjacent Five Points area between 1989 and 1992,[56] and perceptions of Underground as a dangerous place by white office workers and suburbanites. The riot in the wake of the Rodney King verdict in late April 1992 and the looting incidents during the Freaknik celebrations of April 1995 reaffirmed the "dangerous" nature of the area in the eyes of many whites. While this is no doubt a factor in the poor performance of bars and other nighttime venues, the location has not hurt the popularity of the adjacent World of Coca-Cola, which enjoys long lines on virtually every day of the week. Left unsaid is that, in addition to numerous other factors, Underground is simply an unappealing space. A major part of the popularity of similar Rouse-ified zones in Boston, New York, Baltimore, et al., lies not in the sumptuousness of their food courts, the Disneylike quality of their historic restorations, or the all-too-standardized "diversity" of their retail mix, but in the semi-salubrious nature of their harborside or riverside sites. Even with the most formulaic street furniture, waterfront sites provide both a sense of openness and framed views that contrast quite markedly with the closed-in feel of the surrounding urban fabric. While railroads did indeed perform the same function in Atlanta as harbors did in Boston, Baltimore, and New York, the same cannot be said for the dim, claustrophobic spaces beneath the viaducts.

The inhospitableness of Underground extended far beyond the features of its built environment. Despite significant minority participation during the construction phase and in the ownership of UFI, Underground was far from being a hospitable place to minority and female tenants. Many of the recipients of AEDC's loan program to first-time minority entrepreneurs were out of business within a few years.[57] In the spring of 1994, complaints of biased treatment against minority and female tenants prompted a city council audit of Underground's operational practices. The audit could not definitively corroborate the charges, but it did raise questions about Underground's finances. Plagued by high vacancies and turnovers, especially on the above-ground section along Upper Alabama Street, and problems in collecting back rent, the audit concluded that Underground was unlikely to survive without a city bailout and/or major restructuring of debt.[58]

Underground's perilous financial situation has left its management entity and the city scrambling for remedies. One of the more desperate suggestions involved the enclosure of the entire complex beneath an air-conditioned glass dome,[59] as if the problem with Underground was that people did not feel enclosed *enough*. Presumably if they were more emphatically cut off from the surrounding "dangerous" area, people would feel safer and freer with their wallets. While this ludicrous plan to put Underground under glass was soon abandoned, in May of 1995 UFI did come up with a complex restructuring plan that called for ceding the five parcels it owns within the complex (all on troubled Upper Alabama Street) to the city in lieu of repayment of a $10-million loan. This proposal would give the city complete ownership of the entire complex, a state of affairs that was met with great uneasiness in the city council.[60] The chairman of the council's Finance Committee even suggested that the complex "is never going to be self-supporting" and should be sold.[61] As the city and UFI went back to the negotiating table, the latter hired a new manager to oversee operations. By the end of 1995, the city and UFI had finally worked out an arrangement by which Underground's debt was restructured well into the next millennium. In the meantime, UFI, the city, and other interested parties are hoping that the Olympics will stabilize Underground through 1996, and that the completion of the nearby Federal Center in 1997 will come to the rescue of the city's sizeable investment.

HERE COME THE FEDS

The closing of Rich's downtown store in 1991 deeply undermined efforts to stabilize the southern CBD. Faced with the loss of a key anchor to Underground Atlanta, the Atlanta Economic Development Corporation and the Downtown Development Authority spearheaded a controversial project to build a $300-million, 1.9-million-square-foot Federal Center (the city's largest office building) on the Rich's site. The proposal came under intense criticism from many in the local real estate industry, who argued that the new complex would virtually empty the eight older structures scattered throughout the Central Area that housed federal agencies and greatly depress what was already expected to be a depressed post-Olympic real estate market. As more than one prominent member of the industry noted, the project violated all common sense. Atlanta's long-beleaguered preservationist community also protested against the demolition of yet another civic landmark. Meanwhile in Washington, some legislators were skeptical of whether or not the project offered the most economic solution to the federal government's need for additional office space.

Despite all these varied sources of opposition, backers of the project were able to prevail. In order to make it more palatable to members of Congress and the General Services Administration, the size and cost of the complex were scaled down by some 300,000 square feet and $80 million, respectively. Meanwhile, in order to placate preservationists, most of the store's Beaux Arts main building was incorporated into the design rather than demolished. In one of the last effective maneuvers of his mayoralty, Maynard Jackson got Central Atlanta Progress to come out grudgingly in favor of the project (largely because of its lifesaver role for Underground), while congressional approval was obtained via the persuasive politicking of Representative John Lewis and Senator Sam Nunn, as well as a surreally optimistic estimate of the future downtown real estate market. A key assumption of the latter projection was that the downtown office vacancy rate would drop to 6 percent from the then current 26 percent by 1997. Although the downtown vacancy rate had slipped below 15 percent by late 1995, given the vast amount of space absorbed by Olympic-related tenants that will be dumped back on the market after 1996, not to mention the space vacated by federal tenants, this figure is even less realistic than Underground Atlanta's conjured sense of place. In fact, the real estate industry expects that almost half of downtown's Class-B space, i.e. office buildings constructed before the 1980s, will be vacant after the Federal Center opens. Equally unrealistic are the assumptions that the Federal Center will serve as the salvation of the southern CBD or that it will somehow save Underground Atlanta by its mere adjacency. Consisting of four pedway-linked, unrepentantly modernist buildings of varying heights arranged around an eleven-acre green space, the Federal Center is just another enclaved mini-arcology, not unlike Peachtree Center or the Omni. With its own food court and retail zone, and without any physical linkages to Underground or other nearby buildings, it is questionable whether many of the estimated 8,000 employees will venture outside the complex except to go home.

Even after plans for the complex were approved and construction begun, the Federal Center remained a center of controversy. Questions were raised about the multimillion-dollar payment made to the private real estate company, Prentiss Properties, that was developing the complex in a partnership with the Atlanta Economic Development Corporation. During the fall of 1994, Prentiss and the city engaged in a bitter legal battle over the disposition of funds left over from the sale of bonds to finance the complex, as well as a second lawsuit on an unrelated project. Although both suits were settled out of court in July 1995, the incident served to tarnish the already sullied reputation of the AEDC, the Downtown Development Authority (DDA), and the city within the business community.

FAIRLIE-UNPOPULAR

Despite the inclusion of the southern CBD and the West End in the CAS-II game plan, the examples of Underground and the Atlanta Federal Center indicate that the southern boundary of the Central Area has migrated considerably northward since 1988. Although the city council has not given up on plans for the southern CBD, CAP's attention since the bank withdrawals of 1990–92 have been directed north of Five Points, and in particular to a 23-block area called the Fairlie-Poplar Historic District. Although this area comprises the single largest chunk of "historic" buildings remaining downtown, "Fairlie-Poplar" is a quite recent designation coined by Central Atlanta Progress in an effort at "making place." Prior to the late 1970s, the smallest of the three original street grids platted in the 1850s was not distinguished by name from the wider Five Points business district. Following a trend started in the urban renewal era (Bedford-Pine, Rawson-Washington, etc.), when the first move in redevelopment was to rename and symbolically cleanse an area of past associations, Fairlie-Poplar takes its moniker from the two narrow axial streets that intersect at its center. It is located between the three major downtown nodes – Peachtree Center, Omni/World Congress Center, and Underground – and is bordered by Peachtree Street, Marietta Street, Spring Street and Carnegie Way.

It was a residential area for most of the nineteenth century, and the majority of its existing five- to fifteen-story buildings were constructed between 1895 and 1930. The district's economic degeneration during the 1960s and 1970s inadvertently preserved a wide variety of architectural styles ranging from Beaux Arts to Art Deco and Business Gothic, except for the western edge along Spring Street, which was razed for parking garages and lots. The area was marked by a diversity of uses. Office buildings predominated in the southern and eastern parts of the area along Broad and Marietta Streets, while Luckie Street served as an axial corridor for hotels and restaurants. In fact, with its considerable number of theaters and bars, the Luckie Street area was Atlanta's central entertainment zone through the 1960s. Restaurants like Herren's and Emile's served as club houses for politicians, journalists, lawyers, and other downtown power brokers, as well as servicing the tourist and convention trade. In 1961, banker Mills Lane championed the construction of the Commerce Club Building, in whose dining rooms the power structure plotted the urban future (not so well, it turns out) over luncheons of prime rib.

In the latter part of the 1960s the district's role as a hotel center was eroded by the construction of new facilities in the Butler Street urban renewal zone and, later, near Peachtree Center. In 1967, downtown's finest hostelry, the Piedmont Hotel on Peachtree Street ("Atlanta's only New York Hotel") was demolished to make way for the black steel and glass box of the new Equitable Building. The latter replaced the original Equitable Building – the city's first skyscraper – which had been located on the other side of what came to be Central City Park. Designed by noted Chicago architects Burnham and Root, the old Equitable Building was razed for the new white marble headquarters of the Trust Company of Georgia. Subsequently, many of the remaining hotels in the area were transformed into low-budget facilities or single room occupancy hotels. The Playboy Club, which had been cited as proof of Atlanta's national city status after its opening in the Dinkler Plaza Hotel in 1965, closed only a few years later. The Rialto Theater, the largest in the Southeast when it was built in the early twentieth century and which was completely rebuilt in 1963 at great expense, traded down its first-run films for a mix of martial arts and soft-core porn. A number of the popular daytime bars and restaurants hung on through the mid 1970s, but by that time the area had already developed a reputation for drugs, prostitution, and vagrants.

In 1978, CAP, together with Rouse Corporation's Land/Design Research subsidiary and a local architectural firm, produced a plan to revitalize the area through the creation of a "mall-like atmosphere" that would link the Rich's Department Store south of Five Points with the Macy's branch near Peachtree Center by a pedestrian axis along Fairlie Street.[62] Planners talked boldly of creating something along the lines of New York's Greenwich Village or SoHo or New Orleans's French Quarter – an exciting mix of housing, retail, and office space. The preliminary study was followed by a design and implementation plan that bore a distinctly Rouse-ian stamp. When it was realized that the distance between Rich's and Macy's was greater than most shoppers desired to walk, the axis of redevelopment was shifted to east–west. In the project's first phase, three of the area's key streets (Poplar, Broad, and Forsyth) would be wholly or partially pedestrianized, while a tri-level arcaded "marketplace" would bridge both Peachtree and Broad Streets, linking the Central City Park with the second-story atrium of the renovated Healy Building. The second phase of the project envisioned the redevelopment of Margaret Mitchell Square at the northeastern corner of the area as a gateway to the district from the new downtown at Peachtree Center. Two to four thousand units of housing were penciled in along the Spring Street corridor which, thanks to the oddness of the street grid, connected up with the rear of the Peachtree Plaza Hotel and Portman's expanding mart complex.

Although land values in the area had declined significantly from their past peak, neither of the two phases was considered to be financially viable without massive public subsidies in the form of written-down land costs, property tax write-offs, and a package of local, state, and federal loans.[63] The report did note, however, that many of the buildings met the criteria for inclusion in the National Register of Historic Places (NRHP) and the 25 percent tax credit on rehabilitation costs that such a designation brought. Over the next four years, eleven buildings received NRHP status and were bought and renovated with more than $70 million in private capital. While the city refused to subsidize land costs for residential conversion, it did contribute $7 million in Community Development Block Grants for the installation of appealing "street furniture" on Broad Street and for the redesign of Central City Park, which bordered the area on the east.[64] The rehabilitation of the latter was completed in 1983, and it was renamed Woodruff Park in honor of its "anonymous" benefactor two years later.

To celebrate the area's rebirth, CAP threw a gala black-tie street party – "A Fairlie-Poplar Affair" – in May of 1980. Two years later, they threw the "Broad Street Bash" to celebrate the completion of some of the phase-one streetscapes and the designation of nine blocks in the southern half of the area as a National Historic District. These efforts were far from successful, however. By 1989, virtually all of the renovated buildings were, at best, only half full and many had been or were in the process of being foreclosed. Newspaper reporters lamented that the "dream was dead."[65] Many in the business community like to place the major blame for Fairlie-Poplar's initial failure on the large number of homeless persons, drug addicts, and other "sleazoid" and "undesirable" characters who frequented the area. A number of single room occupancy hotels were located in or adjacent to the district, as were a few disreputable and disorderly establishments. Chief among the latter were the infamous Bumper's video game arcade and the neighboring Rialto Theater. However, while their existence created something of a crime and image problem for Fairlie-Poplar, they did not constitute a sufficient explanation for the failure of the first redevelopment efforts. Attributing a main causal role to crime and undesirable users obscures far more fundamental causes that lie in the realm of market forces, poor planning, politics, and the sleazoid character of some of the early developers themselves.

After the initial flurry of plans, neither the city nor Central Atlanta Progress made the area a priority. Envisioned in the waning phase of the second Jackson administration, Fairlie-Poplar was eclipsed in importance by the efforts to redevelop Underground Atlanta in consultation with another Rouse company, the American City Corporation. In addition to providing a major symbolic commitment to the southern CBD, Underground also presented a far bigger pie with which to whet the appetite of the governing coalition. With the city's and CAP's attention focused on the larger prizes of Underground and the Georgia Dome (arising just to the west of the GWCC), Fairlie-Poplar became an unsupervised playground for a diverse mix of other players seeking to take advantage of the tax incentives that accompanied the rehabilitation of historic structures. These included some old-guard Atlanta families, foundations, and corporate institutions, as well as national syndicates, and a few foreign investors.[66] Property values in the area soared until 1986, when changes in the federal tax code greatly reduced the tax benefits associated with renovation and sent prices crashing.[67] Once renovated, many of the buildings experienced considerable difficulty in attracting tenants in a recessionary market already glutted with affordable space in more upmarket areas like Peachtree Center and Midtown. Although the initial redevelopment plan for the district indicated that creation of a new "attraction" was vitally needed, developers acted as if the renovated buildings themselves would be their own attraction. Prospects for Fairlie-Poplar reached their nadir when three major projects ended in lawsuits or arrests for fraud or securities violations in the late 1980s.[68]

Yet less than three years after reporters wrote its obituary, Fairlie-Poplar was given new life as the exodus from the Five Points area reached biblical proportions. In 1990, a proposal to designate the area a Landmark District under the new city preservation ordinance prompted a negative reaction from owners concerned about limitations being placed on their ability to demolish or alter their properties. Together with the DDA, district property owners commissioned a local real estate consultant to devise a plan to revitalize the district and preserve its historic fabric without designating it a Landmark District. The resultant Fairlie-Poplar Revitalization Plan was inspired by the National Trust for Historic Preservation's Main Street Program. In many respects it provides a textbook case of forced-draft gentrification and of imagineering a sense of "traditional urbanity." Working on the assumption that Fairlie-Poplar had "simply exhausted its natural life cycle," and needed to discover a new role for itself in the urban economy, the plan sought to identify a number of new market niches for the district.[69] Chief among these was the creation of an arts and education zone centered on the Rialto Theater, which had posed such a problem for previous redevelopment efforts. It was envisioned that the conversion of the theater into the site of either Georgia State University's arts program or the headquarters of the city and county arts bureaucracy would spin off a whole host of new retail and residential uses.

The example of New York City's loft-living, art-dealing SoHo district has been wistfully invoked by many a Fairlie-Poplar booster, but the comparison is highly misleading. The gentrification of SoHo, as well as the nearby Lower East Side of Manhattan, was initiated by artists and bohemian cultural producers seeking cheap rents; both groups were later displaced as the area was discovered, domesticated, and intensively commodified by the joint action of the real estate and culture industries.[70] Lacking this crucial first wave, redevelopers of Fairlie-Poplar would have to seed "culture" directly to stimulate the simultaneous growth of the deep money veins of retail and residential development. To supplement the revitalizing potential of an arts and entertainment district, the plan also called for the creation both of a design/market center in the Walton Street corridor and of housing through both adaptive reuse and new construction. While the plan was generally amenable to preservation, it also required the demolition of three non-historic office buildings in the block between the Rialto complex and Woodruff Park, so as to create a gateway that would "help define the district's identity."[71] Finally, the plan called for an organizational entity to coordinate redevelopment and market the area; it also suggested that the district be renamed to escape its extant negative connotations.

Inspired by the plan, Mayor Maynard Jackson reconstituted the Fairlie-Poplar Implementation Task Force in May 1992 to spearhead the redevelopment of the district. In addition to the major area property owners and real estate brokers who had belonged to the original task force constituted in 1978, the body included a sizeable contingent from nearby Georgia State University. The inclusion of Georgia State in the plans for Fairlie-Poplar marked a major shift both in GSU's vision of itself and in the downtown redevelopment game more generally. Among the members of the task force's steering committee was GSU's new president, Carl Patton, a professor of urban planning who had previously worked as a consultant to CAP. Prior to taking over the reigns at GSU, Patton had been involved with urban revitalization efforts in downtown Milwaukee and Toledo. His commitment to the idea of a new enhanced role for GSU in downtown redevelopment was symbolized by his stated intention to move his official residence from a Buckhead mansion to a yet-to-be constructed loft apartment in Fairlie-Poplar. By this move alone, Patton marked a major departure from the isolationist island strategy pursued by his more good ol' boy predecessors.

Patton's appointment was only one dimension of GSU's penetration into Fairlie-Poplar. In 1991, the C&S Bank had donated its landmark-designated (and hence unmarketable) building to the university, which moved its College of Business there. Shortly thereafter, GSU embarked on a $14-million project to convert the Rialto Theater into a state-of-the-art performance venue and the neighboring Haas-Howell and Standard Buildings into the new home for the university's music school. With the state Board of Regents reluctant to get involved in the downtown real estate business (quite unlike other "urban" universities), funding for the Rialto project came from a variety of sources, including the Woodruff Foundation, private corporations, contributions from alumni and staff, a bond issue, as well as from the reallocation of monies from GSU's program budget. In addition to the Rialto, some of the nearby low-budget and SRO hotels were contemplated for conversion into dorm space. Students were seen as a pioneering first wave that would attract the supporting retail, such as bars, cafés, and restaurants which, in turn, would help confirm Fairlie-Poplar's identity as a desirable place for the much sought after upper-income residents. The new plan for GSU was very much in keeping with past claims of Atlanta being the New York or Chicago of the South. As one account put it, GSU's new vision seeks to create "an Atlanta-style New York University anchoring a sort of a Greenwich Village–Washington Square, Hyde Park–University of Chicago environment."[72]

The emphasis in the previous description should be on the "sort of," as the last thing that either GSU or the remainder of the safety- and order-obsessed downtown business community is interested in fostering is anything remotely resembling the intense and, at times, anarchically diverse array of peoples and activities associated with these places, especially Washington Square Park. Exactly what aspects of these legendarily urbane domains are to be appropriated is unclear (the analogies were made by a journalist and not project planners), but one can rest assured that ganja-dealing Rastafarians, homeless encampments, and vocal political activists are not among them. Indeed, given the frequency and ease with which Atlanta boosters evince desires to conjure up energetic and exciting SoHos and Washington Squares in their midsts – while simultaneously holding to the vision of a safe, clean, and graffiti-free user-friendly city – one wonders if any of them have ever been to the places they so easily metaphorically appropriate.

With Georgia State set to inherit the 2,000 beds of the Olympic Village located near Georgia Tech after the 1996 Games, efforts to build dorms in Fairlie-Poplar have languished due to the lack of interest by both the Board of Regents and local financial institutions. Instead, developers have gone completely upmarket with plans for moderate- and upper-income loft-style housing in buildings around Five Points and in that section of Fairlie-Poplar between the Rialto and Woodruff Park known as the Muse's Block. The latter takes its name from the former flagship store of one of the city's old-guard clothing retailers, George Muse and Company. The redevelopment of the triangular block reveals a good deal of the problems and prospects of Fairlie-Poplar, as well as downtown gentrification as a whole.

The seven-story, neo-Italianate Muse's Building towers awkwardly over the three- to four-story structures that range northward between Peachtree and Broad Streets. Like their taller neighbor to the south, the six buildings were originally used for retail, before converting to fast-food establishments in the course of the 1970s. By mid 1992, the entire block had been vacated except for a pizza parlor on the ground floor of one building. In the early 1980s, the block had been considered by C&S Bank as the location for a new headquarters tower. After initially acceding, Muse's backed out of the deal and sent C&S searching for an alternative site. In the meantime, the rest of the block was bought by a local philanthrope, the J. Bulow Campbell Foundation, to keep it in safe hands if the C&S deal was revived.[73] Muse's remained adamant about its decision, though, and C&S eventually acquired a parcel near the intersection of North Avenue and Peachtree Street for its new 55-story headquarters. Advertised as the tallest building in the Southeast, the building is now known as NationsBank Plaza, after the North Carolina-based institution that merged with ailing C&S in 1991. The failure to build on the Muse's parcel is widely viewed in the business community as the decisive beginning of Five Points' death spiral as a banking center. In 1991, Muse's filed for Chapter Eleven reorganization and the building and two adjacent parcels came under the control of Wachovia Bank, which put it up for sale. The appeal of the small site was rather limited. Moreover, with its ownership of the remainder of the block, which would be required for any significant redevelopment of the property, the Campbell Foundation exercised veto power over what could be done with the Muse's property.

As Wachovia Bank entertained offers from developers in the spring of 1994, GSU president Patton made good on his earlier intention to move his official residence from a mansion in a swanky section of Buckhead to a penthouse apartment in the Muse's Building. However, the plan also required the sale of the Buckhead mansion, which the Board of Regents was, to put it mildly, loath to do. Indeed, as their tepid enthusiasm for the Rialto project had demonstrated, the Regents were particularly reluctant to get involved in the real estate business at all. After a California developer declined to exercise his option on the property, two groups of local developers expressed an interest in redeveloping the block with a mix of upscale lofts and dorms for Georgia State students. Both were well known for their previous adaptive reuse projects, and one – Winter Properties – was the codeveloper of the Rialto Theater project with GSU. Winter's partner in the joint venture, Cecil Phillips, also enjoyed a tie-in with GSU, having just recently completed the conversion of the former Ramada Inn near the Atlanta-Fulton County Stadium into housing for students from Georgia State and the Atlanta University Center.

Winter Properties acquired the Muse's Building in February 1995 for less than half the $1.8-million asking price. After Phillips's plan for a 400-bed dormitory and parking garage failed to find favor with both the banks and the Board of Regents, Winter purchased the rest of the block from the Campbell Foundation at an equally bargain basement price. Rather than razing the low-rise structures, Winter is restoring their 1920s facades and renovating them for ground-level retail with apartments on the floors above. The Muse's Building itself will be converted into seventy luxury apartments, along with a penthouse suite for GSU's president.

Soon after the Muse's Building was sold, two other relatively young developers with a track record for adaptive reuse announced their own projects to convert two largely vacant office buildings at Five Points – the William Oliver and Georgia Federal buildings – into more than 200 loft-style apartments. The three Five Points rehousing projects give something of a new twist to gentrification as a process in which the symbolic capital of central location is appropriated to revitalize depressed property values. Whereas gentrification is usually manifest in terms of the conversion of working-class spaces (in the form of either factories or working-class residential neighborhoods) into middle- and upper-income housing, as well as the displacement of working-class residents, these projects seek to use vacant and formerly high-end office and retail space.

It would seem, on the surface, that the residential redevelopment of Fairlie-Poplar/Five Points is a win/win situation for all concerned: owners experience the revitalization of property values, aspiring urban gentry find suitable lodging, and Georgia State students and faculty might yet be able to enjoy the delights and diversions of the much-celebrated "urban lifestyle." Most importantly, with the adaptive reuse of derelict office buildings, the usual victims of gentrification, the urban poor, are lacking. Fairlie-Poplar, however, is not without its present or potential displacees. The western part of the district is home to a number of single room occupancy (SRO) hotels, and if the proposed developments are successful, these establishments would be likely to be considered undesirable and unprofitable uses. One hotel, the Atlantan, is being renovated to house an outpost of a national chain of economy hotels. Another SRO, the Walton House, will no doubt soon find itself under strong pressure to relocate. Even with the conversion of the Imperial Hotel north of Peachtree Center into an SRO, the successful revitalization of Fairlie-Poplar will do nothing to ameliorate the shortage of low-income housing and homelessness in the central city. Both the task force and Central Atlanta Progress steadfastly refuse any responsibility for constructively dealing with the problem of the homeless and the urban poor, preferring instead to dump this "public" burden on the steps of city hall.

Although the city government nominally supports the Fairlie-Poplar plan, its lack of purposive activity in the process of the area's redevelopment indicates something of an ambivalence as well. This was best displayed in an ill-fated effort to build an underground parking garage beneath Woodruff Park. The garage would have gone a long way towards removing one of the main roadblocks to the successful conversion of Fairlie-Poplar into a residential neighborhood; the narrow streets of the city's smallest grid were neither designed for, nor are capable of handling in their present form, the movement and storage of automobiles. During the winter of 1993–94, the task force entered into negotiations with a Spanish company to build an underground parking deck, similar to those found in Paris and a number of other European cities, as part of the renovations of Woodruff Park. Despite the lobbying effort of a number of city councilmen on the task force to "fast-track" approval for the garage, the plans met with effective opposition within the city government – which had its own plans for building more downtown parking garages, although not at the Woodruff Park site – and were ultimately abandoned in the spring of 1994. The subsequent renovation of the Park has effectively foreclosed the possibility of building subterranean parking any time in the near future.

As the redevelopment of Fairlie-Poplar proceeded, the task force was absorbed into a renewed Central Atlanta Progress, which hired a full-time revitalization manager to coordinate marketing, urban design, and overall redevelopment efforts. A design guideline for local property owners was produced and circulated to help ensure continuity in the district's historic streetscapes.[74] While hopes for a marketing/design center have been abandoned for the time being, the expansion of Georgia State University and the adaptive reuse of three office buildings into housing offer the prospect of bringing the "right" people back downtown to live, work, and spend money. A recent survey commissioned by CAP indicated that as many as 25,000 persons would be willing to consider living downtown.[75] Most of these, however, indicated a preference for the already established quasi-colonial cantonments in Bedford-Pine. With rents projected to start around $1 a square foot, the redevelopers of Fairlie-Poplar/Five Points appear to be concentrating on the high end of the market that is currently dominated by Buckhead, Midtown, and intown neighborhoods like Virginia-Highland. All three of these areas have established and quite lively entertainment districts, along with appealing housing and supporting retail. Whether the promised safety and cleanliness of the redevelopments will be enough to overcome the area's lack of energy and excitement, not to mention secure parking, is unclear at this point. Despite all the talk of the area's "SoHoification," the vision of "the urban lifestyle" offered for sale in Fairlie-Poplar/Five Points (as well as Bedford-Pine) is essentially a bland simulation of a simulation (for even SoHo has itself long been a hyper-commodified shadow of its "original" refigured self), a vision that seeks to trade gritty diversity and vernacular attractions for a safe, clean, and fun environment – a theme park of sorts, yes, but one without many interesting rides.

In an effort to "add some rides" to Fairlie-Poplar, developers are toying with the idea of building a mixed-use entertainment center on the western edge of the district, bordering the new Centennial Olympic Park and CNN Center after 1996. At the time of writing, plans are sketchy, but one variant involves some kind of interactive venue featuring some of the cultural properties owned by Turner Broadcasting System which, if its merger with Time-Warner meets with the approval of federal regulators, will be even more extensive than they are at present. Such a project, however, is hardly the stuff of even a Rouse-ian version of "traditional urbanity." Then again, the public appetite for safe, delirious, urban spectacle has grown so voracious such a project might well prove popular, if only for the tourist trade. What kind of urban gentry, one wonders, would wish to live in the midst of a such a dedicated tourist zone? Despite backers' claims that the proposed entertainment complex would be "synergistic" rather than competitive with Underground Atlanta, the project would probably be the *coup de grâce* for the already deeply troubled festival marketplace.

The gentrification of the Fairlie-Poplar/Five Points area is only one, albeit central, dimension of the efforts to revitalize downtown. Under former Portman lieutenant Sam Williams, Central Atlanta Progress has rededicated itself to the CAS-II goals of making downtown into a "24-hour city." Even more than housing, parking, and new attractions, CAP's paramount preoccupation is with redressing the perception and actuality of crime and danger. Moving beyond the CAS-II notion of a "safeguard" or "hospitality zone," in mid 1995 CAP orchestrated a successful effort to convince a majority of the 400 area property owners to vote for the designation of a 120-block area bordered by Peachtree Center, the Georgia World Congress Center, and Underground Atlanta as a Downtown Improvement District, or DID. Another example of the seemingly inexorable privatization of public space, the improvement district concept has already been employed in a number of other cities, including New York, Dallas, and Baltimore. As in these other cities, Atlanta's DID is financed by an additional tax on area property owners, with the revenue going to insure that the central city is "clean, safe, and fun."[76]

The roughly $2 million generated annually by the levy will be used to hire a private security and sanitation patrol linked to Atlanta police by radio. These uniformed, but unarmed "goodwill ambassadors" will assist visitors, scrub away graffiti, and sweep up trash, in addition to dealing with minor quality of life crimes, such as those committed by the area's significant homeless population. Indeed, from listening to the way in which not only CAP officials but otherwise liberal journalists speak of the homeless, it appears that the latter are considered to be nothing more than a variety of urban litter, something to be swept out of the way, without regard for where it goes. The DID includes no provision for social services for the homeless, which CAP adamantly insists is the (largely unmet) responsibility of the public sector, and not private business. While CAP is right on target in criticizing the dearth of city efforts to deal constructively with the homeless population, it doth protest too much, for it has exhibited little reticence in usurping otherwise "public" functions — security, sanitation, etc. — not performed to its satisfaction.

SPACE WARS IN WOODRUFF PARK

Just to the east of Fairlie-Poplar and smack dab in the middle of the DID lies Woodruff Park, a putatively public space that owes its existence to private initiative. In 1971, Coca-Cola president Robert Woodruff anonymously bought the four-acre parcel between Peachtree Street, Edgewood and Peachtree Center Avenues, and the Candler Building, and donated it to the city for use as a park. Opened in 1973, it quickly proved a popular site for daytime office workers, as well as the poor and the homeless. These different populations maintained an uneasy coexistence in the park, with the latter group dominating after the end of the business day and during the weekends. In 1980, the park was renovated by the city using federal CDBG money. The new design, however, was not a very pleasing one for many users. Described by one critic as "a Tootsie Roll Pop with the Tootsie missing,"[77] the new improved park featured a large central brick and concrete plaza surrounded by a screen of berms and trees that made it difficult to see into and out of the area. To the north of Auburn Avenue, a small bunkered amphitheater was intended as a site for lunchtime concerts.

The steady emigration of office workers from the surrounding area during the 1980s changed the mix of users and helped to contribute to the perception of it as an unsafe area. There were legitimate grounds for this perception, as significant amounts of petty crime, particularly purse-snatchings and overly aggressive pan-handling, occurred with some regularity. Still, in many respects, the park was considerably more dangerous for the "predatory" homeless than for office users. Thirteen deaths, most from exposure and a few from fights between homeless persons, were recorded in the park between 1992 and 1993 alone.[78] In the 1980s, homeless support agencies began using the park as a site for a soup kitchen, a mobile medical clinic, and other activities at times when the park was devoid of other users, such as in the evenings and on the weekends. These activities attracted upwards of one hundred persons at times. Even though these uses did not occur during prime daylight hours, the park was popularly perceived by office workers as having been "taken over" by the homeless during the daytime as well.

This perception of a homeless "conquest," however, did not necessarily accord with the facts on the ground. Periodic observations conducted between 1992 and 1994 revealed that the vast majority of daytime users, especially at lunchtime, were office workers and GSU students and faculty. Aside from occasional incidents of purse-snatching and panhandling, these mainstream groups usually coexisted rather uneventfully with the several dozen homeless persons who regularly inhab-ited the space. In addition, the park provided a setting for everyday urban dramas featuring hellfire and damnation-spouting street preachers straight out of some Flannery O'Connor story, silent, grim-faced characters practicing their martial arts, and the city's finest charcoal-fired hotdog stand, Barker's. In short, despite its "worn, dirty, and somewhat dysfunctional"[79] appearance, Woodruff Park had evolved into a somewhat authentically diverse urban space.

After five in the afternoon and on weekends, however, the park definitely belonged to the homeless, except during major conventions, when they were swept from the street for the weekend. In the early 1990s, the park became the principal zone where the new anti-homeless ordinances were most visibly put into effect. The park's 11 p.m. closing time was more aggressively enforced and during the daytime the rousting of sleeping homeless persons by horse-mounted police officers was a common sight. Citations for begging and urinating in public were also stepped up. With the city budget strapped for maintenance, the upkeep of the park suffered. In 1993, the Atlanta Downtown Partnership (ADP), a private group of nearby businesses, hired a temporary caretaker to keep up appearances during a scheduled tour by then mayor Maynard Jackson. Impressed by his efforts, the ADP hired him full time. Dubbed by the press as the "Ambassador of Woodruff Park", the multilingual ex-army veteran helped police the homeless population.[80] His was only an interim tenure, however, as the city and business groups were already contemplating more extensive measures to take back the park.

In 1994, Woodruff Park underwent a massive facelift as part of the Olympic renovation of "the public character" of the city. The revised park is an aggressively earnest New Age "civic" space replete with statuary, tasteful plantings, and two new water features, including an International Peace Fountain and a seventeen-foot-high curved waterwall nearly two hundred feet long. Even more than water features, statuary is essentially to civicness, and the new park incorporates both old and new pieces of public art. In the southwestern corner closest to Five Points stands an 18-foot-high statue of a woman (symbolic of Atlanta's feminine essence) holding the city's totemic phoenix aloft to the heavens. Called "Atlanta from the Ashes," it was originally given to the city by Rich's Department Store in 1969 to commemorate the city's 125th anniversary. Since then, a photograph of it has appeared in most of the soft-core coffee-table books celebrating the city. Originally located near the store, the statue had been made homeless by the construction of the Federal Center. Further up the park's northern edge, is another, much less distinguished piece of sculpture bequeathed to the city by one of its entrepreneurs, the founder of a successful chain of chicken sandwich franchises. Meant to commemorate the power of knowledge, the chunky bronze "Chick-Fil-A Arch" stands across the street from the park, forming a ceremonial gateway into Fairlie-Poplar.

Despite the claims of advocates for the homeless, the city and the park's designers steadfastly insist that the park renovation was not part of a conspiracy to rid the city center of the homeless. Instead, they emphasized the need for enhanced security and, by way of an aside, noted that this will make the park less welcoming to the homeless. To this end, the renovation leveled the high berms and fences that made it difficult to see into and out of the park and installed new lighting to better illuminate the space. To take advantage of these well-lit lines of surveillance,

Georgia State University has relocated its central police station to a building on the southern edge of the park itself. Designers are counting on these panoptical strategies, along with hardened features like intermittent sprinklers and sleep-proof benches, to make the park less amenable to those wishing to use it as a temporary abode.

The renovations were not limited to the park itself. With Underground in dire financial straits, and UFI lobbying for greater connectivity to downtown, plans were drawn up for a pedestrian corridor that would directly link the main surface plaza at Underground with the park along the east side of Peachtree Street. While the State Building Authority (SBA) was in charge of the project, the funding for the pedway was another gift from the Woodruff Foundation, who ponied up the needed $3 million. First called Enlightenment Plaza, it has since been renamed Five Points Pedestrian Plaza.

In addition to drawing attention to the privatization of public space, the pedestrian plaza also reveals a good deal about the difficulties of historic preservation even after the passage of the 1989 ordinance. Two historic buildings anchored each end of the proposed plaza, between which lay a short block of undistinguished low-rise nineteenth-century structures with ground-floor retails. At the south end, directly across the street from Underground, was the Peters Building, which had been built in the late 1880s by one of the city's largest real estate developers next to the magnificent Queen Anne-style Kimball House Hotel. In the 1920s, the Wall Street viaduct buried the Palladian entrance of the Peters Building below grade. Forty years later, after the Kimball House fell to the wrecker's ball to make way for a parking garage, the facade of the Peters Building was covered over with white concrete panels in a vain attempt to give it a sleeker, more modern look. This camouflage was quite effective, as most people were unaware that it is actually one of the older buildings in the city. The structure passed into the hands of SBA sometime in the 1960s. After it was vacated by the state in the 1980s, the building became a derelict eyesore above ground, although its original architecture was apparent to the few who wandered below the viaducts. Nonetheless, it was demolished with nary a whisper of notice from the various city and state preservation agencies, who had their hands full with trying to save the landmark-designated Olympia Building that stood at the opposite end of the proposed plaza.

The Olympia Building was built in 1937 and housed a number of small retail and fast-food establishments. Although the Art Deco structure had received landmark status in 1990, the protection came via a city ordinance that the Building Authority, as a state entity, was not obliged to respect. Building Authority designers proposed to lop off twenty to sixty feet of the western part of the building in what they flippantly referred to as a "nose job."[81] The authority's assistant director for planning justified the plan on the grounds that the alteration of the structure was in the civic interest: "We're attempting to make public space here."[82] Preservation advocates mounted a spirited opposition, proposing instead a "nostril enlargement" that would preserve the upper floors of the building while creating an open-air arcade at ground level.[83]

After six months of negotiation, the parties hit upon a compromise. Despite opposition from some critics that the building would leave a "psychological barrier" to the free and easy movement of pedestrians, the preservationist alternative was accepted. A well-lit arcade will run through the ground floor, but despite the claims of the SBA's assistant planning director it will only be a quasi-public space. Underground Festival, Inc. (UFI) is leasing the arcade and the entire pedestrian corridor. UFI will be in charge of leasing space to pushcart vendors and other merchants and will be able to erect a large sign on the Olympia Building's roof. In effect, the corridor becomes Underground's new "front door" and extends the facility's simulated space out into the cityscape. As the president of UFI noted, "What this all means is that if we can't bring Woodruff Park to Underground, maybe we can bring Underground to Woodruff Park."[84] Indeed. Built and managed by a quasi-public state entity (the Building Authority) with funds provided by the city's chief philanthrope (Woodruff Foundation) and leased to a private entity (UFI) that has already been the beneficiary of massive public largesse (DDA's bond issue), the plaza project marked a new level in the theme parking and privatization of Atlanta's public domain, although these have since been exceeded by still more spectacular developments.

MORE PIECES

The plans for Woodruff Park and Fairlie-Poplar are of a piece with those for two other ornamental nodes that are being envisioned for CAP's downtown game board. One of these is the Multimodal Transportation Center to be located in the "railroad gulch" adjacent to the Five Points MARTA station; the other is a new arena for the Atlanta Hawks basketball team to be built on the site of the present Omni Coliseum. The latter is to be connected to the multimodal station and Underground via ten acres of pedestrian plazas and walkways in the remaining section of the gulch. As noted in the previous chapter, filling in the gulch has ben an unrealized aim of downtown visionaries since Haralson Bleckley proposed his City Beautiful plaza in early 1909.[85] In the early 1980s, Omni developer Tom Cousins envisioned building a quarter-mile-long elevated walkway to link his then ailing mixed-use complex with the Five Points MARTA station. Cousins had still not realized this plan when he finally sold the Omni to Ted Turner in 1986. However, the idea of a quarter-mile-long pedestrian bridge/mall was resuscitated as a possible Olympic-related redevelopment project after Atlanta was awarded the Games in 1990. The city-owned Corporation for Olympic Development in Atlanta (CODA) even went so far as to secure right of way for the project from property owners, but prospects evaporated when the necessary funding was not forthcoming.[86]

The multimodal station was the first of the two projects to be discussed publicly. In the early 1990s, city leaders and state Department of Transportation officials desperate to find a solution to Atlanta's traffic problems unveiled plans for a heavy commuter rail system linking the city with its far-flung suburbs, as well as other regional cities, like Augusta, Savannah, even Charlotte, North Carolina. Where possible, the system would use already existing rails owned by freight systems such as CSX, thus minimizing costs. Federal transportation funds would provide much of the needed funding for the most expensive part of the system, a new downtown terminal that would house not only heavy rail, but local and interstate buses as well. In an ironic twist that politicians and newspaper accounts alike failed to mention, the proposed station was to be built on the former site of one of Atlanta's earlier rail terminals that was razed in the early 1970s. The DOT's support for heavy rail marked quite a break from its previously exclusively automobile-oriented solutions to regional transportation problems. Yet, even the support of Governor Zell Miller was not enough to win legislative approval for the state's $13-million contribution to the project, and plans for the station were put on indefinite hold in 1993. The decision was a vivid reminder of the legislature's anti-Atlanta bias and a cruel blow to boosters who saw the station as a key bolster to downtown's ailing economy and a solution to already overcrowded highways.

Less than a year after the Georgia Assembly's refusal to back the multimodal station, Atlanta Hawks president Stan Kasten – who also presided over the Braves baseball team – announced that the team was going to relocate from the Omni to a yet to be determined suburban location. Such a move, which would also involve the city's minor league hockey franchise and dozens of concerts, would effectively turn the city-owned facility into Atlanta's "next dead elephant"[87] and further undermine efforts to revitalize downtown. Kasten's decision was motivated by a host of economic factors, including the claim that 80 percent of the team's paying fans lived in north Fulton, Gwinnett, and Cobb counties, as well as what he perceived as a lack of cooperation from city officials. The most intense reaction came not from the city, however, but from other downtown business interests. Several members of the Chamber of Commerce, for example, stridently accused Hawks (and Braves) owner Ted Turner of "opportunism and abandoning the downtown that had made him."[88]

By comparison, the initial reaction from city officials was rather muted. While Mayor Bill Campbell hoped that the Hawks would remain downtown, he admitted that "it may be that we're not able to keep the Hawks."[89] The city's public ambivalence about the Hawks' likely move marked quite a shift from the desperate maneuverings it engaged in in 1989 and 1993, when Kasten threatened to move the Braves to the suburbs. In an effort to keep the baseball team, city officials made significant concessions to the organization. But the Hawks were not the same kind of prestige item as the Braves, who had dominated the National League since 1992. Chronic underperformers, the Hawks suffered from an embarrassing inability to fill the 16,510-seat arena, even during the playoffs. Hawks officials claimed that the arena's location kept fans away, ignoring their often questionable personnel decisions and their failure to field competitive teams. On many occasions, visiting teams – such as the New York Knicks – enjoyed more vocal support from their expatriate fans than the Hawks did from Atlantan fans.

Although Kasten indicated that Hawks owner Ted Turner was ready to shoulder the $125-million cost for building a new 20,000-seat arena without public assistance, his threat to move was somewhat weakened by the lack of enthusiasm from suburban officials, who had been more than eager to lure the Braves. The Hawks were also constrained by federal pollution regulations stipulating that any new arena had to be built with good access to mass transit, or risk losing federal funding for the infrastructure needed to build it.[90] This requirement dramatically limited the number of possible alternative sites to north Fulton or DeKalb, as neither Cobb or Gwinnett was part of MARTA. Confident that Kasten was bluffing, and still smarting from having been outmaneuvered over the Braves, the city embarked on low-key negotiations aimed at supposedly ensuring that Atlanta taxpayers would be spared the massive debt incurred by other cities in building new sports facilities. In this, the city was bucking national trends, as all but one of the twenty-six arenas that housed National Basketball Association (NBA) franchises, and virtually all of the recently built ones, involved some kind of significant public subsidy, including written-down land costs, infrastructure improvements (road, sewer, power), or low-interest bonds guaranteed by the municipal treasury.[91]

Accepting Kasten's claim that the Omni had become obsolete (it is the smallest arena in the NBA, and possesses only sixteen of the prime income-generating luxury box suites), city officials initially proposed three alternative sites. These included the railroad gulch area to the west of the proposed multimodal station, the moribund Atlantic Steel factory just north of Georgia Tech, and the former Gullstedt-owned dead zone near the Biltmore Hotel in lower Midtown. None of these, however, was owned by the city and the Hawks continued to explore suburban options. One of the most appealing of the latter was in northwestern DeKalb

County adjacent to the Doraville MARTA station. After negotiations stalled in the spring of 1995, the city upped the ante by saying that the Omni itself could be torn down to build a new facility.[92] From the city's perspective, the Omni site was the most appealing as it was burdened by a number of constraints in financing a new arena in whole, or in part. Under the existing operating agreement at the Omni, the Atlanta-Fulton County Recreation Authority (which also owns the baseball stadium and the Georgia Dome) "cannot finance or aid in the financing of, or operate any competing facility within a 20-mile radius of the Omni."[93] There were ways around the restrictions, however, if the Hawks would commit to remaining downtown.

Constrained by their pledge not to stick area residents with the bill for a new stadium for Turner, city officials were forced to entertain other options. In early 1995, they raised the idea of assessing a $1 surcharge on entertainment tickets to raise the necessary money for a new downtown arena. Such a prospect, however, stimulated active, and effective, opposition from the Atlanta entertainment industry and the Georgia legislature, most of whom were loath to use a tax to subsidize billionaire Ted Turner.[94] While it was rejected, the overture was most encouraging to the Hawks, as it indicated that the city's hardball stance was beginning to soften a bit. Negotiations continued outside the glare of the media spotlight until early December 1995, when the city and Turner proudly unveiled plans for building a new arena on the Omni site.

While the original Omni was a neobrutalist concrete bunker with a rust-colored roof, the new facility had more than a touch of Disney about it. Not so much an arena as "entire entertainment complex with a skin that will entertain,"[95] the slant-roofed concrete and glass structure will feature 21,500 seats and 100 of the lucrative luxury suites, as well as enormous external video walls onto which programming from a variety of Turner networks will be projected. Designed by a joint venture of Miami-based Arquitectonica (the imagineers behind Bedford-Pine's playful Rio shopping center) and Atlanta's own Rosser International (designers of the nearby Georgia Dome), part of the arena's walls would retract, opening up on a retail plaza featuring kiosks, vendors, and other design features conducive to creating a "fair-like atmosphere."[96] The complex would be linked to the Five Points MARTA station and the proposed multimodal terminal by two new office buildings and a pedestrian walkway and retail corridor bridging the railroad gulch. Plans for these peripheral developments, however, were sketchy at best, being only "possible," rather than "proposed."

Despite the city's initial vow to limit taxpayer liability, financing for the $200-million complex is to be provided by two city- and county-backed bond issues. By razing the Omni and retiring its debt, the city was able to transcend the legal barriers to funding a new facility. Funding for the arena itself would come from revenue bonds issued by the Atlanta-Fulton County Recreation Authority, which would be repaid by future arena revenue, while the $65 million in needed public improvements would come from revenue bonds subsidized by a 3 percent tax on car rentals, as well as up to $15 million from Turner Broadcasting. Both Turner and city officials justified the arrangement by pointing out that a few million dollars in interest would be saved by using the tax-exempt city/county bonds and that, since the bonds were secured by future arena revenue, city and Fulton County taxpayers would not be stuck with the tab (unless for some reason the arena's revenue fails to meet projections, as in the case of Underground Atlanta). Nor would they bear the burden of the second bond issue, as visitors, and not residents, account for the vast majority of car rentals in the Atlanta area. Unlike the entertainment industry which so successfully opposed the ticket tax, the car rental industry lacks a large army of lobbyists. At the time of writing, however, these arrangements have yet to pass muster with the state legislature and local governments. Given the legislature's previous reluctance to subsidize Turner, acceptance is far from certain, albeit likely. However, a far more pitched battle is more likely to be fought between the city and Turner over how the arena's profits are to be split, and other "nitty-gritty details."[97] If the past is any guide, Turner should fare quite well in these negotiations.

As with a number of projects before it, such as Underground Atlanta, the Fairlie-Poplar district, the Atlanta Federal Center, and Woodruff Park (as well as the Centennial Olympic Park, to be discussed in Chapter 5), the new arena has already been touted by civic and business leaders as *the* savior of downtown, as well as the keystone of "the most fabulous sports complex in the world."[98] According to the city's main negotiator, the project will stimulate development that will realize Atlanta's cherished goal of becoming a "24-hour city," although in the fine fashion of the Atlanta Spirit exactly how it would do so was not specified.[99] City officials are banking heavily on the fact that the arena will become an attraction in itself, apart from any events going on within, and that people might even want to live nearby. With its giant video walls and observation decks offering dramatic views of Atlanta's skyline, it is not inconceivable that the arena will become a tourist attraction of sorts. Yet it is dubious, at best, to think that the arena will be able to generate the sort of round-the-clock activity that boosters hope for, even if the "possible" pedestrian mall becomes a reality. Perhaps they think people will come to watch television on the building's giant external screens on the approximately half of the nights of the year that the arena is not occupied by concerts, sporting events, and revival meetings. Other than that, it is hard to conceive of many licit functions for this latest "downtown wonder."

Perhaps the most glaring limitation of the proposed arena is that, despite the facility's stated centrality to downtown, there is no plan that links it to the other spectacular developments envisioned for downtown. Indeed, the multitude of projects reflect a "disjointed incrementalism"[100] as profound as that occurring on the exurban periphery. Instead, the new arena, Underground Atlanta, Fairlie-Poplar, and Woodruff Park are no more than an unconnected assemblage of flashy stage sets intended to bedazzle and bamboozle the multitudes into believing that some sort of "traditional urbanity" has been rediscovered downtown. All four are demonstration projects of the new kind of urban space that uses "sumptuous architectural imagery, fictional information, entertainment, and spectacle"[101] to blur the boundaries between public and private space and interest until these polar opposites merge into one delirious celebration of the commodity form. Of course, as T.J. Clark and David Harvey remind us, the shapeshifting phantasmagoric urban spectacle has been firmly with us since at least the late nineteenth century.[102] Yet, the plans for renovating the public character of downtown Atlanta are so programmed and earnestly "fun!" as to make the fabricated urbanity to be found along the boulevards of Haussmann's Paris and in the neon-lit hustle of New York City's Times Square seem positively genuine and emancipatory.

PUTTING THE INNER RING BACK INTO PLAY

If the various downtown projects are hardly connected with one another, they at least appear together on the colorful maps that regularly appear in Atlanta's newspapers and glossy promotional brochures.[103] The same cannot be said for the depressed neighborhoods of what was once known as the inner ring. However, even some of these areas are currently experiencing the magic touch of privatized redevelopment.

During the latter part of the 1980s, gentrification came to some of the industrial zones that paralleled the rail corridors extending north, south, and east from downtown. These areas were full of the late-nineteenth and early-twentieth-century warehouse and factory space that constituted the necessary raw material for loft conversion. Beginning in the mid 1980s, artists and a few small developers began rehabilitating vacant structures in the Castleberry Hill area, just to the south of the Omni/World Congress Center/Georgia Dome. By the early 1990s, demand for these units greatly exceeded supply, sending rents skyrocketing and sparking the conversion of additional factory buildings into loft apartments. With its utter lack of amenities and blasted streetscapes, the Castleberry area – which had been home to the shantytown of Snake Nation in the 1850s – seems more a backdrop for a post-apocalyptic science fiction thriller than urban pioneering. The allusion is more than metaphorical, as the neighborhood has served as a film set for such recent urban dystopiads as *Kalifornia*, *Robocop III*, and *Freejack*. The success of Castleberry Hill inspired other developers to cultivate loft-living in nearby areas. Indeed, if Atlanta can be said to possess a SoHo, this is it. Several old factories along Marietta Street between Coca-Cola and Omni have been converted into high-priced residential units and gallery space. At least six other projects promise if not loft, at least loft-style, living. By far the biggest of these involves the eleven-acre Fulton Bag and Cotton Mill property, which Winter Properties (of Fairlie-Poplar fame) proposes to redevelop into a mixed-use complex featuring residential, retail, and office space.

Yet, despite these localized revitalizations (of real estate values, if not a sense of community), most residential neighborhoods within the inner ring have experienced dramatic free-falls in standards of living. Although located close-in to downtown and adjacent to the Atlanta University Center, the high hopes for the gentrification of the West End have not panned out. With the exception of Summerhill (whose comprehensive redevelopment plan authored by the Urban Land Institute will be discussed in depth in Chapter 5), most other neighborhoods lack the leadership, organization, and political connections to make redevelopment happen. In addition, the malign neglect of the 1980s generated great collective distrust and resentment of both the city and the business community among neighborhood residents. The business community returned the feeling many times over, while the city simply ignored the area as best it could.

CAS-II's call for the creation of community development corporations, however, marked a change in the attitudes and actions of the business community towards inner-city neighborhoods. Beginning in 1991, two major Olympic-related initiatives were unveiled to spread the revitalization fever to the disenfranchised areas of the city. As might be expected from the changing national mood and the increasingly entrepreneurial mode of government, both of these efforts are best construed as "private–public" partnerships, with an emphasis on "private." The most high-profile of these was Jimmy Carter's Atlanta Project (TAP), which saw itself as creating poverty-fighting partnerships, not between business and government, but "between the haves and the have-nots." TAP's goal was to empower residents to deal with problems in their own communities by collaborating with government agencies, businesses, philanthropes, and social service groups. However, as was described in Chapter 2, despite a great deal of laudatory media hoopla in its first year, TAP tended to work more from the top-down than from the bottom-up, and has been somewhat less than successful in empowering communities.

Although it received the greatest media attention both within and outside of Atlanta – as proof that Atlanta was serious about doing something about poverty – TAP was preceded by another private–public effort at realizing neighborhood

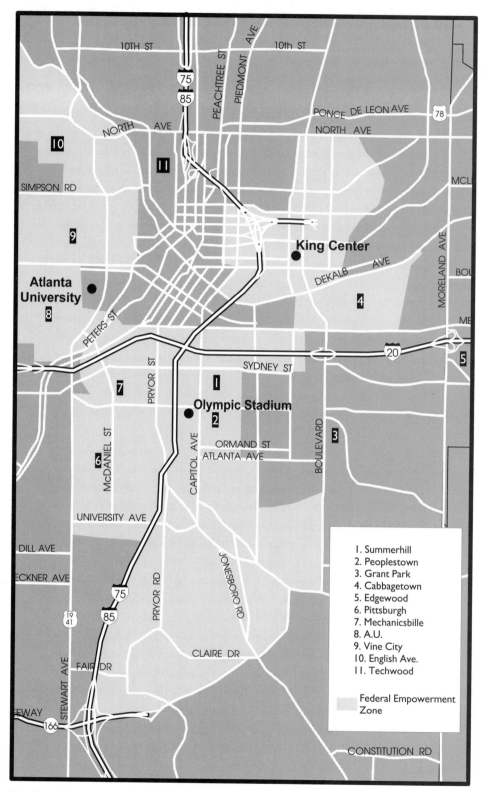

Map 9:   Olympic Ring Neighborhoods

development, the Atlanta Neighborhood Development Partnership, or ANDP. First proposed in 1990, the ANDP was created in 1991 by the joint action of the quasi-public Atlanta Economic Development Corporation and the Atlanta Chamber of Commerce. It was envisioned as sort of a master community development corporation (CDC) to funnel public and private money and expertise to neighborhood CDCs. Most of the money it has received has been private, with significant contributions coming from major banks (Bank South, First Union, Wachovia, Trust Company, NationsBank) and other local corporate patrons (e.g. Bell South, Delta, Georgia Pacific, Home Depot, etc.). The ANDP also received support from James Rouse's Enterprise Foundation, which was established by the developer in 1987 to facilitate the revitalization of low-income neighborhoods.

Unlike the Atlanta Project, the ANDP does not subscribe even rhetorically to the ideology of community empowerment. Decision-making, like money and gravity, flows top-down, rather than bottom-up. Its board, like that of TAP (indeed, their boards and corporate sponsors are to a great extent interlocking) is dominated by representatives from the business community. Seventeen of the twenty-seven board members are from corporations, while the remainder are from large institutions and non-profit agencies.[104] Although the ANDP portrays itself as proof that business cares about revitalization of neighborhoods, there are no board members from these communities. According to one study of the ANDP's operations, this was done so that the board could talk freely about neighborhoods without word getting back to the neighborhoods themselves.[105] Critics have charged that the ANDP acts as a "shadow government" that usurps the traditional role of the city and organizations such as the National Association for the Advancement of Colored People and the Urban League in community redevelopment.[106] While accurate in describing the ANDP's functions, this criticism fails to acknowledge that these traditional institutions had been considerably less than active during the 1980s. It could very well be argued that even a flawed program with good intentions is better than none. However, again much like TAP, the ANDP's actions differ widely from its stated intentions. More of its resources have been spent on administrative costs than on grants to neighborhoods, and there is considerable doubt as to whether the flow of corporate contributions will continue after 1996.[107]

Although ANDP officials emphatically deny that the organization was put together to put an Olympic figleaf over the city's more embarrassing parts, most of its awards have been given to areas near Olympic venues, such as Summerhill, Vine City, and Mechanicsville. More importantly, however, most of the new housing built or under construction in these areas is for mixed- or middle-income families. In other words, the money that is finding its way into these neighborhoods is subsidizing gentrification rather than improving and increasing housing for the poor.

Coupled with plans for privatizing and downsizing a number of public housing projects into mixed-income communities (namely Techwood/Clark Howell and East Lake Meadows), these projects will *decrease* the amount of low-income housing in the central Atlanta area.

The third and latest entry in Atlanta's neighborhood revitalization sweepstakes is the most "public" of the ventures. The federally funded Empowerment Zone project represents probably the last big disbursement of US government monies before the Department of Housing and Urban Development (HUD) is eviscerated by a Republican-majority Congress. A Clintonian riff on Congressman Jack Kemp's Urban Enterprise Zone concept, the Empowerment Zone emphasizes human development as well as tax breaks for businesses investing in the area. The latter will receive some $150 million in exemptions, while HUD will provide $100 million in cash to build housing and otherwise "empower" the community by enhancing childcare, job training, and other vitally needed services.

While the zone is a new concept, it covers familiar territory to those who remember the urban renewal and Model Cities programs. The roughly U-shaped area comprises slightly more than nine square miles, embracing thirty neighborhoods in which over half of the population live below the poverty line and nearly a fifth are unemployed. Approximately 40 percent of the zone population live in substandard public housing.[108] Although it covers a lot of the same ground, the Empowerment Zone is intended to be different from past federally funded efforts, a true attempt at bottom–up development that is to be set in motion by plans generated by the communities themselves. Indeed, one of the requirements of the application procedures was that the proposal be drafted by residents of the zone, assisted by city and state officials. To this end, a Community Empowerment Board composed of neighborhood leaders was selected, many of whom were veterans in the struggle against more than two decades of malign neglect from city hall. Rather than outlining specific plans, the proposal described a number of benchmark goals — decent housing, jobs, services, etc. — that would help transform the targeted neighborhoods into "self-sustaining villages." To realize these goals, projects from individual neighborhoods would be solicited, instead of forcing various localities to conform to a general unyielding plan. As far as community involvement in the proposal goes, the Empowerment Zone may have realized greater bottom-up involvement that the much-lauded Atlanta Project.

The extent of community participation in the operation of the program remains an open question, however. The federal funds are to be distributed through a non-profit Empowerment Zone Corporation, run by a seventeen-member board chaired by the mayor himself. In contrast to the ANDP board, the business community has only two seats, as compared to six from the Community Empowerment

Board that helped draft the proposal. However, the balance of power lies with the mayor and his nine appointees from among the usual suspects of public institutions and non-profits including the Atlanta Housing Authority, the Atlanta Board of Education, Fulton County, the state planning authority, and the Atlanta Project. By insisting on the unhindered ability to hire and fire board members without review, Mayor Campbell has made it quite clear that it is he, rather than the Community Empowerment Board, who is running the show. Community leaders, however, have a different understanding of the situation, seeing the Empowerment Zone project as creating new rules and a new game in which the neighborhoods no longer reflexively do what the city says.[109]

Unfortunately, it seems that the old rules are still in effect. As of December 1995, the Empowerment Zone Corporation has moved glacially, spending virtually all of its time fighting over the internal distribution of power and choosing a permanent director rather than setting up a system for vetting and prioritizing proposals coming in from the various neighborhoods. It is quite unlikely than any meaningful effects will be realized from the program by the 1996 Olympics. Despite the presence of an Atlanta Project representative on the board, there does not appear to be any major effort to coordinate activities of the Empowerment Zone with TAP (which is due to terminate in 1996, anyway) or the ANDP. Rather, the city appears to be using the Empowerment Zone Corporation as an attempt to take back the powers of community redevelopment "usurped" by the ANDP. Although the business community is always singing the praises of the beneficial effects of competition in the marketplace, it is unlikely that this pecuniary truth holds for inner-city revitalization programs as well. Left in the middle of this competition between the public and private sectors are the communities they are supposed to be assisting.

Rather than meaningful efforts, it seems that the Empowerment Zone, the Atlanta Neighborhood Development Partnership, and the Atlanta Project are more like high-budget advertisements attempting to sell the message that the federal government, the city and/or the business community are serious about doing something about urban poverty. With high-profile programs in place, the power elites can thus be absolved of any further responsibility in the matter. As Gary Orfield, Clarence Stone, and other scholars familiar with Atlanta's situation have noted, the amounts connected with the three projects are negligible in comparison to the draconian cuts in federal and state spending flowing down the public sector pipeline.[110] With many area residents in near total dependence on public assistance, tax credits for new businesses and new housing for middle-income populations will do little to make up for the elimination of programs like Aid for Families with Dependent Children in favor of federal block grants to the states. In addition, the US Congress is currently considering legislation that would limit its subsidization of private housing for low-income families through Section VIII vouchers to one year, instead of the current three to five years. This is a development of serious significance, as the Section VIII voucher system is the primary means for relocating residents displaced by the conversion of public housing projects into mixed-income communities.

As Atlanta prepares to host the Olympics, it does indeed seem that this unique event has served to revitalize, if not the city, at least parts of its power structure. Many of the CAS-II recommendations, from enhanced security to new housing for urban gentry and the privatization of the urban renewal of poor neighborhoods, are finally in the process of being put in place. Faced with the prospect of unprecedented global exposure, Central Atlanta Progress has, under the hand of a capable maximum leader, rededicated itself to putting what it believes is Atlanta's best face forward. Yet, while CAP has been able to respond to the challenges of the process of power restructuring, at least for the time being, the city government has not. Indeed, the latter – divided by internecine struggles between the mayor and the city council, burdened by a bloated, patronage-ridden bureaucracy, and facing accusations of corruption and incompetence from a not-so-small army of critics reaching from the grassroots to the boardroom – has lost a considerable amount of ground. Rather than reviving the fraying urban regime of the 1980s, the Olympic mobilization of the last five years has served to further divide the once-fabled biracial governing coalition. How this state of affairs has come about is one of the subjects of Chapter 5.

5

OLYMPIC DREAMS

For the people of Atlanta, the XXVIth Olympiad stands over the future like the cloud-capped peak of Mt. Olympus. It is a dream to be grasped a height to be scaled, a movement to be embraced. As a dream, it has drawn the city together in a bond of desire far greater than anything before.[1]

Even before they have taken place, the 1996 Summer Olympic Games have already done many things to Atlanta (as well as promised many more), but, as will be demonstrated in the following pages, enhanced social cohesion and unanimity of vision are not among them. Rather, the preparations for the Games have deepened many of the divides that separate the inhabitants of the metro region, and created some new ones as well. Depending on the social and geographical positions they occupy, Atlantans dream of different things. The corporate imagineers at Atlanta Committee for the Olympic Games, the Atlanta Chamber of Commerce, and Central Atlanta Progress, Inc., dream of the billions of dollars in new investment that will flow their way as a result of the unprecedented publicity that will prove Atlanta to be the truly world-class city they have tirelessly claimed it to be. Politicians dream of the political capital to be reaped from a successful staging of the Games, while Atlanta's extensive hospitality industry – not to mention individual homeowners and myriad entrepreneurs – dream of the windfall profits to be made fleecing well-heeled Olympic visitors. At the same time, those Atlantans who rent their domiciles dream of not being displaced by unscrupulously greedy landlords, while the city's homeless dream of not being swept off the street into the new city jail, which one city official rather whimsically noted was "the first Olympic construction project to be completed on time."[2] Despite these differences of vision, however, Atlanta won the right to host the 1996 Centennial Olympic Games partly because it was able to project an image of shared communal enthusiasm on the part of its entire citizenry. Unlike other cities competing for the 1996 Games, such as Toronto, few critical voices were to be heard locally throughout the bid process. The lack of criticism, however, reflected not so much unanimous support for the Olympics as the widespread belief that Atlanta's quest was, as chief Olympic cheerleader Billy Payne freely admitted, nothing more than a "crazy dream."

SELLING THE DREAM

According to the officially sanctioned mythology that has been spun around what is already considered to be the most important event in the city's history since General Sherman burned it to the ground, Payne's idea to bring the Olympics to Atlanta was a dream that had a touch of almost divine inspiration to it. In the version of the story that has circulated in both local and national media, the idea for the Games came to Payne during a sleepless night in 1987, following the successful conclusion of a fund-raising effort that he had led for his Dunwoody church and the dedication of a new organ. According to a slavishly hagiographic profile in *Newsweek*, Payne told his wife "we needed to find another cause to build this experience [of community] again," and bringing the 1996 Olympics to Atlanta was it.[3] This was indeed crazy talk coming from an affluent, but not terribly well-known, real estate lawyer and former college football star who was not a core member of the power structure. Nor was Payne a proven manager: as one profile in the *Wall Street Journal* noted, he had "never directed so much as a high school track meet."[4] This lack of a managerial track record was ominous, since to host the Games Payne was going to have "to build an organization big enough to rank in the middle of the Fortune 500, produce what amounts to three Super Bowls a day for 16 days, and dismantle the entire structure overnight."[5] One of the most important challenges was financial, as Payne needed to raise some $1.5 billion in revenue, while keeping a lid on expenditures, which included over $500 million in new construction.

Despite the media's representation of him as a solitary hero, Payne was far from alone in this gargantuan undertaking. While the Chamber of Commerce showed little interest in his vision, Payne did have a few friends in the power structure. On the private side, the most prominent of these was Horace Sibley, an attorney with strong links to the Coca-Cola Corporation. This connection, and the early backing of Atlanta's best-known and most powerful corporation, led some critics to charge that Coke, not Billy Payne, was the "Real Thing" behind Atlanta's bid, and that the 1996 Olympics might be better termed the "Coca-Cola Games." Along with eight other considerably less well connected "Friends of Billy," Sibley was part of a group known as the "Crazy Atlanta Nine" that formed the core brains trust of the Atlanta Olympic Committee, or AOC. Apart from Sibley, none of the other eight was what you would call a power broker; all had less experience in these matters than their fearless leader.

Billy Payne also enjoyed the early, enthusiastic, and crucial support of then mayor Andrew Young, who was named co-chairman of the AOC. Young's support was critical to the success of the venture, since as former US Ambassador to the United Nations and full-time globe-trotting traveling salesman for Atlanta, Inc., Young enjoyed a panoply of contacts among the world's movers and shakers, as well as with the members of the International Olympic Committee (IOC). After leaving the mayor's office in an attempt to run for the governorship of Georgia, Young was enlisted as "the chief weapon in Atlanta's arsenal to capture the Olympics."[6] As a former lieutenant to Martin Luther King, Jr, Young was also a living embodiment of King's spiritual legacy and of Atlanta's central role in the civil rights movement more generally. A great part of Atlanta's claim to the ideals of Olympism was refracted through its claim to being the human rights capital of the world. Young was able to actualize this claim in a way that Billy Payne could never dream of. His symbolic capital was of inestimable importance in influencing IOC members, especially those from Africa and Asia.

Of course, more than symbolic capital was necessary to field a successful bid. Official accounts made much of the fact that Payne and others quit their jobs, lived off savings, and took out loans to get the bid off the ground. However, considerable additional resources were necessary to fund the quest. Officially, the AOC spent $7.3 million on its efforts between 1987 and 1990, but this is widely considered to be an underestimate.[7] Although the Chamber of Commerce declined to provide initial seed money, local corporate citizens provided contributions in cash and in kind, such as use of corporate jets to whisk AOC members on their global junkets, and fêting visiting IOC dignitaries. The Georgia Institute of Technology contributed a $200,000 three-dimensional multimedia video that took IOC members on a "magic carpet ride" through a virtual Atlanta.[8] When the IOC visited Atlanta in September 1989, the AOC pulled out all the stops, covering the city and the airwaves with promotional advertising, hosting an Olympic road race, and a non-stop series of parties and engagements in between tours of the proposed venues.

While Andrew Young hit the global stump advertising the celestial Atlanta's spiritual virtues, Billy Payne worked the hard sell with the International Olympic Committee. Although trained as a lawyer, Payne found his true calling to be that of the super salesman, winning friends and influencing people on the 96-member body by sweating the details and being generous. When IOC delegates visited Atlanta, they were put up in the Buckhead and Dunwoody homes of AOC members. As with other cities, the AOC showered IOC members with complimentary gifts, some of which were quite valuable. Following Atlanta's selection as host city in September 1990, a number of foreign periodicals, including Germany's *Der*

Spiegel, alleged that IOC members had been bribed for their votes.[9]

Allegations of influence-peddling would be very difficult, if not impossible, to prove, and remain only speculations. Still, the overt aspects of Atlanta's bid were alluring enough to the International Olympic Committee. The AOC's financial forecast made a very explicit appeal to the IOC's desire for profit, which had grown quite pronounced after the 1984 Los Angeles Games realized a surplus of over $200 million, none of which found its way back to IOC coffers in Lausanne, Switzerland. Atlanta's plan was very much modeled on Peter Ueberroth's highly successful corporate-backed game plan for the 1984 Games. The AOC envisioned that three-quarters of the nearly $1.62 billion in projected revenue would come from the sale of television rights and corporate sponsorships, and estimated a profit of some $156 million, most of which would be given to the IOC "to support and develop amateur athletics worldwide."[10] In addition to receiving the majority of the surplus, the IOC would get a significant percentage off the top of the global television rights (which were estimated to command well over $600 million) and a hefty cut of all merchandising revenue. From the perspective of the TV rights, Atlanta was in a very strong position. The eastern time zone of the United States, in which Atlanta is located, is the nation's largest television market, which would allow the Games' signature events to be broadcast in prime time and thus maximize their potential advertising revenue. Since US networks formed the lion's share of the TV rights market, and the price they were willing to pay for the rights was directly connected to how much money they could make, an Atlanta Olympics was quite an inviting prospect for the IOC, although Toronto also was.

The IOC was not the only critical body that needed financial assurance from the AOC; so did the city, county, and state governments, especially the latter. The Georgia Assembly had historically been quite tight-fisted when it came to providing money for Atlanta, and much like its opposite number in California in 1984, was haunted by the specter of Montreal's billion-dollar debt from the 1976 Games. Taking a page from Ueberroth's play book, Payne and company won the support of Georgia legislators by assuring them that the Olympics would be staged exclusively with private money, but would nonetheless leave Atlanta with a major material and spiritual legacy. The latter took the form of a harmonic convergence with the ideals of Olympism and to "motivate the youth of Georgia to strive for excellence in all areas of their lives."[11] Never one to miss an opportunity to let loose with a blast of spirit-filled rhetoric, Andrew Young even claimed that the Olympics offered the "divine potential" of giving a conflict-ridden world the opportunity to learn from the harmonious lesson of Atlanta. "Could it be," Young wrote in a memoir, "that Atlanta could play a special role in the plan of God?"[12]

While a determination of such a spiritual legacy will no doubt have to wait until after the End of Days, the material Olympic legacy was both more immediate and tangible. Among the most concrete Olympic endowments were a bevy of new sporting venues, highlighted by a new stadium for the Atlanta Braves baseball team. Moreover, it was argued that the Olympics would enhance Atlanta's reputation as a "world-class city," and attract untold billions in footloose global investment capital in years to come. Much like the Cotton States and International Exposition of 1895, the Olympic Games were a "demonstration project"[13] of the *New* New South Creed. Perhaps the most tangible aspect of the Olympic legacy, however, was the short-term economic impact of hosting the Games on the Georgian and metropolitan Atlantan economy. A study commissioned by the AOC from the Selig Center for Economic Growth at the University of Georgia (alma mater to many in the Georgia legislature) estimated the total economic impact of the Games at some $3.5 billion between 1990 and 1996.[14] The study also noted that the Olympics, which it called "Georgia's Second Gold Rush"[15] would add more than 83,000 jobs to the Georgian economy and create more than $200 million in additional tax revenue for the state. As the Games approached, and costs mounted, the estimate was revised to project a total economic impact on the state of $5.1 billion and nearly 80,000 jobs.[16]

Although state legislators demurred at putting any of the more than $200-million tax "windfall" towards putting on the Games, they did consent to let the AOC use state-owned land for Olympic sporting venues and housing for athletes. Indeed, the plan the AOC submitted to the IOC called for two-thirds of the Olympic venues to be located on, or make use of, state property (the Georgia World Congress Center, the Georgia Dome, and Stone Mountain Park). While it was not widely talked about at the time, the choice of these locations would oblige the State of Georgia to expend significant funds to support the Games. The largest single contribution was made by the Board of Regents of the University System of Georgia, who agreed to spend approximately $120 million to build a part of the Olympic Village, which would be used after the Games as dormitories for students of Georgia Tech and Georgia State University.[17] Despite Payne's assurances that only private money would be used to stage the Games, by 1995 over $350 million in public funds (local, state, and federal) had been expended in direct connection with the Olympics. The State of Georgia accounted for the single largest share of this spending – $146.6 million – followed by the federal government ($92.2 million), and the City of Atlanta ($53.5 million). The remainder was expended by municipal, county, and state governments associated with the handful of outlying venue sites.[18] ACOG explained this away by stating that it had only said it would stage the Games without taxpayer dollars, not pay for the cost of government.[19] Indeed, it was not until late fall 1995 that the city and ACOG were able to come to an agreement on how much the latter was going to compensate the former for expenses incurred in hosting the Games, such as police overtime and the like.

While inspired by the 1984 Los Angeles Olympics, Atlanta's Olympic organizers were not content merely to follow a successful playbook. Rather, in the finest fashion of the Atlanta Spirit, they intended to dramatically improve upon the example set by LA. This meant not just more events, but more promotion, more new construction, etc. Whereas Los Angeles organizers sold hundreds of sponsorships at $4 million apiece, the AOC raised the price of being a full-fledged sponsor to $40 million. However, despite the hype of being the ultimate marketing event in world history (indeed, the competition between rival corporations has proved as compelling, in some ways, as the Games themselves), these Olympic-sized sponsorships proved a hard sell to corporations still reeling from the effects of the 1990–91 recession. As revenues failed to mount and expenses rose, ACOG was obliged to create two additional tiers of less costly, and exclusive, sponsorships.[20]

Another area in which Atlanta planned to exceed Los Angeles was in new construction, although the key part of the success of the LA effort lay in the use of existing venues, thus avoiding the spectacular expenses involved in building new facilities. By contrast, Atlanta's organizers planned to spend approximately half a billion dollars on building new venues, including a $209-million track and field stadium that would be converted after the Games into the new home for Atlanta's professional baseball team, the Braves. This conversion would involve tearing down almost half of the Olympic Stadium, as well as the current home of the Braves, the adjacent Atlanta-Fulton County Stadium. This act of Olympic philanthropy would solve a crucial problem for the city, as the Braves were threatening to move to a new facility in the suburbs (built by an all-too-obliging county government) unless the city provided a new one for them. As will be detailed below, however, plans for the stadium were exceedingly complex and proved to be a key point of conflict between and amongst Atlanta's Olympic organizers, the city government, and neighborhoods in the surrounding area.

The AOC's plan differed from that of Los Angeles in still another crucial respect. While LA's organizers dispersed their venues all over the metro area, Atlanta's concentrated on nine major venues holding nineteen of the thirty sporting events in a five-kilometer-wide (three-mile) circle situated in Atlanta's urban core. Known as the Olympic Ring, this magic circle encompassed all of downtown and much of Midtown, as well as a large swathe of Atlanta's poorest neighborhoods. Although these latter areas were inside the ring, they were "outside the fence" as far as Olympic organizers were concerned. The AOC was on record that its attention, and money, would be limited to the venues themselves, which were distributed among six distinct clusters inside the ring.

At the core of the ring was the Olympic Center zone, which consisted of the

Georgia Dome, the Georgia World Congress Center, and the Omni Arena. One mile to the north of the Olympic Center was the campus of the Georgia Institute of Technology, which would be home to the new Natation Center (swimming and diving) and the Olympic Village. Between the Olympic Center and the Olympic Village lay the Techwood/Clark Howell public housing projects, which were among the oldest in the country (Techwood was the first public housing project in the US, built in 1936). Indeed, initial plans for the Olympic Village involved razing part, if not all, of the Techwood projects. As will be detailed below, this proved to be another point of intense conflict between not only the city, ACOG, and residents but the Atlanta Housing Authority and the federal Department of Housing and Urban Development as well. Another poor neighborhood, Vine City, separated the Olympic Center from the five institutions that comprised the Atlanta University Center, whose athletic facilities constituted a third zone of activity.

The remainder of the venues within the Ring were located at some distance from the Olympic Center in three areas that had been razed and reconstructed during 1960s urban renewal. The two stadiums, for example, were located in the Summerhill neighborhood, which had been partly obliterated by construction of the Atlanta-Fulton County Stadium in 1965–66. The latter was contemporary with the Atlanta Civic Center, which, together with the adjoining gentrified enclave of Bedford-Pine, had been built on the bones of the poor African-American community known as Buttermilk Bottom. The Civic Center was a fairly minor venue, though, hosting only the weight-lifting competition. Georgia State University, whose late 1960s "platform campus" had eradicated the bawdy African-American entertainment zone along Decatur Street, also was host to just one sport – badminton. The remaining eleven sports would take place outside the Ring at Stone Mountain Park (archery, cycling, and tennis), Savannah (yachting), Ocoee River, Tennessee (white-water canoeing), and at two suburban sites, Wolf Creek in southwest Fulton (shooting), and Conyers in Rockdale County (rowing and equestrian).

One consequence of the ring strategy went largely unremarked at the time the original plan was released. Never had Olympic organizers concentrated so many people in so limited a space – not to mention a central business district that employed some 125,000 workers on a daily basis. ACOG itself projected that the population of the Olympic Ring would swell to more than half a million during the Games. Although they prided themselves on developing the first Olympic transportation plan that would encompass the "Olympic Family" (athletes, officials, etc.) and spectators, the effects on what ACOG referred to as the "background traffic" (everyone else) seem not to have been considered. ACOG's conceptual traffic plan assumed that the background traffic could be minimized, so as to allow the Olympic

Family to be moved around by a massive fleet of leased vehicles, while the spectators utilized MARTA. The traffic plan proved to be a point of considerable conflict as the Games approached, as downtown employers were extremely reluctant to follow ACOG's injunctions to "go on vacation" during the three weeks of the Games.

FROM AOC TO ACOG

In early 1991, the Atlanta Olympic Committee reconstituted itself as the Atlanta Committee for the Olympic Games, or ACOG, a private non-profit (sic) corporation. However, the Letter of Agreement worked out between ACOG and city and state governments clearly spelled out that ACOG was working on behalf of the latter, who assumed no financial responsibility for undertaking the Games. ACOG was thus yet another in a series of Atlanta's public–private partnerships, even though it had steadfastly maintained that it is an exclusively private entity. As such, it claimed to be exempt from Georgia's "Sunshine Law" and routinely refused to release information on its decision-making process or any aspect of its internal operations, including the salaries of its top officials. ACOG's penchant for secrecy also proved to be increasingly problematic as the mobilization for the Games took place.

Many of the Crazy Atlanta Nine went on to assume top managerial positions in ACOG, although a few lacked experience in the corporate world. To nobody's surprise, Payne was designated president, while Andrew Young remained on board as co-chairman. The other co-chair was Bob Holder, president of one of the city's largest construction firms. For the crucial role of chief operating officer, Payne turned to A.D. Frazier, Jr, a former Atlanta banker and Carter administration insider known for his take-no-prisoners management style. Payne also hired William Moss, builder of Disney's Epcot Center, to head up the construction effort, and selected Patrick Glisson, Atlanta's chief financial officer in the Andrew Young administration (1982–89), as his CFO. Indeed, the lesser ranks of ACOG's management structure were stocked with veterans of both Young's and Maynard Jackson's administrations, leading more than one observer to note the existence of a "revolving door" between ACOG and city hall.[21] Upper management, however, remained, with the exception of Andrew Young (who was not involved in day-to-day decisions), largely a study in "many shades of white."[22] Until the appointment of Shirley Franklin, Andrew Young's former chief of staff, as senior policy advisor in 1993, there was only one African-American and one Hispanic in the upper management cohort, along with three white women. The inner circle, however, was still (and remains) composed of "white, male, middle-aged Protestant businessmen and lawyers."[23] ACOG's board of directors, which was picked by the governor, the mayor, the business community, and other powerful interests, is considerably more integrated than ACOG management, although it lacks a single Jewish, Hispanic, or Asian member.[24]

The lesser ranks of ACOG, however, were considerably more diverse than the mostly pale, male leadership cabal atop its summit. Early in the organization process, ACOG voluntarily adopted an affirmative action policy regarding the hiring of minorities, women, and the disabled, although they were a little slower to extend the policy to procurement. After city officials stressed that minority involvement in the Olympic process was important,[25] ACOG unveiled an Equal Economic Opportunity Plan which they claimed was "unprecedented in the private sector."[26] The Plan was intended to assure that minority- and female-owned businesses would have the fullest opportunity to receive Olympic-related contracts. In 1992, 42 percent of Olympic contracts went to female- and minority-owned businesses, a considerably higher figure than the 33 percent of city contracts that went to the same kind of firms. However, this sector share of ACOG contracts declined to 31.7 percent by 1994, and continued to drop. In addition, the Atlanta Business League – an organization of minority-owned companies – was deluged with complaints that Olympic contracts rarely went to those without contacts within ACOG's closed world.[27]

Similar patterns were evident in hiring, even with ACOG's commitment to affirmative action. In 1992, female and minority employment levels at ACOG stood at 58 percent and 37 percent, respectively.[28] As with the 1992 contract figures, these figures were comparable to or higher than those of the public sector. However, as noted above, these employees were concentrated in the lower and middle sectors of the organization. As ACOG expanded, "and the need for specialized skills and experienced personnel"[29] increased in subsequent years, the percentage of women and minorities in the organization decreased to 54.7 percent and 33.4 percent, respectively.

With over a billion dollars in expenses to shell out, ACOG's most immediate and pressing concern was money. With a decision on the US television contract not due until 1993, initial emphasis was placed on lining up corporate sponsors, who had been tasked to provide nearly a third of ACOG's revenue stream. Working through the good offices of Andrew Young, Payne and Frazier met with Hugh McColl, whose Charlotte, North Carolina-based NationsBank had just swallowed up one of the pillars of the Atlanta financial community (and Frazier's former employer), Citizens & Southern Bank. In an earnest display of good corporate citizenship, McColl not only signed on as one of the Olympic sponsors, but extended the boys from ACOG a half-billion-dollar line of credit, with the revenues from the TV rights as partial collateral.[30] The remainder of the credit line was unsecured, however, thus opening up NationsBank to significant risk if the Games failed to live up to financial expectations. The Letter of Agreement between ACOG, the City of Atlanta, and the State of Georgia specified that ACOG, rather than either of the two public parties, were financially responsible. In other words, there would be no public safety net if ACOG either went egregiously over budget or was unable to raise sufficient revenue. Despite the oft-made assurance that the Games would be staged without relying on public dollars, most Georgians remained leery of the prospect of a taxpayer bailout.

MAOGA

Public concerns were stoked by the fact that the arrangement between the city, the state, and ACOG stipulated that the last was working for the first two. In fact, the official signatory to the agreement with the IOC that designated Atlanta as host city of the 1996 Games is not ACOG, but the Metropolitan Atlanta Olympic Games Authority, or MAOGA. Created by an act of the state legislature in 1989, MAOGA was charged with approving ACOG's major construction contracts (i.e. those over $250,000), and all changes in venue. It also was the "owner" of the Olympic Stadium and could "even summon armed troops in an emergency."[31] The twelve-member MAOGA board was headed by George Berry, a vice-president of one of Atlanta's (and the state's) largest real estate development firms, Cousins Properties. Berry was also a former aviation commissioner and ex-director of the Georgia Department of Industry, Trade, and Tourism, the state's chief marketing arm. MAOGA's executive director was Richard Monteilh, an alumnus of both the Jackson and Young administrations and a career urban mandarin whose résumé included a stint overseeing the revitalization of the "notorious" downtown of Newark, New Jersey.[32]

Despite its strategic authority, MAOGA adopted a fairly low-key and laid-back approach to its mission, leading one newspaper reporter to call it "the Rodney Dangerfield of Olympic agencies, a largely anonymous collection of public officials and private citizens who have a hard time getting respect."[33] This reputation proved quite deserved. With the lone exception of the Olympic Stadium controversy, which will be discussed below, MAOGA proved to be more of a puppy dog than a watchdog agency, essentially licking ACOG's face and allowing the latter to make free and liberal use of its fire hydrants. As one knowledgeable Olympic observer noted rather late in the game, the characterization of MAOGA as a watchdog was a creation of the media and city hall, as Billy Payne never accepted the overseeing role of what was nothing more than a "paper municipality."[34] The myth of MAOGA autonomy was further eroded by the fact that ACOG, and not the State of Georgia, provided MAOGA's annual operating budget, and offered free passes to all Olympic events to MAOGA board members.[35] Nor did MAOGA make much of its state-chartered powers to finance the gargantuan mission of "outside the fence" redevelopment. Although MAOGA eventually did make some relatively minor land condemnations to clear the way for building housing in low-income neighborhoods, like Summerhill and Peoplestown, it did not take a lead role in community revitalization or other Olympic redevelopment efforts.

ERUPTION AND AVALANCHE ON MOUNT OLYMPUS: THE CITY'S FIRST EFFORTS AT REDEVELOPMENT

Although MAOGA was never more than a symbolic fig-leaf covering the interests of Georgia taxpayers, the city of Atlanta lagged even further behind in establishing its own entity to realize the task of "outside the fence" redevelopment. A great deal of the problem was due to the chaotic political climate that followed Andrew Young's departure from the mayor's office in 1989. Young had worked closely with both the city's business community and with ACOG, while Jackson's previous two administrations had been marked by frequent conflict between business interests and city hall. Jackson was deeply unhappy with the Letter of Agreement worked out by Young, as it essentially gave carte blanche to ACOG to focus exclusively on the venues themselves, without regard to the impact of these activities on the neighborhoods outside the fence, but inside the Olympic Ring. In addition, the agreement explicitly forbade city officials from getting involved in building Olympic venues. This constituted a major break in Atlanta's much-celebrated pattern of civic–business partnerships. Still, as long as Atlanta's Olympic bid was considered a "crazy dream," little attention was directed to the potential impact of the Games on the city. However, after the announcement of "It's Atlanta" in September 1990, tensions deepened between Jackson and ACOG. At the award ceremony in Tokyo, the mayor articulated his vision of the "twin peaks of Mount Olympus" – staging the best games in Olympic history and demonstrating to the world that Atlanta was the best city. While the former was out of Jackson's hands (and ACOG missed no opportunity to remind him of that fact), realizing the latter was an even more impossible task, as it entailed revitalizing inner-city neighborhoods that had been systematically underdeveloped during the previous two decades of the metro area's storied growth.

ACOG stubbornly resisted any effort to broaden its scope of operations, and wheeled out its "special weapon" yet again – Andrew Young. Wearing the crown of the co-chair of ACOG rather than the mantle of a former mayor, Young asserted that the Olympics were "not a welfare program, [they are] a business venture. If they [the city government] wanted to be more involved they should've voted to pay their own expenses."[36] This comment was more than a little disingenuous. The "they" Young referred to was the Atlanta City Council, circa 1989, which had been reluctant to contribute money that it did not have to support the Olympics. ACOG, for its part, wanted nothing to do with the eighteen-member body, which it deemed to be a den of corrupt iniquity. According to Young, the Letter of Agreement excluded city officials from the Olympic process because there was "an anti-city council, anti-politician mood at the time" and ACOG wanted to keep the Olympic process "unpoliticized."[37] Given the number of scandals and incidents of financial impropriety engaged in by several council members, ACOG's concerns were far from groundless.

Yet, the city council was also representing (for a change) the views of the electorate, who were in no mood to see their taxes raised to host the Olympics. It was highly unlikely, for example, that Atlantans would have voted for a bond issue to fund Olympic-related redevelopment, or, for that matter, would have voted to have the Olympics in Atlanta at all. Of course, quasi-public city entities such as the Downtown Development Authority could issue bonds without voter approval. However, since the late 1980s, the DDA had already subsidized putatively "private" ventures like the Georgia Dome and Underground Atlanta to the tune of approximately $400 million. At the time of the Olympic bid, Atlanta's municipal debt burden was exceeded only by New York City's among US cities.[38] When he made that comment in 1992, Andrew Young seemed to have conveniently forgotten Atlanta's penurious condition, along with the reality that he was one of the "they" at the time the agreement between the city and ACOG was reached. Despite his impressive credentials as a civil rights leader, and a mother lode of rhetoric about the semi-divine spirituality of Olympism, at no point did Young use his crucial importance to AOC/ACOG as leverage for getting a better deal for the poor neighborhoods that would be most directly affected by Olympic construction.

As ACOG mobilized in 1991 and much of 1992, the city's responses to the Olympic challenge were fragmented and ultimately unsuccessful. Together with CAP, the city invited the Urban Land Institute (ULI) – a Washington DC-based research group funded by major developers – to work out a redevelopment plan for the Summerhill neighborhood, which had been devastated by the construction of the Atlanta-Fulton County Stadium in 1965–66 and the subsequent conversion of vast stretches of the surrounding area into parking lots. In 1988, community leaders had formed Summerhill Neighborhood, Inc. to plan for the neighborhood's revitalization. ULI planners proposed more than $100 million in improvements that would convert Summerhill into a model mixed-income community. They further argued that the proposed Olympic stadium would have a positive rather than a negative impact on the neighborhood, as long as the old facility was demolished after the Games. Where the money would come from to finance Summerhill redevelopment, however, was unspecified.

Along with Summerhill, the Techwood/Clark Howell public housing projects were among the neighborhoods most dramatically affected by ACOG's plans. Following the model that had driven downtown redevelopment over the previous two decades, the city created a non-profit, quasi-public corporation to lead the revitalization of a 209-acre parcel that included both the housing projects and an adjacent area of vacant lots and small businesses that local real estate practitioners called "the Badlands" or "the Void." To head the entity known as Techwood Park, Inc. (TPI), Jackson named Joseph Martin, who had just finished seeing the complex Underground Atlanta project to a successful completion. On paper, Martin seemed a ideal choice for the job — one newspaper reporter had referred to him as the "poster boy of public–private partnerships in Atlanta." Endorsing a plan developed by a private consultancy group hired by the Atlanta Housing Authority (AHA), Martin proposed to privatize the public housing and use tax increment financing to redevelop the entire area for a mix of residential, retail, and commercial uses. Initially it was hoped that some of the new housing in Techwood Park would be used to house Olympic athletes; however, TPI was not able to work out an effective plan to meet ACOG's deadline of October 1991. In fact, TPI was never able to come up with an acceptable plan at all. The privatization of the Techwood-Clark Howell projects was effectively resisted by the then president of the Atlanta Housing Authority, Earl Phillips, as well as tenants groups who feared (rightly) that they would be displaced. The future of Techwood would be determined by the AHA, not TPI. Martin resigned in protest in late 1991, and took up the presidency of Central Atlanta Progress, which, after an extremely short tenure, he left to reassume the presidency of the company that managed Underground Atlanta. After Martin's angry exodus, TPI essentially closed up shop, until reopening in much diminished form in 1994.

Despite the collapse of TPI's plans to build new housing to be used as Olympic dormitories, Techwood remained the preferred site for parts of the Olympic Village. The AHA hoped to sell a 4.5-acre parcel to the Board of Regents of the University System of Georgia, who would raze the 114 units and construct student dormitories that would be used to house 4,000 Olympic athletes in the summer of 1996. Earl Phillips hoped to realize as much as $7 million from the sale of the property, which would be used to fund replacement housing and to spur his plans for redeveloping the rest of the community. Although the Board of Regents were solidly behind the project, the federal Department of

Housing and Urban Development rejected the AHA plan in September of 1992 for failing to provide adequate replacement housing for residents of the affected parcel.[39] HUD's opposition vanished by the early spring of 1993, when it agreed to AHA's sale of the 4.5-acre parcel to the University System of Georgia for $2.6 million, a considerably lower sum than Phillips had anticipated.

Still, while it met with HUD approval, the relocation plan was far from adequate. By the time the deal was reached, only 65 of the 114 units remained occupied. This was far from coincidental, as former residents complained that the AHA stepped up arbitrary and capricious evictions after 1991 in order to clear the way for its redevelopment plans.

AHA plans called for the remaining residents to be relocated to a privately owned middle-income apartment complex in a largely African-American section of northwest Atlanta. This move was strongly resisted by residents of the complex, and the AHA was obliged to find other means of relocating the former inhabitants of the Techwood Olympic Village parcel.[40] The AHA was still working to find permanent replacement housing for many of the displacees more than a year and a half after the sale.[41] By this time, however, the controversial Earl Phillips had been replaced as director of the AHA by Rene Glover, who was busy trying to work out plans to use the $42 million allocated by HUD for the rehabilitation of the remainder of the Techwood/Clark Howell projects. These plans were dogged by many of the same issues that characterized the redevelopment of the Olympic Village parcel, to which I shall return later in this chapter.

END OF THE HONEYMOON

In the course of 1992, Jackson's relations with ACOG, the business community (represented by Central Atlanta Progress and the Chamber of Commerce), and his own city council deteriorated markedly. Led by CAP, the business community argued for the creation of a new public–private agency to coordinate Olympic-related civic improvements that would operate "outside" of city politics, while Jackson wanted an entity that would involve the departments of public works, housing, and planning, as well as the Atlanta Economic Development Corporation (AEDC). This last entity, which had a key role in putting together the Underground Atlanta deal, was not well regarded by CAP. The local real estate industry was also particularly displeased by AEDC's plans to build a mammoth office building that would consolidate US government offices downtown, and in the process empty out the eight existing buildings in which they were housed (see Chapter 4). Local newspapers desperately called for an "Olympic Czar" to take charge. The problem was that none of the competing power centers could agree on who such a "maximum leader" would be. The city's bargaining position was greatly diminished when Jackson underwent coronary bypass surgery in late summer 1992, after returning from the Barcelona Olympics. Without Jackson at the helm, the city drifted.

As mentioned in the introduction to this volume, the Barcelona Games served as a wake-up call for all of those concerned with getting Atlanta ready for 1996. The Whatizit debacle, together with the lack of a coherent redevelopment plan and open conflict between the civic and business elite, instilled a new sense of urgency amongst leaders as well as the citizenry at large. While a considerable amount of public animus was directed at the city government, for the first time a sense of popular critical resentment was openly directed towards ACOG, which even local reporters were referring to as overly secretive and arrogant. While residents of some of the neighborhoods most affected by ACOG's plans, such as Summerhill, had been organizing protests since 1991, these efforts increased in scope and intensity and got more media attention in the fall of 1992. The major protest groups included Atlanta Neighborhoods United For Fairness (ANUFF), the Olympic Conscience Coalition, and the Task Force for the Homeless. Olympic boosters remained unswayed and clueless; one business leader complained that the protesters lacked the proper "cooperative spirit."[42] By far the largest protest, though, was mounted by the organized labor movement, which marched several thousand people through downtown Atlanta on 18 September 1992 in protest at ACOG's lack of commitment to use union labor to build the venues. At a rally, speakers led by Jesse Jackson and local labor leader Stewart Acuff articulated fears that ACOG would instead make extensive use of labor pools, composed largely of homeless persons, and illegal immigrants. Their fears turned out to be accurate, as ACOG's contractors made extensive use of day labor in their construction programs.[43] The use of poorly paid and highly exploitative labor pools, which in many cases were composed principally of illegal immigrants, harked back to the extensive use of convict labor to build the facilities for both the 1881 International Cotton Exposition and the 1895 Cotton States and International Exposition.[44] Although the march ultimately had little impact on ACOG, it was noteworthy in that it constituted the strongest denunciation of ACOG yet recorded.

TOO MUCH "NEW," NOT ENOUGH "SOUTH"

Criticism was also directed towards ACOG's image as much or more than its practices. As already noted in Chapter 1, Billy Payne's choice of the Whatizit mascot sparked a storm of ridicule and protest. While national and international critics focused their derision on the image's tackiness, the response from around the

South was much more pointed and "close to home." Newspapers from all over the region decried ACOG's abandonment of Southern themes and images in favor of neutered technopolitan fantasies. The latter went far deeper than the choice of Whatizit. Although ACOG's bid books emphasized Atlanta's position as capital of the South, and the uniqueness of the region vis-à-vis the rest of the nation (a number of observers even quipped that ACOG had almost made the South out to be a separate country), the Olympic organizers' emphasis, much like that of CAP and the Chamber of Commerce, was on Atlanta's modernity and orientation towards the future. Several regional newspapers asserted that ACOG was embarrassed by, and sought to run away from, its Southern heritage. The latter, however, was a deeply contested and controversial notion, as it was strongly associated with the South's history of slavery, as well as the not-so-distant past of segregation and massive resistance to civil rights. For many people, a Southern identity referred to an exclusively white South, or at least a region defined in large measure by a pervasive ethos of white supremacy. ACOG's emphasis on the future allowed it, as well as Atlanta's boosters more generally, to avoid dealing with the problematic issues of Southern history, which it preferred to reduce to the unproblematic notion of "hospitality," while simultaneously playing up the city's civil rights legacy from the 1960s. In this latter orientation, however, ACOG was not completely consistent, as it had chosen Stone Mountain Park, a state-built and -owned "Monument to the Confederacy," as a key venue site.

During the winter of 1992 and into the summer of 1993, Atlanta newspapers devoted a great deal of space to the issue of Southern identity. The debate over Southernness was highlighted, but not created, by the Olympics, and was not limited to Atlanta. The rapid growth and modernization of large swaths of the former Confederacy, and the immigration of millions of Yankees, Midwesterners, and even more exotic "foreigners" over the last thirty years had led many to question whether the South remained a distinctive region at all. However, the biggest challenge to the symbols of regional identity came from African-American civil rights groups like the Southern Christian Leadership Conference and local chapters of the National Association for the Advancement of Colored People. Both the SCLC and the NAACP led drives against what they considered to be "public glorifications of the Confederacy."[45] These included the playing of "Dixie" at public events and the naming of streets after Confederate leaders, and certain monuments as well, such as the grave of Ku Klux Klan founder, Confederate General Nathan Bedford Forrest, in Memphis, Tennessee. For the most part, however, the NAACP distinguished between historical markers and monuments, such as those that stood in virtually every community in the South, and "living symbols," such as state flags and banners.[46] "Although one NAACP leader noted that "we certainly don't propose to dig up the landscape of the South," a few black leaders did propose covering the carving on Stone Mountain during the Olympics.[47]

Since 1988, however, the NAACP had led efforts to change the Georgia state flag, which incorporated the Confederate battle emblem (often mistakenly referred to as the Stars and Bars). Supporters of the flag countered that the banner was an essential part of their Southern heritage and history and not a racially offensive symbol. Aside from the dubious logic that held that since it was part of Southern heritage it could not be racially offensive, this point of view implied that the emblem had long been part of the state flag. In fact, the banner was of rather recent origin, having been selected by the Georgia legislature in 1956, ostensibly in tribute to the memory of fallen Confederate soldiers. However, at the time most read the flag change as a major symbolic stand against desegregation and civil rights, or as one state legislator noted: "This will show that we in Georgia intend to uphold what we stood for, will stand for, and will fight for."[48] The efforts of the NAACP and black state legislators received a major boost in May 1992, when Georgia Governor Zell Miller proposed to change the Georgia flag "back" to the pre-1956 original (which itself had been modeled on the Confederate national flag – the actual Stars and Bars), boldly calling the current flag "the last remaining vestige of days that are not only gone, but also days that we have no right to be proud of."[49] He was supported in his effort by many fellow Democratic politicians, especially from Fulton and DeKalb counties, and business leaders from around the state.[50] Not surprisingly, Miller was opposed by virtually all Republican legislators, as well as conservative rural Democrats like Tom Murphy, long-time State House Speaker and political king-maker. However, he was also running against popular opinion, as polls indicated that 56 percent of Georgians opposed changing the flag, while less than a third supported the move.[51]

Miller persevered through March 1993, but abandoned his principled stand when it became clear that it threatened his chances for re-election in 1994. The flag re-emerged as a center of controversy, however, in January 1994, when Atlanta hosted the Super Bowl. Civil rights advocates used the national media spotlight that the US football championship focused on the city to press their efforts to change the flag, threatening a state-wide boycott of businesses that flew the flag and threatening to organize a boycott of the 1996 Olympics by African nations.[52] They received support from the *Atlanta Constitution* (although not from its more conservative sibling, the *Atlanta Journal*), which urged a change in what it referred to as "Georgia's corporate logo."[53] City and state politicians, including Zell Miller, preferred to sidestep the issue, however, as did ACOG leaders Billy Payne and Andrew Young. As two-thirds of the Olympic venues made use of state-owned land and/or facilities, the flag controversy had serious implications for ACOG, which feared both a boycott and alienating the State Assembly. Olympic organizers took a "wait and see" attitude, although two Olympic sponsors – Holiday Inn Worldwide and McDonalds – either asked or gave its franchisees the opportunity not to fly the flag. Holiday Inn's decision sparked a counter-protest from flag advocates, although a threatened boycott never materialized. Since then, ACOG has maintained its hands-off approach to the matter, even in the face of a possible boycott by black and African athletes, delegating responsibility for "all decisions involving the Georgia state flag to those whom we citizens elect and empower to deal with these issues."[54] By 1995, even anti-flag advocates had toned down their rhetoric and scaled back their efforts, although these were likely to be renewed as the Olympics drew closer.

The winter of 1994 brought protests and the prospects of an Olympic boycott from yet another group. As mentioned in Chapter 2, the Cobb County Commission passed a resolution condemning "the gay lifestyle" as contrary to family values and had cut off financing to arts groups in response to the staging of a play in Marietta that portrayed homosexual characters in a positive light. ACOG had planned to stage the preliminary rounds of the Olympic volleyball competition in Cobb's Galleria Center. Local and national gay rights groups protested against the commission's decision and threatened to organize extensive protests before and during the Games if ACOG persisted in its plans to stage volleyball in Cobb. Unlike the flag controversy, ACOG responded in a more direct and proactive fashion, aggressively lobbying the commission to rescind the ordinance. While this proved unsuccessful, the Cobb Commission voted against letting ACOG use the county-owned facility for volleyball or any other purpose, thus sparing ACOG the necessity of moving the competition out of Cobb. ACOG's image of social progressivism was short-lived, however. Later efforts by gay rights groups to prevent the Olympic torch relay from passing through Cobb were unsuccessful.

TURF BATTLES

The early skirmishes in the fight over the state flag served to heighten an incipient racial dimension to the city's struggles with both ACOG and the business community. In order to restore some sense of order to an increasingly chaotic situation, a still not completely recovered Maynard Jackson called a summit meeting of Olympic organizers and top elected officials in late September 1992. In addition to ACOG, those invited included Governor Zell Miller, city councilors, business and neighborhood leaders, and officials from Fulton County and the Atlanta Housing Authority. Little came of the meeting, as ACOG remained obstinate and refused to broaden its scope of activity. One of the few things that came out of the conclave was that there would be no Olympic redevelopment "czar." Jackson remained firmly committed to the idea that the entity would be city-controlled, which alienated the business community, who were being asked, along with county and state officials, to put up much of the money. As the president of the Chamber of Commerce noted at the time, "You've got to give the people who give the dough a chance to write the plan . . . If they write it, they will underwrite it."[55]

Critics of Jackson in and outside the business community portrayed the mayor as being motivated solely by ego, as selfishly wanting to take credit for whatever was accomplished. This is a far too convenient explanation, however. There is no disputing that Jackson's sense of self-aggrandizement greatly exceeded his ample bulk, and that he, as much as any other politician, wished to take as much credit as possible – and then some – for any improvements to Atlanta, but he was far from being the only player on the field with an elephantine ego (an imperial sense of self, it seems, is part of the job description for the power elite). Rather, Jackson was also arguing for the by no means novel, but certainly dated, notion that the elected government officials should have a major say in shaping major redevelopment projects within city boundaries. There is no disputing that Atlanta's municipal government was, and still is, a warren of internecine conflicts tainted by the "perception" of corruption, but it is disingenuous at best to assert that by keeping city government out of it, the redevelopment process is any way "depoliticized." Such a claim projects the bogus notion that the private sector lacks its own interests and agendas and is motivated solely by an enlightened volition to maximize public welfare instead of its own profit, or rather, that the maximization of private profit is equally beneficial to the public good.

POSTMODERN-DAY BABBITTRY

Jackson's Olympic summit was followed by an "Image summit," organized by the city's first marketing director, Joel Babbitt. Appointed by Jackson in July, 1992, the rather aptly named Babbitt was an iconoclastic Atlanta-born ad executive who had recently left the New York firm of Chiat Day Mojo. Answerable only to Jackson, Babbitt was not well received by the Atlanta City Council, which from the start he alienated with his brash and arrogant manner. The purpose of the summit was to bring together the two dozen or so entities with a stake in the "vision thing,"[56] including ACOG, the AEDC, the Metropolitan Atlanta Rapid Transit Authority (MARTA), and the Atlanta Project (TAP), in addition to Central Atlanta Progress, the Chamber of Commerce, and the Atlanta Convention and Visitors Bureau (ACVB). Babbitt was concerned that there was far too little coordination of efforts between these various entities and that efforts would be undermined by discordant visions. Just like any other product, he argued, Atlanta needed a single slogan. Each of the city's principal marketing entities had its own pet line, however, as did Babbitt. The ACVB preferred "Look at Atlanta Now," while ACOG leaned toward the more manifestly international "Atlanta: What the World is Coming To." Babbitt's own slogan eschewed globality for more of a national/regional/communitarian feel: "Atlanta: Hometown to the American Dream." None was able to generate much enthusiasm outside its partisan creators, who each perceived the others as "too generic." Not surprisingly, the summit ended with a rather indecisive commitment "to continue to work towards efforts at generating consensus." In short, what was needed was something that helped create a more authentic image rooted in place.

The ACVB assumed the pivotal role in the effort to generate consensus about a new slogan. To this end, it commissioned a group of local advertising and public relations experts, who in fine forward-thinking Atlanta fashion called themselves the 1999 Group. They vowed that they would allow "the community to have ownership in the process"[57] of picking a new slogan. Still, as befitting Atlanta's status as a world-class city, the ACVB's idea of who comprised the community was both locally limited and grandiosely global. It was also very hi-tech. Using the Atlanta Project's computer system, which allowed for the anonymous polling of focus groups, fifty of the most influential local decision-makers would be surveyed to determine a series of "positioning statements" that would then be run past a broad sample of Atlantans and a thousand influential people around the world.[58] Then, the 1999 Group would crunch the numbers and render the winning decision by March 1993. For a variety of reasons (not the least of which was that local movers and shakers were far more involved in dealing with the more pressing and tangible matters of debating an organizational structure that would realize a material legacy for the Games) the interviewing process did not begin until February 1993.

Seven months later, the 1999 Group revealed five "marketing platforms" that managed to exceed the earlier proposed slogans in utterly banal vacuity: Atlanta: Anything is Possible; Atlanta: A Great Place to Live and Work; Atlanta: Claiming Its Own International Destiny (because, presumably, no one else would); Atlanta: A Canvas for Creative, Intellectual, and Social Expression; and Atlanta: A City of Immense Pride.[59] Even though the 1999 Group took great pains to emphasize that these were general "platforms" rather than specific "slogans" (the implication was that the latter would inevitably emerge from the former), the response from city and business leaders was, to put it politely, "underwhelming."[60] The reaction from the local media and the national advertising industry was particularly scathing. A columnist in *Advertising Age* suggested that Atlanta was "The City Too Dumb to be Ashamed."[61] The hunt for a slogan was quickly turning into a Whatizit redux.

Sent back to the drawing boards, a by now desperate 1999 Group finally began to seriously examine the more than 5,000 entries from around the world, which included such gems as "Atlanta and the World: Yes!"; "Watch Atlanta Transmogrify"; "Atlanta: An Island in a Sea of Rednecks"; and "Atlanta: A City Too Stupid to Find Its Ass with Both Hands If Its Life Depended on It." As the national and international ridicule mounted, the various entities associated with the vision thing began to go their own ways. By the time the ACVB decided upon the vaguely Babbitt-like "Come Share Our Dream" in February 1995, the Chamber of Commerce and the Georgia Department of Industry, Trade, and Tourism had embarked on their own separate campaigns. As one newspaper columnist perceptively noted in 1993, the inability of Atlanta's fractious interests to agree on a message was the most profound, and revealing, symbolic statement that Atlanta could make about itself.[62]

CODA

Two weeks after the inconclusive summit meeting, Jackson held a press conference announcing the creation of the Corporation for Olympic Development in Atlanta, or CODA. This non-profit, quasi-public corporation was charged with planning, funding, and implementing the master plan to revitalize neighborhoods within the Olympic ring. CODA was co-chaired by Jackson and a yet to be determined representative of the business community. They presided over a 21-member board, which consisted of representatives from the Atlanta City Council, Fulton and DeKalb counties, ACOG, MAOGA, neighborhood groups, local philanthropists, the business community, and organized labor. After a brief search, Shirley Franklin, who had been the chief operating officer in Andrew Young's mayoral administration, was named president. One problem from the outset was that, for it to be effective, the CODA board had to achieve broad consensus on means and ends, something that was unlikely given the group's diverse composition. Moreover, the private sector co-chair had to be someone well respected in the business community. With only three members on the board from the latter group, however, local businessmen felt that CODA was stacked against their collective interests. Even after the appointment of the well-respected businessman John Aderhold as co-chair (among whose accomplishments were coordinating public and private sector efforts to build the Georgia Dome), CODA enjoyed little support from the private sector, including the all-important philanthropists like the Woodruff Foundation, upon whom it was counting for financing. Not only was the private sector alienated by Jackson's efforts to run the show, but CODA lacked a plan, and even a set of guidelines. Even the normally generous Woodruff Foundation was reluctant to commit itself without a plan.

Even more troubling than lack of a plan was the matter of where the financing for proposed improvements would come from. Various estimates put the bill for dealing with the city's vital infrastructure needs (sewers and viaducts), as well as neighborhood redevelopment and sundry amenities like parks between $500 million and $1 billion. None of the options proposed for generating that kind of money was particularly viable, however. Unlike MAOGA, CODA did not have the authority to issue bonds. Several other quasi-public entities did, but the bonds had to be backed with some sort of future revenue. Proposals to levy a surcharge on Olympic tickets or temporarily increase the local sales tax met with the disapproval of ACOG and the Georgia Assembly, respectively. The city could also put a bond issue before the voters, but this was considered to be political suicide for any politician who proposed it.

Desperate for revenue, the irrepressible Joel Babbitt proposed to take a page from ACOG's playbook and get corporate sponsors to pay for improvements. In return, sponsors would be able to rename the enhanced streets, parks, and neighborhoods in their own image. The resulting outcry was intense and broad-based. Critics inside city government indignantly responded that Babbitt's plan would demean its image before the world.[63] Their outrage was nothing, however, compared to the reaction from ACOG, which was having its own problems lining up corporate sponsorships for the Games. Not only would Babbitt's plan place the city and ACOG in direct competition for funds in an economy still struggling to grow out of a recession, but it opened up the frightening prospect of "ambush marketing" by corporate rivals of Olympic sponsors. When Babbitt offered American Express the right to be the "official credit card of Atlanta," Olympic sponsor Visa quickly, and angrily, ponied up $2 million to avoid being bushwhacked by its competitor.[64]

True to form, Babbitt did not shrink from the critical response. "Look, we need the money," he said to a reporter. "I don't see any difference in us taking money from Coke and renaming a street Coca-Cola Boulevard and Michael Jordan wearing a Nike hat on the beach."[65] There was no small amount of pecuniary truth to Babbitt's observation. Like the good ad man he was, he presciently realized that "all things float with equal specific gravity in the constantly moving stream of money"[66] and that, to a certain extent at least, all commodities are created equal. However, by making explicit what most advertisers take great pains to conceal, or at least make less obvious (not to mention casting his buckets into ACOG's revenue stream), he committed an ultimately fatal error. Attacked from both inside and outside city government, Babbitt's days were numbered. The killing blow came in the spring of 1993, after he proposed raising money by selling advertising space on a mile-long mylar balloon that would be launched into geosynchronous orbit over

Atlanta, for which the city would receive a 20 percent cut. The city council responded by banning orbital advertising over Atlanta, even though, as Babbitt himself sarcastically noted, such matters were outside the body's jurisdiction. Under fire, Babbitt resigned to take up a position with entrepreneur Chris Whittle's fledgling, but ultimately ill-fated, Channel One national educational television network.

Babbitt's departure did little more than please his scores of detractors and lessen the entertainment value of Atlanta's Olympic-related follies. His firing did little to improve the prospects for CODA, which was further weakened by the resignation of Shirley Franklin in mid May 1993. Significantly enough, Franklin moved on to become Billy Payne's senior policy advisor at ACOG. The impact of Franklin's departure on CODA was ameliorated somewhat by the fact that she had accomplished virtually nothing during her short tenure. Eight months after its creation, CODA still lacked a list of specific projects, not to mention financing and political support. The state legislature hostilely rejected a proposed one cent addition to the sales tax to fund Olympic-related redevelopment, and prospects for federal funding were dim. Jackson did, however, have close ties to the Clinton administration through commerce secretary Ron Brown, transportation secretary Frederico Pena, and housing and urban development secretary Henry Cisneros. Atlanta's ties to Clinton also ran through Governor Zell Miller, who was widely considered to have "delivered" the state to his former fellow governor in the 1992 elections. These connections ultimately bore fruit, although not much of it was destined for CODA's plate. The beleaguered entity was the beneficiary, however, of a National Park Service plan to spend nearly $12 million on improvements to the Martin Luther King Historic Site (the controversy over which was discussed in Chapter 2) and transportation funds for streetscape improvements.

The lion's share of federal monies, however, flowed to other entities. In October 1993, HUD granted the Atlanta Housing Authority $42 million to rehabilitate the Techwood public housing project, even though a plan to direct this revitalization had yet to be devised and accepted. Mayor Jackson, Congressman John Lewis, and Senator Sam Nunn were also able to get the General Services Administration to agree to consolidate most of the federal offices in Atlanta in the new Federal Center that a partnership of AEDC and Dallas-based Prentiss Properties was proposing to build downtown on the site of the old Rich's Department Store. Jackson's Washington contacts also helped to put Atlanta in a favored position to receive one of the six coveted designations as an Empowerment Zone city. Atlanta received the designation in December 1994, but little if any of the $100 million in grants and $150 million in tax credits would be actually used in time for 1996. In the spring of 1993, however, none of these was on the horizon, and with the exceptions of the Martin Luther King and streets projects, few would be started, and none would be completed, by the time the Olympics came around. Nor would any of these large federally funded projects do much to help CODA, whose hopes were dashed even further in June 1993, when Jackson announced he would not seek re-election in the fall.

TRADING A KING-DOM FOR A STADIUM

Jackson's decision not to run for re-election was ostensibly prompted by his family's concerns for his health. While he had made a full recovery from heart surgery, the winter of 1992–93 and the following spring found him at the center of two pitched battles that no doubt influenced his decision a great deal. The fight over CODA found him locking horns, unsuccessfully, with the business community, ACOG, and the neighborhoods. However, in the spring, CODA's problems were overshadowed by an intense multisided battle shaping up over the Olympic Stadium. Estimated at $209 million, the stadium was to be the single largest venue, and by far the most complex. Preliminary plans called for the construction of an 85,000-seat oval stadium to house the track and field competition and the opening and closing ceremonies. Neither of the two extant stadiums – Atlanta-Fulton County and the Georgia Dome – was suitable for track and field. After the Games, part of the Olympic Stadium would be demolished to convert it into a state-of-the-art baseball facility for the Atlanta Braves, while the old stadium would be demolished for parking. In the bid book submitted to the IOC in 1990, the stadium was originally envisioned as a "spaceship-like" interpretation of a classical Greek venue, with part of the stands *below* field level. Later, however, the plans changed to a more "traditional" brick and steel park such as those recently constructed in Cleveland, Baltimore, and Denver that would "pay homage to baseball's past."[67]

As of fall 1992, no deal had been struck between the six key parties involved in the construction of the stadium. ACOG had responsibility to design, build, and convert the new stadium, as well as demolishing the old one after the Games. In its role as official watchdog agency, MAOGA needed to approve ACOG's design and cost estimates, and be the principal signatory on the construction contract. While MAOGA was the temporary titular owner of the stadium, it actually belonged to the Atlanta-Fulton County Stadium Authority, which had to negotiate a lease with the Braves before MAOGA could begin construction. The Authority, however, was owned jointly by the city (two-thirds) and Fulton County, both of whose executive bodies had to approve the deal as well. While they lacked the power to veto the deal, both the Summerhill neighborhood association and the larger Neighborhood Planning Unit also had a role to play.

Various neighborhood groups, like ANUFF, had been protesting against the new facility ever since the location was revealed in 1990, even staging a candlelit vigil outside Billy Payne's Dunwoody home. By late 1992, the Summerhill neighborhood association and the Neighborhood Planning Unit V (which included the communities of Pittsburgh, Mechanicsville, and Peoplestown, as well) had shifted from a rejectionist strategy to one that sought to make the stadium aid in the process of neighborhood revitalization. To this end, they wanted a cap on the number of additional parking spaces (indeed, the uncontrolled proliferation of parking for the first stadium had proved almost as destabilizing as construction of the facility itself), a significant share of parking revenues, and a street-level retail complex oriented to the community. Summerhill residents were in no mood to experience a replay of 1965–66, when construction of the first stadium and associated parking displaced 10,000 of the neighborhood's approximately 12,500 residents.

Neither ACOG nor the Braves nor the Stadium Authority appeared to be very interested in taking the neighborhood's concerns into account when formulating their plans. The Braves were especially unwilling to settle for anything but exclusive control of concessions, parking, and associated retail. ACOG made much of the fact that the construction firm that would build the stadium was minority-owned, and that its president, Herman Russell, had been born and raised in Summerhill, as if this fact somehow constituted a giving back to the neighborhood. Meanwhile, details of negotiations between ACOG, the Braves, and the Stadium Authority remained hidden behind a veil of secrecy even the compliant watchdogs at MAOGA objected to.

The final plan was revealed to the public in mid February 1993 and was one sweetheart of a deal for the Braves. They got not only free use of the stadium and 60 luxury box suites, but total control of stadium operations, 10,000 parking spaces (3,500 more than originally designed) and nearly all of the parking revenue, and the right to name the post-Olympic stadium. Most importantly, the Braves assumed no financial liability whatsoever. The Stadium Authority, and by extension Atlanta and Fulton County taxpayers, were liable for any cost overruns associated with building and converting the stadium, as well as demolishing the old facility. This was no minor matter, as many observers believed that the $209-million figure that ACOG estimated for the complex task was a considerable underestimate of the true costs. Even MAOGA chief George Berry condemned the stadium pact, and the Fulton County Commission, despite the efforts of commission chairman Michael Lomax, rejected the lease arrangement.

The commission's chief opponent of the deal was Commissioner Martin Luther King III – the son of the slain civil rights leader – who criticized the stadium deal as unfair to county taxpayers. He was joined by an unlikely alliance of black Democrats and anti-tax Republicans from north Fulton County. King used the occasion to deliver a wider criticism of ACOG's activities, complaining that "greed, exclusivity, and elitism have become symbols of the Atlanta Olympic movement – all things that my father fought against – and they are all reflected in the deal proposed before us."[68] He went on to condemn the way in which ACOG had used the symbol of his father to sell Atlanta, then relegated his legacy to "the prop room" after the city was selected.[69] Some commissioners angrily noted that ACOG's upper management, who all lived in either Dunwoody or Buckhead, lacked "a basic understanding of the city between Five Points and the airport."[70] Others accused ACOG of being racist, as its top management team lacked a single African-American, with the exception of Andrew Young. ACOG's plans to have a "demonstration" of Olympic golf at the lily-white Augusta National Golf Club were also cited as an example of ACOG's racial insensitivity. Even the *Atlanta Constitution* joined in the critical chorus, describing the stadium controversy as "a familiar Atlanta stew of lingering sores from segregation and days of paternalistic white dominance."[71]

Payne and other members of the ACOG brains trust were flummoxed. They considered their bestowal of a "free" Olympic Stadium to be an act of enlightened civic philanthropy on their behalf that was not appreciated by their critics. However, their construction timetable was such that they could not wait much longer without risking that the stadium would not be completed on time. MAOGA could not sign the contract until the Braves lease was approved. If an agreement could not be worked out, soon, ACOG would have to make other arrangements and the city risked losing the team to the suburbs. While they returned to the negotiating table, ACOG leaders also began scouting alternative sites for a temporary stadium, which would have to be dismantled after the Games, as there was no "end-user" who could assume its operating costs. One of these was a 140-acre parcel on the old Atlantic Steel property located just to the north of the Georgia Tech campus; the other was "the Badlands" just to the south of the Techwood/Clark Howell public housing projects.

After several days of furious negotiations, Martin Luther King III abandoned his principled opposition, and along with the three other dissenting commissioners, supported a revised stadium deal that featured some concessions by both ACOG and the Braves. The new deal capped taxpayer liability for capital improvements at the new stadium to $50 million, reducing parking spaces from 10,000 to 8,900, and allocated 8.5 percent of gross parking revenues to a community development fund. For its part, ACOG agreed to hire a top black administrator answerable directly to Billy Payne and hire eight other African-Americans to top administrative positions. It also agreed to enhance the role of the Atlanta University Center in staging Olympic events and housing athletes, as well as stepping up its minority contracting program, and providing a modest jobs training program for residents of the neighborhoods near the stadium. King was satisfied by these concessions, although they seemed more symbolic than substantive. A little more than two months after the stadium imbroglio, ACOG hired Shirley Franklin away from her job as president of CODA to fill the newly created post of senior policy advisor. ACOG also dropped its plans to have an Olympic Golf event at the Augusta National Club, although only after IOC head Juan Antonio Samaranch came out strongly against it.

WHILE THEY REIGN, IT POURS: THE MAYORAL RACE AND THE INFRASTRUCTURE CRISIS

Franklin was eventually replaced at CODA by Clara Axam, another former city hall insider with limited urban redevelopment experience. However, with neither firm plans nor funding, CODA essentially remained dead in the water. Its circumstances were not improved by Maynard Jackson's decision not to run for a fourth term in the November 1993 elections. None of the contenders for his position, all of whom were African-American, enjoyed a wide base of public support. Most of Atlanta's business community supported Fulton County Commission chairman Michael Lomax, who had been a key supporter of the civic–business alliance that peaked during Andrew Young's mayoralty. Lomax had unsuccessfully challenged Jackson in the 1989 elections and had few allies among the city's grassroots, possessing what pollsters referred to as "high negatives." A native of Los Angeles, and possessing a Ph.D in English Literature, Lomax was not considered to be a man of the people. Moreover, he had angered many Atlantans by pushing through the construction of an elaborate downtown headquarters for Fulton County government in the late 1980s. Because of its extensive use of marble, and glassed-in palm court, Lomax's critics referred to the structure as the "Taj Mahal."

Lomax faced competition from three other contenders: Police Commissioner Eldrin Bell, and council members Myrtle Davis and Bill Campbell. Of this trio, Campbell was by far the favorite, being something of a Jackson protégé, although he lacked the personal connections with the African-American grassroots that his mentor enjoyed. Instead, Campbell possessed closer ties with the white, gentrified neighborhoods on the city's eastside. Still, Jackson's organization threw its support behind Campbell in his race against Lomax and his "Buckhead Boys." Neither Bell nor Davis had much of a machine behind him, and both were essentially out of the race by midsummer. Interestingly enough, none of the four candidates evinced specific proposals for Olympic redevelopment, although all talked of the need to get the city ready for 1996.

Jackson's status as a lame duck mayor further clouded CODA's future as a viable entity. In addition to the spectacle of a mayoral race, the attention of the city government leaders was distracted by an ongoing federal probe into corruption at Hartsfield International Airport. Former city council finance chairman and aviation commissioner Ira Jackson (no relation to the mayor) had been indicted on numerous charges, including accepting kickbacks and maintaining secret ownership of some of the airport concessions he was supposed to supervise. The probe was widening to encompass other members of the council, including president Marvin Arrington and mayoral aspirant Bill Campbell. No more indictments of council members were handed down, but the incident raised further questions about the already suspect integrity of the body.

While CODA and the rest of the city steered aimlessly about, the severity of Atlanta's unseen infrastructure crisis was made apparent a week after Jackson's announcement in early June 1993. Just before the morning rush hour began, a deluge of water caused by an especially heavy rainstorm caused a major sewer line just north of the campus of Georgia Tech to collapse, creating a massive "sinkhole" underneath the parking lot of a Marriott Courtyard hotel. Two hotel employees were sucked to their deaths and the crater expanded to take in some adjacent businesses. The tunnel, which was built in 1915, had been greatly overburdened by the added runoff produced by the extensive development of Midtown in the 1980s and had never been intended to support the fifty feet of fill on top of it, much less a large parking lot. A Georgia Tech study the previous year had warned the city of the compromised status of the Orme Street trunk, as well as the perilous condition of many other major sewer lines throughout the city.[72] Most of the road viaducts that spanned the city's central "railroad gulch" south of Five Points were in similarly decayed states, in some cases unable to support buses and heavy trucks.[73]

For a city supposedly characterized by its state-of-the-art infrastructure, Atlanta was looking more than a little frayed around the edges in the summer of 1993. The sorry state of the city's unseen, but necessary underpinnings was the consequence of decades of malign neglect. Successive administrations skimped on maintaining roads, sewers, and bridges, while encouraging development that increased the burdens placed on that aging infrastructure, some of which dated back to the 1890s. For their part, city voters were unsupportive of bond issues that would address some of the most glaring problems. By 1993, it was estimated that the total cost of needed improvements to Atlanta's infrastructure ran to approximately a billion dollars.[74] Despite the vast sums involved, candidate Campbell argued that the necessary repairs could be made without resorting to increased taxes.[75]

Atlanta was by no means unique in its neglect – the catastrophic condition of New York City's bridges and sewers, for example, is well known – but it was a relatively young city. Atlanta's problems were not limited to the structural integrity of its sewers, but included its inability to deal with what passed through them. For several years, the city had been in violation of the Environmental Protection Agency's limits of phosphorous in its waste water and paid fines totaling several thousand dollars a day. In addition to constituting a drain on the treasury, this lack of compliance threatened to trigger a complete ban on all new sewer hookups as of 1 July 1996, unless the city has taken steps to comply with the regulations, something which, at the time of writing, does not seem likely. The result will effectively be a halt to all development in the city of Atlanta and those areas served by its sewer system.

Atlanta's infrastructure crisis was a direct outgrowth of its permissive development policies. Successive city administrations failed to pass along the costs of improving needed infrastructure to private developers, out of concern for worsening the city's business climate. Assessing impact fees on potential investors, it was assumed, would just make the suburban areas all the more alluring to them. Besides, infrastructure was a quintessentially public domain of responsibility. Nor were city voters – who already labored under one of the highest tax burdens in the metro area – keen on approving a bond issue to upgrade the city's aging water, sewage, and road systems. However, a series of lesser sinkholes over the remainder of the summer, coupled with a number of water main breaks during the winter of 1993–94 (one of which left much of the city without water for one memorable January day), made the infrastructure crisis one of the first orders of business for the newly elected Bill Campbell, who had by now backed off from his campaign stance on a bond issue. After two attempts to schedule a referendum on an infrastructure bond issue were successfully thwarted by taxpayer groups, one was approved in the early summer of 1994. Although most of the money was directed at fixing viaducts, some $17 million was allocated to CODA, which had finally drafted an action plan. The bond issue allocation represented the single largest chunk of that long-suffering agency's budget and allowed it to qualify for federal matching funds for streetscape improvements.

Until the bond issue was approved, CODA was essentially bereft of major financing for the extensive list of projects it had developed during the summer and early fall of 1993. Under the direction of Randal Roark, chairman of the Department of Architecture and Urban Planning at Georgia Tech, CODA had drafted a $220-million revitalization plan that embraced fifteen neighborhoods and twenty-four "pedestrian corridors" within the Olympic Ring. Within the wider plan was a $100-million shortlist of projects. These included spending $41 million on the six neighborhoods closest to the Olympic venues (Summerhill, Vine City, Mechanicsville, Peoplestown, Atlanta University, and Sweet Auburn/MLK) and

$59 million to spruce up five corridors (Auburn Avenue, Atlanta University Center, Capitol Avenue, International Boulevard, and Peachtree Street) and rebuild two parks (Woodruff Park, and Freedom Park at the Carter Presidential Center). The corridors were to receive extensive streetscape improvements, such as new paving, enhanced lighting, and more appealing street furniture. Woodruff Park would get new landscaped gathering places, a Peace Fountain, and an Enlightenment Plaza linking it with Underground Atlanta. In the neighborhoods, CODA planned to fix up substandard housing, condemn and rehabilitate tax delinquent property, demolish abandoned buildings, and begin to implement the ULI redevelopment plan for Summerhill.[76]

The CODA plan had a number of sources of inspiration, incorporating aspects of plans developed by Central Atlanta Progress, the city's Bureau of Planning, and the Rural/Design Assistance Team (R/UDAT) from the American Institute of Architects that had visited the city in October 1992. CODA's plans for Peachtree Street, Auburn Avenue, International Boulevard, and Woodruff Park mingled aspects of the R/UDAT report with the winning plans of design competitions held in the late 1980s under the auspices of CAP and the Bureau of Planning. On a conceptual level, CODA's plans for these areas seemed hard to argue with, calling for more public spaces, enhanced pedestrian environments, landscaping, historic preservation, and safety. However, there were no extant plans to guide the revitalization of poorer neighborhoods, with the exception of the ULI plan for Summerhill. The "action agenda" of the R/UDAT report focused on corridors and gateways linking different parts of the city rather than on the more complex and controversial issues of neighborhood redevelopment.[77]

Although CODA vowed that plans for neighborhood redevelopment would be accomplished through "cooperative partnerships" with community organizations, the CODA plan ran into intense opposition from the neighborhoods it was intended to help. Local opposition to the CODA neighborhood plan climaxed in a series of public meetings in mid November 1993. Neighborhood residents were extremely skeptical about CODA, which they viewed as just another in a long line of city agencies that had intervened in their communities with less than positive results. Community opposition was galvanized by CODA's designation of the Olympic neighborhoods as "slums." A slum or redevelopment area designation was necessary to give the city the special powers and tools to undertake redevelopment plans, as well as making the neighborhood eligible for certain types of funding assistance.[78] However, the designation did *not* give CODA the legal powers to buy or demolish property without the consent of the owner.[79] Residents emphatically denied that their neighborhoods were slums and questioned the motivations behind the CODA effort. They also used the occasion to blast other city agencies and the Atlanta police. Many participants in the meeting also voiced their discontent with neighborhood planning units, which would bear principal organizational responsibility for preparing neighborhood redevelopment plans. It seems that one of the crucial problems facing CODA, in addition to the justifiable skepticism about its and the city's intentions, was the lack of consensus and unity among neighborhood residents themselves. Similar problems were evident in other community revitalization programs organized by the Atlanta Project and the Atlanta Neighborhood Development Partnership. The beleaguered and generally well-intentioned CODA staff found themselves in the unenviable position of being disliked and distrusted by both the communities they were organized to serve and the institutions they relied upon for funds to carry out the work.

The winter and early spring of 1994 proved little better for the embattled agency. The state legislature rejected a proposal for a one-cent rise in the Fulton County sales tax to fund CODA projects, and the mayor's effort to stage a referendum on the infrastructure bond issue was twice delayed by the adroit legal maneuvers of tax protesters. Another wounding blow came in May, when John Aderhold, the businessman appointed as co-chair by Maynard Jackson, resigned to take up the chairmanship of a major downtown development firm, Winter Properties. The company was deeply involved in a number of adaptive reuse projects in the downtown area, including Georgia State University's renovation of the Rialto Theater in Fairlie-Poplar, and Aderhold wanted to avoid any real or imagined conflict of interest. Although he was replaced by banker Joseph Prendergast, Aderhold's departure further clouded an already ominous view of CODA's prospects.

The successful passage of the bond issue in June of 1994 breathed new life into CODA's efforts. Some $32 million of CODA's final $72-million budget came from the bond issue, with the remainder coming from the federal government ($25 million, including the $11.8 million for the MLK site) and private sources ($16 million, of which $7.5 million came from the Woodruff Foundation alone). With the neighborhoods hostile to CODA's intentions, 90 percent of its spending went to downtown parks, streets, and pedestrian corridors; only $7 million went to areas beyond the venues, and most of that went for streetscape improvements. Efforts to help build town homes in the Summerhill neighborhood foundered because the CODA plan ignored city zoning laws.[80]

ACOG-GATE

While the city seemed to take three steps back for every step forward throughout much of 1993, ACOG fared only a little better. The Whatizit fiasco and the stadium imbroglio had tarnished its image among most Atlantans, and its credibility was further compromised by its penchant for secrecy. From its well-guarded hi-tech lair in the Inforum, ACOG regularly refused to provide details about its operations, pointing out its status as a private entity and the need to keep aspects of its decision-making confidential. The information blackout pertained not only to crucial marketing decisions, but to providing information about the salaries of top officials. When reporters successfully pressed home the claim for information under Georgia Sunshine Law, ACOG retitled the positions of its management group to evade compliance. Finally, after several months of increasingly negative publicity, ACOG revealed that its top managers were being paid quite handsome salaries, comparable to top corporate officers. On the face of it, this was not altogether surprising. However, ACOG's reluctance to reveal this information fueled public speculation that it was hiding something from the public.

The keenest, and most critical, speculation focused on the dubious shape of ACOG's finances, which were closely tied to the sale of television rights and corporate sponsorships. Both of these key generators of revenue were performing below expectations. Only six of the $40-million sponsors had signed on by April 1993. While this would improve, the sale of US TV rights – by far the largest component of this revenue stream – had come in more than $150 million *under* what had been expected. Payne had anticipated that US broadcast rights might fetch more than $600 million. However, top bidder NBC, which had taken a steep loss in covering the 1992 Barcelona Games (largely on account of an ill-fated experiment in offering more extensive pay-per-view service in addition to its regular broadcasts) took advantage of ACOG's desperate financial situation to offer a low-ball figure. Without any public subsidies, ACOG was dependent on the US television contract to underwrite the construction of the Olympic Stadium, for which ground had to be broken no later than the summer of 1993. ACOG leaders were indignant that the national broadcast networks would not fall as easily into line behind their plans for the Games as city and state officials. ACOG's perilous financial situation led to increased public skepticism that no public bail-out would be necessary. ACOG's allies in the media began grousing about how the lack of a public sector commitment was responsible for Atlanta missing a critical opportunity to revitalize itself.[81] Rumors began to circulate in Atlanta that the IOC was even considering moving the Games to an alternative host city.

Fears of such a doomsday scenario were highly irrational, but they reflected the fundamental insecurity that lay at the heart of the blustering Atlanta Spirit. Indeed, it does not take a psychoanalyst to see that the over-the-top braggadocio of Atlanta boosters concealed their deep disbelief that the city was what they claimed it to be. ACOG's money troubles continued through the winter of 1993–94. In February 1994 it issued a revised financial forecast that for the first time indicated that no surplus would be realized from the Games and that the contingency fund or "cushion" for the $1.6-billion venture had been reduced from $100 million to $60 million.[82] In addition, almost half of ACOG's revenues had yet to be secured. To compensate for the underperformance of television rights, ACOG was forced to rely more on corporate sponsorships and revenues realized from staging the Games itself, such as tickets, merchandise, etc. With many corporations reluctant to commit themselves to a $40-million expenditure, ACOG was obliged to create additional, less expensive sponsorships in the $10–$20-million range. ACOG's uncertain financial outlook led the IOC's chief liaison to ACOG, Richard Pound, to state that the Olympics would never again be given to a city that "has no significant public sector commitment, either in the form of a financial contribution or, at the very least, a guarantee to meet the necessary costs of organizing the Games." Pound further argued that the lack of a public safety net had caused ACOG to "focus unduly on the revenue-generating aspects of the Games."[83]

As questions about ACOG's financial situation mounted in the fall of 1993, the local media's criticism of the Olympic effort ebbed. In October, the outlook for outside the fence redevelopment brightened considerably when the federal Department of Housing and Urban Development (HUD) announced it was allocating $42 million for the rehabilitation of the Techwood/Clark Howell housing projects. The only problem with this otherwise wonderful news was that the Atlanta Housing Authority lacked a plan to put the money to use. The Techwood redevelopment was soon overshadowed by more momentous news. On his way back from HUD's announcement ceremony in Washington DC, Billy Payne had his second Olympic epiphany, although it would remain a closely guarded secret for more than a month. Cruising serenely at 34,000 feet, Payne decided to abandon his pledge to keep ACOG's attention "inside the fence" of the venues themselves, and build a privately funded, $100-million Centennial Olympic Park in the Badlands south of the projects.

THE CENTENNIAL OLYMPIC PARK

The official media-ordained account of "how Billy Payne got his park" has it that he sketched out the idea that evening on a piece of paper, but this historic document has never been made available to the public.[84] Although Payne himself later acknowledged that the vision for the park did not begin with him, the Atlanta media continues, to this day, to refer to the Centennial Park as Billy Payne's "gift" to the city of Atlanta.[85] However, Payne's brainstorm was only the latest in a long line of ideas for redeveloping the area lying between the Techwood/Clark Howell public housing projects, the Omni/Georgia World Congress Center, and the

Peachtree Center hotel-convention district. The roughly triangular expanse of parking lots, single room occupancy hotels, homeless shelters, and small manufacturing enterprises had long been coveted by speculators, who had purchased numerous parcels during the previous two decades in the expectation of future redevelopment. The first dreams for the area go back to the mid 1960s, when a local architecture firm sketched out plans for a "Golden Mile" of mixed residential, commercial, and retail development along Marietta and Luckie streets between the Central Business District and Georgia Tech.[86] As with many other "visions" for downtown, nothing came of the plans, which included a large "Central Park" as well as a megastructure featuring a 100-story hotel. The depressed state of the downtown real estate market after the mid 1970s, the continued existence of more than 2,000 units of low-income housing nearby, and the allure of the Golden Crescent along the top end of the Perimeter, stymied efforts at redevelopment of the area.

In 1986, as part of its Central Area Study II, Central Atlanta Progress prepared a "concept plan" for the area that it referred to as the Marietta Street Subarea.[87] The plan proposed a mix of high-rise apartments and town homes in most of the area, with a commercial–retail zone on the western edge, bordering the World Congress Center. Recognizing that the Techwood/Clark Howell public housing project posed an impediment to developing the desired middle- and upper-income housing, the report suggested separating the two zones with a moat – the actual term used was a "water feature" – including a waterfall that would take advantage of the naturally occurring sixty-foot drop in elevation across the terrain, but it was much more of a defensive than an aesthetic installation. In keeping with the division of labor within the public–private partnership, CAP authors insisted that, even with low land costs, substantial public subsidies were necessary to make the project work. These included not only long-term tax abatements, but provision of infrastructure (streets, sewage, etc.) and written-down land costs. Such inducements were not forthcoming from the city, which was more interested in developing housing in the south Central Business District around city hall. For that matter, CAP's attention at the time was directed to the east of downtown and connecting the Bedford-Pine redevelopment area – which it owned through a non-profit subsidiary – to downtown and lower Midtown. It was not until 1990 that the city and CAP seriously turned their attentions to the long-neglected westside of downtown. The intention behind Techwood Park, Inc., was a clear outgrowth of the vision sketched out in the 1986 Marietta Street Subarea Housing Study. The inability of TPI to make redevelopment happen, however, indicated that the once-vaunted partnership between public and private interests was something less than it had once been.

A number of other parties had Olympic dreams about this piece of strategic real estate, however. In June 1993, a local businessman proposed using fifty to seventy-five acres for an International Cultural Center. The centerpiece of the project would be a 2 million square foot complex celebrating the world's cultural diversity and demonstrating Atlanta's commitment to being an international city. Other features would include a 1 million square foot World Museum, stocked with works on loan from the world's best private and public collections and a 35-acre sculpture garden. To be funded by local, state, and federal governments and private investors, as well as foreign countries, what backers called "a permanent cultural world's fair" was expected to create 30,000 jobs and attract 15 to 20 million visitors a year.[88] A short time later, a former associate of architect/developer John Portman, Tom Tabor, stated his intention to use the same parcel of land for an "Epcot-like global village" called Expo '96, that would feature a series of corporate and government-sponsored pavilions. Unlike the International Cultural Center, Expo '96 was conceived of as a temporary venture, to be followed after the Olympics by new development of unspecified proportions. Neither of these two projects had the sanction of ACOG, CAP, or the city. After a brief, solitary mention in the *Atlanta Constitution*, plans for the International Cultural Center were not heard of again, while a much scaled-down Expo '96 is – at the time of writing at least – scheduled to arise on twenty acres of leased parking lots to the east of the park area.

Given ACOG's penchant for secrecy, it is unclear exactly when its brains trust started cogitating about filling the void in the middle of the Olympic Ring, but it was most certainly well before Billy Payne's high-altitude epiphany in October 1993. The area was, literally, right outside the window of ACOG's headquarters. From their well-secured offices atop the Inforum (John Portman's unsuccessful effort to build a wholesale trademart for the computer/electronics industry), Billy Payne, A.D. Frazier, and other top ACOG honchos looked out over what the president of the Chamber of Commerce (whose offices were situated on the other side of the area from the Inforum) called "a cancer on Downtown Atlanta."[89] Located between the Olympic media headquarters and key athletic venues of the Omni/GWCC and the hotel district, the Badlands would be all too visible to visitors and viewers during the Games. It is almost inconceivable that ACOG leaders suddenly came to the realization of the problematic nature of this area some *three years* after Atlanta's selection as the Olympic city. However, with the veil of secrecy that remains around ACOG one can only speculate when plans for the area first emerged.

The "when" of the Centennial Olympic Park plan, however, is nowhere as important, interesting, or revealing as the "how," "what," "who," or "why." In keeping with its unremittingly hostile and patronizing attitude towards city government,

ACOG developed its plan without consulting the city. Indeed, top officials, including the planning commissioner, the mayor, and the mayor-elect, only learned of it when the public did, as a result of a story leaked to the *Atlanta Constitution* during Thanksgiving week, 1993. ACOG's explanation for its stealthiness was that it wanted to work out all the details and financing before revealing it to the public, sometime "early" in 1994.[90] However, it is clear that ACOG wanted to minimize any potential opposition to its plans by keeping the project secret as long as possible. Payne had no compunction about meeting first with Coca-Cola chief Roberto Goizueta and Governor Zell Miller in late October and early November, but saw no need to inform the city government of his plans for a key chunk of real estate that lay within its boundaries. Resentful of what they saw as Maynard Jackson's efforts to muscle in on their Olympic action, and contemptuous of the city council, ACOG leaders were determined to keep the city, and CODA, as far out of the park project as possible. They were joined in their antagonistic attitude towards the city government by members of the business community, who, in the course of a series of quasi-public focus groups on the project, made it clear they wanted the city to have nothing to do with the park. For a city that prided itself on the harmonious marriage of civic and business interests, the park project marked a major refiguring of the concept of the public–private partnership. In this case, the "public" in the partnership was constituted by the State of Georgia, and its quasi-public entities like the Georgia World Congress Center (GWCC), and not the city government, much less the citizenry the latter represented.

The initial reactions of the beneficiaries of Payne's beneficence ranged from muted praise to stunned silence. Whatever city officials must have really thought, given the inability of CODA to secure funding and neighborhood resistance to its plans, the political establishment had little choice but to embrace it. Besides, the speculative renderings in the newspaper – of trees, fountains, pavilions, and a thirty-acre lake – made a most appealing image for a city that lacked any of these features. A signature open space would go a long way, it was argued, to convincing skeptics that Atlanta was truly the great world-class city it claimed to be. Besides, who could argue with the idea of a park in a city that had such a long-term aversion to open public space? What better way to "renovate the public character of the city"? Never mind who would pay for it, maintain it, what its effects would be, or what would happen to those inhabiting the area. Indeed, one of the most compelling aspects of the plan was that the area was widely perceived as an empty, worse than useless space and that nobody would be displaced. But, as the anthropologist Gary McDonogh has noted, empty spaces are rarely truly "empty"; rather they tend to be zones of conflict between different groups and are usually full of undesirable and/or unacknowledged uses and users.[91]

Protests by small business owners and advocates of the homeless subsequently demonstrated that the Void was not empty after all. These protests had little effect locally, although they did receive a sympathetic hearing in a series of articles in the *New York Times*, including an op-ed piece by *Fortune* magazine associate editor and third-generation Atlantan, John Huey.[92] The critical treatment in the *Times* sparked indignant responses from ACOG officials, which appear to have had some effect, as subsequent coverage by the national paper of record has been decidedly less critical of ACOG's efforts. The change of tune was even more evident in Atlanta's print and electronic media, which during the dark days of 1992–93 had often adopted a critical tone towards ACOG, as well as the city. While such negativity did not completely vanish from local newspapers and television stations, they tended, with the notable exception of the free weekly *Creative Loafing*, to have far fewer critical stories. Indeed, the *Atlanta Journal* and *Constitution* (which were both owned by Cox Enterprises and were located near the park area) took a lead role in selling the park idea to the public, although they still provided coverage of opposition to the park. The shift in tone was most marked on the editorial pages and in the work of some of the papers' most "liberal" columnists. By the end of 1993, ACOG had been replaced as the favorite target of the latter's critical opprobrium by Atlanta's homeless population, onto whose shoulders virtually all of the responsibility for downtown's decline was heaped. As the city mobilized to host the Super Bowl in late January 1994, local media joyously joined in the task of producing the most positive image of Atlanta possible, and reacted quite pointedly to the critical barbs directed at the city by visiting reporters.

The demonization of Atlanta's homeless by the press was ironic, as they were among the most deeply affected by the Centennial Park and other Olympic-related redevelopments. Estimates of the city's homeless population vary widely, with advocates of the homeless citing figures of as many as 20,000.[93] Even allowing for some inflation on the latter's part, it is undeniable that the number of homeless greatly exceeds the available shelter space, which is provided exclusively by private agencies and Fulton County. More than ten percent of the city's shelter beds were located in the park area, as well as one large single room occupancy hotel.[94] At the time of writing, these facilities have yet to be replaced, and it is unlikely they will be by the summer of 1996, if ever. As noted in the previous chapter, the homeless were also major targets of CODA's efforts to renovate Woodruff Park near Five Points. Financed by a $5-million grant from the Woodruff Foundation and funds from the infrastructure bond issue, the smaller park had been one of the principal gathering points for the homeless community until it was closed for renovations in October 1994.

Opposition from community activists, who said the money would be better spent revitalizing their nearby ravaged neighborhoods, also fell on deaf ears. The lack of recognition given to concerns of the urban poor and the homeless indicates that these groups are not part of "the public" in whose name the park is being constructed. Indeed, "special measures" will be employed in both the Centennial Park and nearby Woodruff Park to make them less amenable to Atlanta's homeless population. These measures range from such design features as sleep-proof benches and automatic sprinkler systems to intensified policing and the criminalization of a number of homeless behaviors, such as loitering, trespassing (including walking through parking lots in which one does not have a car) and aggressive panhandling.

While both the city and ACOG have joined forces to exclude the homeless from a place in the public realm, ACOG was just as adamant about excluding the city from a role in building "its" park. Rather than being players, the city and its panoply of development agencies have been reduced, essentially, to bench-warmers at best, mere spectators at worst. Bypassing local officials completely, ACOG went directly to Governor Zell Miller, who smiled benevolently and, in January 1994, directed the state-owned World Congress Center Authority to coordinate activities to realize the park. Among the authority's powers were the ability to condemn property, should selfish owners balk at doing their part for the common weal. Owners of parcels within the proposed park area, which included small business owners, speculators, and old-guard Atlanta families, presented the most serious opposition that park planners had to face. Unlike the poor and the homeless, they had market forces and high-priced legal talent on their side. Proponents of the park responded by trying to portray them negatively in the media, claiming that some owners were seeking "unreasonable" prices for their parcels that would make the necessary assemblage of property impossible.[95] Land acquisition proceeded slowly during 1994 and 1995, although most of the more than 100 property owners came to terms with the state by April 1995.

As with most visionary ideas, the park underwent a series of revisions in the course of its realization. After preliminary surveying work was completed in early 1994, it was soon discovered that the actual extent of the proposed area was only sixty rather than seventy-two acres. After a lengthy property appraisal process and a feasibility study that included six focus group meetings with various constituencies with an interest in the area, the park was further scaled back to twenty-two acres and was designed to be built in two phases. Downsizing the extent of the park reduced the cost of property acquisition and development of the first, or Olympic, phase to some $50 million. Cutting the price tag in half was essential for keeping true to ACOG's (and the state legislature's) mantra of "no taxpayer dollars." Funding for the park remained exclusively private, although the state, acting through its GWCC Authority, assembled the land and will own the park during and after the Olympics. Approximately half of the necessary money was projected to come from the Woodruff Foundation and other local philanthropists, with another $10 million to be raised by the Chamber of Commerce, and at least $15 million coming from ACOG via the nationwide sale of commemorative brick pavers provided by Olympic sponsor Home Depot, Inc.

In the course of 1994, the area immediately to the north of the downsized Centennial Park between Simpson and Alexander streets was acquired by the Coca-Cola Corporation, operating through its Athena Properties subsidiary. Coke's purchase and short-term lease of the properties helped set the price for parcels throughout the park area. With its corporate headquarters campus lying just to the northwest of the park area, Coke's interest in the project was hardly surprising. The Atlanta-based soft drink colossus intended to use the land for an amusement/promotional venue during the Games. Originally conceived of as a state-of-the-art "Hollywood" theme park to be built in conjunction with Busch Entertainment (creators of the Busch Gardens complex in Tampa, Florida), Coke was forced to scale back plans for the complex when budget projections for the interactive/virtual reality venue exceeded $100 million. In the end, the company decided on a much simpler, and much less permanent, $20-million design for an Olympic City: an eight-acre entertainment area featuring a 1,500-seat, globe-like amphitheater, a miniaturized replica of the Olympic Stadium, and a facility in which visitors will be able to "compete" against video footage of famous athletes. Although coordinated in look with the adjacent Centennial Park, the Olympic City was planned as a separate gated venue requiring paid admission. Coke officials were vague about their post-Olympic plans for the site. However, as will be discussed below, the area has figured prominently in highly speculative plans for building middle- and upper-income housing after 1996.

The downsizing of the Centennial Park also freed up a large section of land along the western edge of the original parcel, which lies directly across the street from the Georgia World Congress Center. In keeping with Atlanta's claims to being an "international city," some especially well connected developers were quick to come up with a particularly global use for the area. The fifteen-acre site was designated as a "special district" by the Immigration and Naturalization Service as part of a little-known program that seeks to attract foreign capital, particularly from Hong Kong, in exchange for green cards for immigrant investors and their families.[96] In the spring of 1994, the site was acquired by a syndicate of local developers who planned to build a Holiday Inn Crowne Plaza on the site with capital attracted through the immigrant investor program. A number of the interested parties enjoyed close ties to ACOG: one of the developers formerly chaired the finance committee of the AOC, and the president of the company chosen to build the hotel, Holder Construction, was one of the co-chairs of ACOG.[97] This situation was far from exceptional, as most of Atlanta's major architecture, engineering, and construction firms received the lion's share of Olympic construction contracts and the park project in particular. Still, despite the consummate insider connections of the developers, lack of interest by prospective immigrant investors dashed hopes to build the hotel before 1996. Instead, the owners will allow ACOG to use the property as a "corporate hospitality village" during the Games.[98]

The original plans for the Centennial Park advertised it as a mini-world's fair, with an amphitheater for live cultural performances, and lots of food and merchandising featuring the wares of official Olympic sponsors. One of the initial key focal points of the park was to be a Festival of the American South, featuring exhibits by each of the eleven states of the former Confederacy. While the festival is a temporary event, an idealized image of Southern culture was literally inscribed in the spatial organization of the park. Olympic imagineers chose the "quilt" as the primary visual motif for the "Look of the Games," and park designers divided the 22-acre expanse into a patchwork grid of brick pathways. At the southern end of the park was the 10,000-square-meter Centennial Plaza, where the sweaty Olympic multitudes could mill about for the benefit of the television cameras located on top of adjacent buildings (indeed, roof space around the park emerged as one of the most dynamic, if ultimately ephemeral, real estate markets in 1995). At the center of the plaza is a computer-controlled dancing fountain in the shape of the Olympic rings. While early plans for a thirty-acre lake were scrapped, the final plan for the park included a large reflecting pool along the northern edge of the Centennial Plaza, and a narrow, stream-like "water feature" meandering along the eastern edge of the park.

Despite having the sanction of all the powers that were, progress on the park was much slower than anticipated. Although three-quarters of the site had been acquired by January 1995, a number of owners were still holding out (rather successfully it turned out) for higher prices, and this greatly increased the costs of land acquisition. At the same time, fund-raising for the park had encountered numerous snags. The Chamber of Commerce's $10-million campaign was behind schedule (although eventually completed), but ACOG's commemorative brick program, which was run by Atlanta-based Olympic sponsor Home Depot, Inc., proved to be a major disappointment. Flush with its success in peddling commemorative license plates to Olympic-spirited Georgians, ACOG had originally expected to sell as many as two million engraved bricks. However, sales managers at Home Depot evidently believed that the $35 bricks would sell themselves without advertising. By late February 1995, only 88,000 had been sold, and ACOG was obliged to scale back its estimate to one million bricks. However, even with an expanded advertising campaign it seemed highly unlikely that ACOG would sell the 750,000 bricks necessary to break even. Although brick sales surged during the spring, reaching some 160,000 by the end of July, ACOG began to consider novel measures. Shortly after the city celebrated a year to go until the start of the Games, it was rumored that Japanese businesses might purchase as many as 100,000 of the outstanding bricks.[99]

Although Atlanta liked to think of itself as an international city, one local columnist felt "almost Third World" at the notion of having the park bailed out by foreigners.[100] In the end, however, ACOG turned to more domestically palatable, but still controversial, measures to meet the shortfall in revenue. In September 1995, it was revealed that in return for a payment of $10 million, AT&T Corporation would be allowed to construct a Global Olympic Village and an 8,500-seat amphitheater inside the park. The Village will consist of a football-field-sized three-story structure, surmounted by a 12-story communications tower. The top two floors are to be a "place of refuge" for athletes and their families, "who will be able to phone home for free."[101] The public portion of the village will feature live entertainment, a giant video screen broadcasting the day's highlights, and a studio for Olympic broadcaster NBC. AT&T is not the only corporate sponsor to buy space in the park. Swatch, the official Olympic timekeeper, is erecting an eighteen-foot-high "Swatch O'Clock" to showcase its timing technology, and Anheuser-Busch will have a hi-tech beer garden. Billy Payne, who had continually vowed not to over-commercialize the Games, justified these "sponsor footprints," on the grounds that they "are not just advertisements," but showcases of "state-of-the-art technology [that] people will be seeing for the first time."[102] While these footprints may sound a lot like advertisements, Payne is indeed correct (although not for the reasons he wants us to believe), for to refer to these hypermediated spectacles as mere ads is like calling a fabric-covered biplane and the Space Shuttle both airplanes. Rather, the Centennial Olympic Park is of a piece with the World of Coca-Cola and Disney's Epcot Center, conjured realms in which the boundaries between advertisement, entertainment, and education have been permanently effaced by a more profound pecuniary truth.

The colonization of the park by corporate sponsors is the least odious and sinister of the revisions to Atlanta's signature Olympic gathering place, however. Originally billed as a public open space, in its full Olympic drag the Centennial Park will be neither open nor all that public. In mid September 1995, ACOG announced that the Centennial Park would be surrounded by a fence, "to control the crowds and keep out the riffraff."[103] The full extent of this latter category was not fully specified, save for the much-maligned homeless population. Olympic security chief Bill Rathburn was quite clear about the nature of the space: "This will not be a public park. We will establish conditions of admission."[104] Rathburn had earlier in the summer demonstrated his keen appreciation of, and respect for, civil liberties by announcing that Olympic security's working definition of "terroristic behavior" would be expanded to include groups of unruly teenagers. On the other side of the social spectrum, Rathburn noted that Olympic sponsors, their guests, and VIPs would enjoy unrestricted access to the park, although this privilege was soon revoked by Billy Payne. Despite this assertion, it seems highly unlikely that the members of the elite group will be made to stand in line for hours on end with the remainder of sweat-soaked humanity who meet the yet to be completely specified "conditions of admission." Once inside, they will find themselves in a totalized environment "synchronized to keep people moving through the park, never lingering long at any one place."[105]

Park officials defended their decision to fence and limit access to the park on the grounds of public safety. Depending on the formulas one uses, the park area can hold only between 40,000 and 60,000 persons at any one time.[106] By contrast, between 500,000 and 750,000 people are expected to be within the Olympic Ring on the peak days of the Games, of whom approximately 200,000 will be ticket holders. The rest will be media people, VIPs, and general gawkers, as well as downtown office workers and other "others," who together comprise what ACOG likes to call the "background traffic." The math is as simple, and disturbing, as ACOG's attitudes towards who has a right to be in "its" park. ACOG has given seemingly little thought as to how the hordes who will be "outside the fence" of the park and the venues will be managed. As with the matter of outside the fence development more generally, this will be the city's problem.

POST-OLYMPIC DREAMS

The fence around the park, like that surrounding the adjacent Olympic Center area (the Omni/World Congress Center/Georgia Dome complex), is only a temporary feature that will be removed after the Games. Corporate and city leaders wistfully imagine the park as a major catalyst for the post-Olympic redevelopment of the surrounding area. Peeking beneath the veneer of civic virtue and Olympic necessity, the park project is nothing more than urban renewal 1990s style, a nifty way of unifying 100 or so parcels not only for a signature Olympic gathering place, but, more importantly, to create a post-Olympic playing field for the downtown redevelopment game. Most of the media coverage up to this point has focused on the matter of how big the park will be and what it will look like during the Games, rather than what will occur after. However, the latter matter is a far more interesting and important question.

Not surprisingly, information on the post-Olympic future is highly speculative, in both the literal and figurative senses of the term. Although the Centennial
Park is described as "permanent," it is unclear if all of its 22-acre extent will remain
sylvan space. The northern third of the site will be minimally developed during the
Olympic phase of construction and, most importantly, sources for financing for the
park's second phase have not yet been identified. This is a crucial problem, for the
Olympic masses will trample the small amount of green space in the park into a
dusty and/or muddy red clay oblivion, and it is questionable at best to expect that
either the state or private interests are going to be willing to devote the $25–$50
million necessary to complete the vision of the firm that designed the park. Just to
the north of the park, developers are eyeing Coke's Olympic City parcel for
middle- and upper-income housing. One block north of the Olympic City, the
Techwood/Clark Howell public housing projects are slated for conversion into a
privatized mixed-income community, although the funds allocated by HUD are
only sufficient to complete the transformation of Techwood Homes. A prime target of Congressional Republicans, HUD has already indicated that additional grants
to rehabilitate the larger Clark Howell projects will not be forthcoming beyond an
additional outlay of $19 million. The lack of funds, however, has not stopped the
AHA from emptying Clark Howell through stepped-up evictions and relocations.
This process of displacement, which will ultimately involve a total of some 558
families, has gone completely without mention in the local media.[107]

To the southeast of the park is the Fairlie-Poplar Historic District. As noted in
Chapter 4, developers wistfully envision Fairlie-Poplar as the new SoHo of Atlanta,
with loft apartments, cafés, and upscale street-level retail clustering around Georgia
State University's new Rialto Theater School of Music complex and Five Points.
Still, despite the interest of the real estate community, the exact size of the market
for downtown housing is still not well known. While a housing study commissioned by CAP revealed that slightly more than a quarter of downtown workers
surveyed would be interested in living downtown, it remains to be seen whether
those numbers will manifest themselves on the ground.[108] More importantly, previous studies of the area, such as the Marietta Street subarea study of 1986, indicated
that residential development was not economically viable without written-down
land costs and other incentives. As the park has already raised adjacent land values
substantially, such public subsidies are now even more important. If such supple-
ments to "natural market forces" fail to emerge to support surrounding
development, the park could very well fail in its intended role as a catalyst for
downtown revitalization. However, the prospect of a post-Olympic let-down does
not disturb developers with a long-time horizon, for as one noted: "Just by demolishing [the Void] and building the park we are improving that area a hundredfold."

Indeed, a post-Olympic fallow period might well be necessary to allow inflated land values to return to more reasonable levels. Then again, the conveniently vacated and located (it stands between the Coke's Olympic City and the Georgia Tech campus) Clark Howell property might well provide some of the needed publically subsidized land.

As mentioned above, even before the park has been completed, it has already served to revitalize property values in surrounding areas. By midsummer 1995, CNN Center, which is located on the southwestern edge of the park area, saw its assessed valuation increase some 26 percent from the previous year. Other properties saw an even greater percentage increase. The eight-acre parcel originally intended for the Holiday Inn Crowne Plaza hotel, for example, more than tripled in value between 1994 and 1995, increasing from $1.3 million to $4.8 million.[109] Overall, the increase in assessed land values due to the park was almost three times as high as the tax revenue lost to the city by the transfer of the park property into the tax-exempt coffers of the state-owned Georgia World Congress Center Authority.

As plans for the Olympic phase of the park assumed more coherent, if disturbing, form, more sustained attention was directed at envisioning the park's post-Olympic future. In a display of belated unity, the city and Central Atlanta Progress sponsored a study by a team from the Urban Land Institute. The ULI was no stranger to Atlanta, having produced the 1991 redevelopment plan for Summerhill – which among other things downplayed the negative effects of Olympic Stadium construction on the neighborhood – as well as a study of the main challenges to metropolitan growth for the Atlanta Regional Commission in 1994. After a week-long study period in late July–early August 1995, the ULI presented its findings to an audience of major downtown business leaders. The conceptual plan envisioned a series of developments, phased in over a period of two decades, to help Atlanta realize its goal of becoming a 24-hour city. The ULI team determined that a mix of residential and entertainment uses, along with a technology park, provided the greatest opportunities and market potentials. Of these uses, residential was the most central, with a minimum of 3,000 new housing units to be built in a variety of forms (detached home, townhouse, apartments) and for a mix of income levels (students, low, middle and upper). A number of the consultants had worked for Disney and explicitly utilized a set of Disney criteria in imagineering a conceptual plan. These included scrupulous attention to "arrival sequences" and "wayfinding," elimination of streetside clutter and incompatible uses, and stringent attention to upkeep and maintenance.

CAP president Sam Williams had asked the team to utilize "out of the box" thinking, by which he meant bold new ideas. While many of the components of the ULI plan were not all that novel, the ULI group did take a very expansive idea of the project boundaries. Much like the original Techwood Park plan, the ULI plan encompassed not only the area covered by the Centennial Park and Coke's Olympic City but the land covered by Techwood/Clark Howell homes, and the western edge of Fairlie-Poplar. For the plan to be successful, ULI planners were adamant that the Techwood/Clark Howell homes and the Olympic City area be linked to form "one total new community." Rather than redevelopment and revitalization, the ULI team referred to their task as stimulating "re-neighboring." Their non-binding vision called for building a series of diverse, mixed-income neighborhoods clustered around small village greens and squares linked by a network of streets that conformed to the contours of the topography. Given the close proximity of both Georgia Tech and CNN, the western edge of the zone was viewed as an ideal location for a technology research park. Neither the residential nor the hi-tech research dimensions of the ULI plan were particularly novel; both ideas had figured in formal plans and/or the imaginations of local developers for some time.

The most dramatically different aspect of the ULI plan involved the western edge of Fairlie-Poplar, specifically the area around the old Baptist Tabernacle. An imposing structure with a large auditorium, the tabernacle had been acquired in 1994 by a veteran local developer who intended to lease it as either corporate hospitality space or an entertainment venue during the Games. ULI proposed that the church be redeveloped as the core of a hi-tech entertainment/retail complex called Tabernacle Square, that could, for example, make intensive use of intellectual properties belonging to the nearby Turner Broadcasting System. Other possible tenants for the square included an aquarium (long on downtown boosters' wish lists), a multiplex theater complex, and high-end retailers like Banana Republic, Laura Ashley, etc. Although ULI planners claimed that the project would be "synergistic" to nearby Underground Atlanta, it's difficult to imagine that, if built, it would not prove to be parasitic, and ultimately fatal to the festival marketplace once heralded as the savior of downtown Atlanta. Beset by red ink and an image as a dangerous place, Underground's continued existence is highly dubious as it is, even without the prospect of new competition.

It will be some time, however, before Tabernacle Square or any other aspect of the ULI plan gets translated into reality. Meanwhile, Olympic-related building projects give sections of the city the look of a giant construction site and provide Atlantans with a taste of the snarled traffic and other unpleasantries that await them. In the remainder of this chapter, I shall try to summarize some of the key developments and conflicts that marked the final year and a half of preparations and their different effects on a variety of groups in Atlanta, including but not limited to the city government, the business community, and the residents of neighborhoods both inside and outside the Olympic Ring.

AMONG THE BILLBOARDS THERE EXISTS A CITY?

The use of the Centennial Olympic Park as a large corporate advertising space is well in keeping with the overall emphasis of the ACOG. Despite Billy Payne's vow not to over-commercialize the Games, ACOG has gone all out to promote the Olympics as the greatest global marketing event of all times – a sort of cosmic advertisement – to prospective sponsors. ACOG took great care to protect the intellectual property rights of itself, the IOC, and their sponsors. This was especially so regarding the word "Olympic." One hapless Greek restaurant owner was forced to change the name of his business, the Olympic Restaurant, even though he opened it well before the idea of the Games ever entered Billy Payne's head. ACOG's early hostile reaction to Joel Babbitt's stillborn plan to raise money by selling its own corporate sponsorships is another good example of ACOG trying to protect its monopolistic domain. In the summer of 1995, the city made yet another, more successful effort to poach on ACOG's turf, to which I shall return shortly. However, these latter efforts were preceded by a very revealing episode in which ACOG attempted, and for a time succeeded, in getting the city to protect its monopolistic advertising interests.

Indeed, one of ACOG's first orders of business was to attempt to limit the ability of non-Olympic sponsors to advertise in Atlanta's public domain during the Games. In 1991, Payne requested that downtown property owners not allow advertising banners to be hung from or on their buildings and attempted to get the city's billboard industry to offer Olympic sponsors first rights on all its available boards.[110] The latter effort proved unsuccessful, since the industry stood to make a killing on its valuable space. Although ACOG was seeking to maximize its own profit, it saw no discrepancy in asking local businesses to make a considerable sacrifice on its behalf, or, rather on behalf of the noble Olympic spirit. Such hypocritical double standards became one of ACOG's most defining features. While it stubbornly refused to open its books to public scrutiny or its coffers to poor neighborhoods on the grounds that it was a private business venture, ACOG was quick to portray itself as acting in the public's, even all of humanity's, interest when it came down to others doing unto it what it was trying to do itself. This was a well-nigh impossible job, because asking Atlantans to pass up an opportunity to make a buck flew in the face of the Atlanta Spirit.

As part of its effort to restrict outdoor advertising, ACOG funded a study to help the city to draft a new city sign ordinance. The explosion of outdoor advertising when Atlanta hosted the Super Bowl in January 1994 further impelled ACOG to find some way of limiting the possibilities for "ambush marketing" by corporate rivals of official Olympic sponsors. Unfortunately for ACOG, the consultant took

Olympic organizers at their word when they said they wanted to prevent excessive "visual pollution." The resulting ordinance, which was passed by the city council in August 1994, sharply limited *all* kinds of outdoor advertising, including that of ACOG and its corporate sponsors. Although existing signs would be "grandfathered in," under the ordinance, new signs would be greatly limited in size, while new billboards would be banned from all but industrial zones. The ordinance was even more remarkable given the fact that Atlanta already had the highest per capita concentration of billboards in the world. So strict was the ordinance, one newspaper account claimed, it would even consider an opened logo-ed umbrella on a sunny day to be an illegal portable sign.[111]

In characteristically imperious fashion, ACOG proposed another ordinance exempting it and its sponsors from the limits of the sign law. Together with local corporate colossus Coca-Cola, ACOG was able to exert the "political arm-twisting" necessary to push the law through council.[112] Less than three weeks after enacting one of the most restrictive sign laws in the country, the council passed a second bill permitting ACOG and its sponsors to pay a trifling amount to erect up to fifty 10-story "super signs" in non-residential "concentrated sign districts" near the stadiums, the airport, Centennial Olympic Park, and Peachtree Street.[113] After public outcry, the council lopped two stories off the signs and reduced their number by half. One city official attempted to put a festive spin on the council's craven retreat thus: "This would allow sponsors to decorate the city, albeit in a huge way."[114] Although the signs were described as "temporary," the ordinance actually allowed them to be up for at least two years. Council members defended the bill as a revenue opportunity, but at $1,500 for a permit fee, the total income for the city was a less than Olympian $75,000. An ACOG spokesperson defended the controversial measure thus: "The Olympics is [sic] the ultimate world bazaar – a full stage of people with competing needs and siren calls to visitors. They [the sponsors] are paying the bill for the Games for their right to have their wares displayed vividly and dramatically."[115]

Olympic sponsors were not the only ones with rights, though, even if they ponyed up tens of millions of dollars to ACOG. Local billboard companies were quick to argue that the ordinance constituted an unfair restraint of trade. In May of 1995, a federal judge struck down the ACOG-friendly ordinance for violating the free speech rights and equal protection guarantees under the First and Fourteenth Amendments to the US Constitution.[116] The judge let stand, however, the first ordinance limiting visual clutter, as it did not restrict the content of a sign, only its size and location. There was no immediate public reaction from either ACOG or Coca-Cola. Prior to the ordinance being enacted, Coke had secured permission for a 15-story mural on the side of a building near the Olympic Stadium. Although this sign, which features the visages of forty famous Georgians in addition to the corporate logo, was grandfathered in, the judge's ruling prevented the company from installing others it had planned. As the first ordinance greatly limited the ability of the city to grant exemptions from the law, Atlanta may well indeed be marked by considerably less visual clutter than Barcelona. However, there appears to be far too much at stake for ACOG to let the matter stand. While there has been virtually no public mention of the matter since May 1995, Olympic organizers and their powerful corporate allies are no doubt working quietly behind the scenes to selectively free up Atlanta's public spaces for corporate expression.

Although Coke suffered a setback with the revocation of the second sign ordinance, this by no means diminished its influence on the workings of its home town. This was made abundantly clear in an unrelated incident that took place during the summer of 1995. In 1994, Atlanta-based Visioneering International announced plans for a signature tourist attraction called GeoNova, which would be located on a yet to be determined site in Midtown. The 15-story, $40-million sphere would feature a wide variety of entertainment venues, including an interactive museum, a theater in the round, restaurants, and a nightclub. The most unique and controversial feature of GeoNova, however, was its exterior. In addition to a highly detailed rendering of the globe, the sphere's special illuminated skin would be able to project film, video, and computer-generated images, including advertising messages. As part of their campaign to raise the necessary capital, the project's backers argued that GeoNova would be a unique attraction that would symbolize Atlanta's status as an international city.[117] Mayor Bill Campbell threw his support behind the project, even taping a video promotion predicting that GeoNova would become Atlanta's No. 1 tourist attraction, as did former US president Jimmy Carter.[118]

In mid September 1995, Visioneering International announced that the Pepsi-Cola Corporation had agreed to sponsor the sphere, which would be located on one of two sites near arch-rival Coca-Cola's headquarters. Both Coke and ACOG reacted harshly to what they saw as a particularly offensive act of ambush marketing, although GeoNova backer's were quick to claim that they had courted Coke for almost two years, but to no avail.[119] The day after the announcement, a visibly irked Mayor Campbell not only withdrew his support for the project but vowed that he would act to insure that Pepsi would not be able to display outdoor advertising.[120] How the ban would be accomplished short of preventing the construction of the project was unclear, as even with its new highly restrictive sign ordinance, the city lacked the ability to control the content of advertising. Indeed, as the fate of the second sign ordinance indicated, federal courts were reluctant to approve the granting of special rights to a select handful of companies. Atlantans were spared such a potentially entertaining judicial spectacle when Visioneering International announced that construction of GeoNova would be postponed until after the Olympics, when the threat of ambush marketing would no longer exist.

SON OF BABBITT: SELLING THE CITY II

Although the city was quick to quash the threat to Coke's marketing interests, this development by no means indicated a lessening of tensions between it and ACOG. Shortly after the federal appeals court ruled the ACOG sign law unconstitutional, it was revealed that the city itself had entered into an agreement with a German firm that would blanket the urban landscape with nearly three hundred illuminated "lollipop" signs. The signs were part of the deal struck with Wall City Design, Inc. to install a dozen state-of-the-art pay toilets on city sidewalks. The addition of these self-cleaning marvels of German sanitary engineering will go part of the way towards addressing the utter lack of public relief facilities in Atlanta, without dipping into public coffers to do it. Standing some eight feet tall, and made of granite and enameled steel, the signs will carry advertising on one side and urban wayfinding information on the other.[121] The city, however, will realize only the revenue from the toilets themselves, as all advertising revenues will go to Wall City Design. ACOG and its allies at CAP and in the wider business community were upset at the perceived double standard that the toilet contract represented (ACOG itself will be providing some 1,800 advertisement-less and presumably free portable toilets near Olympic venues). At the time of writing, however, it is unclear if these hi-tech privies will actually be deployed, as the city and Wall City Design cannot agree about where they will be located.

The controversy over the toilets and lollipop signs, however, was nothing compared to the ruckus raised over the city's marketing plans devised by mayoral crony and local entrepreneur Munson Steed. His plan, while much more down to earth than Joel Babbitt's idea of leasing space on gigantic orbiting billboards, nonetheless bore a spiritual kinship to the visions of the city's first marketing director. Indeed, in terms of sheer entrepreneurship, Steed's plan goes one better than Babbitt's in that he personally stands to receive a hefty cut of the $20 million he estimates can be realized from leasing retail carts and kiosks to companies willing to pay fees ranging from $20,000 to $1 million.[122] ACOG and the IOC were quick to condemn the city's marketing plan as a threat not only to ACOG's ability to make its budget, but to "the Olympic movement's fund-raising future."[123] Proponents of the plan responded by noting that Olympic sponsors would be contacted first, to minimize the prospects for ambush marketing.[124] Steed, though, is close to working a deal with Fuji Film, arch-rival of official sponsor Eastman Kodak, as well as other corporate competitors of Olympic sponsors. ACOG has referred to Steed's plan as "parasitic" rather than mere "ambush marketing."[125] This, of course, is reminiscent of Babbitt's earlier efforts to get Olympic sponsor Visa to agree to pay an additional $2 million for the right to be Atlanta's "official credit card." However, whereas Babbitt's maneuver was resoundingly condemned by the city council, most council members supported Steed's plan. Unlike on the previous occasion, dissenting council members were upset not by the selling of the city's good name, but by the apparent cronyism displayed by the mayor's choice of Steed.

Proponents of the city's marketing plan also claimed that it would allow for more small, minority and female-owned businesses – who could otherwise not afford to participate in ACOG's expensive marketing program – to get a share of the Olympic largesse.[126] This assertion does not stand up to sustained scrutiny, as it is unlikely, to say the least, that many local small businesses will be able to come up with such hefty fees. In fact, the Steed plan clearly discriminated against the city's oft-beleaguered cohort of street vendors, who for the most part were unable to afford even such "bargain" rates. In July of 1995, an organization of the city's street vendors, most of whom are African-American, filed suit in federal court against the city, ACOG, MAOGA, and several other entities for restraint of trade. At the time of writing, no decision has been made, but given the court's rejection of the ACOG-backed sign ordinance, vendors are hopeful.

RAZING/RAISING THE DUMP

Even without resorting to Godzilla-sized billboards or giant illuminated spheres, corporations enjoyed a number of ways of making dramatic contributions to the Atlanta landscape that served their promotional interests. In December 1994, Daimler-Benz, the manufacturer of Mercedes-Benz cars and the supplier of automobiles to the International Olympic Committee, announced plans to purchase and renovate the house in which Margaret Mitchell wrote *Gone With the Wind*. Mitchell, who lived there between 1925 and 1932, referred to the Tudor-style house turned apartment building as "the Dump." Located near the corner of Peachtree and 10th streets and unoccupied since the late 1970s, the Dump occupies a strategic parcel of land in Midtown and had been the object of a battle between developers and preservationists for more than a decade. In the 1980s, the property was acquired as part of land assemblage for a large mixed-use development, but passed into the hands of a Japanese bank when the developer went bankrupt. As it was the house in which the legendary book was written, and was one of the few extant places with a direct connection to its author, the Dump held a special place in the hearts of *Gone With the Wind* aficionados. For several years, the non-profit Margaret Mitchell House, Inc. had been attempting to raise funds to purchase and restore the dwelling. These efforts had proved unsuccessful, in large measure because the run-down condition of the building led many to consider it an eyesore not worth preserving.

In mid September 1994, the building was severely damaged in a fire set by an unknown arsonist. At the time of the blaze, the Dump had been covered by a blanket of 50,000 inflated condoms as part of an installation for the annual Arts Festival held in nearby Piedmont Park. With only three walls left standing, and the interior completely gutted, preservation efforts appeared at an end. However, notice of the fire caught the eye of the people at Daimler-Benz, who were looking for a place in which to entertain guests during the 1996 Olympics. Company officials donated $5 million to the non-profit organization that will buy and restore the structure to its "original" condition.[127] After the Olympics, the restored Dump will no doubt jump to the head of the roster of Atlantan places venerated by *Gone With the Wind* cultists.

GOING FOR THE OLYMPIC GOLD

The city, ACOG, and large transnational coporations were not the only ones seeking to take advantage of the unnatural market forces set in motion by the Olympics. In the summer of 1995, it seemed that nearly every property owner and prospective entrepreneur in the city of Atlanta was consumed by Olympic fever. Commercial property owners near the core of the Olympic Ring benefited greatly from the demand for corporate hospitality and promotional space. Led in large measure by Olympic-related leases, the downtown office vacancy rate in the fall of 1995 had shrunk to less than half of 1992's stratospheric rate of more than 30 percent, its lowest rate in more than a decade.[128] Owners of downtown street-level retail space jacked up rents and refused to renew leases so as to clear out existing tenants to make way for the anticipated wave of high-paying renters.

The frenzied anticipation in the commercial sectors was paralleled, and even exceeded in some ways, by that in the residential rental market. With ACOG taking 80 percent of the 55,000 hotel rooms in the Atlanta area to host the "Olympic Family" (VIPs, sponsors, media), and most of the remainder set aside for corporate clients or booked by large travel agencies,[129] most of the anticipated 250,000 daily visitors during the seventeen-day Olympic period face the prospect of either finding hotel rooms in cities as far away as Chattanooga, Tennessee and Birmingham, Alabama (2–3 hours' drive), or delving into the private housing market. ACOG officials anticipated that they alone would require some 6,000 homes and 7,000 apartments, totaling some 33,000 beds, in addition to the 44,000 hotel rooms they had already secured.[130] Homeowners near Olympic venues and throughout the intown neighborhoods were positively giddy with the prospect of renting out their homes at rates starting at a minimum of $200 per bed per night. In choice areas like Buckhead, real estate professionals were indicating that a per-bed figure of $500 per night "was not unreasonable."[131] One enterprising, and optimistic, suburbanite was anticipating getting $925 per bed.[132] In early June, an *Atlanta Constitution* poll found that 17 percent of homeowners surveyed were interested in renting part or all of their homes to Olympic visitors. Nearly three-quarters, however, lived outside the Perimeter, rather than in the more desirable Buckhead and Midtown locations.[133]

Ever in search of additional revenue, as well as more beds for members of its "family," ACOG set up its own Private Housing '96 operation late in 1994. In return for a 55 percent commission, ACOG would find a suitable tenant for houses that met its rather demanding set of criteria (separate bathroom for each bedroom, etc.). In typically imperious fashion, ACOG figured it could charge more because it would control the majority of the demand for high-end rentals.[134] As with many of their other assumptions, however, this did not prove to be the case. In an effort to entice more homeowners into its pool, it cut its commission by 10 percent in the spring of 1995. However, at 45 percent, ACOG was at a considerable disadvantage vis-à-vis competitors charging commissions as low as 20 percent. Large brokers and corporations descended upon Midtown, Buckhead, Dunwoody and other posh areas in search of large blocks of rooms. Several Midtown condominiums and apartment complexes were leased in toto. Although areas closest to the Olympic Ring fetched the highest prices, the search extended well into Cobb, north Fulton, and Gwinnett. Residents of one upscale subdivision near Marietta were offered a guaranteed $1,000 per night for use of their homes for a month.

As might be expected in such a hot-house climate, rental rates for Atlanta residents in many close-in neighborhoods skyrocketed. In Midtown, rents increased by some 14 percent over 1994 levels, while the rate for single-family homes in many intown neighborhoods increased as much as 20 percent.[135] In addition, many landlords specified that tenants could not sub-lease and/or must vacate during the Olympics. The worst offender in this regard was Intown Properties, which managed a large number of units in older complexes in Virginia-Highland and Buckhead. In June, 1995, Intown notified its tenants that they would have to either vacate for up to four months or pay rents of $3,000 a month. In return, tenants were promised 30 percent of the profits, but no specific figure was guaranteed. Many of these units were small spaces without air-conditioning, much less the upscale amenities in demand by Olympic visitors, that previously rented for $500 to $600 a month. Such maneuvers were legal, for although the Georgia Assembly had passed a law prohibiting price gouging by hotels, no such protection was provided for Atlanta residents who rented their domiciles. Despite the state attorney general's observation that Intown's price increases were "immoral,"[136] no steps were taken to make this extreme profiteering illegal. Disgruntled residents of Intown's apartments formed Residents Outraged About Rental Rape, or ROARR, and staged a demonstration outside the State Capitol, where legislators were meeting in special session to decide on Congressional redistricting. Although the legislature declined to act, a wide range of the city's high and mighty, from the mayor to Billy Payne to the editorial staff of the *Atlanta Constitution*, took turns castigating Intown's decision. Faced with a tidal wave of negative publicity, in a midsummer aboutface the company made compliance with the program "voluntary." Rental rates throughout the city, however, continued to climb at faster than average rates.

Despite the intense hype about the need for tens of thousands of beds to house the arriving multitudes, most prospective properties remained without tenants at the end of 1995. As of December, ACOG's official housing operation had leased only 751 apartments and 377 homes out of an inventory of 7,500 residences.[137] Many of the older properties in intown neighborhoods lacked the amenities that commanded the high prices their owners dreamed of receiving, and several real estate operators, remembering the experience of Los Angeles in 1984 – when many homes went without renters – began to revise their optimistic figures downward. At the time of writing, the full extent of this "correction" has yet to be realized. Indeed, a number of developments have occurred to make the prospect of renting less appealing. Current federal and state tax regulations allow owners to rent their homes for as many as fourteen days a year without tax liability, but legislation has been introduced in Congress to do away with this loophole. Moreover, some homeowners are beginning to realize that after paying brokers' commissions, and the inconvenience and expense of finding alternative living arrangements, coupled with the cost of providing amenities (food, utilities, maid service, etc.) and the potential of damage, the profits of renting are nowhere as high as initially anticipated.

The total number of persons displaced by the rental controversy in the intown neighborhoods is hard to estimate at this point, but it could total a couple of thousand persons if those obliged to leave because they cannot afford the increased rent are included, along with those who will be temporarily displaced for Olympic tenants. While no systematic study of these displacees has been conducted, from anecdotal evidence it appears that this group is a fairly diverse, although mostly white, one, ranging from struggling college students to comparatively prosperous young professionals. Particularly among the latter, the controversy over Olympic rentals has opened up the previously invisible class divide between owners and renters, and provided the relatively privileged with an experience that, in Atlanta at least, has been historically confined to mostly African-American working-class and poor populations. However, this experience is hardly likely to build bridges across the divides of race and class. Indeed, more public attention has been focused on potential Olympic-related displacements in the intown neighborhoods, than on actual displacements from inner-city neighborhoods and public housing projects.

While total numbers are lacking, figures from the Atlanta Housing Authority indicate that as many as 2,200 families could be displaced from public housing between 1994 and 1996. The breakdown is as follows: 114 from Techwood, 558 from Clark Howell, 340 from Eagan Homes, 470 from East Lake Meadows, 64 from John Hope Homes, and 30 from the Martin Street Plaza complex in Summerhill. In addition, 363 families were displaced from private housing in the Summerhill neighborhood.[138] Relocation activities have largely consisted of residents being offered either accommodation in other public housing or Section VIII vouchers that subsidize the cost of private housing. Assuming an average family/household size of approximately four persons, the displacements could involve as many as 10,000 persons. However, not all of these displacements are directly connected with the Olympics, nor will they be completed by the summer of 1996. While the Eagan and John Hope Homes are located within the Olympic Ring, they, along with East Lake Meadows, are being emptied in the course of separate renovation projects set in motion by the AHA and private developers, respectively. The Summerhill, Techwood, and Clark Howell displacements enjoy a much more direct connection with Olympic redevelopment efforts. Having already described the plans for turning Techwood/Clark Howell into privatized "mixed-income" communities, I turn my attention to Summerhill, which has been billed as a showcase for neighborhood redevelopment in Atlanta.

Along with Buttermilk Bottom – which has been replaced by the upscale communities of Bedford-Pine – Summerhill was one of the neighborhoods most dramatically affected by 1960s urban renewal, and one of the centers of protest against it. Although it was included in the Model Cities program, little improvement was registered by the time the program ended in 1973. Little positive change was forthcoming with the subsequent Community Development Program either, as much of the available federal CDBG money was funneled to other parts of the city. In 1988, community leaders formed Summerhill Neighborhood, Inc. (SNI) to further the prospects for redevelopment. SNI was Atlanta's first neighborhood redevelopment corporation and was the beneficiary of a plan conceived by the Urban Land Institute for its revitalization. The ULI plan, which had a total estimated cost of some $100 million, envisioned the creation of clusters of new residential and retail developments throughout the community.

The largest of these residential/retail nodes was a 30-acre area just to the east of the stadiums to be known as Greenlea Commons. Named after one of the recently deceased founders of SNI, the Greenlea Commons project consisted of a corridor of townhomes, apartments, stores, and a park running along Capitol Avenue and Fraser Street. Divided into a northern and southern half along Georgia Avenue, the total development would have upwards of 250 units of housing and cost some $27 million. Initial plans called for CODA to condemn the land and the housing to be built with a combination of bonds from the state-chartered Urban Residential Finance Authority and private sources. SNI planned to have the units completed in time for the Olympics, so as to be able to rent them out to Olympic sponsors for $40,000. As this was termed to be an Olympic usage, it was MAOGA, rather than CODA, that actually condemned the land for the 116 townhomes of the Greenlea North development. For a complex array of reasons, not the least of which was the lack of financing, the rest of the project was delayed until after the Olympics.

SNI envisioned that the profits realized from the Olympic rentals would not only pay its operating costs, but be used to fund an endowment that would subsidize the mortgages of low-income Summerhill residents who wished to purchase the $85,000 townhomes after the Games, i.e., if a resident qualified for a $65,000 mortgage, the endowment would cover the $20,000 downpayment. It is unlikely, however, that many of the neighborhood's current low-income residents will qualify for a $65,000 mortgage, especially given local financial institutions' odious track record in providing mortgages in depressed areas of the city.[139] Indeed, the Summerhill plan was explicitly based on the premise of limiting the number of low-income residents in the new, improved Summerhill. Instead, SNI hopes to attract middle- and upper-income households to the area, which, in turn, would attract neighborhood businesses, that had completely disappeared during the area's post-urban renewal decline. While no one has used the "G word" in reference to Summerhill redevelopment, the SNI plan is a clear attempt at gentrification. Neighborhood leaders and property owners would be quick to point out that they have just as much right to revitalize their neighborhood as do their opposite numbers in Virginia-Highland and Candler Park. Indeed they do: there is no reason why Summerhill should remain blighted while owner/residents in largely white intown neighborhoods experience dramatic enhancement of their property values and have the choice of two dozen places to enjoy a properly made tall skim latte. The principal problem with the SNI plan, especially if it is to be used as a model for other neighborhoods, is one common to gentrification: it does not address specifically the questions of how and where low-income populations are to live.

The implicit assumption of the SNI plan is that the way to deal with the problem of low-income housing is simply not to build any low-income housing and get some unspecified "others" to build some elsewhere, or, as with Section VIII vouchers, to rely on the existing private housing market to provide it. However, there are far fewer "elsewheres" these days. While the negative impact of such a plan might be limited in a small neighborhood that has already been drastically depopulated, such as Summerhill, the effects will be much greater if this kind of plan is adopted by larger poor neighborhoods. Moreover, it is questionable whether or not Summerhill will be successful in attracting urban gentry. Efforts to gentrify the Victorian homes and cottages of the mostly African-American neighborhood of West End during the booming 1980s proved of only limited success.

In the current national mood, the prospects for publically subsidized housing are grim. The much-celebrated conversion of the Techwood, Clark Howell, and East Lake public housing projects into privatized mixed-income communities will result in 40 percent fewer, if nicer, units for low-income families. The reality of the situation is that the number of low-income units in the city of Atlanta will be greatly decreased, and that few, if any, new low-income units will be built anywhere in the metro area. Even if the Empowerment Zone plan is effective in creating significant new employment opportunities in this area, it is highly unlikely that its low-income population will decrease in numbers. Instead, they will be merely redistributed in space, preferably, from the point of view of city and neighborhood leaders, outside their boundaries. Indeed, as the suburbanization of poverty in southwestern DeKalb indicates, this process is already well advanced.

ASSESSING THE OLYMPIC LEGACY

Compared to the massive displacements that accompanied the Olympics in Seoul (1988) and Barcelona (1992), the demolitions and removals occasioned by the 1996 Centennial Games in Atlanta are relatively minor. For example, several hundred thousand people were displaced by the Korean government's efforts to make its capital a showplace for its new-found economic prosperity. Barcelona, too, utilized the occasion to relocate large numbers of its poor, although it did so as part of a comprehensive vision that included building a twenty-first-century urban infrastructure for itself. In the case of Atlanta, a good deal of damage has already been inflicted by three decades of renewal, redevelopment, and revitalization, although the fundamental unevenness of these processes has often been obscured by the metropolitan area's fervid, long-lasting boom and the manifold labors of myriad imagineers.

What is highly ironic, given the course of subsequent events, is that Atlanta got the Games, in part, on the basis of what the AOC and city leaders liked to call its peerless modern infrastructure. By this they referred not to the city's roads, sewers, and viaducts — which actually proved in need of approximately a billion dollars in repairs — but such things as the MARTA rail system, Hartsfield International Airport, the Georgia Dome/World Congress Center complex, and the most extensive fiber-optic network in the world. Aside from the $150 million realized from the bond issue, which probably would have not been passed without the occasion of the Olympics to provide the motive force, most of the monies expended on infrastructure improvement will be spent to provide the World Congress Center with a new parking deck and International Plaza ($30 million) and the airport with a flashy new $300-plus-million postmodern ambience. The State Assembly declined, however, to provide the necessary 10 percent of expenses (the federal government would have provided the rest) to build a central multimodal station for a heavy rail system that would have ameliorated the metro area's unwholesome addiction to the automobile. Instead of an integrated commuter rail network, Atlanta's Olympic transportation legacy (aside from seeing if MARTA can work beyond its designed capacity for three weeks) will be the neo-Orwellian Advanced Transportation Management System and high-occupancy vehicle lanes for the expressways within the Perimeter.

While neighborhood revitalization will be limited to some showpiece developments in the vicinity of the stadium such as Summerhill's Greenlea Commons North and Mechanicsville's Street of Dreams (another pod of thirty upscale townhomes), the material legacy of the Games will consist of the venues, the Centennial Olympic Park, and the articulated network of pacified corridors and green spaces wrought by CODA, along with the controversial redevelopment of the Martin Luther King Historic Site. The Atlanta University Center will get three new athletic venues, while Georgia Tech gets a spanking new Natation Center and several hundred new dorms. Georgia State University gets an improved gym, as well as the Techwood Olympic Villages to utilize as dormitories. Unfortunately three of the dorm buildings were constructed with defective foundations and are settling at an accelerated rate (over nine inches within the first year). The University System of Georgia — and, by extension, state taxpayers — will be liable for dealing with these "minor" problems. Ted Turner's Atlanta Braves are, however, the greatest beneficiary of Olympic largesse, receiving a new stadium with all the trimmings, and sticking Fulton County taxpayers with a bill that they had little say in negotiating. Indeed, it is quite likely that the latter will be ultimately responsible for the cost of converting the Olympic Stadium into a baseball facility and demolishing the existing Atlanta-Fulton County Stadium.

The Olympic/Braves stadium, along with non-Olympic plans for the new Hawks arena to be built on the bones of the existing Omni Coliseum, provide good examples of both Atlanta's lingering fascination/compulsion for not-so-creative destruction (a condition with its origin in General William Tecumseh Sherman being "a little careless with fire") and the accelerated dynamic obsolescence of the built environment in our contemporary era. While the market-driven urban landscape has always been by nature "restless," the increasingly frequent proclivity for building demolition into the construction plans for large civic structures verges on hyperactivity. Despite all the talk of the Olympic's material legacy, many of the venues are, in fact, temporary constructions. In addition to the northern third of the Olympic Stadium, the rowing venue at Lake Lanier and the velodrome and the archery facilities at Stone Mountain will disappear after the Games, along with the water polo pool at Georgia Tech's Natation Center. Almost a quarter of a million bleacher seats will be erected and dismantled (including the 52,000 at Atlanta-Fulton County Stadium), along with one million square feet of tent space and twenty-four miles of fencing. Indeed, the 1996 Olympics will be the most transient ever, leading one observer to refer to them as "the Disposable Games."[140] Without end-users, such as the State of Georgia and local governments, agreeing to assume the cost of maintaining these facilities after the Olympics, it was cheaper for ACOG to build ephemeral venues that only give the appearance of permanence.

The financial legacy of the Games is its most complex and elusive to pin down. The latest estimate of the Olympics' impact on the Georgian economy amounts to $5.1 billion between 1990 and 1996, with most of that accruing in the Atlanta area, as well as some 80,000 jobs. The $5.1-billion figure includes everything from ACOG's expenditures to those of the various governmental agencies to the estimated $900 a day that the average family of four will spend to attend the Games. Where that money will go and how much of it will affect the run of the mill Atlantan is unclear. Certain segments stand to benefit, and already have benefited, more than others. The construction industry, for example, has received an enormous boost from Olympic-related building, although its extensive use of labor pools limits its positive impact on construction unions. In addition, the Olympic construction boom has dramatically raised the price of materials in the metro area, which have been passed on to the consumer in a multitude of ways. This "invisible add-on," however, is nothing compared to the anticipated rise in the cost of living, if restaurateurs and other retailers jack up their prices to fleece the Olympic hordes, as is widely expected. Property owners in or near the Olympic Ring stand to profit considerably during the Games from Olympic-related rentals, but that picture is nowhere near as rosy in the post-Olympic future, as millions of square feet of office and retail space will be dumped back on the market.

Despite the billions coursing through the local economy, "the questions" still remain. That is, will ACOG break even, and if it does not, will taxpayers be stuck with the tab? ACOG leaders have been insistently answering "Yes" to the first question, and emphatically "No!" to the second. Public concern deepened in February 1995, when ACOG announced it was delaying its final financial report until the fall. When the forecast was released in late October, ACOG chief operating officer A.D. Frazier pronounced it was "just about bulletproof."[141] That is, ACOG was assured of no worse a fate than breaking even. However, in early November 1995 this assertion was contested by the normally complacent watchdogs at MAOGA, whose accountants noted that ACOG's revenue projections were on the high side of ambitious, and could easily be penetrated by the armor-piercing rounds of economic reality. Given the controversy that has surrounded the issue from the start, however, it is extremely unlikely that taxpayers will be directly responsible for bailing out ACOG if the worst-case scenario does indeed occur. That dubious honor falls to NationsBank, which extended an Olympian line of credit to Payne and Company. Still, if the city and ACOG are unable to come to agreement about the latter's reimbursement of the former for municipal services necessitated by the Games, such as police overtime, sanitation, etc. (as is possible given their intense disagreements over the city's marketing program), Atlanta's already overburdened taxpayers will ultimately be the ones to foot that particular bill.

ACOG has been reluctant to conclude an agreement on paying for city services, arguing that the tax windfall the city stands to reap more than offsets the cost of what the city will spend. Indeed, holding to the line that it has maintained since 1990, ACOG argues that it is really doing the city and people of Atlanta an enormous favor by staging the Olympics, indeed, that the Olympics are the best thing that ever happened in, and to, Atlanta. Although they like to emphasize the material aspects of the Olympic legacy, Billy Payne and A.D. Frazier are quick to emphasize that enhanced "image, prestige, and pride are the real residuals."[142] Payne even went as far as claiming that the Olympics will establish Atlanta "as one of the top cities in the world; right up there with the Parises, and the Tokyos, and the New Yorks, and the Moscows, and the like. We're in for a quantum leap in terms of image and reputation."[143] Many other non-ACOG business leaders agree that the unprecedented publicity and media attention will inevitably result in increased tourism, investment, and business growth, especially from abroad. While it is by no means inevitable, such a scenario seems likely, though if current development trends are any indication, much of the new investment and activity will take place out on the peripheries in Gwinnett, Cobb, north Fulton, and Buckhead rather than in the urban core. In addition, Payne and Co. seem to truly believe that there is no such thing as bad publicity. Approximately 15,000 journalists will be descending upon Atlanta in the summer of 1996, an unspecified percentage of whom will have the express purpose not of covering the Games, but of demonstrating how Atlanta is not really what it claims to be.

The aspect of the Olympic legacy that has received the least amount of public attention is easily among the most important. A crucial component of Atlanta's success over the past two decades has been the development of a biracial civic–business partnership, which reached its apogee in the mayoralty of Andrew Young. The bestowal of the Olympics coincided with several independent developments that deconstructed the fabled coalition. The re-election of Maynard Jackson in November 1989, and his succession by a protégé elected without either strong ties to the African-American grassroots or the support of the business community, coupled with the intensifying perception of the city council as bloated and corrupt, divided and demeaned the public sector. Meanwhile, the absorption of major local corporate citizens by larger national concerns, and the siphoning away of the private sector's sunk investment in the core to the new downtowns of the periphery increasingly fragmented "the" business community. Nonetheless, enough fragments of the latter have endured to constitute what former city councilman Jabari Simama and fellow investigative reporters from Atlanta's free weekly *Creative Loafing* have called a "shadow government."[144] Though it is an ephemeral, nominally private corporation, the Atlanta Committee for the Olympic Games evolved as an organizational entity that drew heavily on personnel used to working with each other from the heyday of the 1980s public–private partnership. How these persons will be reintegrated into the governing coalition that emerges after 1996 remains to be seen, but the intense hostility that has emerged between city hall and ACOG in the course of the preparation does not bode well for an easy or early return to business as usual.

Indeed, if the circumstances surrounding the creation of the Centennial Olympic Park are any indication, we may well see the emergence of a new kind of urban regime in Atlanta, one in which the city is reduced to the status of junior player or partner, while the crucial decisions are made by a coalition of private business leaders and quasi-public state authorities. Just as decision-making has been privatized, or at the very least removed from public accountability, the park itself is exemplary of contemporary tendencies towards the privatization and spectacularization of public space. Sold to the people of Atlanta as a state-of-the-art open gathering place, the park, in its Olympic manifestation at least, is neither all that open nor public, nothing more than an ephemeral simulation of a public open space of an earlier age. The failure to address the problems of adjacent poor neighborhoods, public housing projects, and the homeless raises the prospect of the park becoming as empty and objectionable to the business community as the current "void" is, if not more so given the heightening of expectations. Then again, the lack of linkage between specific projects and the surrounding urban whole is a general failing of virtually all ongoing efforts at urban redevelopment in Atlanta and elsewhere.

But all of these consequences lie in the not-so-distant future, on the other side of the Olympics. As 1995 drew to a close, the attention of most Atlantans was fixed on efforts to get the city ready to handle the two million visitors who were expected to arrive in a little more than six months. The banner of the the the local newspaper bore a running countdown of the "days to go." At key points around the city, digital clocks provided an even more precise accounting of the days, hours, minutes, and seconds until the Games. As I write these words, the sense of anxiety and uncertainty is as pervasive as construction cranes and blocked roads near the major venues, and provides an almost irresistible motive force for endorsing whatever is necessary to get the city ready, regardless of the consequences. There is literally no time for argument or serious rethinking of priorities. As in the case of Whatizit, Atlanta's Olympic imagineers, faced with a product of dubious appeal, have focused their resources on a superficial makeover, leaving a complex and troubling set of problems to be "rediscovered" in 1997.

SO WHAT?

My intentions for this volume were rather modest: to provide a critical introduction to the political, economic, and social realities of Atlanta, to describe some of the ways in which the 1996 Olympic Games reinforced, revised, and transcended both the profane and profound dimensions of the status quo, and to provoke what I hope will be a lively, constructive, and truly *public* discussion of what Atlanta has been, is, and can be. As I have indicated, there is an awful lot to be critical about, much more, in fact, than I was able to include in my narrative. At the risk of penning yet another jeremiad about the death of the city, and completely offending the legendarily thin-skinned powers that happen to reside in this particular one, I have lingered on "the critical" in part because of the giddy and effusively celebratory tone of much of what has been written, imaged, and broadcast about Atlanta. To paraphrase Italo Calvino (without a reference to whom no book on the late-twentieth-century city would be complete), Atlanta's imagineers have both willfully and inadvertently confused the city with the words (and images) they have used to describe it. Invariably, the latter substitute a wishful vision of how the city might be (if their critics would just be quiet) for a cold hard look at what the city actually is, and how it came to be that way. Consequently, boosters have avoided acknowledging those aspects of the city, and its population, that do not fit neatly into their bright, shiny, and hopeful Atlanta of the next millennium. By not acknowledging them, or rather, the processes that bring them into being, boosters delude themselves and ultimately reinforce the decidedly "unheavenly" nature of Atlanta, even as its peripheries glimmer with the celestial glow of new investments and affluent residents.

In focusing all of my attention on critique, I have not left much room for sketching out an alternative vision of and for Atlanta. Such a monumental task defies inclusion in what is, I fear, an already far too lengthy "introduction." That, as we academics are wont to say, is another book (or several, nay, a life's work), not to mention a problem of almost impossible complexity. I have always taken a dim view of utopian schemes that purport to find "the" answer to the challenges of the urban future in either the magic workings of the unregulated marketplace or the beneficent (and often oppressive) wisdom of technocratic planners. In some ways, the inexorable play of contradictory and uncontrollable forces that define our contemporary world makes even the most well-intentioned effort at comprehensive planning an exercise in folly, at best. Nonetheless, even the latter seems desirable compared to the sprawling and fundamentally unequal chaos created by the reigning ideology of "disjointed incrementalism."[145]

To be effective, as well as equitable, the planning process needs to be inclusive as well as comprehensive. Planning and urban design, such as they exist in Atlanta and much of the rest of the United States today, reflect the vision of private, rather than public, interests. Although the Atlanta Regional Commission has taken steps to incorporate many different constituencies in its "thirty-year plan" – better known as Vision 2020 – the effectiveness of this endeavor is limited by the political–economic context in which the ARC operates. As the decision to build the Outer Perimeter indicates, despite all its efforts at inclusiveness, the ARC ultimately reflects the interests of the suburban politicians and developers who dominate its board. Moreover, the ARC includes only part of the metropolitan area and, as the case of Gwinnett County ignoring its recommendations indicates, has only an extremely limited ability to regulate local land use. Nor, as a predominantly suburban body, can the ARC be said to very much concerned with the plight of the "whole in the center." In the ARC, private interests enjoy an even more untrammeled influence through such entities as the Atlanta Committee for the Olympic Games, Central Atlanta Progress, and the Atlanta Neighborhood Development Partnership, as well as through a host of quasi-public authorities that exist to subsidize the private sector's activities. Bloated by a patronage-heavy bureaucracy and forced to compete with other centers for much-needed investment, the City of Atlanta has been reduced to at best a junior partner in what is now more accurately described as a *private*–public partnership that is largely free of public oversight and accountability. In this, of course, Atlanta is far from unique, but that makes it no less troubling, especially for a city that advertises itself as the "world capital of human rights." If private entities truly wish to act in the public interest – a development that by all means should be encouraged – there is no reason why they should not be held accountable by those they claim to serve.

NOTES

INTRODUCTION

1. G. Clay, *Close-Up: How To Read the American City*, 1973, Chicago: University of Chicago Press, p. 11.
2. R. Hughes, "Fetus, Don't Fail Me Now," *The New Yorker*, 5 October 1992, pp. 67–68.
3. Quoted in *Atlanta Journal Constitution* (hereafter *AJC*), 24 October 1993.
4. Atlanta Committee for the Olympic Games, "The 1996 Olympic Games Mascot" in *The Olympic Spirit: History of the Games and the Atlanta Committee for the Olympic Games, Volume I*, 1992–93, Atlanta.
5. Other contenders included Peter Peachnut, a weird combination of Georgia's two main cash crops – peaches and peanuts; CenTen, a goofy-looking flame; Friendly the Fawn, a white-tailed deer in a tracksuit; and Fox, inspired by Atlanta native Joel Chandler Harris's Brer Fox.
6. *AJC*, 30 August 1992.
7. *AJC*, 29 September 1993.
8. *AJC*, 11 August 1994.
9. *AJC*, 24 October 1993.
10. *AJC*, 17 July 1993. The Braves were the first thing that came to mind to 13 percent of respondents, followed by the South/history 7 percent, the airport 6 percent, business 6 percent, Olympics 6 percent, peaches 5 percent, and civil rights 4 percent.
11. Atlanta Committee for the Olympic Games, *Atlanta: City of Dreams, Volume II of Atlanta's Official Bid for the 1996 Olympic Games*, Authorized Commemorative Edition, 1990, Atlanta: Peachtree Publishers, p. 12.
12. Some representative examples include: M. Christine Boyer, *The City of Collective Memory*, 1994, Cambridge: MIT Press; M. Davis, *City of Quartz: Excavating the Future in Los Angeles*, 1990, London: Verso; R. Fishman, "Megalopolis Unbound: America's New City," *Wilson Quarterly*, 1990, winter, pp. 25–45; D. Harvey, *The Condition of Postmodernity*, 1990, Oxford: Blackwell; S. Zukin, *Landscapes of Power*, 1991, Berkeley: University of California Press; and M. Sorkin's edited collection, *Variations on a Theme Park*, 1992, New York: Hill and Wang.
13. M. Webber, "The Urban Place and the Nonplace Urban Realm," in M. Webber, et al., *Explorations into Urban Structure*, 1964, Philadelphia: University of Pennsylvania Press, pp. 79–153.
14. M. Castells, *The Informational City*, 1989, Oxford: Blackwell.
15. S. Fjellman, *Vinyl Leaves*, 1992, Boulder: Westview Press, p. 319.
16. For a discussion of the "doughnut complex," see W. Sharpe and L. Wallock, "From 'Great Town' to 'Nonplace Urban Realm': Reading the Modern City," in Sharpe and Wallock, *Visions of the Modern City: Essays in History, Art, and Literature*, 1987, Baltimore: The Johns Hopkins University Press, pp. 37–9. In Atlanta, this term has sometimes been racistly amended to read "the *black* hole in the center of the doughnut."
17. M. Davis, "The Infinite Game: Redeveloping Downtown LA," in D. Ghirardo, ed., *Out of Site: A Social Criticism of Architecture*, 1991, Seattle: Bay Press.
18. M.C. Boyer, "The City of Illusion: New York's Public Places," in P. Knox, ed., *The Restless Urban Landscape*, 1993, Englewood Cliffs, New Jersey: Prentice Hall, pp. 112–26.
19. The term "Jim Crow" was initially used in the early nineteenth century to refer to a dance routine and a black-face character in minstrel shows. Over time, it developed as a reference to African-Americans

more generally. It was first used to describe segregated facilities and accommodations in the pre-Civil War North, although it is best known as a label for the system of legal segregation that flourished in the former states of the Confederacy from 1877 onward. See C.R. Wilson, "Jim Crow," in *Encyclopedia of Southern Culture*, 1989, Chapel Hill, and London: University of North Carolina Press, pp. 213–14; and C.V. Woodward, *The Strange Career of Jim Crow*, 1955, Chapel Hill: University of North Carolina Press.

20. See, for example, A. Trachtenberg, "Mysteries of the Great City," in *The Incorporation of America*, 1982, New York: Hill and Wang; N. Smith, "Gentrification, the Frontier, and the Restructuring of Urban Space," in N. Smith and P. Williams, eds, *Gentrification of the City*, 1986, Boston: Allen & Unwin, pp. 15–34.

21. For examples of the former, see S. Mintz, *Sweetness and Power*, 1985, New York: Norton; and E. Wolf, *Europe and the People Without History*, 1982, Berkeley: University of California Press. For examples of the latter, see M. Taussig, *Colonialism, Shamanism, and the Wild Man*, 1986, Chicago: University of Chicago Press.

22. Exceptions include R. and S. Price's *Equatoria*, 1992, London: Routledge, and D. Foley's *Learning Capitalist Culture*, 1990, Philadelphia: University of Pennsylvania Press.

23. R. Rotenberg, "Introduction" to R. Rotenberg and G. McDonogh, *The Cultural Meanings of Urban Space*, 1993, South Hadley, Mass.: Bergin and Garvey, p. xiii.

24. In films ranging from *Ice Man* to *Cannibal Women in the Avocado Jungle of Death*, anthropologists have invariably associated with "primitive" non-Western peoples.

25. With a few noteworthy exceptions, a good deal of the first wave of what became known as "urban" anthropology consisted of finding the traditional in the modern, of conceptualizing the *favelas, barrios*, and neighborhoods of Latin American, African, and Asian cities as discrete "urban villages." Not surprisingly, our focus of study, more often than not, was on migration, social networks, and poverty, on describing "urbanization without breakdown," and, as the 1960s wore on, the reproduction of social inequality. These topical concerns persisted as anthropologists began to stay home in greater numbers during the late 1960s and directed their attentions towards North America's turbulent central cities. Urban ethnographers played a crucial role in first unwittingly advancing and later definitively shattering the thinly veiled racist shibboleths of the notion of the "culture of poverty" and related concepts that blamed the urban, mostly minority poor for their impoverishment without the slightest regard for the structural causes of inequality. Although it was not conceptualized as such at the time, in retrospect there is no better sign of the transformation of the North American inner city into a colonial frontier than the presence of increasing numbers of anthropologists, regardless of the progressive politico-theoretical axes many were attempting to grind there.

The rediscovery of the city by anthropologists ushered in a brief golden age of urban anthropology during the 1970s. The emergence of yet another adjectival anthropology was part of a decades-long reconfiguration of the discipline away from "national" theoretical schools – e.g., "British" structural-functionalism," "American" historical-particularism and culture and personality, "French" structuralism, etc. – to a more Balkanized assemblage of theoretical, topical, and geographic subfields held loosely together by variations on the age-old master dialectic of neo-Platonic idealism and vulgar, and not-so-vulgar, materialism. Like any of the other sub-, or sub-sub-fields, urban anthropology was marked by the emergence of new texts, compilations, journals, conferences, and professional associations. Yet, despite this incipient institutionalization, by the early 1980s urban anthropology (much like both the discipline of anthropology as a whole *and* the sociocultural phenomenon it took as its focus of study) was decidedly less coherent than it had been a decade earlier.

26. W. Gibson, *Neuromancer*, 1984, New York: Dell Books.

27. B. Anderson, *Imagined Communities: Reflections on the Origins and Spread of Nationalism*, revised edition, 1992, New York and London: Verso, p. 6.

28. M. Sorkin, "Introduction," *Variations on a Theme Park: The New American City and the End of Public Space*, 1992, New York: Hill and Wang, p. xiv.

29. M.C. Boyer, *Dreaming the Rational City*, 1983, Cambridge: MIT Press.

30. My colleague Tim Crimmins has previously drawn attention to the "palimpscestuous" nature of Atlanta's urban landscape, see "The Atlanta Palimpsest: Stripping Away the Layers of the Past," *Atlanta Historical Journal*, 1982, vol. 26, pp. 13–32.

31. Italo Calvino, quoted in P. Patton, "Imaginary Cities: Images of Postmodernity," in S. Watson and K. Gibson, *Postmodern Cities and Spaces*, 1995, Oxford and Cambridge: Blackwell, p. 112.

32. G. McDonogh, personal communication.

1. BUILDING THE IMAGINARY CITY

1. J. Raban, *Soft City*, 1974, London: Hamish Hamilton, p. 10.
2. K. Robins, "Prisoners of the City: Whatever Could a Postmodern City Be?," *New Formations*, 1991, winter, vol. 15, p. 10.
3. S. Zukin, *Landscapes of Power*, 1991, Berkeley: University of California Press, pp. 258–9.
4. I have appropriated the term from Martin Amis, see his *Money: A Suicide Note*, 1981, New York: Pantheon.
5. Although the last thing the world needs is another neologism, the World of Coca-Cola facility does not fit neatly into the existing category of kinds of places. As a facility dedicated to celebrating one of the world's best-known commodities (as well as a symbol of US economic and cultural hegemony – "coca-colonization"), it combines narrative features of the museum, with the purpose, sensibility, and production values of an advertisement. Indeed, a good part of its display consists of the visual history of Coca-Cola advertisements.
6. U. Eco, *Travels in Hyper Reality*, 1983, New York: Harcourt Brace Jovanovich, p. 8.
7. See for example the contrasting accounts in the Work Projects Administration (WPA), *Atlanta: A City of the Modern South*. Compiled by the Workers of the Writer Program of the Work Projects Administration in the State of Georgia, American Guide Series 1942, Board of Education of the City of Atlanta, reprinted in 1973 by Somerset Publishers, St Clair Shores, Michigan; and F. Garrett, *Atlanta and Environs: A Chronicle of Its People and Events*, Volume I, 1954, Athens: University of Georgia Press.
8. See, for example, E.Y. Clarke, *Atlanta Illustrated: Containing Glances at its Population, Business, Manufacture, Industries, Institutions, Society, Healthfulness, Architecture, and Advantages Generally . . .*, 1881 [orig. 1877], Atlanta: Jas. P. Harrison and Company.
9. Quoted in D. Thomas, *Atlanta: A City for the World*, 1989, Northridge, Cal.: Windsor Publications, p. 16.
10. A low-level controversy has raged for the better part of a century as to whether the actual name of the Creek settlement was Standing Peachtree or Standing Pitch (or pine)tree. Peach trees are not indigenous to the region, while pine trees are. Peaches do thrive when planted, however, and a number of white accounts from the late eighteenth century refer to a peach tree on the site. For a comprehensive account of the naming controversy, see Garrett, Volume I, 1954, pp. 9–12.
11. Ibid., pp. 183–4.
12. W.E.B. DuBois, "On the Wings of Atalanta" in *Souls of Black Folk* (1903), in *Three Negro Classics*, 1965, New York: Avon Books, p. 263.
13. The term "Atlanta" was coined by J. Edgar Thompson, the chief engineer of the Western and Atlantic Railroad, who responded to a request by Richard Peters, local superintendent of the W&A (and soon to be the city's leading real estate speculator) thus: "Eureka – Atlanta, the terminus of the Western and Atlantic Railroad – Atlantic masculine, Atlanta feminine – a coined word, and, if you think it will suit adopt it." Quoted in Garrett, Volume I, p. 225. Seen from the point of view of the Western and Atlantic Railroad, which sought to connect lines from the Atlantic and Gulf coasts with the Ohio Valley and the West, the choice of Atlanta would seem to indicate the advertisement of "Atlanta" as the interior's gateway to the Atlantic.
14. Clarke, 1881, p. 36.
15. Ibid., p. 36.
16. The Creeks were forced to cede the land around the current city of Atlanta to the state of Georgia in 1821. The Cherokees who occupied the northern part of the metro area were forcibly displaced from their lands by the Georgia militia and federal troops in the winter of 1830–31 and sent to Oklahoma via "the Trail of Tears."
17. WPA, 1942, p. 14.
18. J. Hornady, *Atlanta: Yesterday, Today, and Tomorrow*, 1922, American Cities Book Company (no place of publication listed), pp. 10–15.
19. Presently, the site of Slab Town has been eradicated by an expressway, while the site of Snake Nation is now known as Castleberry Hill, where artists and real estate developers have turned turn-of-the-century factory buildings into much-desired loft apartments.
20. Hornady, pp. 138–9.
21. Quoted in W. Ellis and J. Amos, "Atlanta: Pacesetter City of the South," *National Geographic*, 1969, February, 135/2: p. 247.

22. WPA, 1942, p. 17.

23. D. Doyle, *New Men, New Cities, New South*, 1990, Chapel Hill: University of North Carolina Press, p. 35.

24. ACOG, Atlanta: *City of Dreams, Volume II of Atlanta's Official Bid for the 1996 Olympic Games*, Authorized Commemorative Edition, 1990, Atlanta: Peachtree Publishers, p. 49.

25. This federal government agency was set up in 1865 to mediate the transition between slavery and freedom for the South's newly emancipated African-American population.

26. Clarke, 1881.

27. Garrett, Volume I, 1954, pp. 836, 908–9; WPA, 1942, pp. 162–3.

28. WPA, 1942, p. 162.

29. Ibid.

30. S. Hertzberg, *Strangers in the Gate City*, 1978, Philadelphia: Jewish Publication Society of America, p. 232.

31. Ibid.

32. These were the Atlanta University (1867), the Atlanta Baptist Seminary (1867, after 1913 known as Morehouse College), Spelman Seminary (1881, later Spelman College), Clark University (1877, changed to Clark College in 1940, later merged with Atlanta University to form Clark-Atlanta University, Morris Brown College (1885), Gammon Theological Seminary (1883).

33. D.L. Lewis, *W.E.B. DuBois: Biography of a Race*, 1993, New York: Henry Holt and Company, p. 214.

34. P. Gaston, *The New South Creed: A Study in Southern Mythmaking*, 1970, Baton Rouge: Louisiana State University Press.

35. E. De Leon, "The New South: What it is Doing and What it Wants," *Putnam's Magazine*, 1870, 15, p. 458.

36. D. White and T. Crimmins, "How Atlanta Grew: Cool Heads, Hot Air, and Hard Work," in A.M. Hamer, ed., *Urban Atlanta: Redefining the Role of the City*, 1980, Atlanta: Georgia State University, College of Business Administration, Research Monograph No. 84, p. 26.

37. I. Allen, *Atlanta From the Ashes*, 1928, Atlanta: Ruralist Press, p. 8.

38. White and Crimmins, 1980, p. 31.

39. J.S. Wilson, *Atlanta As It Is: Being a Sketch of Its Early Settlers*, 1871, New York: Little, Rennie and Co.

40. Clarke, 1881, p. 107, emphasis in the original.

41. Oglethorpe University opened in 1870, but was forced to close two years later. The Georgia Institute of Technology did not open until 1888, Emory University not until 1914.

42. Garrett, Volume I, 1954, pp. 908–9.

43. Chief among the latter was the purchase of the model cotton factory by a major New England textile manufacturer, Inman and Company of Boston, which renamed it the Exposition Mills. Although their interests were worldwide, the Inman family relocated to Atlanta, diversifying their holdings into banking, insurance, and real estate and quickly becoming part of the city's ruling elite. A short time later, industrialist Jacob Elsas opened the Fulton Bag and Cotton Mill just to the east of the city, building a mill town for his Appalachian workers that became known as Cabbagetown. Other industries making use of Georgia's other abundant resources – ceramics, furniture, chemicals – followed in the course of the 1880s. However, with few exceptions (principally that of Coca-Cola and, after 1909, the Ford Motor Company), the city's economy remained principally dedicated to trade and transportation rather than manufactures, especially after 1900.

44. Doyle, 1990, pp. 44–6.

45. W. Mixon, "Resistance to Industrialization," in C.R. Wilson and W. Ferris, eds, *Encyclopedia of Southern Culture*, 1989, Chapel Hill and London: University of North Carolina Press, p. 725.

46. Of these, the poets Frank Stanton and Thomas Holley Chivers, and humorist Charles Smith, writing as "Bill Arp," are perhaps the best known.

47. Appreciative Atlantans celebrated Harris and his work with not one but two holidays through the mid twentieth century – The Uncle Remus Festival in May and, following his death, a memorial service every December. His Queen Anne-style home in the southwestern suburb of West End, which he called the Wren's Nest, was deemed one of the city's premiere points of interest through the 1960s. With the West End now a largely African-American neighborhood, Harris's home now is neighbored by the Shrine of the Black Madonna and Islamic book stores.

48. P. Hales, *Silver Cities: The Photography of American Urbanization, 1839–1915*, 1984, Philadelphia: Temple University Press.

49. The tone of *The Gate City* was echoed in I. Avery, *City of Atlanta: A Descriptive Historical and Industrial Review of the Gateway City of the South, Being the World's Fair Series on Great American Cities*, 1892–3, Louisville, Ky.: Inter-State Publishing Co.

50. E.R. Carter, *The Black Side: A Partial History of the Business, Religious, and Educational Side of the Negro in Atlanta, GA, 1894*, Atlanta, reprinted in 1971 by Books for Libraries Press, Freeport, NY, p. 17.

51. Ibid., p. 16.

52. Unlike Daniel Burnham's neo-classical structures for the Chicago Exposition's "White City" two years earlier, lead architect Bradley Gilbert preferred the more stolid Romanesque style for five of the six main buildings he designed, "with the idea of showing stability." Quoted in Cotton States and International Exposition, *The Great Atlanta Exposition, 1895: Reached Via the Holly Springs Route*, 1895, St Louis: Cairo Short Line, Illinois Central Railroad, unpaginated. For other contemporary accounts of the event, see *Souvenir Album of the Cotton States and International Exposition, Atlanta, Ga., 1895*, 1895, Portland, Maine: Leighton and Frey Souvenir View Co.; and W.G. Cooper, "The Official History of the Exposition," *The Cotton States and International Exposition and South, Illustrated*, 1896, Atlanta.

53. R. Rydell, *All the World's a Fair*. Chicago: University of Chicago Press, 1984, p. 85.

54. Ibid.

55. Ibid., pp. 95–6.

56. Ibid., p. 95.

57. Garrett, *Atlanta and Environs: A Chronicle of Its People and Events*, Volume II, 1954, Athens: University of Georgia Press, pp. 329–31.

58. Allen, 1928.

59. Ibid., p. 39.

60. Hertzberg, 1978, p. 203.

61. W.E.B. DuBois, "The South," *Crisis*, 1917, April, Vol. 13, pp. 268–70.

62. See, for example, E.P. Ansley, *Atlanta: A Twentieth Century City*, 1903, Atlanta: Foot and Davies Co.

63. Quoted in M. Sindeman, "William-Oliver Building's Five Points Role," *Atlanta Business Chronicle* (hereafter *ABC*), 1 April 1991.

64. Although much of the building boom would take place after World War I, this spirit was well established by the turn of century. See, for example, "Atlanta by Night," *Harper's Weekly*, 10 October 1903; S.H. Kress, Co., *Souvenir of Atlanta and Vicinity*, 1904, Portland, Maine: L.H. Nelson Co.; and Anonymous, *Atlanta in a Cotton Bale*, 1904, Atlanta: John Miller Co. In the 1920s, the Atlanta Convention and Visitors Bureau began publishing its *Official Guide to the City of Atlanta*.

65. K. Luehrs and T. Crimmins, "In the Mind's Eye: The Downtown as Visual Metaphor for the Metropolis," *Atlanta Historical Journal*, 1982, summer/fall, pp. 177–97.

66. Atlanta Chamber of Commerce, *Report of the Forward Atlanta Commission, 1926–1929*, 1929, p. 54.

67. Ibid., pp. 86, 90.

68. See C.A. McMahan, *The People of Atlanta*, 1950, Athens: University of Georgia Press. As the Forward Atlanta campaign claimed, the city was first and foremost the domain of the open shop, with less than 7.5 percent of its non-agricultural workforce belonging to unions in 1930. Still, despite these meager numbers, which constituted fully one half of all union members in the state, organized labor had, in fact, enjoyed increasing strength in the first three decades of the twentieth century. As early as 1900, railroad and newspaper workers had unionized, along with many of the skilled trades. One of the city's largest and strongest unions was of the street railway workers, who had won recognition from the Georgia Power Company after a series of bitter strikes between 1916 and 1918. The textile industry proved especially resistant to unionization, however, and organized labor suffered a series of reverses in the late 1920s that significantly limited its ability to expand. For a more detailed account of labor in early-twentieth-century Atlanta see WPA, 1942, pp. 64–71, and D.L. Smith, *The New Deal in the Urban South*, 1988, Baton Rouge and London: Louisiana State University Press.

69. Ivan Allen, *The Atlanta Spirit: Altitude + Attitude*, 1948, Atlanta: Ivan Allen-Marshall Company.

70. Ibid. p. i.

71. *Report of the Forward Atlanta Commission*, 1929, p. 74.

72. The colonial analogy has often been noted by Southern writers. See J. Persky, "The South as 'Colony,'" in C.R. Wilson and W. Ferris, eds, *Encyclopedia of Southern Culture*, 1989, Chapel Hill and London: University of North Carolina Press, pp. 723–4.

73. Quoted in J.T. Farrell, ed., *H.L. Mencken Prejudices: A Selection*, 1958, New York: Random House, p. 73.

74. W.E.B. DuBois, *Darkwater: Voices from Within the Veil*, 1921, New York: Harcourt Brace, p. 21.

75. See J.T. Kirby, *Media-Made Dixie: The South in the American Imagination*, 1978, Baton Rouge and London: Louisiana State University Press.

76. McMahan, 1950.

77. D. White, "The Black Sides of Atlanta," *Atlanta Historical Journal*, 1982, summer/fall, pp. 210–13.

78. P. Miller, *Atlanta: Capital of the Modern South*, 1949, New York: Dutton, p. 31.

79. The most detailed, although non-analytic, description of the riot is to found in Garrett, Volume II, 1954, pp. 500–504.

80. WPA, 1942, p. 31.

81. E.J. Hughes, "The Negro's New Economic Life," *Fortune*, September 1956, pp. 248, 251.

82. See White, "The Black Sides of Atlanta," 1982; C. Stone, *Regime Politics: Governing Atlanta, 1945–1988*, 1989, Lawrence: University of Kansas Press.

83. See M. Warner, et al., *Community Building: The History of Atlanta University Neighborhoods*, 1978, Atlanta: Department of Budget and Planning.

84. See K.T. Jackson, *The Ku Klux Klan in the City, 1915–1930*, 1967, New York: Oxford University Press.

85. Hertzberg, 1978, p. 210.

86. Ibid.

87. Ibid.

88. See White and Crimmins, 1980, pp. 33–4, and C. Kuhn, et al., *Living Atlanta: An Oral History of the City, 1914–1948*, 1990, Atlanta, Athens, and London: The Atlanta Historical Society and University of Georgia Press.

89. Hornady, 1922, p. 340.

90. See Jackson, 1967, p. 37, 262n; White and Crimmins, 1980, p. 33; Kuhn, et al., 1990 pp. 313–16.

91. Smith, 1988, p. 27.

92. Ibid.; WPA, 1942, p. 68.

93. Smith, 1988, p. 42. For a comprehensive account of the Herndon case see J.H. Moore, "The Angelo Herndon Case, 1932–1937," *Phylon*, 1971, vol. 23, pp. 60–71; C.H. Martin, *The Angelo Herndon Case and Southern Justice*, 1975, Baton Rouge: Louisiana State University Press.

94. Ibid., p. 42.

95. The group, which included historian John Crowe Ransom and writer/critic Robert Penn Warren, presented their views in a volume by "twelve Southerners" called *I'll Take My Stand: The South and the Agrarian Tradition*, 1930, New York and London: Harper.

96. See Kirby, 1978.

97. Pioneer Citizens' Society of Atlanta, *Pioneer Citizens' History of Atlanta, 1833–1902*, 1902, Atlanta: Byrd Printing Co., p. 9. The authors opened their "Introductory" with this quote from George Washington.

98. Miller, 1949, p. 224.

99. In this regard, see especially, C.E. Cantrell, *Holy Stone Mountain*, 1975, Atlanta: privately printed, ms. in the collection of the Atlanta Historical Society.

100. R.W. Harllee, "Custodians of Imperishable Glory: the Stone Mountain Controversy," 1980; MA thesis, Emory University; Stone Mountain Confederate Monumental Association (SMCMA), *Custodians of Imperishable Glory*, 1925, Atlanta: SMCMA.

101. See SMCMA 1925; G.W. Johnson, *The Undefeated*, 1927, New York: Minton, Balch and Company.

102. Harllee, 1980, p. 19.

103. H. Kenimer, *The History of Stone Mountain (The Eighth Wonder of the World)*, 1993, Atlanta: Kenimer Publishing, p. 28.

104. Ibid., p. 30.

105. The term is actually that of Borglum's successor, Augustus Lukeman.

106. K. Mixon, *The Mountain of Controversy*, 1970, Atlanta: privately printed, ms. on file in collection of the Atlanta Historical Society.

107. Kenimer, 1993, p. 7.

108. A. Lukeman, "An American Monument to Surpass the Pyramids: An Article on the New Plans for the Stone Mountain Memorial," *The World's Work*, 1926, March.

109. Ibid., p. 3.

110. Ibid., p. 9.

111. See Harllee, 1980.

112. In 1956, Mills Lane, president of Citizens and Southern Bank and key member of the downtown power structure, was elected chairman of a group that envisioned developing the memorial park as a private undertaking. See Kenimer, 1993, pp. 13–15.

113. R. Harwell, "Introduction," *Gone With the Wind as Book and Film*, 1983, Columbia: University of South Carolina Press, p. xv.

114. White and Crimmins, 1980, p. 27.

115. D.A. Pyron, Preface to *Recasting: Gone With the Wind in American Culture*, 1983, Miami: University Presses of Florida, p. ix.
116. See especially, Pyron, "*Gone With the Wind* as History," and R. King, "The 'Simple Story's' Ideology: *Gone With the Wind* and the New South Creed," in Pyron, 1983, pp. 117–22 and pp. 167–83.
117. E. Granberry, "The Private Life of Margaret Mitchell," in Harwell, 1983, pp. 46–55.
118. Y. Gwin, *Yolanda's Atlanta: From the Historical to the Hysterical*, 1983, Atlanta: Peachtree Publishers, p. 17.
119. T. Cripps, "Winds of Change: *Gone With the Wind* and Racism as a National Issue," in Pyron, 1983, p. 140.
120. Mitchell noted in a letter that she would be "upset and mortified if Left Wingers like the book," and they did not disappoint her. Both the *Daily Worker* and the *Socialist Appeal* were effusive in their critique. Reaction from the NAACP and the mainstream black intelligentsia was considerably more muted. See Cripps, "Winds of Change," pp.43–4.
    On the other extreme, "Vanderbilt agrarian" John Crowe Ransom was alone among prominent "neo-Confederates" in criticizing the novel as "overly Southern" in its treatment of Reconstruction. See Pyron, "The Critical Setting," in Pyron, 1983, p. 6.
121. Granberry, in Harwell, 1983, p.53.
122. Gwin, 1983, p. 18.
123. Ibid.
124. Miller, 1949, p. 187. The post was first honored with a bronze plaque by the United Daughters of the Confederacy in 1919. The plaque was replaced by a less partisan one celebrating the 125th anniversary of the city in 1971.
125. Ibid.
126. Ibid., p. 36.
127. Gwin, 1983, p. 12.
128. See especially H. Martin, "Atlanta's Most Brilliant Event," *The Atlanta Georgian*, 16 December 1939.
129. R. Flamini, *Scarlett, Rhett, and a Cast of Thousands: The Filming of Gone With the Wind*, 1975, New York: Macmillan, p. 330.
130. Gwin, 1983, p. 19.
131. D. O'Briant, *Looking for Tara: The Gone With the Wind Guide to Margaret Mitchell's Atlanta*. 1994, Atlanta: Longstreet Press.
132. The battle to save the Dump is directly related to Olympic revitalization efforts and will be discussed further in Chapter 5.
133. O'Briant, 1994, p. 57.
134. *Atlanta Journal Constitution* (hereafter *AJC*), 10 October 1993.
135. Ibid.
136. *AJC*, 22 March 1995.
137. Miller, 1949, p. ix.
138. Ibid.
139. See H. Jenkins, *My Forty Years on the Force, 1932–1972*, 1973, Atlanta: Center for Research in Social Change, Emory University.
140. See Stone, 1989, pp. 25–50.
141. V. Hein, "The Image of 'A City Too Busy to Hate': Atlanta in the 1960s," *Phylon*, 1972 33/3, p. 205.
142. Ibid.
143. Ibid.
144. Ibid.
145. In H. Martin, *Atlanta and Environs: A Chronicle of Its People and Events*, Volume III, 1987, Athens and London: The University of Georgia Press, published in conjunction with the Atlanta Historical Society.
146. See V. Hein, "The Image of 'A City Too Busy to Hate'," pp. 205–21.
147. Ibid.
148. F. O'Connor, "The Artificial Nigger," in *The Complete Stories of Flannery O'Connor*, 1971, New York: Noonday Press p. 251.
149. J. Baldwin, *The Evidence of Things Not Seen*, 1985, New York: Holt, Rinehart, and Winston, p. 2.
150. P. Garland, "Atlanta: Black Mecca of the South," *Ebony*, 1971, August, pp. 152–7.
151. D. Lockerman, *Discover Atlanta*, 1969, Atlanta: Longstreet Press.
152. See, for example, C. Jamison, B. Galphin, N. Shavin, K. King, *Atlanta: A Celebration*, 1978, Atlanta:

Perry Communications; and C. Sibley and P. Beney, *Atlanta: A Brave and Beautiful City*, 1986, Atlanta: Peachtree Publishers.

153. Sibley and Beney, 1986, p. iii.

154. Jamison, et al., 1978, p. 5.

155. Lewis, 1993, p. 217.

156. Representative examples of this genre include W. Williford, *Peachtree Street, Atlanta*, 1962 [1973], New York: Ballantine Books, and C. Sibley, *Peachtree Street, U.S.A.* 1963, Garden City, NY: Doubleday.

157. C. Kuhn, "Introduction," in Kuhn, et al., 1990, p. xiii.

158. Ibid., p. xv.

159. D. White and T. Crimmins, "Urban Structure, Atlanta," *Atlanta Historical Journal*, 1982 (26), pp. 6–8. The article was an introductory essay for a special issue of the *Journal*, which featured the work of a number of scholars working in the new, critical vein. See also Kuhn, et al., 1990.

160. C. Patton, "Industries of the Mind," *AJC*, 18 July 1993.

161. The best-known example of Emory's academic head-hunting involved the luring of nearly the entire French Department – lock, stock, and graduate students – from the Johns Hopkins University.

162. J.S. Haydock, "Organized Participation in the Atlanta Hippie Community, 1971," unpublished MA thesis, Emory University.

163. Ibid. see also D. Beck, "The 14th Street Area," 1969, Community Council of Atlanta.

164. *Time*, 10 October 1969.

165. *AJC*, 19 July 1976.

166. As in other cities, gay gentrification was in part pioneered by small real estate developers who themselves were gay. Lower Midtown was also home to the highest concentration of gay bars and discos in the Atlanta area, as well as numerous cruising spots.

167. See for example, R. Hudspeth, *Living, Loving, Laughing, Dying, and Crying on Peachtree*, 1980, Atlanta: Peachtree Publishers.

168. *AJC*, 20 June 1995.

169. Stone, 1989, pp. 103–7.

170. I. Allen, Jr, with P. Hemphill, *Mayor: Notes From the Sixties*, 1971, New York: Simon & Schuster.

171. However, due to the age distribution of the population, whites still held a slim electoral majority. See Stone, 1989, p. 77.

172. See G. Orfield and C. Ashkinaze, *The Closing Door: Conservative Policy and Black Opportunity*, 1991, Chicago: University of Chicago Press; B. Holmes, *The Status of Black Atlanta, 1993, 1994*, 1994, 1995, Atlanta: Southern Center for Studies in Public Policy, Clark-Atlanta University.

173. See Holmes, 1994.

174. For an in-depth account of Young's mayoralty, see Stone, 1989, pp. 109–59.

175. S. Carlson, "Spatial Aspects of Homicides in the City of Atlanta," MA thesis, Georgia State University, 1978, p. 3.

176. Baldwin, 1985, p. 1.

177. Ibid.

178. M. Curriden, "The Case that Shook Atlanta Rises Again," *The National Law Journal*, 17 January 1994, 16/20, p. 8.

179. Since Atlanta's initial claim to internationality in the early 1970s, an Institute for the Study of International Cities has opened up for business in Montreal and promulgated a list of thirteen main characteristics of an international city:

   1. The city has a geographically international exposure

   2. It is the recipient of capital, manpower, and services from abroad and is engaged in trade

   3. It hosts foreign and/or international institutions and their representatives

   4. Its "local" firms have a presence abroad

   5. It has direct transportation links to foreign countries

   6. It is significantly engaged in social communications with foreign countries

   7. It has an outward-looking support services network (convention facilities, hotels, etc.)

   8. Its mass media have an international presence/audience abroad

   9. It hosts, regularly, major international events

 10. It is the locus of national/regional/local institutions of international scope (international associations, universities, museums, etc.)

 11. Its institutions have agreements of cooperation with foreign or international institutions (sister-cities agreements)

12. Its local government has the ability to conduct city paradiplomacy
13. Its population has an international composition.
180. For three different discussions of these transformations see M. Castells, *The Informational City*, 1989, London: Basil Blackwell; D. Harvey, *The Condition of Post-Modernity*, 1989, London: Basil Blackwell; and S. Sassen, *The Global City*, 1991, Princeton, NJ: Princeton University Press.
181. Quoted in *AJC*, 10 June 1995.
182. L. Hepburn, "Politics and Government," in L. Hepburn, ed., *Contemporary Georgia*, 1987, Athens: Carl Vinson Institute of Government, University of Georgia, p. 154.
183. CNN International, "Key Facts," 1994.
184. Cable News Network, 1990.
185. Long frustrated in his efforts to acquire one of the three major broadcast networks (in part due to the opposition of Time-Warner and TeleCommunications Inc., both of which controlled key chunks of TBS stock), Turner (along with TCI's John Malone) instead negotiated hard for a controlling interest in Time-Warner.
186. See Thomas, 1989.
187. *AJC*, 23 May 1995.
188. *AJC*, 20 June 1995.

2. ONE, TWO, MANY ATLANTAS

1. Anonymous, *Atlanta in a Cotton Bale*, 1904, Atlanta: John Miller Co., unpaginated.
2. A. Downs, *Key Aspects of the Future of the Atlanta Region*, 1994, Washington DC: The Urban Land Institute, p. 18.
3. V. Coppola, "Atlantans," in M.E. Zenfell, ed., *Insight Guides: Atlanta*, 1995, New York: Houghton Mifflin, p. 68.
4. The city of Atlanta's current population is a matter of dispute. The figure of 424,300 is an estimate of the Atlanta Regional Commission as reported in the *Atlanta Constitution* on 24 August 1995. The figure is based not on actual counts of people, but on social and economic formulas derived from such things as housing starts and commercial activity. The 1990 census put the city's population at 394,000, a figure which the city contested as a considerable undercount. In December 1990, the city of Atlanta filed suit challenging the accuracy of the census (*City of Atlanta, et al. v. Mosbacher, et al.*) and joined in another suit filed by a number of other cities, (*City of New York, et al. v. United States Department of Commerce*, No. 88CIV3474 (E.D.N.Y.)). Until the litigation is resolved, it is official city policy to use the estimated population figure of 437,300. See City of Atlanta, Bureau of Planning and Development, Department of Planning, *1993 Comprehensive Development Plan*, 1992. The ARC, by contrast, estimated the city's 1990 population at 415,200, down from 424,922 in 1980.
5. In 1994, the population of the 20-county metro area was estimated at 3,284,979, see *Georgia Trend*, 1995, April, 10/8, p. 24. At least, 75,000 people were expected to move into the region during 1995.
6. This figure is based on the population estimates of the Atlanta Regional Commission. Using these figures, the city of Atlanta accounted for only 16 percent of the ARC region's population in 1990, but only 12.5 percent of the total MSA population by 1995. According to the city's estimates, however, it enjoyed an 18 percent share of the metro area population in 1990. See City of Atlanta, Bureau of Planning, 1992, p. 6.
7. Unlike Atlanta, both Memphis and Charlotte have been successful in annexing their expanding unincorporated suburban fringes.
8. T. Hartshorn and K. Ihlanfeldt, *The Dynamics of Change: An Analysis of Growth in Metropolitan Atlanta Over the Past Two Decades*, 1993, Atlanta: Research Atlanta, Inc., Policy Research Center, Georgia State University.
9. Ibid., pp. 57–67.
10. Downs, 1994, p. 3.
11. Ibid. see also Hartshorn and Ihlanfeldt, 1993.
12. *Atlanta Journal Constitution* (hereafter *AJC*), 24 August 1995.
13. *Atlanta Business Chronicle* (hereafter *ABC*), 1 January 1993.
14. *AJC*, 29 October 1995.
15. Hartshorn and Ihlanfeldt, 1993, p. 6.
16. The term refers to urban development that apparently "just happened" owing to "market forces, chance, and countless uncoordinated decision." Downs, 1994, p. 8.

17. Quoted in I. Gournay, "Urbanism and Architecture in Atlanta, A Personal View," in G.W. Sams, ed., *AIA Guide to the Architecture of Atlanta*, 1993, Athens and London: University of Georgia Press, p. xxv.

18. P. Lewis, "The Galactic Metropolis," in R.H. Platt and G. Macinko, eds, *Beyond the Urban Fringe*, 1983, Minneapolis: University of Minnesota Press, p. 35.

19. Power centers are large shopping complexes housing one to several mammoth low-cost retailers such as Home Depot and Wal-mart.

20. D. Thomas, *Atlanta: A City For the World*, 1989, Northridge, California: Windsor Publications, p. 94.

21. B. Braden and P. Hagan, *A Dream Takes Flight: Hartsfield International Airport and Aviation in Atlanta*, 1989, Atlanta, Athens, and London: The Atlanta Historical Society and University of Georgia Press, p. 109.

22. The 1948 terminal was constructed out of a large war surplus hangar formerly used by the Army Air Force. Inside it boasted the world's longest ticket counter and large color murals featuring scenes from Joel Chandler Harris's *Uncle Remus: His Songs and Sayings*. The airport's restaurant featured an elderly black man who sat by the doorway and recited anecdotes from the Uncle Remus tales. See Ibid., pp. 115–18.

23. For a description of the wrangling involved in the construction of the super-airport see Ibid., pp. 148–94.

24. Ibid.

25. See, for example, W. Schivelbusch, *The Railway Journey: The Industrialization of Time and Space*, 1986, Berkeley: University of California Press; and S. Kern, *The Culture of Time and Space, 1880–1918*, Cambridge, Mass.: Harvard University Press.

26. See L. Mumford, *Technics and Civilization*, 1963, New York: Harcourt, Brace, and World.

27. The term is from H.L. Preston, *Automobile Age Atlanta: The Making of a Southern Metropolis*, 1979, Athens: University of Georgia Press.

28. H.L. Mencken, "The Sahara of the Bozart," in J.T. Farrell, ed., *H.L. Mencken Prejudices: A Selection*, 1958, New York: Random House.

29. M. Sorkin, "Introduction," *Variations on A Theme Park: The New American City and the End of Public Space*, 1992, New York: Hill and Wang, p. xi.

30. See R. Bayor, "Roads to Racial Segregation," *Journal of Urban History*, 1988, 15/1, pp. 3–21.

31. See D.M. Smith, *Inequality in an American City: Atlanta, Georgia, 1960–1970*, 1981, London: Department of Geography, Queen Mary College, University of London, Occasional Paper No. 17.

32. Hartshorn and Ihlanfeldt, 1993, p. 19–27.

33. US Bureau of the Census, *1990 Census of Population and Housing*.

34. See G. Orfield and C. Ashkinaze, *The Closing Door: Conservative Policy and Black Opportunity*, 1991, Chicago; University of Chicago Press.

35. Hartshorn and Ihlanfeldt, 1993, p. 41.

36. *AJC*, 14 December 1995.

37. *AJC*, 27 December 1995.

38. S. Hertzberg, *Strangers in the Gate City*, 1978, Philadelphia: Jewish Publication Society of America, p. 230.

39. A small number of German Jews actually began arriving in the late 1840s. See ibid.

40. Hertzberg, 1978; see also, Work Projects Administration, *Atlanta: Metropolis of the New South*, 1942, p. 4.

41. C.A. McMahan, *The People of Atlanta*, 1950, Athens: University of Georgia Press, p. 51.

42. C. Hill, "Adaptation in Public and Private Behavior of Ethnic Groups in an American Urban Setting," *Urban Anthropology*, 1975, 4/4, p. 336.

43. J. Saindon, et al., *Multi-Purpose Center Feasibility Study: A Study of the Feasibility of a Centralized Service Center for Refugees and Immigrants in Metropolitan Atlanta*, 1992, Atlanta: Center for Applied Research in Anthropology, Georgia State University, p. 8.

44. Ibid.

45. Ibid.

46. *AJC*, 27 July 1994.

47. US Census of Population and Housing, 1990.

48. Ibid. Four percent of immigrants came from places "not reported."

49. For a good example of this attitude, see Thomas, 1989.

50. Saindon, 1992.

51. Source: Center for Applied Research in Anthropology, Georgia State University, 1995.

52. Ibid.

53. Moreland, also known as "Tom More Asphalt," was the commissioner of the Georgia Department of Transportation in the 1960s and presided over the largest road-building program in the state's history.
54. S. Zukin, *Landscapes of Power*, 1992, Berkeley: University of California Press.
55. This is one of Atlanta's oldest suburban developments, originally planned by developer Joel Hurt in the 1890s, but completed by financier and textile magnate Samuel Inman in the early 1990s.
56. *AJC*, 17 September 1995.
57. Ibid.
58. *AJC*, 15 October 1995.
59. Ibid.
60. *AJC*, 12 November 1995.
61. Hartshorn and Ihlanfeldt, 1993.
62. Quoted in the *New York Times,* 1 August 1994.
63. Ibid.
64. Ibid.
65. T. Barry, "Edge Cities," *Georgia Trend*, February 1995, p. 24.
66. *AJC*, 20 August 1995.
67. *AJC,* 29 July 1994.
68. Quoted in *New York Times*, 1 August 1994.
69. Ibid.
70. Ibid.
71. By contrast, a recent survey by MARTA found that almost three-quarters of those who rode the CCT buses from Atlanta were traveling to Cobb to work. *AJC*, 18 August 1995.
72. *AJC*, 29 July 1994.
73. *Creative Loafing*, 6 May 1995.
74. *AJC*, 29 July 1994.
75. Barry, "Edge Cities," p. 24.
76. *AJC,* 13 November 1994.
77. *AJC*, 24 August 1995.
78. Hartshorn and Ihlanfeldt, 1993, p. 14.
79. *AJC*, 11 December 1993.
80. *AJC,* 13 November 1994.
81. Ibid.
82. *AJC,* 26 October 1995.
83. *AJC* 29 October 1995.
84. Thomas, 1989.
85. Hartshorn and Ihlanfeldt, 1993, p. 42.
86. Source: Atlanta Regional Commission, 1993.
87. J. Grimes, "Southern Crescent Forging Forward – With a Difference," *Georgia Trend*, February 1995, p. 57.
88. Source: Center for Applied Research in Anthropology, Georgia State University, 1995.
89. *AJC*, 4 April 1993.
90. Ibid.
91. *AJC*, 20 July 1995.
92. Blazer is a long-standing member of the Forum, the current incarnation of Werner Erhard's EST program. Until a 1989 lawsuit by eight former employees ended the practice, Blazer required that all of his workers attend Forum's quasi-religious seminars at their own expense. See *Wall Street Journal*, 31 May 1989.
93. Quoted in T. Anderson and M. Witsaman, "Ethnicity as Commodity: The Myth of the DeKalb Farmers' Market," unpublished ms.
94. Ibid.
95. Ibid., p. 13.
96. Ibid.
97. J. Yang, "Mallticulturalism," *Village Voice*, 20 September 1994, p. 27; see also, DeKalb Chamber of Commerce, "A Preliminary Feasibility Study for the Development of an International Village in DeKalb County," n.d.
98. Ibid.
99. The term was coined by Margaret Crawford, see M. Crawford, "The World in a Shopping Mall," in

M. Sorkin, ed., *Variations on a Theme Park*, 1992, New York: Hill and Wang, pp. 3–30.

100. Yang, 1993.
101. Ibid., p. 31.
102. See, for example, the collection of essays in Sorkin, 1992; as well as S. Zukin, *Landscapes of Power: From Detroit to Disneyworld*, 1992, Berkeley: University of California Press; and S. Watson and K. Gibson, *Postmodern Cities and Spaces*, 1995, Oxford and Cambridge, Mass.: Basil Blackwell.
103. Zukin, 1992.
104. M. Castells, *The Informational City*, 1989, Oxford and Cambridge, Mass.: Basil Blackwell.
105. H. Preston, *Automobile Age Atlanta*, 1979, Athens: University of Georgia Press, pp. 50–51.
106. *Creative Loafing*, 22 April 1995.
107. Ibid., p 23.
108. E.J. Hughes, "The Negro's New Economic Life," *Fortune*, September 1956, pp. 248, 251.
109. F. Garrett, *Atlanta and Environs: A Chronicle of Its People and Events,* Volume II, 1954, Athens: University of Georgia Press, p. 820.
110. Atlanta City Code, Section 6–3012.
111. The term is used by the Claritas marketing firm to describe upwardly mobile African-American households.
112. City of Atlanta Bureau of Planning and Development, *City Trends 1991*, 1992.
113. Ibid.
114. Ibid.
115. *AJC,* 30 June 1994.
116. *AJC,* 17 September 1992.
117. *AJC,* 16 February 1995.
118. *AJC,* 20 May 1993.
119. Ibid.
120. L. Porter, "From Bedroom Community to Suburban Business Center: a Geographical Analysis of the Buckhead Community in Atlanta, 1920–1988, 1989," unpublished MA thesis, Georgia State University, p. 51.
121. F. Brown and B. Sehlinger, *The Unofficial Guide to Atlanta*, 1994, New York: Prentice Hall Travel, p. 26.
122. Porter, 1989, p. 51.
123. Ibid.
124. P. Williams and N. Smith, "From 'Renaissance' to Restructuring: The Dynamics of Contemporary Urban Redevelopment," in N. Smith and P. Williams, *Gentrification of the City*, 1986, Boston: Allen & Unwin, pp. 204–24.
125. Atlanta Urban Design Commission, *Atlanta's Lasting Landmarks*, 1987, p. 110.
126. See B. Cutler, "Coming Home to Downtown," *Historic Preservation*, 1984, 36/1, pp. 40–45; *AJC,* 19 May 1993, 3 November 1994, 7 May 1995.
127. The King site and Sweet Auburn neighborhood are overlapped by a complex array of local and federal designations.
128. *AJC,* 13 November 1993.
129. *AJC,* 21 January 1995.
130. *AJC,* 11 August 1994.
131. *AJC,* 21 January 1995.
132. *Creative Loafing*, 14 January 1995.
133. Quoted in ibid.
134. *AJC,* 15 January 1995.
135. *AJC,* 1 February 1995, 7 February 1995.
136. *Creative Loafing*, 12 September 1992.
137. *AJC,* 24 April 1994. The account was written by the chairwoman of Freaknik '83.
138. *AJC,* 25, 26 April 1994.
139. *AJC,* 19 April 1995.
140. *AJC,* 18 May 1995.
141. *AJC,* 25 April 1995, 29 April 1995.
142. *AJC,* 29 September 1995.

3. CITY OF HYPE, 1837–1975

1. Quoted in the *Atlanta Georgian*, 19 April 1924.
2. B. Dunlop, "Atlanta: An Accidental City With a Laissez Faire Approach to Planning," *AIA Journal*, Special Convention Issue: *Learning From Atlanta*, 1975, April, pp. 53–5.
3. T. Crimmins, "The Atlanta Palimpsest," *Atlanta Historical Journal*, 1982, vol. 26, pp. 21–5.
4. T.H. Martin, *Atlanta and Its Builders: A Comprehensive History of the Gate City of the South*, 1902, Atlanta; see also Crimmins, 1982.
5. F. Garrett, *Atlanta and Environs: A Chronicle of Its People and Events*, Volume I, 1954, Athens: University of Georgia Press, p. 809.
6. D. Klima, "Breaking Out: Streetcars and Suburban Development, 1872–1900," *Atlanta Historical Journal*, 1982, vol. 26, p. 68.
7. Ibid., pp. 68–70.
8. Ibid., pp. 79–80.
9. Atlanta Preservation Center, Piedmont Park Walking Tour.
10. Ibid.
11. Quoted in F. Garrett, *Atlanta and Environs: A Chronicle of Its People and Events*, Volume II, 1954, Athens: University of Georgia Press, p. 180.
12. S. Hertzberg, *Strangers in the Gate City*, 1978, Philadelphia: Jewish Publication Society of America.
13. Ibid.
14. H. Preston, *Automobile Age Atlanta*, 1979, Athens: University of Georgia Press, p. 84–5.
15. See E. Lyon, "Business Buildings in Atlanta: A Study in Urban Growth and Form," 1971, unpublished PhD dissertation, Emory University; and E. Lyon, "Frederick Law Olmsted and Joel Hurt: Planning for Atlanta," in D.F. White and V.A. Kramer, eds, *Olmsted South: Old South Critic/New South Planner*, 1979, Westport: Greenwood Press.
16. *Atlanta Journal Magazine*, 10 October, 1929.
17. K. Luehrs and T. Crimmins, "In the Mind's Eye: The Downtown as Visual Metaphor for the Metropolis," *Atlanta Historical Journal*, 1982, vol. 26, p. 188.
18. See Preston, 1979, pp. 74–108.
19. Ibid., p. 106.
20. A. DeRosa Byrne and D.F. White, "Atlanta University's 'Northeast Lot': Community Building for Black Atlanta's 'Talented Tenth,'" *Atlanta Historical Journal*, 1982, vol. 26, pp. 155–75.
21. Preston, 1979, p. 105; see also A. Meier and D. Lewis, "History of the Negro Upper Class in Atlanta, Georgia, 1890–1958," *Journal of Negro Education*, 1959, vol. 59.
22. However, the area around the Union Depot had been briefly used as a public open space in the 1850s. See Garrett, 1954, Volume I.
23. B. Brownell, "The Commercial-Civic Elite and City Planning in Atlanta, Memphis, and New Orleans in the 1920s," *Journal of Southern History*, 1971, vol. 41, pp. 339–68.
24. Ibid.; see also R. Bayor, "Roads to Racial Segregation: Atlanta in the Twentieth Century," *Journal of Urban History*, 1988, 15/1, pp. 3–21.
25. Bayor, 1988, pp. 14–18; see also G. Orfield and C. Ashkinaze, *The Closing Door*, 1991, Chicago: University of Chicago Press, pp. 69–102.
26. See Garrett, Volume II, pp. 700–706.
27. Preston, 1979, pp. 98–102.
28. Brownell, 1971; Preston, 1979, p. 149.
29. J. Beeler, *Report to the City of Atlanta on a Plan For Local Transportation*, 1924, Atlanta: Foot and Davies, Inc.
30. Preston, 1979, pp. 62–4.
31. Palmer documented his crusade in *Adventures of a Slum Fighter*, 1955, Atlanta: Tupper and Low, just as renewed plans for massive slum clearance were being discussed.
32. This gives municipal governments the power to condemn private property in the "public interest." It was extensively used during urban renewal to assemble large parcels of land, which would then be sold at a deeply discounted or "written-down" cost to private developers.
33. See C. Stone, *Regime Politics*, 1989, Lawrence: University of Kansas Press, pp. 16–17.
34. See Brownell, 1971.
35. Fred Powledge, "Atlanta Begins to Sense the Loss of Its Seeming Immunity to Urban Problems," *AIA Journal*, 1975, vol. 34, p. 46.

36. See B. Frieden and L. Sagalyn, *Downtown, Inc. How America Rebuilds Cities*, 1989, Cambridge, Mass.: MIT Press; and D. Harvey, "From Managerialism to Entrepreneurialism: The Transformation of Urban Governance in Late Capitalism," *Geografiska Annaler*, 1989, vol. 71, pp. 3–17.

37. See H.W. Lochner and Company and DeLeuw Cather Co., *Highway and Transportation Plan for Atlanta, Georgia*, January 1946.

38. Stone, 1989, pp. 34–42.

39. See Bayor, 1988, pp. 8–9.

40. Metropolitan Planning Commission, *Up Ahead: A Regional Land Use Plan for Metropolitan Atlanta*, 1952, Atlanta.

41. Ibid., p. 5.

42. This last option was actually proposed two years after the 1954 study, although by the original plan's authors. See H. Martin, *Atlanta and Environs: A Chronicle of Its People and Events*, Volume III, 1987, Atlanta, Athens, and London: The Atlanta Historical Society and University of Georgia Press, pp. 241–242.

43. Metropolitan Planning Commission, 1952, p. i.

44. Metropolitan Planning Commission, 1954, p. 32.

45. Jane Jacobs, *The Death and Life of Great American Cities*, 1961, New York: Doubleday.

46. The term is Mike Davis's. See "The Infinite Game: Redeveloping Downtown L.A.," in D. Ghirardo, ed., *Out of Site: A Social Criticism of Architecture*, 1991, Seattle: Bay Press, p. 86.

47. By contrast, even with white flight, the population of the city of Atlanta alone was over 495,000 in 1970, in a total metro population of some 1.6 million. By 1980, the city population had decreased to some 425,000, while the metro population had increased to slightly more than 2.2 million. Source: *US Census of Population and Housing 1980, 1990*.

48. Martin, 1987, p. 316.

49. Ibid.

50. F. Hunter, *Community Power Structure: A Study of Decision Makers*, 1953, Chapel Hill: University of North Carolina Press.

51. Atlanta Chamber of Commerce, "Metropolitan Atlanta – The First Million," cited in Martin, 1987, p. 317.

52. C. Stone, *Economic Growth and Neighborhood Discontent*, 1976, Chapel Hill: University of North Carolina Press, p. 226; T. Hartshorn, et al., *Metropolis in Georgia: Atlanta's Rise as a Major Transaction Center*, 1976, Cambridge, Mass.: Ballinger Publishing Co., p. 44.

53. Stone, 1989, pp. 60–73.

54. Ibid., p. 63.

55. Indeed, a nationwide survey conducted in 1992 found that the Atlanta Braves baseball team was far and away the most characteristic feature associated with the city, ahead of even the iconic representation in *Gone With the Wind*. See Chapter 1 for more on the shifting mythologization of Atlanta.

56. See Stone, 1976.

57. Ibid.

58. "Written-down land" refers to property that has been assembled by a public redevelopment agency (out of a series of smaller, privately owned parcels) and resold to private developers at a below market value cost.

59. See C. Stone, "Partnership New South Style: Central Atlanta Progress," *Proceedings, The Academy of Political Science*, 1986, 36/2, pp. 100–110.

60. In Stone, 1989, p. 10.

61. R. Hebert, *Highways to Nowhere: The Politics of City Transportation*, 1972, Indianapolis: Bobbs-Merrill.

62. American Institute of Planners, *Urban Design: Atlanta*, 1977, Atlanta: PRM Law Publishers, p. 29.

63. C. Kuhn, et al., *Living Atlanta: An Oral History of the City, 1914–1948*, 1990, Atlanta and Athens: Atlanta Historical Society and the University of Georgia Press, p. 301.

64. L. Ford, *Cities and Buildings*, 1993, Baltimore: The Johns Hopkins University Press.

65. *National Real Estate Investor*, 1975–1978, Central Atlanta Progress, *Central Area Study*, 1971.

66. Central Atlanta Progress, *Central Area Study*, 1971.

67. G. Sams, *AIA Guide to the Architecture of Atlanta*, 1993, Athens and London: University of Georgia Press, pp. 14–15

68. F. Jameson, "Postmodernism, or the Cultural Logic of Late Capitalism," *New Left Review*, 1984, 146, pp. 53–92.

69. J. Portman and J. Barnett, *The Architect as Developer*, 1976, New York: McGraw Hill, p. 25. For a

comprehensive critique of Portman's design philosophy, see E.W. Henry, Jr, "Portman, Architect and Entrepreneur: The Opportunities, Advantages, and Disadvantages of His Design and Development Procedures," 1985, unpublished PhD dissertation, University of Pennsylvania School of Architecture.

70. R.F. Kenzie, J.F. Rinehart, H. Dessau Bunn, *Cain Street Station Area Development Plan*, 1975, Atlanta: Bureau of Planning, p. 104.

71. D. White and T. Crimmins, "How Atlanta Grew," in A.M. Hamer, ed., *Urban Atlanta: Redefining the Role of the City*, 1980, Atlanta: College of Business Administration, Georgia State University, Research Monograph No. 84, p. 37.

72. Trevor Boddy, "Underground and Overhead: Building the Analogous City," in M. Sorkin, ed., *Variations on a Theme Park*, 1992, New York: Hill and Wang, pp. 123–53.

73. *The Economist*, 11 March 1978.

74. The Krofft brothers were creators of that *ur*-Barney the Dinosaur, H&R Puffenstuff.

75. *Business Week*, 27 February 1978, pp. 33–4.

76. T. Barry, "Thomas G. Cousins: Georgia's Most Respected CEO of 1995," *Georgia Trend*, June 1995, vol. 10/10, pp. 23–7.

77. The term is Ed Soja's; see his "It All Comes Together in Los Angeles," in *Postmodern Geographies*, 1989, London: Verso.

78. *National Real Estate Investor*, May 1978.

79. American Institute of Planners – Georgia Section, *Urban Design Atlanta*, 1977, Atlanta: PRM Law Publishers, pp. 14–16.

80. A. Downs, *Key Aspects of the Future of the Atlanta Region*, 1994, Washington DC: Urban Land Institute, p. 8.

81. CAP, *Central Area Study*, 1971.

82. Ibid., p. 8.

83. Ibid., p. 54.

84. Ibid., p. 57.

85. Stone, 1989, p. 80.

86. Ibid.

87. Ibid., pp. 77–98.

88. Powledge, 1975, pp. 46–7; see also *Creative Loafing*, 16 December 1995.

89. Atlanta Institute of Planners – Georgia Section, 1977.

4. PLUGGING THE WHOLE IN THE CENTER, 1975–95

1. Anonymous saying from the nineteenth century.

2. John Huey, managing editor of *Fortune* magazine, quoted in *Atlanta Journal Constitution* (hereafter *AJC*), 10 June 1995.

3. *AJC*, 9 October 1994.

4. T. Hartshorn and K. Ihlanfeldt, *The Dynamics of Change: An Analysis of Growth in Metropolitan Atlanta Over the Past Two Decades*, 1993, Atlanta: Research Atlanta, Inc., Policy Research Center, Georgia State University, p. 57.

5. See L. Ford, *Cities and Buildings: Skyscrapers, Skid Rows, and Suburbs*, 1994, Baltimore: The Johns Hopkins University Press, p. 65.

6. See G. McDonogh, "The Geography of Emptiness," in R. Rotenberg and G. McDonogh, eds., *Cultural Meanings of Urban Space*, 1994, South Hadley, Mass.: Bergin and Garvey.

7. Although Atlanta had earned the dubious distinction of being the most violent city in the nation in 1993 (see *AJC*, 3 October 1993), much of the violent crime was concentrated in a swathe of neighborhoods south and west of downtown. See *AJC*, 6 September 1992, 13 November 1994, 16 November 1994.

8. Atlanta's lack of opposition to the Games during the bid process contrasts markedly with the experiences of two of its principal rivals, Toronto and Sydney, and it is said greatly strengthened the city's favorable impression in the eyes of the International Olympic Committee. For a more detailed account of this, see Chapter 5, this volume.

9. C. Stone, *Regime Politics: Governing Atlanta, 1946–1988*, 1989, Lawrence: University of Kansas Press.

10. J. Logan and H. Molotch, *Urban Fortunes*, 1987, Berkeley: University of California Press.

11. See G. Orfield and C. Ashkinaze, *The Closing Door: Conservative Policy and Black Opportunity*, 1991, Chicago: University of Chicago Press; Hartshorn and Ihlanfeldt, 1993; B. Holmes, *The Status of Black*

Atlanta, 1994, Atlanta: The Southern Center for Studies in Public Policy, Clark-Atlanta University.

12. Until the early 1990s, the growth of Atlanta-based banks was limited by the lack of state-wide banking possibilities. See Hartshorn and Ihlanfeldt, 1993, p. 57.

13. In an op-ed piece in the *AJC*, GSU president Carl Patton defined these industries as "businesses that produce information, concepts, and images" such as the arts, communications and technology, and educational institutions and related agencies, such as accrediting bodies, academic associations, and foundations. See *AJC*, 18 July 1993.

14. N. Peagram, "Why the Foreigners Flock in to Atlanta," *Euromoney*, 1984, December, pp. 115–16.

15. Ibid.

16. See D. Thomas, *Atlanta, A City For the World*, Northridge, Cal.: Windsor Publications, 1989, p. 162.

17. See Stone, 1989, pp. 109–59.

18. *National Real Estate Investor*, 1987, vol. 29, November, p. 32.

19. Ibid., and *National Real Estate Investor*, 1989, vol. 31.

20. American Institute of Planners – Georgia Section, *Urban Design: Atlanta*, 1977, Atlanta: PRM Law Publishers, pp. 18–20.

21. E. Sams, ed., *AIA Guide to the Architecture of Atlanta*, 1992, Athens: University of Georgia Press.

22. *AJC*, 26 October 1978.

23. *Sunday Times Observer*, 27 May 1962.

24. *Business Week*, 27 February 1978.

25. Stone, 1989, p. 130.

26. Quoted in ibid., p 130.

27. *AJC*, 21 September 1991.

28. *AJC*, 10 July 1993.

29. *The Economist*, 11 March 1978.

30. *AJC*, 21 September 1991.

31. *AJC*, 10 July 1993.

32. *AJC*, 12 September 1993.

33. Stone, 1989, pp. 120–22, 138.

34. Central Atlanta Progress, *Report of the Upper Downtown Task Force*, 1983.

35. Atlanta City Council, *Report of the South CBD Housing Task Force*, 1986.

36. Central Atlanta Progress and the Bureau of Planning, *Transit Area Housing. Mixed-Use Study*, 1985.

37. City of Atlanta Art Program, "Atlanta City Detention Center," n.d., mimeo.

38. C. Boyer, *Dreaming the Rational City*, 1983, Cambridge, Mass.: MIT Press.

39. Central Atlanta Progress, *International Boulevard Design Competition*, 1985.

40. See for example, ACOG, *Atlanta: City of Dreams*, 1992, pp. 71–2.

41. Central Atlanta Progress, *Central Area Study II*, "A Cooperative Effort of the City of Atlanta, Central Atlanta Progress, and Fulton County," 1988, p. 16.

42. Ibid.

43. For an unpacking of Marx's notion, see D. Harvey, "Money, Time, Space, and the City," in *Consciousness and the Urban Experience*, 1985, Baltimore: The Johns Hopkins University Press, pp. 1–35.

44. This recommendation was not included in the general CAS-II Final Report released in February 1988, but is to be found in the Executive Summary of the Public Safety Task Force Final Report, July 1987, pp. 5–7, Appendix III.

45. *AJC*, 23 October 1994.

46. R. Collins, E. Waters, and A. Dobson, "Atlanta," in *America's Downtowns: Growth, Politics, and Preservation*, 1991, Washington DC: Preservation Press, p. 29.

47. Ibid.

48. To be determined by a three-member economic review panel consisting of one member appointed by the UDC, one by the property owner, and the third by the first two appointees. Their decision could be over-ruled by a three-fourths majority of the UDC.

49. Ibid.

50. Stone, 1989, p. 139.

51. *AJC*, 5 July 1995.

52. *AJC*, 28 April 1994.

53. *AJC*, 13 May, 1995.

54. *AJC*, 25 May 1994.

55. Ibid.

56. Haddow and Company, *Revitalization Plan for the Fairlie-Poplar District, Atlanta, Georgia*, 1991, Atlanta, p. 1A.

57. *AJC*, 28 April 1994.

58. *AJC*, 25 May 1994.

59. *AJC*, 9 June 1994.

60. *Atlanta Business Chronicle* (hereafter *ABC*), 30 June–6 July 1995.

61. *AJC*, 13 July 1995.

62. Robert and Company, *Fairlie-Poplar Planning Report*, 1978, Atlanta, p. 36.

63. Ibid.

64. *AJC*, 27 March 1980.

65. *AJC*, 26 March 1989.

66. Haddow and Co., 1991, p. 4.

67. Ibid.

68. *AJC*, 26 March 1989.

69. Haddow and Co., 1991, p. 2.

70. For an analysis of SoHo, see S. Zukin, *Loft Living: Culture and Capital in Urban Change*, 1982, Baltimore: The Johns Hopkins University Press. For the Lower East Side, see Neil Smith, "Gentrification, the Frontier, and the Restructuring of Urban Space," in N. Smith and P. Williams, *Gentrification of the City*, 1986, Boston: Allen & Unwin, pp. 15–34; and "New City, New Frontier: The Lower East Side as Wild, Wild West," in M. Sorkin, ed., *Variations on a Theme Park*, 1992, New York: Hill and Wang, pp. 61–93.

71. Haddow and Co., 1991, p. 17.

72. *Creative Loafing*, 19 November 1994.

73. Although he was not an employee of the company, much of Campbell's wealth came from the ownership of vast blocks of Coca-Cola stock.

74. Fairlie-Poplar Implementation Task Force, *Fairlie-Poplar, The Heart of Atlanta: Design Guidelines*, 1994.

75. Arthur Anderson Real Estate Advisory Services Group, *Downtown Atlanta Housing Study*, Spring 1995.

76. *AJC*, 8 October 1995.

77. *AJC*, 16 October 1994.

78. *AJC*, 13 January 1994.

79. *AJC*, 16 October 1994.

80. *AJC*, 13 January 1994.

81. *AJC*, 9 August 1994.

82. Ibid.

83. *AJC*, 10 August 1994.

84. *AJC*, 9 June 1995.

85. One study has described no fewer than six proposed projects for the area since 1958 alone. See Atlanta Institute of Planners, 1977, pp. 49–62.

86. See Chapter 5 this volume for a indepth discussion of CODA and its revenue-raising travails.

87. *Creative Loafing*, 21 May 1994.

88. Ibid.

89. *AJC*, 6 November 1994.

90. Ibid.

91. *AJC*, 25 September 1994.

92. In this case, the Hawks would temporarily play in either the Georgia Dome or Georgia Tech's Alexander Memorial Coliseum until the new arena was completed.

93. *Atlanta Business Chronicle*, 27 May–2 June 1994.

94. *ABC*, 3–9 February, 1995.

95. *AJC*, 10 December 1995.

96. Ibid.

97. Ibid.

98. Ibid.

99. Ibid.

100. A. Downs, 1994.

101. M. Christine Boyer, "The City of Illusion," in P. Knox, ed., *The Restless Urban Landscape*, Englewood Cliffs, NJ: Prentice Hall, p. 126.

102. See T.J. Clark, *The Painting of Modern Life: Paris in the Art of Manet and His Followers*, 1985, London: Thames and Hudson; D. Harvey, "The Urban Face of Capitalism," in J.F. Hart, ed., *Our Changing Cities*, 1991, Baltimore: The Johns Hopkins University Press. Both authors limit themselves to an

analysis of capitalist urbanism, yet it is clear that the "urban face of socialism" – while not shaped by the restless, community-dissolving dynamics of market forces – is as enamored of the manipulative spectacle and the control of space.

103. The most recent addition to this stable of publications is the exceedingly cheerful *CITYBEAT* (capitals in original).

104. *Creative Loafing*, 22 July 1995.

105. Ibid.

106. Ibid.

107. Ibid.

108. *AJC*, 3 June 1994.

109. *AJC*, 8 September 1994.

110. Quoted in *AJC*, 26 December 1994; *Creative Loafing*, 3 December 1994.

5. OLYMPIC DREAMS

1. Atlanta Committee for the Olympic Games, *Atlanta: City of Dreams*, Volume II of the Official Commemorative Edition, 1992, Atlanta: ACOG

2. Quoted in Empty the Shelters, *Spoilsport's Guidebook to Atlanta*, p. 21.

3. M. Starr and V. Smith, "No Payne, No Games," *Newsweek*, 17 July 1995, p. 65.

4. *Wall Street Journal*, 11 June 1993.

5. Ibid.

6. *Atlanta Journal Constitution* (hereafter *AJC*), 5 July 1990.

7. *AJC*, 12 July 1992.

8. *AJC*, 30 August 1989.

9. *AJC*, 12 July 1992.

10. *AJC*, 1 February 1990.

11. ACOG, *General Information: Atlanta 1996, The 1996 Atlanta Centennial Olympic Games*, 1993, unpaginated.

12. Quoted in *AJC*, 14 May 1994.

13. D. White and T. Crimmins, "How Atlanta Grew: Cool Heads, Hot Air, and Hard Work," in A. Hamer, ed., *Urban Atlanta: Redefining the Role of the City*, 1980, Atlanta: College of Business Administration, Georgia State University, Research Monograph No. 84.

14. J. Humphries and M. Plummer, "The Economic Impact of Georgia's Second Gold Rush: The 1996 Olympics," *Georgia Business and Economic Conditions*, 1990, vol. 50/5, pp. 1–4.

15. The first Georgia "gold rush" took place in the north Georgia mountains in 1830s, and provided the impetus for the displacement of most of the indigenous Cherokee nation to Oklahoma along the infamous "Trail of Tears."

16. *AJC*, 15 July 1995.

17. *AJC*, 27 March 1995.

18. Ibid.

19. Ibid.

20. At the apex of the hierarchy are the ten TOP (The Olympic Program), or worldwide, sponsors: Coca-Cola Co., Eastman Kodak, Visa, Bausch & Lomb, Xerox, Sports Illustrated, Panasonic, IBM, John Hancock, and United Parcel Service, or UPS. The second tier of sponsors – "the Partners" – have marketing and advertising rights only within the United States: NationsBank, Champion Sportswear, The Home Depot, IBM, Sara Lee, Anheuser-Busch, McDonald's, AT&T, Delta Air Lines, Swatch, and Motorola. The third category – "Sponsors" – have more limited US promotional rights: American Gas, Avon, BellSouth, Blue Cross and Blue Shield, BMW, Borg-Warner, Georgia Power, General Motors, Holiday Inn, International Paper, Nissan, Ranstad, Scientific-Atlanta, Sensormatic, York Heating and Cooling, and WorldTravel Partners. Included in this category are "Wheel of Fortune" and "Jeopardy," which enjoy the status of official game-shows of the Olympics.

    Nine of the corporate sponsors – Coca-Cola, UPS, Home Depot, Delta, BellSouth, Georgia Power, Holiday Inn, Scientific Atlanta, and WorldTravel Partners – are headquartered in Atlanta, and several others, including AT&T, IBM, NationsBank and Panasonic, have major operations and/or facilities in the Atlanta metro area.

21. *AJC*, 15 October 1994.

22. *AJC*, 25 April 1993.

23. *AJC*, 25 April 1995.
24. Ibid.
25. *Atlanta Business Chronicle* (hereafter *ABC*), 17–23 February 1995.
26. ACOG, "General Information."
27. *AJC*, 26 March 1994.
28. *ABC*, 17–23 February 1995.
29. Ibid.
30. *AJC*, 17 July 1992.
31. Ibid.
32. *AJC*, 7 July 1995.
33. Ibid.
34. *AJC*, 10 November 1995.
35. *AJC*, 7 July 1995.
36. *Creative Loafing,* 12 September 1992.
37. Ibid.
38. C. Stone, *Regime Politics, Governing Atlanta, 1946–1988*, 1989, Lawrence: University of Kansas Press, p. 173.
39. *AJC,* 12 September 1992.
40. *AJC,* 18 April 1993.
41. *AJC,* 31 October 1994.
42. *AJC,* 23 April 1991.
43. Source: Empty the Shelters.
44. R. Rydell, *All the World's A Fair*, 1984, Chicago: University of Chicago Press, pp. 76, 80.
45. *AJC,* 7 March 1993
46. *AJC,* 7 March 1993.
47. Ibid.
48. *AJC,* 29 January 1994.
49. Ibid.
50. *AJC,* 12 July 1992.
51. *AJC,* 29 January 1994.
52. Ibid.
53. *AJC,* 30 January 1994.
54. *AJC,* 24 November 1994.
55. *AJC,* 6 October 1992.
56. *AJC,* 17 October 1992.
57. *AJC,* 27 October 1992.
58. *AJC,* 28 October 1992.
59. *AJC,* 7 August 1993.
60. Ibid.
61. J. Winski, "Marketing Run Amok: The Adman Who Sold Atlanta," *Advertising Age*, 1993, 2 August, vol. 64/32, p. 14.
62. *AJC,* 7 August 1993.
63. In a letter to the editor of the *Atlanta Constitution*, city council president Marvin Arrington argued that selling Atlanta's "good name" was "ill-conceived, dangerous, and potentially very detrimental to the city." 10 February 1993.
64. *AJC,* 12 January 1993.
65. *AJC,* 24 October 1992.
66. G. Simmel, "The Metropolis and Mental Life," in K. Wolff, ed., *The Sociology of Georg Simmel*, 1964, Glencoe, Minn.: The Free Press, p. 414.
67. *AJC,* 31 October 1992.
68. *AJC,* 4 March 1993.
69. Ibid.
70. Ibid.
71. *AJC,* 7 March 1993.
72. *AJC,* 15 June 1993.
73. *AJC,* 26 June 1993.
74. *AJC,* 15 June 1993.

75. *AJC*, 20 June 1993.
76. See City of Atlanta Department of Planning and Development and Corporation for Olympic Development in Atlanta, "Master Olympic Development Program for [sic] City of Atlanta," 19 October 1993.
77. See Report of the Atlanta Rural/Urban Design Assistance Team, October 1992.
78. *AJC*, 11 November 1993.
79. CODA, "Neighborhood Planning Information Sheet."
80. *Creative Loafing*, 15 July 1995.
81. See *AJC*, 7 October 1993, 6 November 1993.
82. *AJC*, 3 February 1994.
83. *AJC*, 29 May 1994.
84. *AJC*, 29 May 1994.
85. Ibid.
86. Atlanta Institute of Planners – Georgia Section, *Planning Atlanta*, 1977, Atlanta: PRM Law Publishers, pp. 163–6.
87. CAP, Marietta Street Subarea Housing Study, 1986.
88. *AJC*, 11 June 1993.
89. Quoted in *AJC*, 19 November 1993.
90. *AJC*, 29 May 1994.
91. G. McDonogh, "The Geography of Emptiness," in R. Rotenberg and G. McDonogh, *The Cultural Meanings of Urban Space*, 1993, South Hadley, Mass.: Bergin and Garvey.
92. *New York Times*, 21 November 1993, 19 December 1993, 20 December 1993.
93. Source: Empty the Shelters.
94. Ibid.
95. *AJC*, 22 January 1994.
96. *AJC*, 4 November, 1994.
97. *AJC*, 16 July 1994, 4 November 1994.
98. *AJC*, 19 September 1995.
99. *AJC*, 30 June 1995.
100. Ibid.
101. *AJC*, 19 September 1995.
102. *AJC*, 15 September 1995.
103. Ibid.
104. Ibid.
105. Ibid.
106. Ibid.
107. Empty the Shelters, citing figures from the Atlanta Housing Authority.
108. Arthur Anderson & Co., *Downtown Atlanta Housing: Opportunities, Barriers, and a Plan for Action*, 1995.
109. *ABC*, 28 July–3 August 1995.
110. *AJC*, 5 April 1993.
111. *AJC*, 30 August 1994.
112. *AJC*, 1 September 1994.
113. Ibid.
114. *AJC*, 30 August 1994.
115. *AJC,* 1 September 1995.
116. *AJC* 4 May 1995.
117. *AJC*, 12 September 1995.
118. Ibid.
119. *AJC*, 13 September 1995.
120. Ibid.
121. *AJC*, 17 May 1995.
122. *AJC*, 21 September 1995.
123. Ibid.
124. *Creative Loafing*, 7 October 1995.
125. *AJC*, 8 September 1995.
126. Ibid.
127. *AJC*, 25 September 1995.

128. Source: Jamison Research, quoted in *AJC*, 12 October 1995.
129. *AJC*, 2 March 1995.
130. *AJC*, 7 April 1995.
131. *AJC*, 23 March 1994.
132. *AJC*, 7 April 1995.
133. *AJC*, 2 June 1995.
134. *AJC*, 7 April 1995.
135. *AJC*, 18 May 1995.
136. *AJC*, 22 July 1995.
137. *AJC*, 1 December 1995.
138. Source: Atlanta Housing Authority.
139. See G. Orfield and C. Ashkinaze, *The Closing Door: Conservative Policy and Black Opportunity*, 1991, Chicago: University of Chicago Press.
140. *AJC*, 8 December 1995.
141. *AJC*, 10 November 1995.
142. Quoted in *ABC*, 7–13 July 1995.
143. Ibid.
144. See *Creative Loafing*, 22 July 1995; 16 December 1995; 23 December 1995.
145. A. Downs, *Key Aspects of the Future of the Atlanta Region*, 1994, Washington DC: The Urban Land Institute, p. 18.

INDEX

THE HAYMARKET SERIES

Already published

ANYTHING BUT MEXICAN: Chicanos in Contemporary Los Angeles *by Rudi Acuña*

THE INVENTION OF THE WHITE RACE: Racial Oppression and Social Control *by Theodore Allen*

PUBLIC ACCESS: Literary Theory and American Cultural Politics *by Michael Berube*

MARXISM IN THE USA: Remapping the History of the American Left *by Paul Buhle*

FIRE IN THE AMERICAS: Forging the Revolutionary Agenda *by Roger Burbach and Orlando Núñez*

THE FINAL FRONTIER: The Rise and Fall of the American Rocket State *by Dale Carter*

CORRUPTIONS OF EMPIRE: Life Studies and the Reagan Era *by Alexander Cockburn*

THE SOCIAL ORIGINS OF PRIVATE LIFE: A History of American Families, 1600–1900 *by Stephanie Coontz*

ROLL OVER CHE GUEVARA: Travels of a Radical Reporter *by Marc Cooper*

SHADES OF NOIR: A Reader *edited by Joan Copjec*

BUILDING THE WORKINGMAN'S PARADISE: The Design of American Company Towns *by Margaret Crawford*

WAR AND TELEVISION *by Bruce Cumings*

IT'S NOT ABOUT A SALARY: Rap, Race and Resistance in Los Angeles *by Brian Cross, with additional texts by Reagan Kelly and T-Love*

CITY OF QUARTZ: Excavating the Future of Los Angeles *by Mike Davis*

PRISONERS OF THE AMERICAN DREAM: Politics and Economy in the History of the US Working Class *by Mike Davis*

THE ASSASSINATION OF NEW YORK *by Robert Fitch*

MECHANIC ACCENTS: Dime Novels and Working-Class Culture in America *by Michael Denning*

NO CRYSTAL STAIR: African Americans in the City of Angels *by Lynell George*

WHERE THE BOYS ARE: Cuba, Cold War America and the Making of a New Left *by Van Gosse*

RACE, POLITICS, AND ECONOMIC DEVELOPMENT: Community Perspectives *edited by James Jennings*

POSTMODERNISM AND ITS DISCONTENTS: Theories, Practices *edited by E. Ann Kaplan*

WHITE SAVAGES IN THE SOUTH SEAS *by Mel Kernahan*

SEVEN MINUTES: The Life and Death of the American Animated Cartoon *by Norman M. Klein*

RANK-AND-FILE REBELLION: Teamsters for a Democratic Union *by Dan La Botz*

IMAGINING HOME: Class, Culture and Nationalism in the African Diaspora *by Sidney Lemelle and Robin D.G. Kelley*

Forthcoming

THE INVENTION OF THE WHITE RACE, VOLUME 2: The Origin of Racial Oppression in Anglo-America *by Theodore Allen*

MIAMI *by John Beverley and David Houston*

THE CULTURAL FRONT: The Left and American Culture in the Age of the CIO *by Michael Denning*

POWER MISSES *by David James*

MESSING WITH THE MACHINE: Modernism, Postmodernism and African-American Fiction *by Wahneema Lubiano*

PUBLIC TRANSPORT *by Eric Mann*

BLACK AVANT-GARDE FILM *by Ntongela Masilela*

QUEER SPACE *by Kevin McMahan*

BEARING NORTH *by Paul Smith*

DANCING ON THE BRINK: The San Francisco Bay Area at the End of the Twentieth Century *by Richard Walker*